COMMERCIAL ACTIVITY, MARKETS AND ENTREPRENEURS IN THE MIDDLE AGES

COMMERCIAL ACTIVITY, MARKETS AND ENTREPRENEURS IN THE MIDDLE AGES

ESSAYS IN HONOUR OF RICHARD BRITNELL

edited by

Ben Dodds *and* Christian D. Liddy

THE BOYDELL PRESS

First published 2011
The Boydell Press, Woodbridge

ISBN 978 1 84383 684 1

The Boydell Press is an imprint of Boydell & Brewer Ltd
PO Box 9, Woodbridge, Suffolk IP12 3DF, UK
and of Boydell & Brewer Inc.
668 Mount Hope Ave, Rochester, NY 14620, USA
website: www.boydellandbrewer.com

A catalogue record for this book is available
from the British Library

The publisher has no responsibility for the continued existence or accuracy of URLs for
external or third-party internet websites referred to in this book, and does not guarantee
that any content on such websites is, or will remain, accurate or appropriate.

Papers used by Boydell & Brewer Ltd are natural, recyclable products
made from wood grown in sustainable forests

Designed and typeset in Aldus with Palatino display by
The Stingray Office, Chorlton-cum-Hardy, Manchester

Printed and bound in Great Britain by
CPI Group (UK) Ltd, Croydon CR0 4YY

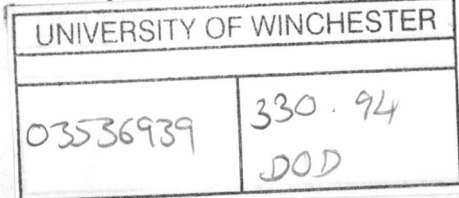

Contents

List of Figures

List of Tables

List of Contributors

....

Mark Bailey	Professor of Late Medieval History at the University of East Anglia
Martha Carlin	Professor of History at the University of Wisconsin–Milwaukee
James Davis	Lecturer in Medieval History at Queen's University Belfast
Christopher Dyer	Emeritus Professor of Regional and Local History at the University of Leicester
John Hatcher	Emeritus Professor of Economic and Social History at the University of Cambridge
Derek Keene	Leverhulme Professor of Comparative Metropolitan History at the University of London
Maryanne Kowaleski	Professor and Director of Medieval Studies at Fordham University
John Langdon	Emeritus Professor of History at the University of Alberta
Peter L. Larson	Associate Professor at the University of Central Florida
John S. Lee	Research Associate at the Centre for Medieval Studies at the University of York
James Masschaele	Professor of Medieval History at Rutgers University
Christine M. Newman	Honorary Fellow in the Department of History at Durham University

List of Abbreviations

....

AgHR   *Agricultural History Review*

AHEW   *The Agrarian History of England and Wales,* general ed. J. Thirsk (8 vols., Cambridge, 1967–2000)

BL   British Library

CCR   *Calendar of Close Rolls*

CChR   *Calendar of Charter Rolls*

CIM   *Calendar of Inquisitions Miscellaneous*

CPR   *Calendar of Patent Rolls*

CRR   *Curia Regis Rolls of the Reigns of Richard I, John and Henry III preserved in the Public Record Office* (19 vols., 1922–2002)

CUL   Cambridge University Library

DRO   Devon Record Office

DUL   Durham University Library

ECL   Exeter Cathedral Library

EcHR   *Economic History Review*

EHR   *English Historical Review*

NH   *Northern History*

P&P   *Past & Present*

PROME   *The Parliament Rolls of Medieval England, 1275–1504,* ed. C. Given-Wilson (16 vols., Woodbridge, 2005)

SR   *Statutes of the Realm* (11 vols., London, 1810–28)

TNA   The National Archives

TRHS   *Transactions of the Royal Historical Society*

Richard Britnell: An Appreciation

....

Ben Dodds and Christian D. Liddy

RICHARD BRITNELL, FBA, will almost certainly be slightly embarrassed by the production of a *Festschrift* in his honour. One of the editors of this volume was supervised by Richard for his doctoral work and remembers, when he became a little overheated in a discussion, Richard's gentle reminder that 'we're not trying to change the world'. And yet, over the course of his distinguished academic career, Richard's work and teaching have indeed changed the world of medieval economic history. The papers collected in this volume, from scholars on both sides of the Atlantic, several of whom are his former students, reflect the impact of Richard's scholarship on the international academic community.

Richard arrived in Durham in 1966 and spent the first part of his career working in the Department of Economic History until its closure in 1985. For most of this period, during which he met his wife Jenny, also a distinguished academic, none of Richard's teaching involved medieval economic history. The focus of the Economic History degree at Durham was the process of modern economic growth through the themes of Land, Labour and Capital. Richard's teaching concentrated upon the last of these. Among his various courses was one with the rather forbidding title, 'Problems in Invention and Business Activity', later rebranded as 'Capital Formation and Technological Change' and, finally, 'Industrialisation in Europe'. In addition, Richard helped to teach a first-year survey course on 'Industrial Britain: Origins and Development', which served as an introduction to economic history and which was a compulsory requirement for all students studying Social Science degrees involving Economics, Politics and Sociology. Richard's teaching load was, therefore, enormous, and time for research limited. To use the present-day jargon, 'research-led teaching' was not made easy for Richard. One colleague remembers his comment that his Special Subject (a final year Honours course) on the eighteenth-century Scottish economy was the nearest thing to medieval economic history that he could find. It was only following the

We should like to thank our colleague, Professor Ranald Michie, for sharing some of his reflections on Richard's early career in Durham.

closure of the Department of Economic History and the merger with the Department of Modern History to form the Department of History that Richard was to enjoy greater freedom to develop his own courses.

Characteristically, Richard made the best of difficult circumstances and used his wide knowledge of more recent economic history and his strong grasp of conceptual issues to inform his work on the Middle Ages. This is most apparent in the ground-breaking 1993 book for which Richard is best known: *The Commercialisation of English Society, 1000–1500*. Richard's description and exploration of the growth of commercial institutions, practices and ideas, and his assessment of the significance of these changes, have become fundamental to our understanding of the Middle Ages. When Richard began studying the medieval economy at Cambridge in the 1960s under the supervision of Michael Postan, work in the field concentrated on demographic change and class conflict. Although both factors have remained prominent in historical scholarship in subsequent decades, our thinking on economic change has been deepened, and in many ways altered, by much greater understanding of the role of the market. Richard's work on the urban and rural economies has been at the centre of this development. Although acknowledging the long phase of expansion from *c.*1000 to *c.*1300 and the subsequent contraction from *c.*1300 to *c.*1550, Richard described and analysed a process of commercialisation that was not always defined by these cycles.

Richard's ideas about the commercialisation of the economy and the wider importance of the market in medieval life permeate many of the contributions presented here. All those working on the late Middle Ages have benefited from Richard's assessment of the significance of commerce in different settings. Maryanne Kowaleski, for example, explores the entrepreneurial skills and business acumen of shipmasters in the port towns of late medieval England, while Peter L. Larson considers the entrepreneurial activities of peasants and their engagement with the land market in three villages in County Durham. Martha Carlin discusses the phenomenon of employee fraud, the dark side of business, while James Davis investigates the development of regulatory frameworks to govern the market. Christopher Dyer's essay reflects a new interest among medievalists in consumerism and the relationship between the buyer and the market.

One of the great strengths of Richard's work is the combination of conceptual rigour with concern for the detail of specific examples. This applied as much to his teaching as to his research. In his popular undergraduate course on 'Italian Towns and Trade', Richard introduced students to the complexities of Malthusian models and political violence while encouraging each student to choose their 'favourite' Italian town. Richard's enthusiasm for detailed and meticulous archival research has been clear from the beginning of his career in his work on regional and local history, culminating in his first book, *Growth and Decline in Colchester, 1300–1525* (1986), which used a case study of an important English town to shed light on wider industrial and commercial developments. Both the conceptual and the archival strands continue to be important in Richard's recent publications. His 500-page *Oxford History of Britain and Ireland, 1050–1530: Economy and Society* (2004), for example, appeared in the same year as a close study of field systems in north-east England. Both approaches are reflected in the papers presented in this *Festschrift*. John Hatcher challenges firmly held beliefs about fifteenth-century wage labour and reassesses the value of familiar datasets drawn from throughout England. John Langdon, by contrast, has selected one particularly important set of records relating to the construction industry to raise questions about the little-understood issues of low wages and unemployment.

No less considerable is Richard's reputation as an urban historian. His work on towns stemmed in part from his broader interest in commercialisation, but it also extended to the character and processes of urban government. One of Richard's earliest published papers (1968) was about the market town of Witham in Essex, since when the study of small towns has become a major strand of English urban historiography. Christine M. Newman's contribution here charts the contrasting economic fortunes of three seigniorial boroughs in County Durham, while Mark Bailey examines, more directly, the relationship between economic and political development in an urban context and argues that small towns, particularly seigniorial boroughs, enjoyed considerably more autonomy in the late Middle Ages than historians have suggested. In separate essays, Derek Keene and John S. Lee address two of the issues critical to the well-being of any town in the late Middle Ages (which Richard also considered in his study of Colchester): relations between the town and its rural hinterland, and urban management of the food supply in the face of the threat of famine.

Richard is also known to many as an important historian of north-east England. His study of feudal reaction in Durham in the aftermath of the Black Death clarified ways in which the economic and political history of the region conformed to wider patterns and ways in which they were distinctive. Richard was one of the first historians to exploit fully the rich archives available locally, which he did through a series of major research grants from the Economic and Social Research Council (ESRC) and the Leverhulme Trust. In the 1990s Richard directed two collaborative projects with Professor A. J. Pollard on the economic and social history of the small Yorkshire market town of Northallerton and on the employees of Durham priory in the fifteenth century. He also co-directed (with Professor Brian Roberts of the Department of Geography at Durham) an innovative interdisciplinary project on the settlement of the wasteland in the region, which produced illuminating evidence from an area outside historians' traditional focus and in which the chronology of development before the Black Death differed markedly from that observed elsewhere. Richard's contribution to the history of the north-east is reflected in the essays of Larson and Newman in this volume, both of which develop Richard's ideas on the interplay between markets and institutional structures.

A further strength of Richard's work is its chronological range. His concern with economic and political developments at the very end of the Middle Ages is pioneering. Unlike their continental counterparts, economic historians of medieval England have tended to concentrate on the thirteenth and fourteenth centuries, periods to which Richard himself has devoted considerable attention. The majority of contributions to this *Festschrift* echo this emphasis. However, Richard's 1997 book, *The Closing of the Middle Ages?*, covers an unusual chronological period and reflects the author's wider interests in political history, especially Cardinal Wolsey, the subject of his Special Subject taught in the Department of History at Durham. The book also incorporates an original and detailed discussion of the economy in the final quarter of the fifteenth century and the first quarter of the sixteenth, including comments on the role of entrepreneurship. Notable in this respect is the essay by Lee, a former student of Richard, whose contribution is a detailed discussion of the response of the city of Coventry to a serious grain shortage in the second decade of the sixteenth century.

Aside from the brilliance and innovation of his work, Richard enjoys a reputation for scholarly generosity within academic circles, and he has helped generations of historians, including all of those whose work appears in this volume. Since 1999 Richard has been joint editor of the Surtees Society with his close friend and colleague, Dr Margaret Harvey. In this capacity Richard has demonstrated his tireless commitment to the publication of archival sources in order to make them widely available to the scholarly community. In 2008 Richard's own edition of the court records of the prior of Durham's borough of Crossgate (*Records of the Borough of Crossgate, Durham, 1312–1531*) was published by the Surtees Society. Richard's awareness of the importance of charters, record keeping and the administrative mechanisms of market exchange is reflected in this volume by the contribution of James Masschaele, who explores the public use of charters in the resolution of legal disputes relating to the transfer of land. Richard's own interest in the interaction between literacy and commercial life led to his edition of a pioneering collection of essays on the subject of *Pragmatic Literacy, East and West, 1200–1330* (1997). It is typical of the breadth and depth of Richard's learning that he took it upon himself to write about Chinese bureaucracy in the Yuan period (thirteenth and fourteenth centuries). Richard's work represents a remarkable combination of high quality documentary analysis and broad reaching synthesis on an increasingly global scale.

Within a short period, Richard, who had been a Lecturer in Economic History at Durham between 1966 and 1985, was appointed to a Readership and then Chair. In the words of a former colleague, Richard had become 'one of the research stars of the Department of History'. He was, for instance, the co-director (with another colleague and friend, Professor Paul Harvey) of two major projects on the peasant land market in southern England, which drew on the wonderfully rich estate records of the bishops of Winchester (Winchester Pipe Rolls). Richard's election as a Fellow of the British Academy in 2005 was a fitting acknowledgement, by the wider academic community, of the significance of his research.

In his dealings with others, Richard has always shown rare levels of modesty and insight, often with a humorous twinkle in his eye. This was particularly apparent at his inaugural lecture following his appointment to a Chair at Durham in 1997. Richard delivered his lecture to a large and enthusiastic audience until, two minutes before the end, a small group of students arrived noisily. When the floor was opened for questions, one of the late-comers raised a hand, observed that he had missed the talk, and demanded a short summary. Many speakers would have been flummoxed by such a cheeky question but, without a second thought, Richard addressed the student and responded with a brief comment on the significance of medieval field systems and their distinctiveness in Durham. The contributors to and editors of this volume present their work here in gratitude to Richard Britnell as a scholar, colleague and generous friend.

Acknowledgements

We should like to thank James Davis for suggesting the cover illustration and Lisa Liddy for preparing the index.

August 2011

1

Unreal Wages:
Long-Run Living Standards and the 'Golden Age' of the Fifteenth Century

....

John Hatcher

Nᴏᴛ ᴍᴀɴʏ ᴅᴇᴄᴀᴅᴇs ᴀɢᴏ the long fifteenth century was a notoriously dark age in English history, neglected because it was located awkwardly between the 'true' Middle Ages and the early modern era. When at last it began to receive the attention it warranted, attempts to dispel the gloom were bedevilled by an ambition to fashion generalisations that fitted the whole experience of the 150 years after 1350, or even the quarter millennium from 1300 to 1550. As a result fundamental disagreements arose, the most notable being whether this era should be characterised by economic growth and prosperity or by recession and decline.[1] However, contention cooled as more research was undertaken, topics on the agenda defined and prioritised, and more manageable chronologies adopted, along with a willingness to identify sub-periods and sectors whose characteristics differed in major respects.[2] Confidence has now increased sufficiently to persuade us that we are close to achieving a full understanding of the economy and society

I am grateful to the Humanities Center, Stanford University, for awarding me a fellowship for the academic year 2008/9, and for providing the ideal environment in which I completed much of the planning and research for this essay. Earlier versions of this essay benefited greatly from constructive comments by members of the Social Science History Workshop at Stanford, the Pre-Modern Economic and Social History Seminar at the Institute of Historical Research, London, and the Core Economic History Seminar at Cambridge. I am also indebted to Mark Bailey, Bruce Campbell, Nick Crafts and Steve Broadberry for reading drafts of the essay and making many valuable suggestions.

[1]   Most notably the differences of interpretation between M. M. Postan ('The Fifteenth Century', *EcHR* 9 (1939), 160–7, and 'Some Economic Evidence of Declining Population in the Later Middle Ages', *EcHR* (1949–50), 221–46) and A. R. Bridbury (*Economic Growth: England in the Later Middle Ages* (London, 1962)).

[2]   For notable more recent contributions to this field by Richard Britnell, see *The Closing of the Middle Ages? England, 1471–1519* (Oxford, 1997); *The End of the Middle Ages? England in the Fifteenth and Sixteenth Centuries* (Stroud, 1998); *Britain and Ireland, 1050–1530: Economy and Society* (Oxford, 2004).

of England at the close of the Middle Ages, and there are distinct signs of a consensus emerging, with optimistic epithets such as 'Economic Growth', 'An Age
of Ambition', 'A Golden Age of Prosperity', 'An Age of Transition', 'A Consumer
Economy' and 'A New Middle Ages' in the ascendant.

However, a little more probing reveals that there is much that remains mys-
terious about the era and paradoxical about attempts that have been made to
describe and explain it. There is a library of economic, social and demographic
theory that tells us what should have happened in the century and a half after
the Black Death, but most of it fails to explain what actually happened. Many
crucial elements of the pictures that have been drawn do not fit together as they
should, and many leading indicators on which great reliance has been placed are
very unusual and in some cases contradictory. Attempts to incorporate the later
Middle Ages into long-term models and data sets of economic and social change
have also faced formidable difficulties. Much of the economic theory that has
been applied to the era is ill suited to the task because it was designed to analyse
modern rather than pre-modern economies and the types of data that illuminate
the workings and measure the performance of modern industrial and industri-
alising economies cannot be extracted with the same confidence from their pre-
industrial equivalents.

Amidst all the uncertainties that remain, however, there is one crucial matter on
which for centuries there has been universal agreement: the long fifteenth century
was 'a golden age' for the mass of the population. The promethean efforts of a host
of compilers of wage and price data have combined to add depth and precision to
observations first made by eighteenth-century political economists, and there is
now a massive statistical archive that attests the prodigious levels attained by the
wages of late medieval workers.[3] And these enthusiastic affirmations have been
taken to confirm the existence of widespread levels of prosperity unparalleled for
a pre-industrial economy. Whether by association, intuition or economic theory,

---

[3]   For England see, for example, J. E. T. Rogers, *The History of Agriculture and Prices* (7 vols.,
      Oxford, 1866–1902); W. H. Beveridge, *Prices and Wages in England*, 1: *The Mercantilist Era*
      (London, 1939); E. H. Phelps Brown and S. V. Hopkins, 'Seven Centuries of Building Wages',
      Economica 22 (1955), 195–206; E. H. Phelps Brown and S. V. Hopkins, 'Seven Centuries
      of the Prices of Consumables, compared with Builders' Wage-Rates', *Economica* 23 (1956),
      296–314, repr. in E. H. Phelps Brown and S. V. Hopkins, *A Perspective of Wages and Prices*
      (London, 1981); D. L. Farmer, 'Prices and Wages', in *AHEW* II, 716–817; D. L. Farmer, 'Prices
      and Wages, 1350–1500', in *AHEW* III, 431–525; J. H. Munro, 'Prices and Wages' in *The Me-
      dieval and Early Modern Data Bank*, ed. R. M. Bell and M. Howell, accessed at www.scc.
      rutgers.edu/memdb; R. C. Allen, 'Data: Wage and Price History', accessed at www.nuffield.
      ox.ac.uk/General/Members/allen.aspx; G. Clark, 'The Price History of English Agriculture,
      1200–1914', *Research in Economic History*, 22 (2004), 41–124; G. Clark, 'The Long March of
      History: Farm Wages, Population, and Economic Growth, England, 1209–1869', *EcHR* 60
      (2007), 97–135.

the fortunes of the unskilled have commonly been taken as a reflection of the exalted material living standards of the bulk of the population.[4] Accepted wisdom has for centuries seen this era as characterised by living standards that were so phenomenally high they were not to be equalled until the mid nineteenth century or even the 1880s, long after the benefits of advanced industrialisation had finally trickled down to the masses.

It is notable that the host of scholars who have diligently laboured in this field have arrived, without exception, at extremely optimistic outcomes. Thorold Rogers, the leading modern pioneer in the collection of price and wage data, was the first to use the term 'golden age', when he concluded in 1884 that 'the fifteenth century and the first quarter of the sixteenth were the golden age of the English labourer, if we are to interpret the wages which he earned by the cost of the necessaries of life. At no time were wages, relatively speaking, so high, and at no time was food so cheap.'[5] The publication seventy years later of the immensely influential Phelps Brown and Hopkins index duly revealed a doubling of the purchasing power of the day wages of urban building craftsmen between the first half of the fourteenth century and the third quarter of the fifteenth, and the most recent contribution, Gregory Clark's computations based on a host of new wage and price data, shows the real wages of agricultural labourers soaring by more than 160 per cent, comparing 1300–49 with the peak reached between 1440 and 1479 (see Figures 1.1, 1.2).[6]

These are striking rates of increase, but even more extraordinary are the absolute levels that living standards are held to have attained in comparison with those of much later times. As Henry Hallam noted, with the approval of Thomas Malthus, in his *View of the State of Europe during the Middle Ages*, first published in 1818:

> There is one very unpleasing remark which everyone who attends to the subject will be induced to make, that the labouring classes, especially those engaged in agriculture, were better provided with the means of subsistence in the reigns of Edward iii [*recte* iv] or of Henry vi than they are at present.[7]

It was not entirely unexpected, therefore, that the peak of the Phelps Brown and

---

[4] For example, the confident statements in G. Clark, *A Farewell to Alms: A Brief Economic History of the World* (Princeton, 2007), 21–2.

[5] J. E. T. Rogers, *Six Centuries of Work and Wages: The History of English Labour* (London, 1949 edn), 326.

[6] The higher rate of increase found by Clark is largely due to his plausible adoption of a substantially lower level of real wages before the Black Death than that calculated by Phelps Brown and Hopkins.

[7] H. Hallam, *View of the State of Europe during the Middle Ages*, iii (11th edn, London, 1855), 96 and fn.

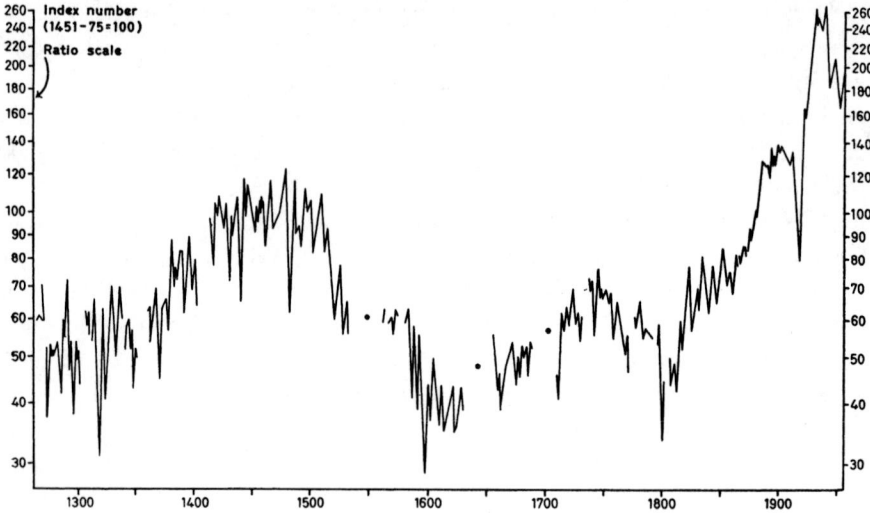

Fig. 1.1: Changes in the equivalent of the wage rate of a building craftsman expressed in a composite physical unit of consumables in southern England, 1284–1954

Source: E. H. Phelps Brown and S. V. Hopkins, *A Perspective of Wages and Prices* (London, 1981), 19.

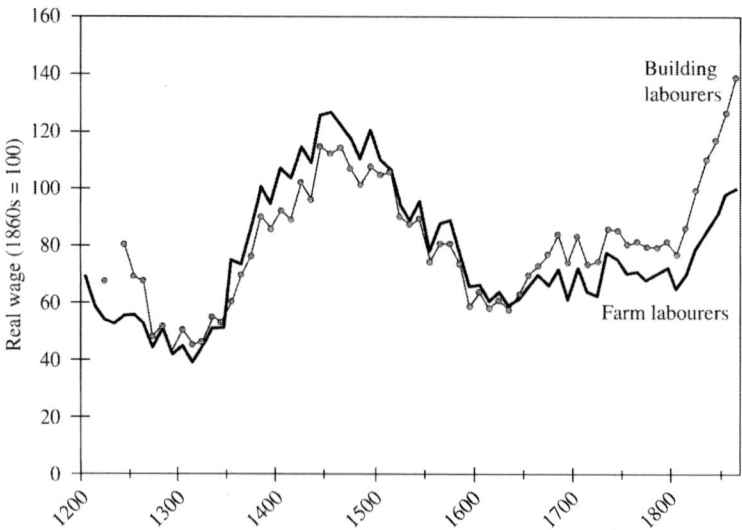

Fig. 1.2: Real agricultural day wages, 1209–1869

Source: G. Clark, 'The Long March of History: Farm Wages, Population, and Economic Growth, England 1209–1869', *EcHR* 60 (2007), 109.

Hopkins index reached in the later fifteenth century was not to be surpassed for more than four hundred years. There have been many adjustments and improvements to this seminal index, as well as a wide range of completely new statistical compilations that span the centuries from the Middle Ages to modern times, but the broad thrust of the original findings have been confirmed rather than supplanted. Indeed, the close similarities shared by the abundant series of long-run real wages that are now available lend great strength to their credibility. The experience of Clark's agricultural labourers, for example, differs relatively little from Phelps Brown's building workers when the purchasing power of their wages in the 1860s are shown to be still twenty per cent short of the exalted levels their fifteenth-century predecessors had achieved.[8]

Results no less stunning have been produced by reversing the standard statistical computations of what a day's wage would buy by measuring improvements in welfare by the amounts of work required to provide subsistence. Farmer's investigations of the money wages of threshers and reapers show that the number of units of work required to purchase a quarter of wheat and a quarter of barley fell by almost sixty per cent between the first half of the fourteenth century and the 1440s,[9] and Allen and Weisdorf have recently computed that, at the money wages that are assumed to have prevailed in the fifteenth century, an agricultural labourer in southern England would have been able to provide for all his basic needs, and those of a wife and two children, from no more than 200 days' work.[10]

There is, therefore, a centuries-old and disciplines-wide consensus that the living standards of ordinary Englishmen and women at the close of the Middle Ages were stupendously high for a pre-industrial economy. This essay will challenge this consensus. It will argue that the towering peak in real wages that dominates the later Middle Ages in all long-term representations of living standards has been grossly exaggerated, and that it does not represent the course that the living standards of either the landless or the landholding majority followed.

Whereas there is no doubt that the real wages of labourers rose very substantially between the crowded and crisis-torn early fourteenth century and the spacious later fifteenth century, rates of improvement should not be confused with absolute levels of income. It will be shown that the real wages of the landless and near landless did not soar nearly as high as it has been conventional to believe, and that it is misguided to believe that the rate of improvement of the real incomes of the lower strata of rural society was representative of the experience of

---

[8]   G. Clark and Y. van der Werf, 'Work in Progress? The Industrious Revolution', *Journal of Economic History*, 58 (1998), 830–1.

[9]   D. L. Farmer, 'Crop Yields, Prices and Wages in Medieval England', *Studies in Medieval and Renaissance History*, 6 (1983), 146.

[10] R. C. Allen and J. L. Weisdorf, 'Was There an "Industrious Revolution" Before the Industrial Revolution? An Empirical Exercise for England, *c.*1300–1830', *University of Copenhagen Department of Economics, Working Papers no. 10–14* (2010), 8.

the majority, whose fortunes improved far less dramatically. Preliminary model-ling indicates that the real incomes of the substantial body of middling peasants with holdings of roughly subsistence size remained relatively stable in the face of dramatic changes in the prices of labour and farm produce, while those of large-scale farmers declined. The golden age of the fifteenth century is in need of a severe dose of debasement.

Real wages are of considerable significance, not just for the fifteenth century but for all periods of history, and they are ensconced at the heart of almost all major descriptions and analyses of long-term economic, social and demographic devel-opment. However, it will be argued here that across much of history the conven-tional measures used to compute them are ill suited to their task.[11]

The daily wage rates of workers and the prices of subsistence commodities are almost universally accepted as the data that can best perform the many cru-cial functions demanded of them. By the simple procedure of converting wage rates and the costs of subsistence into index numbers, and dividing the former into the latter, real-wage indices are created that are precise and consistent, as well as abundantly available.[12] They lend themselves admirably to the mapping of trends and fluctuations across centuries and continents and form the basis of comparisons of not merely the living standards but the economic performance of countries.[13]

However, despite their value in facilitating comparisons between economies and across time, there are many reasons why such crude data cannot bear the weight that is routinely placed on them and why their deficiencies proliferate and deepen the further back one goes in history. The most significant failings may be grouped under three main heads: first, the daily wage rates of labourers and craftsmen and the prices of subsistence goods do not constitute a sound basis for measuring the real incomes of these groups; second, the real incomes of landless or near landless males cannot be used as a surrogate for those of the landholding population at large, for whom daily wages were not the source of all income nor

---

[11] The author is preparing an article that provides more detailed criticisms of current estimates of English real wages before the nineteenth century and presents new methods and data for estimating long-run changes in real incomes and living standards.

[12] For a recent account of the methods of measuring real wages and the value of real-wage data, see R. C. Allen, 'Real Wage Rates (historical trends)', in *The New Palgrave Dictionary of Economics*, ed. S. N. Durlauf and L. E. Blume (2nd edn, Basingstoke, 2008).

[13] Hence: R. C. Allen, 'How Prosperous were the Romans? Evidence from Diocletian's Price Edict (301 AD)', *Oxford Department of Economics Discussion Papers* (2007); W. Scheidel, 'Real Wages in Early Economies: Evidence for Living Standards from 2000 BCE to 1300 CE', *Journal of the Economic and Social History of the Orient*, 53 (2010), 425–62; S. Özmucur and S. Pamuk, 'Real Wages and Standards of Living in the Ottoman Empire, 1489–1914', *Journal of Economic History*, 62 (2002), 293–321.

the market the source of all subsistence; third, the incomes of households are far more informative than the incomes of their male heads.

Henry Phelps Brown voiced these reservations. On the first page of his 'Seven Centuries of the Prices of Consumables compared with Builders' Wage-rates' he stated in an unequivocal manner: 'Nowadays, real wages are commonly estimated by comparing money wages with an index of the cost of living, but there are several reasons why we cannot do that here'.[14] He elaborated, 'all we have is the rate of pay for a day, we do not know how many days' work the builder was getting in the year from time to time, nor what other resources he had ... and we know little or nothing about some important costs'. Phelps Brown continued, 'These things apart, we still could not attach much meaning to "the cost of maintaining a constant standard of living" through seven centuries of social change. So we have not tried to construct any measure of real wages in the modern sense'. Accordingly, he took great care never to use the terms 'real wages' or 'real income' for his findings, and instead he composed the following lengthy title : 'Changes in the equivalent of the wage rate of a building craftsman expressed in a composite physical unit of consumables in southern England'.

Yet, Phelps Brown's admonitions have been repeatedly ignored by those who have used and interpreted his index, or amassed similar data to construct new indices.[15] Time and again comparisons of the nominal daily wage rates of labourers and craftsmen with the prices of baskets of basic consumables have been deemed to constitute not just the real wages of those workers but their real earnings over a period of time, commonly a year. Indeed, their annual earnings are often computed by multiplying the daily wage by a working year of 250 to 300 days.[16] This is not all. Implicitly and explicitly the population at large is commonly assumed to have shared the same experience and benefited from the same rate of improvement in real incomes between the early fourteenth century and the later

[14] Phelps Brown and Hopkins, *Perspective of Wages and Prices*, 23.

[15] For a notable exception, see D. Woodward, 'Wage Rates and Living Standards in Pre-Industrial England', *P&P* 91 (1981), 28–46. Concentrating on building craftsmen in the early modern period, Woodward argues convincingly that the daily wage rates of building craftsmen and the price of a basket of commodities cannot provide an accurate guide to their fortunes by showing that they were not wage earners but small independent businessmen who made money from a variety of sources including the employment of apprentices, the supply of raw materials and sometimes from small-scale farming. He also stresses our ignorance of the number of days they worked and of the income brought in by other members of their households. Woodward's arguments were extended and amplified in D. Woodward, *Men at Work: Labourers and Building Craftsmen in the Towns of Northern England, 1450–1750* (Cambridge, 1995).

[16] See, for example, the transmutation of the purchasing power of an urban day's wage into a ratio of full-time annual income to annual subsistence costs in R. C. Allen, *The British Industrial Revolution in Global Perspective* (Cambridge, 2009), chap. 2: 'The High-Wage Economy of Pre-industrial Britain'.

fifteenth. However, Malthus was not measuring the living standards of the average labourer, still less those of the mass of Englishmen and women, when he compared the money paid to a man for a day's labouring and the price of grain in the fifteenth century with those prevailing in his own day.[17] He was merely computing the quantity of food that a day's labouring at that wage would purchase, and that is precisely what Gregory Clark's newly-produced series of farm labourers' wage rates and living costs does. The sources Clark is forced to use over the greater part of the period his series covers are the same as those available to all other price and wage historians, and they do not reveal how many days in each year the average labourer was employed at these rates, or what other sources of income and subsistence he might have had. There is also the vexed question of whether, when, and how much food and drink labourers received at work.

At first sight the real value of the pay received for a day's work in the later fifteenth century might well appear comparable to that pertaining in the 1880s. But earnings are what really matter. A true comparison must take into account the number of days worked in the two periods, and there can be no doubt that this differed substantially. The labour market in the late Middle Ages, and indeed throughout the early modern centuries, offered far less regular employment than was to be the case subsequently, when the great bulk of the population worked in non-agricultural occupations and the majority of those that remained in the countryside were employed on large farms.[18] In pre-modern times paid employment in the countryside was characterised by its intermittent and piecemeal character: the changing routine of the seasons of the farming year combined with uncertain weather to cause wide fluctuations in the demand for labour and produce short-term and discontinuous working, and this inherent irregularity was accentuated by the fact that both the demand for labour and its supply came overwhelmingly from the occupiers of relatively modest farms. It is particularly regrettable that there is little or no useful information on the terms and conditions on which peasants hired each other because the likelihood remains that much work was undertaken between people in the same village using swap arrangements rather than cash payments.

In the fifteenth century access to land was unusually easy and the proportion of landless in the adult rural population was unusually low. The great bulk of the farmland of England was distributed in relatively small parcels among households that primarily used family labour to farm them, and if these households

---

[17] T. R. Malthus, *Principles of Political Economy* (2nd edn, London, 1836), chap. IV, sec. IV, p. 204, cited by Phelps Brown and Hopkins, *Perspective of Wages and Prices*, 61.

[18] Steve Hindle provides an extremely perceptive and well-documented picture of spasmodic and fragmented labour markets in the countryside of early modern England: *On the Parish? The Micro-Politics of Poor Relief in Rural England, 1550–1750* (Oxford, 2004).

needed to hire additional labour, or had spare labour to market, they bought and sold it on an intermittent and short-term basis. The proliferation of large farms and the rise of an involuntary landless proletariat that came to dominate the agricultural landscape had yet to get under way. Relatively few villagers possessed lands that were sufficiently extensive to make it worthwhile hiring labour on a continuous and full-time basis, and those who did appreciated that their needs could be served better and more cheaply by servants hired by the year and remunerated with a combination of food, lodging, clothing and cash rather than by labourers hired by the day.

So far as the construction of a reliable wage series for the fifteenth century is concerned, it is particularly unfortunate that information has to be compiled exclusively from the demesne accounts of great institutions when by far the greater part of labour was hired by peasants and lesser lords. Not only were these institutions unusually inflexible employers but they progressively abandoned direct farming, so that by the 1440s the sample of accounts supplying data is tiny.[19] There are also serious problems with the most dominant constituents of the agricultural wage series: payments for harvest work and for threshing and winnowing grain. These tasks were chosen because they are well recorded and strictly defined, but they are also untypical and problematical. Harvest work was paid exceptionally well, commonly at double the winter wage, but such employment lasted for only a few weeks a year, while threshing and winnowing constituted only a tiny proportion of labour inputs in agriculture. Even on the largest seigneurial farms with expansive arable acres, threshing and winnowing the whole crop of grains and legumes rarely took more than the equivalent of the annual labour of a single man. Moreover, remuneration for this task was both lower and far more variable between manors than it is usually portrayed, and those who performed it were commonly paid by the piece rather than by the day.[20]

The daily wages paid for casual work during the slack periods of the year are of great significance but, unfortunately, this is when the great demesnes normally used their servants rather than hired labourers and the available data are consequently sparse, disparate and poorly-suited to inclusion in statistical tables. However, there is a body of robust detailed empirical evidence, much of it drawn from

---

[19] Farmer declared his series of agricultural wages to be 'fragmentary and unreliable, 1466–1500': 'Prices and Wages, 1350–1500', 524.

[20] Ibid., 468–71. Clark acknowledges the seriousness of a range of issues connected with the use of piece-rate payments for threshing as a surrogate for day-wage rates, including the fact that the ratio of day wages to threshing payments per bushel change substantially over time. He adopts a number of strategies to bring the threshing rates back into line including positing an increase of around forty per cent in the labour productivity of threshers, who threshed 5.1 bushels a day from 1209 to 1349 but a commendable seven bushels per day from 1350 to 1525; from 1525 onwards, however, the productivity of the threshers apparently sank progressively below the pre-Black Death level ('Long March of History').

extremely informative farm accounts of lesser lords, that convincingly under-mines the current wage series by demonstrating the prevalence of far lower rates of pay and the scarcity of employment for casual labourers during the dominant slack periods of the year. Poos's detailed and resourceful analysis of the labour market in late-fifteenth-century Essex, which he characterises as 'highly episodic and discontinuous', is a particularly enlightening case study.[21] Unusually in-formative records reveal that the great bulk of the work running William Capell's 300-acre mixed farm at Porter's Hall, Stebbing, in 1483–4 was performed not by wage labourers but by eleven year-round servants, who were paid modest cash stipends ranging from 3s. 3d. to 22s. 3d. in addition to their board and lodging. Almost two-thirds of the days worked by the labourers hired at Porter's Hall took place during the few weeks of harvest, when the males were richly rewarded with 4d. per day and food. During the rest of the year, however, tasks such as sowing, weeding, ditching and harrowing required the hiring of far less labour and were remunerated at only 1–2d. per day. Significantly, in the light of the heavy weight contributed by wages for threshing and winnowing in the series that estimates an average wage of 3.55d. per day at this time,[22] the four men who performed these tasks at Porter's Hall earned an average of only 1.6d. per day and laboured for only fifty-one days between them. Overall, the mean employment of the male labourers hired during the year on this farm amounted to just 7.8 days and their mean earnings to 24d. Of course, the records of a single large farm can give only a partial picture of the demand for labour in the region, and most of the labourers hired at Porter's Hall must have found some additional employment elsewhere. However, Poos augments the intermittent employment and modest earnings of the labourers, cottagers and servants revealed by the Porter's Hall accounts with complementary evidence from proceedings under the labour legislation and in wills and tax assessments.[23]

Such informative documentation is rare but not unique, and other sources attest to the prevalence of relatively low wages. On the Newton demesne in Cheshire at the turn of the fifteenth and sixteenth centuries, for example, casual labourers often received only 1d. per day for unskilled work and harvest workers were paid merely 2d., and the same niggardly sum was paid to harvest workers at Millom in Cumberland. The Newton accounts, like those of Porter's Hall, reveal a heavy reliance on servants employed on annual contracts, the cash element of which for males ranged from just 5s. to 13s. 4d.[24] The archive of Durham priory,

[21] L. R. Poos, *A Rural Society after the Black Death: Essex, 1350–1525* (Cambridge, 1991), 213–19.
[22] Clark, 'Long March of History', 100. Clark, however, is only following Beveridge, Farmer and others in relying heavily on the remuneration for these tasks.
[23] Poos, *Rural Society*, 219–22.
[24] D. Young, 'Servants and Labourers on a Late Medieval Demesne: The Case of Newton, Cheshire, 1498–1520', *AgHR* 47 (1999), 158–9. Around the same time cash stipends were 16s. at Elvethall manor, Durham, and from 8s. to 13s. 4d. at Millom, Cumberland: ibid., 152–3.

which contains the names of employees, has enabled Christine Newman to complete a detailed study of workers and wages at the priory and its estates from
1494 to 1519, and she tells a similar story of brief, irregular and piecemeal hirings.
Despite being by far the largest institution in the region, the priory offered substantial employment to very few. Newman's conclusion is that the golden age for
labour was tarnished, for it did not have a 'labour market characterised for most
people by fixed employment, settled patterns or predictable career prospects';
most of the time workers were taking what they could get, which did not amount
to much.[25] This pessimistic view is shared by many other researchers, paradoxically including those who have compiled statistics that paint a far more optimistic
picture.[26]

There are also special concerns about the authenticity of the summit of later
medieval real wages, which, according to almost all the series, was attained from
*c.*1440 to *c.*1479. This was a time when the country was in the throes of a deep
and prolonged slump and the agrarian economy was enduring a most savage retrenchment. It is well known that large-scale farmers faced severe problems from
falling commodity prices and rising wages in the later Middle Ages and that these
led to the abandonment of demesne farming by landlords, frequent chronic in-
debtedness of entrepreneurs who ventured to lease abandoned demesnes, a shift
towards pastoral husbandry and the relative scarcity and short-lived duration of
large-scale peasant farms. In the mid fifteenth century these adverse conditions
profoundly worsened and engulfed substantial peasants and aspiring yeomen as
well as the greater and lesser lords.[27] It is not surprising, therefore, that the main
driver that sent the already elevated real-wage index even higher at this time
was a further sharp fall in the prices of farm produce rather than a rise in money
wages. More than this, there is evidence that the severity of the slump was reduc-
ing the demand for labour and driving employment and pay down.[28]

Thus, there is no substance in the belief that the average agricultural labourer
in the fifteenth century was able to find employment for around 250 days a year
at the exalted wage rates recorded in various published series. Few labourers were
able to find work whenever they sought it, or accepted it whenever it was offered,

---

[25] C. Newman, 'Work and Wages at Durham Priory and its Estates, 1494–1519', *Continuity and Change*, 16 (2001), 375–8.

[26] For example, Farmer writes that, because of an inability to answer a series of basic questions adequately, 'it seems a little incautious to hail the fifteenth century as the "golden age of the English labourer"': 'Prices and Wages, 1350–1500', 490–1. Mavis Mate notes that in the fifteenth century, 'Earnings . . . did not always rise together with wage rates', and that outside of harvest time 'workers might be hired for just a few days': 'Work and leisure', in *A Social History of England, 1200–1500*, ed. R. Horrox and W. M. Ormrod (Cambridge, 2006), 286–7.

[27] J. Hatcher, 'The Great Slump of the Mid-Fifteenth Century', in *Progress and Problems in Medieval England: Essays in Honour of Edward Miller*, ed. R. H. Britnell and J. Hatcher (Cambridge, 1996), 259–62.

[28] Ibid., 262–3.

and it is unwise to assume that all of the work that was available was paid at the extremely favourable rates recorded in the published series. In the unlikely circumstance that a labourer was able to enjoy full employment at the 3.5–3.7*d.* recorded in the Clark index, this lowly member of peasant society would have received an annual income of around £4, which is substantially higher than that of a senior full-time estate bailiff, who was paid a maximum of 60*s.* annually, and only 20*s.* or so below the declared taxable income of the majority of Warwickshire gentlemen in 1436 or the sum paid to the steward of the prior of Durham, who was a member of the gentry.[29] But, even more significantly, such optimistic assumptions would have led to the perverse result that peasants could consistently earn far more from casual labouring than they did from working on their own land.

The calculation of the income tenant farmers received from working their own lands avoids many of the uncertainties and complications that dog attempts to estimate earnings from wages. If the calculation is restricted to arable alone it is able to rest on unusually robust data and non-controversial assumptions, for whereas real-wage series cannot capture the participation rate or the earnings of either landless labourers entirely dependent on wages for their sustenance or the common run of peasant farmers who intermittently engaged in casual work, the physical output of an acre of arable farmland and its monetary value can be estimated with a considerable degree of accuracy, as can the number of days required to cultivate it. Of course, in practice there were no exclusively arable farms and farm labour was shared between growing crops and raising livestock, but the quality of the data and the robustness of the results make this theoretical exercise worthwhile, and for the purposes of illustration it will be based on the cultivation of crops on twenty arable acres, of which a generous fifteen acres are assumed to be under cultivation each year. Focusing on the period from 1450 to 1479, and using the distribution of crops given in Campbell's medieval crop-yields database, it is assumed that 5.7 acres of the twenty acres were under wheat, 4.8 acres under barley and 4.5 acres under oats, with the remaining 5 acres left fallow.[30] Mean yields, net of seed, have been derived from the same database, and the selling prices of grains have been taken from Farmer's series in the *Agrarian History of England and Wales, 1348–1500*.[31] Together these data tell us that on average the gross value of an acre of wheat was 5.8*s.*, after reserving seed for the following year, an acre of barley was worth 4.8*s.* and an acre of oats just 1.8*s.* Thus, the

[29]   D. L. Farmer, 'The *Famuli* in the Later Middle Ages', in *Progress and Problems*, ed. Britnell and Hatcher, 235–6; C. Carpenter, *Locality and Polity: A Study of Warwickshire Landed Society, 1401–1499* (Cambridge, 1992), 57; Newman, 'Work and Wages', 361.

[30]   B. M. S. Campbell, 'Three Centuries of English Crops Yields, 1211–1491' (2007), www.cropyields.ac.uk, last accessed 10/12/2009.

[31]   Farmer, 'Prices and Wages, 1350–1500', 502–5.

total wheat crop would have been worth approximately 33*s.*, the barley crop 23*s.*, and the oats crop 8*s.*, giving a combined sale value of 64*s.* for the produce of the twenty acres. From this sum it is necessary to deduct rent and other seigneurial dues, estimated at 10*s. per annum*, with a further 4*s.* allowed for additional costs arising from the depreciation and maintenance of farm equipment, the costs of milling and suchlike. This gives a net average income of 50*s. per annum* from the twenty acres, before payment of tithes.

Meticulous calculations of labour inputs on the arable land of demesne farms by Karakacili and others indicate that from ten to just under fourteen days annually were spent on each acre, including the fallow.[32] A relatively high figure of thirteen days has been adopted for these calculations, since peasants were likely to have invested more labour on their own holdings than did demesnes. Thus, our theoretical peasant farmer would have expended a total of 260 days working his twenty arable acres, which is conveniently close to the assumed full working year of an adult male, and each day worked would have brought him 2.3*d.*

This is a strikingly low figure, and if tithes are deducted from the crops the farmer's earnings would fall to just over 2*d.* per day, which is not much more than half the wage commonly attributed to casual labourers.[33] Such a pronounced difference between the relative rewards of farming and casual labouring is very difficult to explain and would have been very difficult to sustain in practice. Apart from the fact that farmers would have been reluctant to pay labourers more than they added to the value of the output of the farm, any such gap ought to have been swiftly narrowed by a flow of labour from farming into labouring, which would have been relatively easy to achieve since the great bulk of the rural population commonly combined working for themselves with working for others.[34]

This is not all. Yet further doubt can be cast on the validity of common assumptions about wages and the availability of employment in the late Middle Ages by using the same methods and data to estimate the profitability of com-

---

[32] E. Karakacili, 'English Agrarian Labor Productivity Rates before the Black Death: A Case Study,' *Journal of Economic History*, 64 (2004), 24–60; H. S. A. Fox, 'Exploitation of the Landless by Lords and Tenants in Early Medieval England', in *Medieval Society and the Manor Court*, ed. Z. Razi and R. M. Smith (Oxford, 1996), 544–5; C. Thornton, 'The Determinants of Land Productivity on the Bishop of Winchester's Demesne at Rimpton', in *Land, Labour and Livestock: Historical Studies in European Agricultural Productivity*, ed. B. M. S. Campbell and M. Overton (Manchester, 1991), 205–6.

[33] Not surprisingly, attempts to calculate labour productivity using the purchasing power of nominal wages of around 3.5 to 3.7*d.* produce decidedly eccentric results. See, for example, the huge surge in the productivity of threshers, reapers and mowers in the fifteenth century claimed in Clark, 'Long March of History', 112.

[34] Applying identical methods to comparable data drawn from averages across the first half of the fourteenth century reveals a contrasting set of circumstances in which a farmer cultivating twenty acres of arable would have 'earned' around 2.5*d.* per day when the daily wage of an agricultural labourer was just 1.5*d.*

mercial arable farming. If all the conditions for the operation of the notional twenty acres are held constant, excepting that now it is cultivated entirely by hired rather than family labour, the operation would have produced an average annual loss of around 30s. between 1450 and 1479, before deductions for tithes. The prime reason for this dismal performance, of course, is the high imputed cost of labour. Even at a very low ten days' labour per acre with no reduction in yields, the wage bill would have virtually matched the receipts from selling the complete crop, net of seed. While in practice temporary grazing on the arable would have been of some value to the farm livestock, it would have fallen far short of that needed to meet the additional costs of rent, seigneurial dues, milling, capital depreciation of farm equipment, tithes and so on.

Part of the solution to the paradox these speculations have thrown up is, of course, that few farmers paid wages at these exalted levels outside of the busiest times of the year, and that those like William Capell who had ongoing needs for additional labour hired servants on long-term contracts. The rewards and conditions of service that such servants in husbandry, called *famuli*, received provide a further opportunity to place the reputed wages of day labourers in a broader context, and once again it is sobering. For, rather than soaring in the manner that is claimed for the wages of casual labourers, 'in the later Middle Ages the condition of the *famuli* was inconsistent but [only] gradually improving'.[35] Although information becomes ever scarcer as the fifteenth century wears on, we may be confident that the earnings of such servants were only a small fraction of the approximately 75–80s. a year that a labourer might have earned if he had been able to find continuous employment at the reputed 3.5–3.7d. per day. While the annual remuneration in cash and kind of a very few highly-paid servants with full-time duties might reach 50s., which equates to around 2.25–2.5d. per day for a 250–260 day working year, as we have seen, the great majority of servants were likely to have received a small fraction of this.[36]

The seductive charms of readily available sets of measures that are informative, continuous, internally and externally consistent, and capable of spanning the centuries from the Middle Ages to the present day, as well as many countries of the world, have meant that far too much attention has been devoted to attempting to calculate the real wages of landless male casual labourers rather than of those of the great majority, who were landholders and self-employed artisans. The collection of daily wage rates and the prices of a few basic commodities is

---

[35] Farmer, 'The *Famuli*', 236. Harold Fox has written of the tied labourers' cottages, found on many manors in the south-west of England, as indicating 'some degree of debasement of the condition of some labourers in the so-called "Golden Age" of labour': H. S. A. Fox, 'Tenant Farming and Farmers: Devon and Cornwall', in *AHEW* III, 735–7.

[36] See p. 10 above.

also far less problematic than trying to estimate GDP per head by extrapolating national-income accounting backwards into the past alongside estimates of population size, and in addition the results can be expressed in far simpler terms via the experience of a single worker. But it is far from certain that real-wage indices are a more reliable method of estimating living standards. The prospect of being able to draw broad conclusions from the purchasing power of a day's wage has led to a systematic neglect of the limitations of wage and price data and of the realities of the economies from which they have been drawn. Not only do these failings compromise attempts to measure the incomes of full-time labourers, who were a comparatively small section of late medieval society, they vitiate endeavours to extrapolate projections of the movements of the real wages of labourers to the whole population. While labour economics might state that 'the material living standard of the bulk of the population will be determined by the purchasing power of the wages of unskilled workers',[37] the validity of this proposition is dependent on the existence of modern, highly developed labour markets which possess a host of characteristics that did not exist in fifteenth-century England or for a long time afterwards.[38]

Because the majority of households held land, and consequently did not derive their incomes solely from wages or their subsistence solely from the market, the scale and nature of their income and expenditure varied in accordance with a far broader and more varied range of factors than those conventionally used to determine the welfare of labourers. Most obviously, the price of foodstuffs, predominantly grain, has a massive impact on calculations of the real wages of the landless, because food constituted by far the biggest part of their expenditure, but in the real world the great majority of those who laboured for wages also held some land and engaged in the self-supply of foodstuffs.

At the risk of stating the obvious, the stratification of rural society is of crucial importance in determining average real incomes in the fifteenth as well as in subsequent centuries. For, not only did rural households farm widely varying amounts of land for which they paid varying sums in rents and other dues, they practised diverse forms of agriculture, supplied differing proportions of their own subsistence, and had streams of income that varied in scale and source. All this, and much more, meant that villagers were affected in profoundly different ways by the dramatic changes that occurred in the relative prices of labour, food and land in the later Middle Ages. The robust estimates of the level and distribution of incomes must await the collection of the best data and rigorous modelling, but

---

[37] For example, the central role played by this theory in Clark, *Farewell to Alms*, 21–3.

[38] Labour economics is a relatively new field and primarily applicable to modern economies; there are many reasons why its laws should not be applied indiscriminately to pre-industrial labour markets: J. Jacobsen and G. Skillman, *Labour Markets and Employment Relationships: A Comprehensive Approach* (Oxford, 2004), 1–12.

what can be done now with relative ease is to test current assumptions by undertaking some rough and ready projections.

Table 1.1 presents some rudimentary estimates of the fortunes of a range of representative tenant farmers derived from widely accepted and respected data using apparently reasonable methods. For ease of construction and transparency of method, the modelling has been based on an amended and adapted version of the framework established by Kitsikopoulos for households farming eighteen to twenty acres in England before the Black Death of 1348–9.[39] The table is structured largely in the form of a comparison between the first half of the fourteenth century and the three decades from 1450 to 1479. The range of landholding sizes portrayed, including the landless, probably captures in excess of ninety per cent of the rural population and over three-quarters of the total population. The economic performance given in columns (a) and (b) has been measured in the conventional manner by estimating the income and expenditure of the household, converting these estimates into index numbers and assigning the value of 100 to the period before the Black Death.

Family farms were effectively small businesses practising a mix of arable and pastoral husbandry. The sources and amounts of income and the costs of basic subsistence and of running the holding were modelled by making estimates of the following:

(a) the net yields of the arable acres that were cultivated (after making allowances for seed corn and tithes) and the quantities of dairy produce and meat produced by the livestock. The yields of grain and livestock were kept constant, both between farm sizes and between periods.

(b) the quantities of grain, dairy produce and meat consumed by households, and, if purchased, the cost of these and other basic subsistence items. Levels of consumption of these items has been deemed to be the same for each household, regardless of holding size or period.

(c) the net amount received from the sale of agricultural commodities or spent on their purchase.

(d) the amounts paid out in rent and other seigniorial dues, and the costs of all necessary expenditure on the farm, its equipment and its livestock. These amounts have been varied according to holding size and period.

(e) the earnings received by the household from labouring or the sums paid to hire labourers.

For the purposes of modelling, each household is assumed to have had 260 days of labour to expend annually on its own holding or working for wages. An average of thirteen days of labour is assumed to have been expended on each acre of

[39] H. Kitsikopoulos, 'Standards of Living and Capital Formation in Pre-Plague England: A Peasant Budget Model', EcHR 53 (2000), 237–61.

Table 1.1: Estimates of the economic performance of peasant households

	Real income before 1348–9 (a)	Real income 1450–79 (b)	Increase in net income (a–b)	Surplus/deficit income 1450–79
Landless males	100	239	47s.	39s.
5 acres	100	220	38s.	32s.
10 acres	100	188	27s.	23s.
18–20 acres	100	110	5s.	2s.
36–40 acres	100	69	(45s.)	(35s.)

land held. Following Clark, all labour is assumed to have been employed or sold at 1.5d. per day in the early fourteenth century and 3.7d. per day from 1450 to 1479.[40]

It can be seen at a glance that Table 1.1 contains much that is seriously at odds not only with prevailing assumptions about the fifteenth-century agrarian economy but with common-sense and rational economic outcomes. For example, is it likely that all those who farmed land received substantially lower real incomes than those who, in Langland's memorably contemptuous phrase, 'have no land to liven of but their own hands', or that the more land a household farmed the more its surplus income shrank? Is it plausible that cottagers with around five acres enjoyed surplus incomes sixteen times higher than those accruing to farmers with around twenty acres? To repeat, Table 1.1 is based on widely used data held in high repute to which commonly accepted and not obviously defective methods have been applied, but clearly something is amiss with an economy that produces such a state of affairs, or, more likely, with our reconstruction of it.

At first glance, the rates of change in real incomes between 1300 and 1349 and 1450 and 1479, given in columns 1 and 2, might appear superficially less troubling than the incomes themselves given in columns 3 and 4. Other things being equal, the benefit that households derived from the movements that took place in farm costs and revenues during the later Middle Ages might be expected to vary inversely with the amounts of land that were held. The condition of the poorer strata in society should have improved the most, since the landless and near-landless would have enjoyed the quadruple boon of rising wages, increased employment opportunities, falling food prices and easier access to cheap land. Higher up the landholding scale, however, those with more acres to cultivate had fewer days available for working for wages and, eventually, as the acreage farmed by a household came to exceed what could be worked with its own resources, labour needed to be hired rather than sold and high wages turned from a benefit into a cost. At the same time, the amounts of food that a household needed to purchase declined with each additional acre it farmed, until increasing acreages

[40] Clark, 'Long March of History', table 1, 99–100.

eventually resulted in agricultural surpluses for sale. Yet, because those surpluses fetched less in the fifteenth century than they had before, the incomes of large farmers, particularly those who concentrated on the growing of crops, were harmed by precisely the same price movements that benefited the landless.

However, there would appear to be no plausible explanation for the absolute levels of income reported in the final two columns of the table. While there are a number of premises underlying this table that might be in need of some modification, by far the most powerful drivers of eccentricity are, once again, conventional assumptions about wages and work: namely that work was freely available throughout the year at around 3.7d. per day, that all the assistance hired by employers cost around 3.7d. per day, and that those who had spare time devoted it all to working for hire. It is these deeply ingrained beliefs that have the primary responsibility for generating the bizarre patterns of income reported in columns 3 and 4, just as they have prime responsibility for the twin conclusions, spelt out above, that a late medieval peasant earned well over fifty per cent more from time spent working for wages than he did from cultivating his own arable land, and that farmers regularly paid wages far in excess of the marginal productivity of the labour they hired.[41]

Table 1.2, based on revised wage data, starkly demonstrates how acutely sensitive household budgets throughout the landholding spectrum were to adjustments in wage rates and the number of days worked. Whereas in Table 1.1 the unrealistic assumption was made that each household received income from the full balance of the 260 days of labour that was left after cultivating its own holding at the rate of 1.5d. per day in the early fourteenth century and 3.7d. per day from 1450 to 1479, in Table 1.2 the number of days worked for wages is estimated to have been significantly less than the maximum. In addition, in the latter period rates of pay are assumed to be 4d. per day at peak times but only 2.5d. per day for the rest of the year, resulting in an average wage of 2.7–2.8d. per day rather than 3.7d.[42]

As can be seen, the revisions incorporated into Table 1.2 produce dramatic changes in both the absolute and relative incomes of the various landholding strata. There is a marked reduction in the gains of the landless and smallhold-

---

[41] See p. 13 above.

[42] Landless labourers are assumed to have worked for hire for 150 days rather than 260 days, of which thirty were paid at 4d. per day and 120 at 2.5d.; five-acre householders worked for 140 days (twenty at 4d. and 120 at 2.5d.); and ten-acre householders for one hundred days (fifteen at 4d. and ninety-five at 2.5d.). In the next stratum the cultivation of eighteen to twenty acres is assumed to have required the full labour of the male householders. It has been assumed that the same number of days was worked by each category of landholder in the early fourteenth century, and that the rate of pay averaged 1.5d. per day, but it is likely that the availability of paid employment at this time was significantly lower than in the later fifteenth.

Table 1.2: Estimates of economic performance of peasant households using revised wage data

	Real income before 1348–9 (*a*)	Real income 1450–79 (*b*)	Increase in net income (*a–b*)	Surplus/deficit income 1450–79
Landless males	100	191	17s.	(4s.)
5 acres	100	165	16s.	2s.
10 acres	100	150	14s.	6s.
18–20 acres	100	110	5s.	2s.
36–40 acres	100	87	(15s.)	(5s.)

ers at the bottom, who no longer enjoyed incomes far in excess of those with more acres, and an absolute as well as a relative improvement in the fortunes of the larger landholders. These new outcomes are patently less implausible than those depicted in Table 1.1, but they are in need of substantial further adjustment. However, while precision must await extensive research and comprehensive modelling, certain deficiencies can immediately be identified, of which the most significant have led to an understatement of income for all strata. Most importantly, the model adopted for the construction of both tables takes no account of income earned by female members of households from casual labouring and from home-based crafts or ale-brewing, which was significantly higher in the latter period.[43] The allowance made for the range of subsidiary incomes that could accrue to landholders, especially from subletting acres or accommodation, is also inadequate. Moreover, although there can be no denying that the economic environment for farmers with surpluses to sell had been far more favourable in the era of cheap labour and expensive food that prevailed in the early fourteenth century, the model lacks the flexibility that later medieval farmers displayed when they used servants rather than day labourers, adopted new methods, expanded pastoral husbandry at the expense of arable and hired out assets such as pasture, carts and ploughs.

It must be stressed, however, that although such necessary adjustments would undoubtedly bring estimates of income closer to reality by increasing them, it is difficult to see how any reasonable assumptions could have the effect of raising the net profits of the great majority of households by anything like the 100 to 150 per cent that is claimed for the real incomes of labourers. Indeed, in addition to the certainty that the profits of the majority of large farmers declined

---

[43] For a recent account of the improvement in the labour conditions of women in the later Middle Ages, see T. de Moor and J. L. Van Zanden, 'Girl Power: The European Marriage Pattern and Labour Markets in the North Sea Region in the Late Medieval and Early Modern Period', *EcHR* 63 (2010), 1–33.

significantly, there is the strong probability that the incomes of classic subsistence farms of fifteen to twenty acres, a common size in the fifteenth century,
could not have changed dramatically over time. The reason is obvious, for such
farms were by their very nature geared towards self-sufficiency, which meant that
they engaged relatively little in the market: their food output was likely to match
the consumption needs of the family that farmed it, and the labour required to
work the land they held was likely to match the resources the family could supply. Thus, while the ten per cent increase in income signalled in both of the tables
for these middling landholders is almost certainly on the low side for the reasons
given in the preceding paragraph, the actual figure is unlikely to have been substantially greater. Overall, the inevitable conclusion is that far too much affluence
has been claimed for the fifteenth century.

The fallacy that average real incomes in the later fifteenth century were as high
as or even higher than they were to be in the mid and later nineteenth century is
further exposed by the stark contrast between the structure of the economies of
the two periods. Whereas the empirically-generated income and expenditure patterns found in Victorian England are entirely compatible with the highly indus-
trialised, urbanised and commercialised nation of that time, the similar income
and expenditure patterns conjectured for the fifteenth century are entirely at odds
with an economy in which the urban, commercial and industrial sectors were
stunted.[44] In the later nineteenth century no more than one in four persons was
employed in agriculture, whereas large-scale research into late medieval occupational structures is confirming that well over sixty per cent of the total workforce
regularly found employment in agriculture and closely associated activities, and
a recent investigation has concluded that the proportion of the population living
in towns probably declined in the late Middle Ages.[45] The sharp contrast in occupational structure is, of course, accompanied by an even more dramatic difference
in the range and quality of the goods and services available at the two dates.[46]
    While it is possible that there was some overall growth in the consumption
of manufactures, non-essential items and services relative to the depleted size of

[44] This paradox is discussed without questioning the validity of conventional real-wage estimates in Clark and van der Werf, 'Work in Progress?', 830–1, and J. de Vries, *The Industrious
Revolution: Consumer Behaviour and the Household Economy, 1650 to the Present* (Cambridge, 2008), 90–1.

[45] L. Shaw-Taylor and E. A. Wrigley, *The Occupational Structure of Britain, 1379–1911* (www.
geog.cam.ac.uk/research/projects/occupations/abstracts); S. H. Rigby, 'Urban Population
in Late Medieval England: The Evidence of the Lay Subsidies', *EcHR* 63 (2010), 393–417.

[46] Such a massive improvement in the material standards of comfort and convenience available over the 400 years makes it extremely difficult to conduct a meaningful comparison of
standards of living using traditional methods, as Phelps Brown noted. See J. B. DeLong, 'Cor-
nucopia: Increasing Wealth in the Twentieth Century', *National Bureau of Economic Research
Working Papers* 7602 (March 2000).

the late medieval population, there is nothing to indicate that there was a revolutionary expansion of consumption. Quite simply, the urban, industrial and commercial sectors of late medieval England contain no evidence of the impact that real wages at 'extraordinarily high levels' would have had.[47] The lower social strata were the main beneficiaries of the transformation in the relative scarcity of labour and land, but it is important not to confuse the pace of improvement in their welfare with the absolute levels of income they received. By universal agreement the early fourteenth century was a time of deep poverty when well over half of the population were landless or lived on inadequate smallholdings,[48] and even very substantial improvement would have left much smaller amounts of disposable income in the pockets of the labouring poor of the fifteenth century than it has long been customary to assume. Moreover, it is likely that they spent the greater part of the increased purchasing power they enjoyed on subsistence items rather than genuine consumer purchases: more and better food and drink, including meat and dairy produce; higher-quality bread and ale; more fuel and lighting; and, of course, the freedom to choose when to work and when to spend time and money on leisure and in the alehouse.[49] Naturally, even the households of labourers and cottagers often had some money left over for clothing, furniture, bedding, tableware, cooking pots, and the occasional even more frivolous acquisition, as moralists of the age never tired of claiming. But, the labouring poor simply did not have enough purchasing power to generate a genuine consumer revolution, especially as the consumption of manufactured items was dampened by the fact that their prices rose substantially while those of farm produce fell.[50]

---

[47]   The phrase used by Clark and van der Werf in 'Work in Progress?', 830.

[48]   For statistics showing the proliferation of smallholdings, see J. Hatcher and M. Bailey, *Modelling the Middle Ages: The History and Theory of England's Economic Development* (Oxford, 2001), 44–6, and C. Dyer, *Standards of Living in the Later Middle Ages* (rev. edn, Cambridge, 1998), 126. For discussion of the existence of labour surpluses that were far too substantial to have been absorbed by secondary employments, see Hatcher and Bailey, *Modelling the Middle Ages*, 43–55, 134–7. Calculations of the supply and demand for labour on Ramsey abbey manors in the later thirteenth century suggest that even on the most cautious estimates underemployment would have approached thirty per cent (I am grateful to James Gill for this information).

[49]   As Engels noted, 'the normal diet of the individual worker . . . varies according to his wages' and both the quantity and quality eaten increased with income: F. Engels, *The Condition of the Working Class in England*, ed. and trans. W. O. Henderson and W. H. Chaloner (Oxford, 1845), 45, cited in Allen, *British Industrial Revolution*, 28–9. For evidence of improving diet in the fifteenth century, see C. Dyer, 'Changes in Diet in the Late Middle Ages: The Case of Harvest Workers', *AgHR* 36 (1988), 21–37. For the existence of leisure preference in the later Middle Ages, see J. Hatcher, 'Labour, Leisure and Economic Thought Before the Nineteenth Century', *P&P* 160 (1998), 76–80; G. Persson, 'Consumption, Labour and Leisure in the Late Middle Ages', in *Manger et boire au Moyen Âge*, ed. K. G. Persson (Nice, 1984), 211–23; Dyer, *Standards of Living*, 224–5.

[50]   Precise measurement of the cost of industrial products is bedevilled by the difficulties of en-

Accordingly, local markets reveal a proliferation of butchers and bakers but scant trace of trade in luxuries and semi-luxuries.[51]

The case has been made in this essay that the projections of real wages across seven centuries and more that have for so long been deeply embedded in the historiography do not represent accurately the levels and fluctuations in the incomes of the workers they are meant to record, still less those of the population at large. Most of the criticisms made in this essay of the way in which real-wage indices have been compiled, interpreted and applied have implications that stretch far beyond the fifteenth century.

It needs no stressing that living standards are a key concern of social and economic historians and used as one of the most powerful indicators of the character and performance of economies, or that real-wage data loom very large in attempts to put dimensions to such crucial issues as the nature of pre-industrial and developing economies and the welfare of their inhabitants, the progress of the industrial revolution and the distribution of its fruits, and historical comparisons between the economic development of England and other parts of Europe and the wider world.[52] And, of course, since well before Malthus living standards have been the lynchpin of explanatory frameworks for demographic behaviour.[53]

More than this, real wages are the central pillar of one of the most powerful and enduring tenets in economic history, namely that the history of the world has been divided into two phases. The first phase, termed Malthusian, persisted until the nineteenth century and is characterised by the lack of any long-run trend in real wages. As can be seen from Figures 1.1 and 1.2 above, and from a multitude

---

suring that like is compared with like, but we may be confident that the average increase of around a third in the prices of nails, salt and cloth between the early fourteenth century and the later fifteenth is not an exaggeration of inflation in the sector as a whole. For the prices of nails and salt, see Farmer, 'Prices and Wages, 1350–1500', 512–16; for the price of cloth, see Clark, 'Long March of History', 108, and Munro, 'Prices and Wages'.

51   I am indebted to James Davis, Mark Bailey and Jo Sear for informing me of the results of their researches into the local markets of late medieval East Anglia.

52   For example, real wages are central to the 'Great Divergence' debate: K. Pomeranz, *The Great Divergence: China, Europe and the Making of the Modern World Economy* (Princeton, 2000); R. C. Allen, 'The Great Divergence in European Wages and Prices from the Middle Ages to the First World War', *Explorations in Economic History*, 38 (2001), 411–47; S. Broadberry and B. Gupta, 'The Early Modern Great Divergence: Wages, Prices and Economic Development in Europe and Asia, 1500–1800', *EcHR* 59 (2006), 2–31.

53   Some would see the potential to unlock far more information from these basic data. For example, Gregory Clark believes that by 'using day wages, we can build up a picture of English agricultural history that presents an internally consistent picture of the real wage, the MPL (marginal product of labour), output per farm worker, national population, the share employed in agriculture, and agricultural efficiency in general, from 1200 to 1869': 'Long March of History', 127.

of similar representations, there is no sign of any secular trend towards higher living standards before the industrial era. Instead there was overall stagnation, punctuated by wide swings that were linked to rising and falling population. The explanation for this stagnation is the so-called 'Malthusian Trap', within which high real wages and gains in efficiency were inevitably channelled into population growth, which in turn undermined prosperity. Thus, it was only when the industrial revolution was well under way that the Malthusian cycle that characterised the first phase was finally broken and both real wages and population were able to rise together.[54]

The unparalleled height of the late medieval peak in real wages is a crucial component of this grand and enduring framework, and this and the precipitous plunge that occurred over the ensuing century and a half were by far the most pronounced of the swings that occurred between the 1200s and the 1800s. If, as has been argued in this essay, the height of the late medieval peak and the steepness of the subsequent early modern plunge are drastically reduced, much of the power of the overarching two-phase stagnationist exposition would be lost. In fact a different picture would emerge, and a different model would be required to account for it. With some confidence it can be predicted that the vertiginous oscillations displayed in conventional wage series based solely on estimates of the fortunes of the landless would be substantially moderated by the inclusion of the countervailing forces arising from the incomes of other social and occupational sectors, and that across the centuries a discernible rising trend in average real incomes will emerge.[55]

The long-term course of the real incomes of whole societies cannot be represented by any particular group, since shifts in key indices such as population, prices and wages affected different groups in markedly different and often contrary ways. It is equally true that the huge shifts that took place in the distribution of land and resources over time could be at least as important as fluctuations in wage rates. The bulk of the data on the distribution of land recorded in later-fourteenth- and fifteenth-century manorial rentals, surveys and extents scattered throughout England has yet to be systematically collected and analysed, nevertheless there is no doubt that as the population plunged the average number of acres per head rose sharply, the proportions of the landless and near landless fell steeply, possibly from as much as two-thirds before 1349 to well under half in

---

[54] For a brief description of the two-phase theory and the role of real wages in it, see Allen, 'Real Wage Rates'. For a more detailed analysis of Malthusian theory and pre-industrial economies, see Hatcher and Bailey, *Modelling the Middle Ages*, 21–65.

[55] Real GDP per head data currently being produced from estimates of output, wealth and population size show a modest but generally cumulative trend growth in the half millennium between the later thirteenth century and the mid nineteenth century: S. N. Broadberry, B. M. S. Campbell, B. van Leuwen and M. Overton, *British Economic Growth, 1300–1850: Some Preliminary Estimates* (Working paper, University of Warwick, 2010).

the later fifteenth century, and the proportions of households farming holdings of subsistence size and somewhat greater increased significantly.[56] Therefore, in order to provide reliable national estimates for the late Middle Ages, not only do the rising real incomes of labourers and smallholders have to be set against the relatively inflexible incomes of subsistence farmers and the falling real incomes of large farmers, but the changing proportions in each category have to be taken into account.

All the conventional indices signal that real wages plunged precipitously for most of the sixteenth and early seventeenth centuries as the gains the lower strata made in the preceding era were severely eroded. However, as William Harrison explained with great clarity in the mid 1570s, rising agricultural prices and the falling real cost of labour meant that many farmers and husbandmen were far better off than their predecessors had been despite the substantially higher rents that they paid. Harrison helpfully related the rising incomes of the middling and greater sort directly to a markedly increased consumption of the sorts of goods that feature in the progressively richer and more varied household inventories that have so perplexed historians who would only follow the rapidly deteriorating fortunes of landless adult males.[57]

As the economy subsequently became progressively more developed and differentiated, the occupational structure was decisively altered and along with it the levels of incomes enjoyed by its constituent parts. The provision of robust genuinely national measures of long-term changes in real incomes will therefore necessitate estimating not only the household budgets of all significant occupational groups but the relative size of these groups. In other words, it will involve an exercise not dissimilar to that undertaken by Gregory King when he created his social tables in the 1680s. This will be a far more complex and less precise undertaking than simply recording wage rates and the prices of subsistence goods, but however tentative the findings it produces they are certain to provide a more accurate measure than the crude real wages on which we have for so long placed so much reliance.

[56] For sizes of landholding on individual manors, see, for example, R. H. Britnell, 'Tenant Farming and Tenant Farmers: Eastern England', in *AHEW* III, 614–6; E. King, 'Tenant Farming and Tenant Farmers: The East Midlands', in *AHEW* III, 624; Fox, 'Devon and Cornwall', 724; Dyer, *Standards of Living*, 141; J. Hatcher, *Rural Economy and Society in the Duchy of Cornwall, 1300–1500* (Cambridge, 1970), 226–8.

[57] W. Harrison, *The Description of England*, ed. G. Edelen (New York, 1968), 200–2.

2

Minimum Wages and Unemployment Rates in Medieval England:
The Case of Old Woodstock, Oxfordshire, 1256–1357

....

John Langdon

Many might consider a discussion of minimum wages and unemployment rates in the Middle Ages as hopelessly anachronistic. Certainly medieval people would probably have had considerable trouble in understanding what either of these concepts meant. Unemployment rates — the percentage of the total available workforce who are *not* employed — would certainly puzzle them. In their minds, everyone, even the habitually lazy, would be put to work for family and community, especially at busy times like the harvest. Minimum wages in the way we think of them today would likely have been no easier for them to understand. Certainly, when state attempts to regulate wages were made in the Middle Ages, as after the advent of the Black Death, it was to set a ceiling on wages, not to bring them up to a certain level.[1]

Yet medieval authorities undoubtedly did have a sense at any particular moment of what might comprise a basal or lowest level wage for both skilled and unskilled labour and would also have a sense, although certainly a more vague one, of the current availability of that labour. As a surrogate for these almost instinctively held notions, then, it might be useful, despite the dangers of anachronism, to apply modern concepts such as minimum wages and unemployment rates as conceptual aids for achieving a better understanding of waged labour in the Middle Ages. Unfortunately, most of the work done on medieval wages, from Thorold Rogers onwards, has tended to be unhelpful for establishing such things as basal wages, either because of the focus on *average* wages, as discussed below, or because of a greater emphasis on elite workers, such as craftsmen. The wages of

---

[1] S. A. C. Penn and C. Dyer, 'Wages and Earnings in Late Medieval England: Evidence from the Enforcement of the Labour Laws', *EcHR* 43 (1990), 356–76; D. Farmer, 'Prices and Wages, 1350–1500', in *AHEW* III, 483–90; L. F. Salzman, *Building in England down to 1540: A Documentary History* (Oxford, 1952; reprint. with corrections and additions, 1967), esp. 72–6; B. H. Putnam, *The Enforcement of the Statute of Labourers during the First Decade after the Black Death* (New York, 1907), esp. 1–3.

those we would call manual workers, those who brought relatively limited skills beyond brute physical exertion, have, until recently, been lightly considered for the medieval period, certainly up to the advent of the Black Death, even in the famous series by Phelps Brown and Hopkins.[2] Yet it is these manual workers who were certainly closest to earning what we would call a minimum wage, and it also seems that their daily earnings most closely conformed to what authorities or society at large felt was a proper basal wage.

This unskilled labour was performed by a constellation of people, not only adult males, but also women, adolescents, children, possibly the elderly and infirm, even prisoners,[3] each receiving what might be called a specialised rate, according to what was customarily paid to them or their perceived ability to provide useful work relative to an able adult male.[4] Preferences were clearly at work here, where it seems clear that adult male labour was the 'norm' and would — in most circumstances — be the first hired. Women and other 'marginal' workers served effectively as a reserve work force.[5] As a result, something akin to a crude 'unemployment index' might be to measure over time when this reserve labour was engaged (indicating relatively full employment) and when it was not (indicating a shortage of employment). Certain activities show this variation in labour demand better than others. Agriculture regularly employed women and probably children and other marginal labourers (like the elderly or infirm), so it is difficult to tell whether in any one year that the level of this 'reserve' labour was higher than normal or not. Other activities show the 'reserve' labour more clearly, simply because the appearance of women and children was likely to be less frequent. One of these was building. As in our own time, building activity could fluctuate

---

[2]   E. H. Phelps Brown and S. V. Hopkins, 'Seven Centuries of Building Wages', *Economica* 22 (1955), 195–206. Up to 1350, Phelps Brown and Hopkins were undecided as to whether the wage for labourers was 1½d. or 2d. per day: 'Seven Centuries of Building Wages', table 1 (p. 205) and figure 1 (p. 197). More recently, a more definitive compilation of the daily wages of labourers has been pushed back into the thirteenth century by J. H. Munro, 'Wage-Stickiness: Monetary Changes, and Real Incomes in Late-Medieval England the Low Countries, 1300–1450: Did Money Matter?', *Research in Economic History*, 21 (2003), see esp. table 6 (pp. 342–4).

[3]   Prisoners were employed at Rockingham Castle in the 1270s and 1280s, those with chains being paid ½d. per day, those without chains 1d. per day: for example, TNA, E101/480/20, m. 1; /480/25, m. 1d; /480/28, m. 5.

[4]   For debate in relation to women, see S. Bardsley, 'Women's Work Reconsidered: Gender and Wage Differentiation in Late Medieval England', *P&P* 165 (1999), 3–29; J. Hatcher, 'Debate: Women's Work Reconsidered: Gender and Wage Differentiation in Late Medieval England', *P&P* 173 (2001), 191–8; S. Bardsley, 'Reply', *P&P* 173 (2001), 199–202.

[5]   There is a growing consensus around women in particular often serving as a reserve work force: Bardsley, 'Women's Work Reconsidered', 4–5; R. H. Britnell, *Britain and Ireland 1050–1530: Economy and Society* (Oxford, 2004), 378; M. K. McIntosh, *Working Women in English Society, 1300–1620* (Cambridge, 2005), 7.

dramatically over time, displaying decided 'boom and bust' periods.[6] The sources for tracking building expenditure are rich for the medieval period in England. Building costs routinely appear in manorial accounts for instance, and following these over time can tell us much about phases of building investment.[7] But much more useful sources for building investment — in that expenses for wages and materials were often entered on a weekly rather than a yearly basis (as in manorial accounts) — are the royal works accounts found in the E101 class of records in The National Archives at Kew, which detailed the construction and repair costs of the various royal castles, palaces and houses. Hundreds of these accounts exist for the medieval period, and for specific sites the number of accounts is sizeable (over fifty for the Westminster complex of buildings before 1348–9, for example). They supply labour information of a richness not found in the manorial accounts which make up the wage series of Thorold Rogers, Beveridge, Phelps Brown and Hopkins, Farmer, or Munro. The works accounts also add another dimension to the analysis of wages. They supply considerable material about the casual labour market, as indicated, for instance, by the frequent appearance in the accounts of women, a pointed noted in L. F. Salzman's seminal book on building in medieval England.[8] But no one, including Salzman, has ever tried to examine systematically the shifting nature of this casual labour.

This particular study is meant as a modest pilot project to tease out the information concerning basic manual labour, including the 'reserve' labour of women, the young, and perhaps others like the disabled or elderly, for one particular royal site, the royal manor and park complex at Old Woodstock (henceforward referred to simply as Woodstock) in Oxfordshire, now the site of Blenheim Palace. Woodstock was chosen because it has a reasonably generous survival of accounts and fits more into a rural environment than most other sites covered in the works accounts. Serving largely as a temporary residence-cum-hunting lodge,[9] Woodstock's houses and park fences were continually being refurbished in anticipation of the king's visits, thus explaining the high number of surviving accounts, about as good as any for the royal sites except Westminster. There are many gaps, particularly from 1304 to 1334 in the period we plan to study here, but there are enough accounts to get a sense of the scale and nature of employment on the manor and whether it contained significant amounts of labour from other than adult, able-bodied men. Because of their inconsistency in format and often poor preservation, going through these accounts is demanding on eyesight and

---

[6]   J. Langdon, J. Walker and J. R. Falconer, 'Boom and Bust: Building Investment on the Bishop of Winchester's Estate in the Early Fourteenth Century', in *The Winchester Pipe Rolls and Medieval English Society*, ed. R. H. Britnell (Woodbridge, 2003), 139–55.

[7]   As in ibid.

[8]   Salzman, *Building in England*, 69, 71, 78, 153, 224, 227, 235, 265 and 337.

[9]   See R. Allen Brown, H. M. Colvin and A. J. Taylor, *The History of the King's Works*, I: *The Middle Ages* (London, 1963), 42–8, 81–7, 120–30 and 241–8.

concentration, and so deliberate section-by-section analysis of each account has been limited to the first century or so after the accounts start, that is, 1256 to 1357. Ultimately, the information was obtained for thirty-seven of these years, in part or in full, contained in twenty-two separate accounts.

The 'Minimum' Adult Wage

The first concern of the study was to determine what the basal or minimum wage rates were for the various types of manual labour recorded in the accounts. Usually such information was given in the form of a short statement indicating: (1) the type of person employed — the actual name of the person was almost never given — and often what s/he was doing, (2) the length of employment (usually during a particular week), (3) the total amount paid to the worker for that particular period of time, and — sometimes — (4) the rate per day upon which the total was calculated. Thus, as three examples involving women collecting moss (for bedding tiles or slates during roofing construction or repair):

(a) 'In one woman hired for collecting moss for the same time (that is, the 'whole week' mentioned two statements before), 9d., who took 1½ pence per day' ('In j muliere conducta ad colligendam mossam per idem tempus, ixd., que cepit per diem jd. ob.').[10]

(b) 'And in one woman collecting moss for five days, 5d.' ('Et in j ancilla coligenda mousam per v dies, vd.').[11]

(c) 'And in one woman collecting moss for the whole week, 6d.' ('Et in j ancilla coligenda mousam per totam septimam, vjd.').[12]

In collecting the data for calculating basal rates for unskilled labour, both female and male, a very conservative approach was taken. A statement was not considered as suitable for inclusion in the statistical analysis unless the actual rate per day was give, as in example (a), or could be determined with near certainty from other evidence in the statement, as in example (b), where, by dividing the total amount paid by the number of days worked, it seems obvious that the woman was making 1d. per day. In cases where more than one person was involved, it was assumed that each person received the same wage. Thus, if two women had been collecting moss for five days and were paid 10d., it was assumed that both were making 1d. per day each. However, when the entry described the time period as 'the whole week', as in example (c), the entry was not included in the quantifying process, because of the uncertainty in the number of days worked

---

[10]   For the year 1334: TNA, E101/497/29.

[11]   For the year 1292: TNA, E101/497/19.

[12]   For the year 1293: TNA, E101/497/19.

in the week, even though in the great majority of cases, 'the whole week' seemingly meant six working days (as can be inferred in example (*a*)).

Even with these restrictions, a considerable amount of data for unskilled labour wage rates was drawn together, as indicated in Tables 2.1, 2.2 and 2.3. The tables are arranged by decade and according to the various terms found in the accounts for both men and women. Many wage series tend to give averages only, say year by year or decade by decade,[13] but, as has been done in Tables 2.1–2.3, it is much more revealing to break the data into means, medians and modes in order to get a better sense of the spread of the values, critical here in giving a sense of what was the normative wage for various categories of labour. Only using means gives a false sense that the wages were continually being shaped by the market. In fact, within the limits of the categories in which workers found themselves, deeply entrenched attitudes among the suppliers and consumers of labour largely kept wages stable in preindustrial societies.[14] This was seemingly the case regardless of experience, especially for unskilled workers. An experienced digger, for example, was probably rewarded not by receiving a higher wage, but by being hired more often. As a result, these notional wages dictated largely by custom tend — statistically — to be revealed more clearly by the *mode* (that is, the most commonly occurring value in the data) rather than the mean.

As shown in Tables 2.1–2.3, the terminology used for both male and female workers could vary notably over time. For example, there were four main terms for unskilled male workers in the Woodstock accounts. The most common throughout the entire run of accounts was *homo* (Table 2.1), simply 'man'. In the earlier accounts *operarius* (that is, 'worker') was also common (again, see Table 2.1). Where the gender of the word was revealed in the heavily abbreviated medieval script, it was always masculine, and so it has been characterised as such in Table 2.1. Another very common term for male workers and very redolent of an inferior status was the term *servitor* ('servant'; see Table 2.2), again, when indicated, always masculine. These males tended to support the work of various craftsmen working on the royal manor. Another term, again somewhat unique to the Woodstock accounts and only appearing in the fourteenth century, was *quadrator* or *quarrarius* (see Table 2.2), in both cases meaning 'quarryman'. These

[13] As Beveridge and Farmer did for the medieval period: W. Beveridge, 'Wages in the Westminster Manors', *EcHR* 7 (1936), 22–43; idem, 'Westminster Wages in the Manorial Era', *EcHR* 8 (1955), 18–35; D. L. Farmer, 'Prices and Wages', in *AHEW* II, 768–72, 811–17; idem, 'Prices and Wages, 1350–1500', esp. 474–81, 516–20. Phelps Brown and Hopkins ('Seven Centuries of Building Wages') do a better job of indicating the predominant, rather than mean, values, as does John Munro ('Wage-Stickiness'). Sandy Bardsley also attempted a more subtle breakdown of her wage data than just employing means ('Women's Work Reconsidered', esp. tables 2 and 4, pp. 15, 24).

[14] On this point, see Munro, 'Wage-stickiness', esp. 204–6; see also H. Phelps Brown and S. V. Hopkins, *A Perspective of Wages and Prices* (London, 1981), 2–3.

Table 2.1: Male wages at the royal manor and park at Woodstock, 1256–1357 (part one)

Time period[a]	Homo					Operarius				
	a	b	c	d	e	a	b	c	d	e
1250s [1]	—	—	—	—	—	1.55	1.55	—	2	1.5–1.6
1260s [3]	1.63	1.63	—	2	1.5–1.75	1.44	1.5	1.5 (21)	26	0.75–2
1270s [2]	—	—	—	—	—	1.63	1.5	1.5 (5)	7	1.5–2
1280s [1]	3	3	3 (1)	1	3	1.5	1.5	1.5 (2)	2	1.5
1290s [8]	1.6	1.5	1.5 (100)	140	1–2.5	1.75	1.5	1.5 (3)	4	1.5–2.5
1300s [1]	1.5	1.5	1.5 (9)	9	1.5	—	—	—	—	—
1330s [1]	1.92	2	2 (11)	13	1.5–2	—	—	—	—	—
1340s [5][b]	—	—	—	—	—	—	—	—	—	—
1350s [3][c]	3.18	3	3 (21)	73	1.5–5	—	—	—	—	—

Sources: TNA, E101/497/12–/498/9.

Column headings: a — mean (in *denarii* (pence); henceforward abbreviated to '*d.*'); b — median (in *d.*); c — mode (in *d.*; the number in brackets indicates the number of cases at that value); d — total number of cases; e — range of values (in *d.*).

[a] the number in square brackets indicates the number of accounts making up the decade or time period indicated.

[b] up to and including 1347.

[c] from 1349 to 1357.

Table 2.2: Male wages at the royal manor and park at Woodstock, 1256–1357 (part two)

Time period[a]	Servitor					Quadrator/Quarrarius				
	a	b	c	d	e	a	b	c	d	e
1250s [1]	—	—	—	—	—	—	—	—	—	—
1260s [3]	1.5	1.5	1.5 (2)	2	1.5	—	—	—	—	—
1270s [2]	1.5	1.5	1.5 (2)	2	1.5	—	—	—	—	—
1280s [1]	—	—	—	—	—	—	—	—	—	—
1290s [8]	1.46	1.5	1.5 (63)	72	1–2	—	—	—	—	—
1300s [1]	1.5	1.5	1.5 (3)	3	1.5	—	—	—	—	—
1330s [1]	1.5	1.5	1.5 (4)	4	1.5	1.5	1.5	1.5 (2)	2	1.5
1340s [5][b]	1.05	1	1 (27)	32	1–1.5	1	1	1 (54)	55	1–1.25
1350s [3][c]	2.07	2	2 (16)	38	1–3	2	2	2 (17)	17	2

Sources: TNA, E101/497/12–/498/9.

Column headings: a — mean (in *denarii* (pence); henceforward abbreviated to '*d*.'); b — median (in *d*.); c — mode (in *d*.); c — mode (in *d*.); d — total number of cases at that value); d — total number of cases; e — range of values (in *d*.).

the number in square brackets indicates the number of accounts making up the decade or time period indicated.

a the number in square brackets indicates the number of cases at that value; d — total number of cases; e — range of values (in *d*.).

b up to and including 1347.

c from 1349 to 1357.

Table 2.3: Female wages at the royal manor and park at Woodstock, 1256–1357

Time period[a]	Ancilla					Mulier				
	a	b	c	d	e	a	b	c	d	e
1250s [1]	—	—	—	—	—	—	—	—	—	—
1260s [3]	1	1	1 (3)	3	1	—	—	—	—	—
1270s [2]	—	—	—	—	—	—	—	—	—	—
1280s [1]	1	1	1 (1)	1	1	—	—	—	—	—
1290s [8]	1.04	1	1 (11)	12	1–1.5	—	—	—	—	—
1300s [1]	—	—	—	—	—	—	—	—	—	—
1330s [1]	—	—	—	—	—	1.5	1.5	1.5 (2)	2	1.5
1340s [5][b]	—	—	—	—	—	1	1	1 (1)	1	1
1350s [3][c]	—	—	—	—	—	1.5	1.5	1.5 (1)	1	1.5

Sources: TNA, E101/497/12–/498/9.

Column headings: a – mean (in *denarii* (pence); henceforward abbreviated to '*d.*'); b – median (in *d.*); c – mode (in *d.*); the number in brackets indicates the number of cases at that value); d – total number of cases; e – range of values (in *d.*).

a   the number in square brackets indicates the number of accounts making up the decade or time period indicated.

b   up to and including 1347.

c   from 1349 to 1357.

men were invariably involved in digging up rocks and stones for masons building walls and were the most specialised term among the cohort of unskilled labourers. A few other terms denoting relatively unskilled male workers were evident in the Woodstock accounts, but in small numbers. One was *garcio*, literally meaning 'boy', but often used in accounts and other documents to indicate someone in service, especially when connected to a craftsman,[15] and so perhaps here in the Woodstock case virtually synonymous with *servitor*. In any case, because of its rarity in this particular set of accounts, it has not been included in the statistical breakdown in Tables 2.1–2.3. Finally, *fodiator* ('digger') was very occasionally used as an alternative to *quadrator* or *quarrarius*, but so infrequently that it too was not included in the statistical analysis.

The two main terms for female labour (Table 2.3), *ancilla* and *mulier*, have already been given in examples above. *Ancilla*, found in the accounts up to 1303–4, means 'maidservant' in classical Latin and may have indicated a younger woman,[16] while *mulier* (often translated as 'wife'), found in the 1334–5 account onwards, carried the connotation of an older married woman, although the scribes were employing it in a more general sense to include both married and unmarried women.[17] The term *femina*, often found in accounts for other royal sites, was only occasionally used in the Woodstock accounts examined here and so has not been included in Table 2.3.

As mentioned above, the mode numbers (column 'c' in the tables) are the most revealing in giving the sense both of the 'minimum' wage and the consistency with which it was applied. Among the *operarii* (Table 2.1) — the most frequently used designation in the early accounts — thirty-two of the forty-one 'reliable' cases (or seventy-eight per cent) were exactly at the rate of 1½d. per day, covering work that included digging stones, carrying stones and other material to masons in particular, and mixing mortar, all relatively menial, unskilled jobs.

Those workers termed simply as 'men' (*homines*) tended to vary much more widely in the daily rate they were paid, partly because they also occurred in the more highly remunerated post-plague period but also because the term seemed to cover a broader range of workers. This was clearly very time-specific, so that in, say, the 1290s the term *homo* seems to have been interchangeable with *operarius*; the mode rate for *homines* in that decade was 1½d. per day which occurred in one hundred (or seventy-one per cent) of the 140 trustworthy cases, underlining

[15] See, for example, H. S. A. Fox, 'Exploitation of the Landless by Lords and Tenants in Early Medieval England', in *Medieval Society and the Manor Court*, ed. Z. Razi and R. M. Smith (Oxford, 1996), esp. 521; *Dictionary of Medieval Latin from British Sources*, fasc. IV (F–G–H), prepared by D. R. Howlett (Oxford, 1989), 1050–1.

[16] This certainly is the opinion concerning the term *ancilla* given in P. J. P. Goldberg, 'What Was a Servant?', in *Concepts and Patterns of Service in the Later Middle Ages*, ed. A. Curry and E. Matthew (Woodbridge, 2000), esp. 4–6.

[17] Again, particularly in the 1334–5 account: TNA, E101/497/29.

strongly that the base rate for unskilled adult male labourers, 'men' and 'workers' alike, was probably 1½d. per day. Later on, in the 1330s, the same consistency in rate for 'men' was seen, but at 2d. per day; as we shall see later, this decade seemed to experience a spike in wages. These rates, it should be noted, are more or less consistent with those tabulated recently by John Munro, who lists 'nominal' wages for — presumably male — labourers at 1½d. per day from at least the late 1260s up to 1300, then rising to 2d. per day by 1320.[18] After the arrival of the plague, the rate for the work of *homines* at Woodstock began to vary much more widely. This was especially the case for the period we have classified as the 1350s (actually covering 1349–57), when the work of *homines* seems in many cases to have included that normally carried out by craftsmen. It is possible that, in the depleted labour force after the advent of the Black Death, many 'unaccredited' persons may have done work more normally performed by craftsmen. Certainly, there was no strongly established mode value in the data for *homines* during this 'decade', the actual mode value of 3d. being found in only twenty-one (or twenty-nine per cent) of seventy-three reliable cases.

Much more specific in terms of what they were paid were that group of people called *servitores* in the accounts. It might be possible to consider them as apprentices and so tied to the craftsmen they were serving, especially where a lump sum was paid both for the craftsman and his helper, which was particularly common among those craftsmen who worked in high places (roofers, slaters, tilers and plumbers), who needed a nimble assistant to climb up and down ladders.[19] On the other hand, those cases where the helper was paid separately, especially when serving masons but also often even with roofers, seem to have been more temporary arrangements. The same could be said of the *homines* and *operarii* who were often specifically designated as helping a mason, roofer or carpenter, the term 'man' or 'worker' implying a certain independence from the person they were serving. If the term *servitor*, when paid separately (and as listed in Table 2.2), can be said to fall into the same independent category, thus making apprenticeship unlikely, then it may indicate a more specific category of casual male labour than the less precise 'man' or even 'worker'. As shown in Table 2.2, wages rates for these separately paid *servitores* were very stable, even through the 1330s, when wages as a whole on the Woodstock site seemed to rise. Although the sample is admittedly dominated numerically (in terms of cases) by those drawn from the 1290s, seventy-three (or eighty-nine per cent) of the total of eighty-two reliable cases through to the 1330s set the daily wage rate for the *servitor* squarely at 1½d. per day. For these 'servants', there was a surprising dip in wages during the 1340s, down, in terms of the mode value, to 1d. per day. Munro noted a similar decline in his figures for the wages of both craftsmen and labourers during the late 1330s,

[18]   Munro, 'Wage-Stickiness', 243.
[19]   These cases were not included in Tables 2.1–2.3.

which he has ascribed to severe monetary deflation.[20] As might be expected, the wages for *servitores* at Woodstock rose to 2*d.* per day after the plague arrived. Altogether, those individual males called *servitores* in the record seem normally to have been at the bottom of the male wage scale and perhaps, as we shall see later, qualitatively different from the other male classifications.

Next, we come to that group of males called *quadratores* or *quarrarii* in the accounts, probably best translated simply as 'quarriers'. Their work was restricted to digging stones, presumably for rubble masonry work. Given this narrow definition, it is not surprising that the payment for their work was remarkably consistent within each account. According to the 1334–5 account (representing the 1330s in Table 2.2), they seem to have been paid 1½*d.* per day (although this was only based on two cases), before, as with *servitores*, dipping down to 1*d.* per day in the 1340s, where an impressive fifty-four (or ninety-eight per cent) of the total of fifty-five cases were at that rate. After the advent of the plague, their rate of pay seems to have stabilised at 2*d.* per day. Again, this was remarkably consistent, because all twenty cases extracted from the post-plague period were at that rate.

The wages paid to females working in building construction or repair show the same predilection for a set rate. Although only twenty ironclad cases giving daily wage rates for women were culled from the Woodstock accounts examined in this study, sixteen (or eighty per cent) of these cases were at 1*d.* per day, echoing Thorold Rogers's statement nearly a century and a half ago that the normal payment for women's work before the Black Death was a penny a day.[21] The four exceptions — all at 1½*d.* per day — occurred in readily explicable contexts. One occurred after the Black Death, when wages across the board were increasing. Two occurred in the 1334–5 account when again some male wages at least were also increasing (see Table 2.1). The third occasion occurred in 1293, where it was explained that an *ancilla* collecting moss was paid 7½*d.* for five days, or a rate of 1½ *d.* per day, 'because of the harvest' (*quia autumpnus*).[22] These are all pretty much exceptions that prove the rule: that is, that women employed in building before the Black Death were normally paid a standard 1*d.* per day. Furthermore, when other less secure references are considered, such as those where the women are recorded as working 'for the whole week' (*per totam septimanam*) rather than a specified number of days, the entries are often invariably neatly divisible by six, as for example in example (*c*) given above. There are twenty-six such cases in the accounts up to 1303–4, where *ancillae* were paid by the 'whole week', and if one assumes six days per week, the payment per *ancilla* works out exactly to 1*d.* per

20   That is, he found that, by 1341, the 'nominal' value of craftsmen's wages had dropped from 4*d.* per day down to 3*d.* per day and that of labourers from 2*d.* per day down to 1½*d.* per day: Munro, 'Wage-Stickiness', 209, 243.

21   J. E. Thorold Rogers, *A History of Agriculture and Prices in England* (7 vols., Oxford., 1866–1902), I, 281.

22   TNA, E101/497/19, m. 2.

day. Finally, in a number of thirteenth-century cases where males and females were recorded as working together, the mathematics consistently implies that the men and women were paid 1½*d*. and 1*d*. per day each respectively.[23]

In short, basal wages for labourers, both male and female, often stayed constant for long periods of time. This was particularly the case for the half-century or so up to the beginning of the fourteenth century, where the base wage for a male labourer seems to have been 1½*d*. per day and for a female 1*d*. per day. Given the regularity with which these wages occurred, it seems likely that these were rates for male or female adults. But there was a definite hierarchy, with women taking a decidedly secondary or marginal position to able adult males, as would any male who received similar wages to a woman, indicating that he may have been a child, or elderly, or even disabled.[24] This point has considerable analytical value for elucidating employment cycles. The aim of the rest of this essay is to examine how this might be revealed in the Woodstock accounts.

Marginal Wage Labour

Women

Women are the easiest to see in the marginal labour category. As the examples given already indicate, women's labour was recorded with some frequency in the Woodstock accounts, but, as Table 2.3 in particular has already indicated, its appearance was episodic. Table 2.4 attempts to quantify the amount of female labour in terms of person-days worked by women for each of the calendar-years covered by the Woodstock accounts, the numbers in square brackets beside each year indicating how many weeks of that year the accounts actually covered. For most years, this involved only a part of the year because the account involved started, say, at Michaelmas (29 September), with no account preceding it, or ended at the same feast day and was not followed up by another account.

The gaps in the account run are all too obvious in Table 2.4, but nonetheless enough accounts do survive from 1256 to 1357 to give a sense of how the input of women's labour in building on the manor changed over about a century. In compiling this table on women's labour, the 'certain' references involve those where women were actually mentioned, as in the examples given at the start of the section on the 'Minimum Wage'. In the cases where the number of days was not specifically given, as in those covering 'the whole week', it was assumed that the women worked for six days or were remunerated at 1*d*. per day each, so that if,

---

[23] For example, 'In two workers and three women serving in the same place [that is, helping two masons in lengthening the knights' chamber] for the said six days, 3*s*.' (April–May 1269: TNA, E101/497/15, m. 2). The math is as follows: the two men at 1½*d*. per day for six days would get 18*d*.; the three women at 1*d*. per day for six days would also get 18*d*. The total would be 18*d*. + 18*d*. = 36*d*., which equals 3*s*.

[24] Bardsley has already suggested this in 'Women's Work Reconsidered', 4–5.

Table 2.4: Women-days worked at the royal manor and park at Woodstock, 1256–1357

Year(s) [no. of weeks]	No. of woman-days worked			Comments
	Certain	Possible	Total	
1256 [16]	0	0	0	
1265 [37]	0	22	22	
1266 [13]	6	7	13	
1267 [39]	4	50	54	
1268 [13]	36	12	48	
1269 [39]	85	52.5	137.5	
1270 [3]	8.5	10	18.5	
1271 [40]	154	50	204	
1272 [46]	38	36	74	
1284 [13]	18	17	35	Imperfect account
1285 [39]	45	94	139	Imperfect account
1292 [13]	7	0	7	
1293 [39]	139.5	0	139.5	
1295 [40]	0	0	0	
1296 [39]	0	0	0	
1297 [40]	0	0	0	
1298 [39]	0	0	0	
1299 [39]	0	0	0	
1303 [13]	0	0	0	
1304 [39]	0	0	0	
1334 & 1335 [66]	384[a]	0	384[a]	[a] all for collecting moss
1341 [35]	0	0	0	Imperfect account
1342 [17]	0	0	0	Imperfect account
1343 [?]	0	0	0	*Very* imperfect account
1344 [48]	12	0	12	
1345 [52]	0	0	0	
1346 [52]	0	0	0	
1347 [39]	0	0	0	
1349 [31]	0	0	0	
1350 [52]	0	0	0	
1351 [52]	0	0	0	
1352 [52]	0	0	0	
1353 [52]	12	0	12	
1354 [39]	0	0	0	
1356 [13]	0	0	0	
1357 [39]	0	0	0	

Sources: TNA, E101 497/12–498/9.

say, it was recorded that a woman was paid 12*d.* for collecting moss, she actually worked for twelve days to earn this sum. The 'possible' references are those where women were not actually mentioned, but it seems highly likely that women were doing the work recorded. This is particularly the case with any expenses dealing with the collection of moss which, except for occasional exceptions (see below), seems to have involved the sort of bending and stooping labour that men were normally content to leave to women. Thus, as a specific example, it was recorded for early November 1266 that a woman (*femina*) was paid 6*d.* for collecting moss.[25] In the very next section it was simply stated that moss was collected for 3*d.*[26] It seems likely that this latter payment went to the same woman and probably represented three person-days of work, which was accordingly put in the 'possible' column.

In contrast to the establishment of the minimum adult wages above, there is a certain amount of 'interpretation' in putting together this table of women's work, but it does give a fairly secure sense of when women were more likely to have been employed in building construction or repair at Woodstock, and, by implication, possibly in many other parts of England at the time. One important note of caution needs to be made here. Even if we consider the number of women's working days in the table, especially those in the 'certain' column, as reasonably accurate, it is hardly impressive in terms of actual employment. Thus, for example, the 204 women's working days, both 'certain' and 'possible', for the forty recorded weeks in 1271 was only equivalent to one woman working for most of the year. Thus, even in the best years, working sites were hardly swarming with women. Rather, in the spirit of 'marginal' economics, the presence of *any* woman on the site indicates that the employment situation for men was likely very full. This constitutes the chief analytical value of the table.

With this qualification in mind, Table 2.4 nonetheless does show some marked trends. The period from the late 1260s to the early 1290s seems to have been a time when some women at least regularly found work on building sites. One striking feature of this work was its variety. Not only were women collecting moss, they were also carrying water, carrying stones to masons, making mortar, and manipulating wheelbarrows.[27] If Woodstock is at all typical, then, the overall story is of a period in the late 1260s and early 1270s (certainly compared to the

---

[25] 'In j femina colligente mossam, vjd.': TNA, E101/497/14.

[26] 'In collectione mosse, iij d.': TNA, E101/497/14. Several similar references follow on the same manuscript.

[27] For example, 'In iij ancillis portantibus aquam per vj dies, xviij d.' [May 27 – June 1 1269: TNA, E101/497/15, m. 1]; 'In ij ancillis portantibus petram, xijd.' [May 20–5 1269: TNA, E101/497/15, m. 2]; 'In ij ancillis mortarium facientibus, xijd.' [February 23–8 1271: TNA, E101/497/16, m. 1]; 'In iiij ancillis ferentibus civera per iij dies . . .' [the rest of the entry is missing, because the right-hand side of the manuscript is badly deteriorated; the entry is seemingly for April 9–14 1285: TNA, E101/497/18, m. 1].

mid 1260s and earlier, when women were much less evident on the Woodstock site) when opportunities for women working on building sites like Woodstock increased markedly, an activity still evident in the early 1290s.

Then, just as dramatically as it arose, women's employment for building at Woodstock seemingly disappeared after 1292–3. The accounts covering the period 1295–1304 show no women's employment at all in building at Woodstock. Even the collection of moss, typical of women's work a few years earlier, was now done solely by men, significantly at the increased rate of 1½d. per day (fifty per cent more than the women normally received).[28] For whatever reason, it seems here that the mid to late 1290s ushered in a period of relatively slack employment, at least on a local level, so that women were withdrawn as men turned up to take their place.[29] This may have been because women's labour was seen as ergonomically less efficient,[30] or that patriarchal/pro-male sentiments were just so strong that they militated against the continued employment of women, even if their labour was a bargain. Also, in demographic terms, the boost in family income that might have accompanied the increased employment of women as early as the late 1260s may have created the cash needed for accelerated family formation starting about this time. If so, a subsequent 'baby boom' could have created something of a labour glut in the 1290s.

The gap in the Woodstock accounts from 1304 to the mid 1330s unfortunately does not let us explore these complexities further. During 1334–5, women's labour is again clearly evident, although solely in collecting moss for roof repairs. But the remuneration paid to these women, 1½d. per day, is quite remarkable compared to what they had received in earlier accounts, and coincides with reasonably healthy wages for men at the time, certainly compared to the decade which followed. Indeed the local economy, certainly from the point of view of building employment, was seemingly going through a boom period. An analysis of building on the estates of the bishop of Winchester indicates similarly optimistic conditions for labour in the mid to late 1330s, perhaps associated with the build-up to the Hundred Years' War, while, as mentioned above, Munro's figures show that these heightened wages may have already been in place twenty to thirty years before this.[31]

Wages for building workers at Woodstock seemed to collapse in the 1340s,

---

[28] For example, 'In j homine colligente mussum ad idem [that is, for slating roofs] per idem tempus [five days] vijd. ob. qui capit per diem jd. ob.' (June 1296: TNA, E101/497/21, m. 2).

[29] J. Langdon and J. Masschaele, 'Commercial Activity and Population Growth in Medieval England', *P&P* 190 (2006), esp. 74–5, noted a downturn of economic growth and investment by 1300 at the latest, which would likely have affected employment negatively.

[30] Hatcher, 'Women's Work Reconsidered', esp. 193–4.

[31] Langdon, Walker and Falconer, 'Boom and Bust', esp. 149–50, 151–2, 153; Munro, 'Wage-Stickiness', 243.

perhaps due to monetary deflation, as argued by Munro.[32] The single definite reference to women working (helping roofers in this case) in the 1340s shows their wages reverting back to 1d. per day, a rate that was matched by that for many male workers (see below). But perhaps the most striking feature here is the almost total lack of references to female labour during the 1340s, a pattern which continued after the Black Death. The Woodstock evidence indicates that any shortage in labour after the Black Death did not necessarily extend to women, at least up to 1357. The sole incontestable reference to female labour in the Woodstock accounts during the period 1349 to 1357 involved two women collecting moss at 1½d. per day each for roof repairs during a week in late May 1353.[33] Cartloads of moss were also bought during this period, but it is difficult to say how much women's labour, if any, was wrapped up in these payments.[34] In short, whatever shortage there might have been in adult male labour at Woodstock after the advent of the plague, it does not appear to have been filled by women. And so we are forced to look for other possible sources.

The labour of children and others

Here we consider the possible contribution of children, the elderly and the disabled at times when labour from adult males in their prime was in short supply.[35] Tracking this sort of labour is a much trickier proposition, and indeed, for the elderly and the disabled no concrete evidence — or even hints of it — was surrendered by the Woodstock material. The same could be said of young labour, that of children or adolescents, since neither does the Woodstock material give specific instances of this kind of employment, although at least we can draw upon the evidence of works accounts at other sites where more direct indications of young labour were given. One such case involved a construction gang of masons and helpers working at Corfe Castle (in Dorset) during the week of Monday 19 August to Saturday 24 August 1280. The detailed description of this gang is worth giving in full:

> In the service of Walter Mogg, mason, for that week, 20d. In the service of Richard Mareys, mason, for that week, 18d. In wages of Peter Platel, Robert his son, John of Alfrinton and Robert Brenda, stone-layers (*cubitores*) for that week, 6s., to each one of them 18d. per week. In the service of Richard Bruton, John Catel, John le mere, junior, William the fuller, who made mortar as well as carrying stones and water and drawing sand

---

[32] Munro, 'Wage-Stickiness', 243; Phelps Brown and Hopkins, 'Seven Centuries of Building Wages', 205, show a corresponding decline in wages during this period.

[33] TNA, E101/498/8, m. 1d.

[34] Altogether £2 18s. was spent on numerous cartloads of moss from 1344 to 1357: TNA, E101/498/4–9.

[35] Since it was very unusual, prisoner labour, as in n. 3 above, is not included here.

for that week, 4s., to each one of them 12d. per week. In the service of Hugh Scot making mortar and carrying water and stones for that week, 9d. And to Henry, 'boy' (*garcioni*) of the janitor, collecting (or bringing) small stones (*minutas petras*) to the hands of the stone-layers for four days, 4d.[36]

If we look at the group as a whole, they seem very much to be listed in descending order of status, the masons/stone-layers being followed by their helpers. Of the helpers, the group of Richard Bruton et al. seems to be adults hired at 12d. per week, which, assuming a six-day week, indicates 2d. per day. On that basis the next worker listed, Hugh Scot, was seemingly paid 1½d. per day. He seems to have been in a junior position, perhaps on the cusp in some way, maybe an adolescent or young adult, although he might have been an elderly worker past his prime or perhaps disabled in some fashion. The most interesting in the group is the last, Henry the *garcio* or 'boy' of the janitor. 'Boy' probably meant something closer to 'son' in this instance, while the fact that he only carried 'small stones' suggests that his carrying ability was limited in some way, most likely, it would seem, because he was a prepubescent male. Certainly, if he were an elderly person, he most likely would have been given his full name, rather than being styled a 'boy' or 'servant' of someone else.

That the order in which the various people appeared in the above entry seems to have been determined by skill, experience and perhaps age is supported by a number of references in the next section of the Corfe account for the following week of Monday 26 August to Saturday 31 August 1280. Here Henry, now styled more simply as Henry Janitor, carried small stones for six days for 6d. He was joined by Adam Wydbred (another child?), who carried water and small stones, but only for four days, for which he was paid 4d. Most telling, however, in this section was the reference to the hiring of 'the daughter of the fuller' to help fill the trough (in which the mortar was being made) with sand, for which she was paid 6d. for six days' work. Those making up the account felt they had to add the reason for hiring her, which they expressed as *propter periculum hominum*, which is probably best interpreted as 'because of the perilous shortage of men'.[37] As all of this was happening during the harvest, the supervisors of the construction at Corfe Castle were seemingly calling upon labour from wherever they could get it, and that, in this instance, meant both female and (probably) child labour, both paid 1d. per day.

What can this evidence tell us about the Woodstock situation? Although the Woodstock accounts do not provide cases as suggestive as those for Corfe, the

[36] TNA, E101/460/27, m. 1.

[37] 'In servicio filie le vuelere que iuvabat inplere puteum de sabulo propter periculum hominum per vj dies, vjd.': TNA, E101/460/27, m. 1. 'Fuller' seems the best translation of the oddly spelled *vuelere*.

payments for some at least of the male labourers might indicate they were in the same category as Henry Janitor and others at Corfe, particularly if they were being paid at the same rate as women. Whether described as 'men' (*homines*), 'workers' (*operarii*), 'quarrymen' (*quadratores*/*quarrarii*), or 'servants' (*servitores*), there were times when wages for male labour did drop to the level of that for women.[38] The male labourers most likely to display these characteristics were those called 'servants' (*servitores*). Although generally their wages were equivalent to other adult male workers (see Table 2.2), there were a number of notable occasions when their wages dropped to a level equivalent to that paid to women. One interesting case occurred starting the working week of Monday 20 October to Saturday 25 October ('the week after the feast of St Luke Evangelist') 1292, when two 'servants' were hired for a day to help two masons working on the manor houses, one being paid 1½d. for his work and the other 1d. Given that in this same week a woman (*ancilla*) was paid 5d. for collecting moss over five days, the second 'servant' seems to have received the same daily wage as she did, indicating that he was one of that group of 'lesser' male workers mentioned above. The same pair of *servitores*, paid at the same rates of 1½d. and 1d. per day respectively, showed up again helping two masons working on the manor houses in the last week of January 1293. The crew of masons and helpers working on the park walls, possibly the same as those who worked on the manor houses, also had a 'servant' working for a penny a day until at least mid February 1293. By the end of June in the same year, however, all 'servants' in the crew were making 1½d. per day. As this likely included the 'servant' previously making 1d. per day, it suggests that his work earlier in the year might have comprised a sort of training phase.[39]

After 1292–3, the wages for 'servants' remained strikingly consistent at 1½d. per day in the Woodstock accounts until the 1340s , when the wages for 'servants' showed a marked drop to 1d. per day, a rate shared by the 'quarrymen' during this period. One notable exception to this occurred in June 1344, when extra 'servants' were hired during a spate of abnormally heavy roofing repairs and were paid 1¼ d. per day for a period of four weeks. Significantly, this was when the single certain reference to two women (*mulieres*) being hired during this period occurred, also to help the roofers, where they made 1d. per day each.[40] But this period seems to have been a very temporary one in an otherwise depressed labour market.

After the plague arrived, the situation for labour generally improved, as is a staple in the secondary literature. But, as we have seen, it was not women who

---

[38] Such as the payments made to twelve 'men' (*homines*), all given 1d. per day each, 'for mending the great fish-pond at Everswell', over about a week in 1295, noticeably less than the 1½d. or more paid to all other 'men' working on the manor for this year: TNA, E101/497/20, m. 1.

[39] TNA, E101/497/19.

[40] TNA, E101/498/4, mm. 1–2.

benefited. Rather, it was probably child or adolescent labour that featured significantly. Although wages for 'servants' on average rose like wages for labour generally, there was also a much greater variation in the wages paid to them compared to before the plague. This is reflected in the relatively small number of mode values. In the case of the accounts for 1349–57, the mode value of 2*d.* per day, although the most common wage given to 'servants' during this period, was still found in only sixteen of thirty-eight cases, or less than half, a much smaller proportion for the mode than in any previous period, reflecting a greater spread of data across the 1*d.*–3*d.* per day range. Eight of the thirty-eight cases of wages of 'servants' were in fact 1*d.* or 1½*d.* per day for jobs like helping roofers/slaters or collecting moss. Since these were equal to or less than the one recorded case of women's wages after the Black Death (at 1½*d.* per day; see Table 2.3), it seems that these cases may reflect 'lesser' male labour. David Farmer noted that the differential between a craftsman's wage and that of his helper reached a peak in the period 1347–56.[41] He put this down to the plague putting an extra premium on the skill of the craftsman, but a corollary might be that helpers for the immediate post-plague period at least were getting younger and hence paid less relative to those they were serving. Thereafter, Farmer's figures reveal that the distance between craftsmen's wages and those of their helpers began to diminish sharply,[42] which suggests that the penetration of younger male labour, perhaps even of children, was a temporary phenomenon.

Conclusion:
Towards an Unemployment Index for the Middle Ages?

This detailing of women and 'lesser' male labour in the building industry does give us a clearer picture of the employment situation, at least around Woodstock. Whether the labour of women and children was routinely seen on other building sites in medieval England is a matter for further research, but the evidence presented here does indicate that the period from the late 1260s to the early 1290s, when women's labour and perhaps some young labour in building seemed to be at its most frequent and varied, might well have been a time where employment opportunities were plentiful all round. This time of plenty dried up rather dramatically over the 1290s, possibly because of a 'baby boom', when the previous generation or so of good employment opportunities suddenly produced a glut of labour. Unemployment rates rose, the first casualty of which was the participation of women in building. This seems to have continued for at least ten years, up to 1303–4 according to the Woodstock accounts, but unfortunately the long gap in accounts after 1303–4 does not allow us to see what happened over the next

---

[41]   Farmer, 'Prices and Wages, 1350–1500', 478.
[42]   Ibid., 479.

generation or so. By the time of the 1334–5 account, however, the situation had clearly recovered with relatively high wages being made by male and female la-bourers alike, perhaps, as argued above, as a result of the heightened building ac-companying the lead-up to and start of the Hundred Years' War, although Munro's figures suggest that this period of high wages might have been in place for some decades already.[43] Unfortunately, for Woodstock residents, it did not last long and by the 1340s, women at least were scarcely evident, and wages as a whole seem to have been at a nadir on the royal estate. Although the issue of monetary deflation is a complicating factor here, it is not inconsistent with higher rates of unemploy-ment. In this regard, the plague, for all its horrible human consequences, likely improved matters for those who survived, but, again according to this Woodstock example, the ones who stepped in to make up for the consequent labour shortfalls were not women but probably (male) adolescents and children.

This study has been an exercise to see if tracking 'marginal' workers like women and children might give us a better sense of how employment opportuni-ties fluctuated over time in medieval England, particularly in the century leading up to the Black Death. If enough data can be gathered concerning the employ-ment of women in particular within the medieval English building industry, per-haps this can be built up into a rough index of employment over time. Also, some sense of what the 'minimum' wage was for an adult male labourer at any point of time is essential, because we can use it as a base to analyse lower-price male la-bour, especially as it is likely to have been that of adolescents and children. Work on this subject is only beginning, but, in particular, having a stronger sense of the number of young people in the work force over time will undoubtedly increase our understanding of medieval labour.

[43]   Munro, 'Wage-Stickiness', 243.

3

Crisis Management in London's Food Supply, 1250–1500
....
Derek Keene

Aₛ ɪɴ ᴛʜᴇ ᴀɴᴄɪᴇɴᴛ Gʀᴀᴇᴄᴏ-Rᴏᴍᴀɴ ᴡᴏʀʟᴅ, subsistence crises were common in medieval Europe, but famines, defined as food shortages that occasioned large increases in mortality caused by hunger and disease, were relatively rare.[1] Famines usually arose from harvest failures in a succession of years, in most cases the outcome of abnormal weather and sometimes exacerbated by warfare or political breakdown. Contemporary descriptions did not always make such a precise distinction, but in the commercialised conditions which prevailed from the early eleventh century onwards it was common to characterise the severity of a crisis or famine by reference to the price of wheat. This was the premier and most widely marketed grain and of special significance for the supply of cities such as London, where grain probably contributed about seventy per cent of the calorific requirement of the average inhabitant.[2] Using a new series of wheat prices for London, this essay explores the relative significance of three fairly well-recorded episodes of famine in the later-medieval city — those of 1257–60, 1315–17 and 1438–40 — and the nature of responses to them. Those reactions highlight aspects of the political and moral economy of urban famine and of civic developments over the period.

Several earlier famines recorded both in England and in other parts of Europe are likely to have had a serious effect in London. These were in 793, 975–6, 1005–6, the mid 1040s, 1124–6 and the years 1193–8. England in 1196 witnessed high mortality and mass graves were dug. The price of a quarter wheat in England was said in 1044 to have reached 5s. or more and in 1124–5 6s. or more.[3] Higher

---

[1] Cf. P. Garnsey, *Famine and Food Supply in the Graeco-Roman World: Responses to Risk and Crisis* (Cambridge, 1988), 17–39; P. Garnsey, *Food and Society in Classical Antiquity* (Cambridge, 1999), 34–42. C. Ó Gráda, *Famine, A Short History* (Princeton, 2009) focuses on recent centuries.

[2] B. M. S. Campbell, J. A. Galloway, D. Keene and M. Murphy, *A Medieval Capital and its Grain Supply: Agrarian Production and Distribution in the London region c.1300* (London, 1993), 32–33.

[3] *The Anglo-Saxon Chronicle*, trans. and ed. D. Whitelock, D. C. Douglas and S. I. Tucker

prices, with a maximum of 7s. 9d. per quarter, were paid for royal purchases of wheat between 1201–2 and 1203–4,[4] when entries in a later chronicle that may be derived from a contemporary London source records a price of 12s. and associates it with bad weather in 1202.[5] In Farmer's general series of wheat prices for medieval England these years stand out as a crisis comparable to those of 1257–60 and 1293–6, both episodes noted for exceptional mortality especially among the poor.[6] For not one of the famines earlier than that of 1257–60 do we have any direct information concerning London. That of the 1120s, however, is notable for a contemporary account of the disaster in Flanders, which details the particular experiences of towns (especially Ghent) and public measures taken in response to the shortage of corn, and where the response of Charles the Good, count of Flanders, is portrayed as that of an ideal ruler for charity and effectiveness. In this Charles was partially matched in 1195 by the repentant King Richard of England, to whose court, towns and cities the hungry flowed.[7]

In general, medieval England was well supplied with corn, of which from at least as early the twelfth century onwards it was a significant exporter. As by far the largest and wealthiest city in the realm, London was well placed to draw on that resource in years affected by poor harvests by extending its zone of supply. The city enjoyed good access to productive areas by road, river and coastal ship-

(London, 1961), s.a. 793 (p. 36), 976 (p. 78), 1005 (p. 87), 1040 (p. 105), 1044 (p. 108), 1124–5 (pp. 191–2); Henry, archdeacon of Huntingdon, *Historia Anglorum: The History of the English People*, ed. and trans. D. Greenway (Oxford, 1996), 474–5; *Chronicles of the Reign of Stephen, Henry ii, and Richard i*, ed. R. Howlett (4 vols., Rolls Series, 1881–9), ii, 460, 463, 484–5, 492 (William of Newburgh); for bad weather and high prices in Paris, 1194–6, see *Œuvres de Rigord et de Guillaume le Breton, historiens de Philippe-Auguste*, ed. H. François Delaborde (Paris, 1882), 130, 132, 134; F. Curschmann, *Hungersnöte im Mittelalter: ein Beitrage zur deutschen Wirtshaftsgeschichte des 8. Bis 13. Jahrhunderts* (Leipzig, 1900), 90–1, 107–9, 116–18, 132–6, 156–61.

4   D. L. Farmer, 'Prices and Wages', in *AHEW* ii, 716–817.

5   *Annales Monastici*, ed. H. Richards Luard (5 vols., Rolls Series, 1864–9), ii, 254–5 (the *Annales de Waverleia* record that wheat sold for 12s. a quarter in 1202 and note famine in 1203). *The Great Chronicle of London*, ed. A. H. Thomas and I. D. Thornley (London, 1938), 3, records a price of 16s. a quarter which may ultimately derive from a thirteenth-century source, cf. ibid. 397 n.; see M. Brett, 'The Annals of Bermondsey, Southwark and Merton', in *Church and City, 1000–1500: Essays in Honour of Christopher Brooke*, ed. D. Abulafia, M. Franklin and M. Rubin (Cambridge, 1992), 279–310.

6   Farmer, 'Prices and Wages'; M. Postan and J. Titow, 'Heriots and Prices on Winchester Manors', *EcHR* ii (1957), 392–411; *The Chronicle of Walter of Guisborough*, ed. H. Rothwell (Camden Society 89, 1957), 184, 252; Z. Razi, *Life, Marriage and Death in a Medieval Parish: Economy, Society and Demography in Halesowen 1270–1400* (Cambridge, 1980), 38; cf. Curschmann, *Hungersnöte*, 201–2. For 1257–8, see also below.

7   Galbert of Bruges, *The Murder of Charles the Good*, trans. and ed. J. Bruce Ross (Toronto, 1982), 84–9; *Chronica Rogeri de Houedene*, ed. W. Stubbs (4 vols., Rolls Series, 1868–71), iii, 289–90.

ping, especially along the east coast. Indeed, its demand and that of cities overseas were among the factors which shaped agrarian production in those districts.
From time to time London also drew on neighbouring areas overseas, including
Picardy, Ponthieu and Flanders, while in the fourteenth and fifteenth centuries
Baltic grain became a periodically significant resource. Moreover, the political
setting of London — its position within the relatively extensive and unified kingdom of England — gave it an advantage over many large cities in terms of access
to food supplies. London merchants, along with those of other important English
towns, could trade toll-free throughout the realm, and rival cities could not set
up significant barriers to London's supply. At times of crisis in food supply, the
effective barrier for regulation was at the border of the realm, not at the jurisdictional limit of the city itself. Thus, since at least as early as the twelfth century,
monarchs periodically banned the export of corn when harvests fell short or in
order to deny supplies to an enemy overseas. This political economy shaped the
city's response in important ways. For example, there appears to have been little
need to maintain a public stock of grain within the city. City corn merchants hired
private granaries in London as required, but those same merchants also hired
granaries more cheaply in the market towns of the grain-producing areas which
supplied the city. The greater part of the stock of corn available for consumption
in the city must usually have resided well outside the city itself. There was little
risk of those distant supplies being denied to London when the city needed them.
Consequently, the city appears not to have attempted to establish a staple right,
while even its power to prohibit markets in its vicinity extended no more than
seven miles, hardly more than the customary distance between markets across
the kingdom.[8] It is no surprise therefore that early in the thirteenth century Gervase of Tilbury noted the stability of the city's corn supply.[9] The contrast with the
food wars between cities in northern Italy, where the public stock of grain was
a vital civic resource and where maintaining control of a productive *contado* was
a key element in the commercial and military policies of communes, could hardly
be greater.[10]

---

[8]   N. S. B. Gras, *The Evolution of the English Corn Market from the Twelfth to the Eighteenth
      Century* (Cambridge, Mass., 1915; repr. 1926), 210–17; E. Miller and J. Hatcher, *Medieval
      England: Rural Society and Economic Change, 1086–1348* (London, 1978), 82; Campbell et
      al., *Medieval Capital, passim*; J. A. Galloway, 'One Market or Many? London and the Grain
      Trade of England', in *Trade, Urban Hinterlands and Market Integration c.1300–1600*, ed. J.
      A. Galloway (London, 2000), 23–42; idem, 'Town and Country in England, 1300–1570', in
      Town and Country in Europe, 1300–1800, ed. S. R. Epstein (Cambridge, 2001), 106–31.

[9]   Gervase of Tilbury, *Otia imperiali: Recreation for an Emperor*, ed. and trans. S. E. Banks and
      J. W. Binns (Oxford, 2002), 400–1.

[10] D. Waley, *The Italian City Republics* (London, 1969), 110–22; F. C. Lane, *Venice, A Maritime
      Republic* (Baltimore, 1973), 58–65; P. Jones, *The Italian City-State from Comune to Signoria*
      (Oxford, 1997), 161–72, 486–95, 564–73. For a vivid account of such a struggle, see Salim-
      bene da Parma, *The Chronicle of Salimbene de Adam*, ed. J. L. Baird, G. Baglivi and J. R. Kane

Prices of wheat in the London markets are available for almost every year between 1277 and 1499 (Figure 3.1). There is only one London price for the years 1257–60, but chroniclers record some believable prices within the London region, and these are supported by sale prices at manors belonging to the bishop of Winchester (or markets nearby), several of which are known to have supplied London. The best evidence of London prices between 1277 and 1370 is provided by records of the city's assize of bread — the customary means of establishing a stable supply of this basic food[11] — which after a period of neglect was reformed, probably in 1277, soon after Edward I's arrival in England as king.[12] The records, however, survive in a state of disorder.[13] Normally the assize was undertaken in October (Figure 3.1), when prices reflected the quality of the harvest that year, although they would also have been influenced by the quantity of grain carried over from the previous year and by expectations of shortage or glut to come. In times of shortage, the assize was undertaken several times during the year, so that for some periods it is possible to track prices on a seasonal basis (Figure 3.2).

To judge the significance of these prices as indicators of the severity of crises it is necessary to take account of monetary inflation and changes in the standard of living which might affect the capacity of the inhabitants of London to cope with the effects of harvest shortfall. The wage-rate index for London building craftsmen over the period (Figure 3.1, Table 3.1) immediately reveals that while in terms of absolute prices the episodes of 1315–17 and 1438–39 were similar, the latter was probably a good deal less severe in its impact than the former since Londoners, who now were on average better off than earlier, would have been able to draw on resources which would enable them to survive a crisis in food supply, despite two or three years of poor harvests and livestock mortality and the very high absolute

(Binghamton, N.Y., 1986), 489–91. For conflicts between Flemish towns arising from staple rights in grain, see P. Stabel, *Dwarfs among Giants: The Flemish Urban Network in the late Middle Ages* (Leuven/Apeldoorn, 1997), 163–72.

[11] J. Davis, 'Baking for the Common Good: A Reassessment of the Assize of Bread in Medieval England', *EcHR* 57 (2004), 465–502.

[12] *De Antiquis Legibus Liber: Cronica Maiorum et Vicecomitum Londoniarum*, ed. T. Stapleton (Camden Society 34, 1846), 159; *Calendar of Letter-Books Preserved among the Archives of the Corporation of the City of London at the Guildhall (A–L)*, ed. R. R. Sharpe (11 vols., London, 1899–1912), *Letter-Book A*, 215–16.

[13] In the fourteenth century the earlier folios recording the assize were bound into four separate volumes, three of which also contain much other material. These volumes, in the City of London Records Office and currently administered from the London Metropolitan Archive, are: *Liber de Assisa Panis* (COL/CS/01/004, covering 1283 and years between 1293 and 1437, but not recording prices after 1375) and parts of *Letter-Book A* (COL/AD/01/001, fols. 110–29, covering 1277–92), *Letter-Book B* (COL/AD/01/002, fols. 85–9, covering 1298–1301), *Letter-Book D* (COL/AD/01/004, fols. 170–90, covering 1309–16). The printed calendars of the Letter-Books (see n. 12 above) omit the records of the assize.

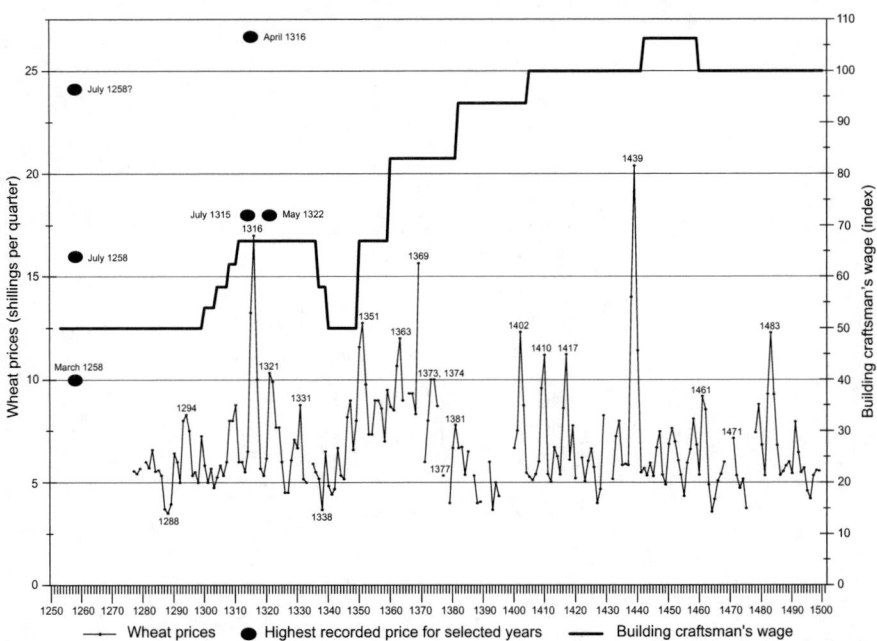

Fig. 3.1: London wheat prices, 1258–1499

Wheat prices: For 1258, see text; the highest price is from the Bermondsey Annals (see n. 16). Between 1277 and 1369, and in 1374 and 1375, most prices are from the records of the assize of bread (see n. 13) and relate to October and to the Pavement market (at Gracechurch or within Newgate, where prices were usually a little higher than those at the riverside markets Queenhithe and Billingsgate); a few relate to November. Between 1369 and 1499 most prices are from annual accounts running from Michaelmas to Michaelmas and cannot be dated within the year; they are attributed to the year in which the account ends. Up to 1399 these concern purchases made by Westminster abbey or sales from the abbey manor of Hyde, close to the city (from accounts in Westminster Abbey Muniments). From 1400 prices are from purchases by the abbey treasurer listed by the late David Farmer (University of Saskatchewan Archives, MG 145, III.C.5).

Wage rate index: Based on decennial means of the day rate paid to a carpenter or mason in London (rate for 1460–1548 is 100). Wage rates in London were higher than elsewhere. Rates for 1361–1548 are from the City of London's Bridge House accounts, for work on houses in the city. Rates for 1264–1380 are based on those in E. H. Phelps Brown and S. V. Hopkins, 'Seven Centuries of Building Wages', *Economica* 22 (1955), 195–206, adjusted upwards according to the proportional difference between their series and the London rate over the subsequent period. For mid-thirteenth-century rates, see *Building Accounts of King Henry III*, ed. H. M. Colvin (Oxford, 1971), 8–12.

(Figure executed by Olwen Myhill.)

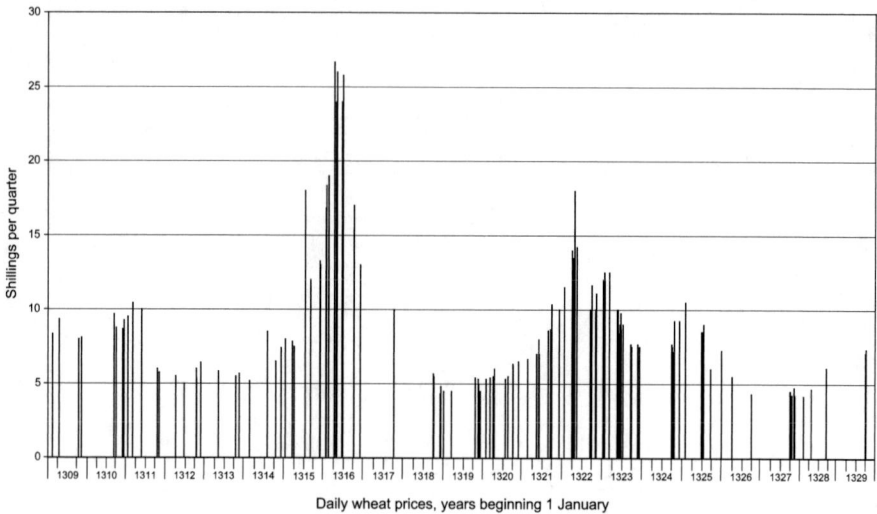

Fig. 3.2: London wheat prices, daily 1309–29

Source: records of the assize of bread (see n. 13), mostly from the Pavement market.

(Figure executed by Olwen Myhill.)

price of grain in the city.[14] Nevertheless, this episode probably struck contemporaries as especially severe since it followed two decades during which corn prices
had been low.

1257 and 1258 were years of very high wheat prices, but the volatility of prices
during such episodes, the difficulty of attributing them to particular dates during
the year and the lack of a continuous English price series before 1268, make it hard
to assess the severity of this famine in relation to that of 1315–17. Several years
of relative abundance in the early 1250s, including the harvest of 1254, mitigated
the effect of difficult weather in 1255, when prices following the harvest were also
low. There was a poor harvest in 1256 and an even worse one in 1257, with the
result that in 1256–7, according to Farmer's series, prices were about sixty per cent
higher than for the mean of the nine years for which they are recorded between
1244–5 and 1254–5, while those for 1257–8 were 118 per cent higher or eighty-
seven per cent higher than the mean of the previous ten annual prices, including

---

[14] London chronicles agree with the London price series in identifying the years 1437–8 and
1438–9 as ones of dearth, with a lower but still unusually high price in 1439–40: *Great
Chronicle of London*, 173–44; *Chronicles of London*, ed. C. Lethbridge Kingsford (Oxford,
1905), 145–6; *The Historical Collections of a Citizen of London*, ed. J. Gairdner (Camden
Society 17, 1876), 181–2. Cf. J. Hatcher, 'The Great Slump of the Mid-Fifteenth Century', in
Progress and Problems in Medieval England: Essays in Honour of Edward Miller, ed. R. Britnell and J. Hatcher (Cambridge, 1996), 246.

Table 3.1: Relative severity of famines measured by peak wheat prices

Famine episode	Date of price (peak year)	Wheat price (s. per quarter)		London building craftsman's wage index	Wheat price in 1316 values (s. per quarter)
		General	London		
1043–6?	1044	5 (ASC)		15?	22.3
1124–6	1124–5	6 (ASC)		20?	20.1
1202–5?	1202–3	7.7 (Farmer)		30	17.3
	1202	12 (text)		30	26.8
1257–60	1257–8	8 (Farmer)		50	10.8
	1257 (Dec)	10		50	13.4
	1258 (March)		9	50	12.1
	1258 (July)		15	50	20.1
	1258 (July?)	20 (at Northampton)		50	26.8
1293–6	1293 (Oct)		8	50	10.7
	1294 (Oct)		8.3	50	11.1
	1295 (c.April)		9.3	50	12.5
	1295–6	9.2 (Farmer)		50	12.9
	1295 (c.April)		14	50	18.8
1315–17	1315–16	16.6 (Farmer)		67	16.6
	1315 (July)		18	67	18
	1315 (4 Dec)		13.3	67	13.3
	1316 (April)		26.7	67	26.70
	1316 (Oct)		17	67	17
	1317 (Oct)		10	67	10
1321–3	1321 (Oct)		10.3	67	10.3
	1322 (May)		18	67	18
	1322 (Oct)		9.9	67	9.9
	1323 (March)		12.5	67	12.5
	1323 (Oct)		7.7	67	7.7
1438–40	1438–9		20.4	100	13.7

Sources: General wheat prices: ASC, *Anglo-Saxon Chronicle*; Farmer, 'Prices and Wages'; text. London wheat prices: see text and Figure 3.1. Wage index: see Figure 3.1; for 1202–3, representing a rate of 3*d*. a day paid in Southwark, see *The Pipe Roll of the Bishopric of Winchester, 1208–1209*, ed. Hubert Hall (London, 1903), 60; the values for 1044 and 1124–5 are guesswork.

that for 1256–7.[15] This suggests that the famine of those years was among the worst of those recorded in England and probably comparable to that of 1315–17 (Table 3.1). Chroniclers record storms and floods for June 1256; rains, storms and extreme cold for late December that year; disturbed weather and floods between February and March 1257 and continuous rain during the summer and autumn of 1257 — also noted in Central Europe — causing a poor harvest, an immediate shortage of corn and abnormal mortality. Wheat was said to sell for 10*s*. a quarter in December 1257 and in February 1258, but in March for '9*s*. or more' in London. In February a great cold began, continuing until June. In London wheat prices rose to 15*s*. a quarter in about July. In Norfolk and Suffolk they were said to be between 15*s*. and 20*s*. a quarter, while the Dunstable chronicler noted that they rose to 20*s*. in Northampton, 17*s*. in Bedford and 13*s*. 4*d*. in Dunstable. Late June was marked by heavy rain, snow, ice, thunder, lightning and floods, but July was marked by heat and thunderstorms. Heavy rain in the autumn caused much of the harvest of 1258 to be lost. There was a further storm in December. In these years, at both Dunstable and Tewkesbury, the land market was especially active, presumably as people raised money to purchase food by selling off holdings. We have no records of prices from then until 1262–3, but disease and high mortality unexpectedly returned in early summer 1259. The harvest of 1260 was poor following a very dry summer which ended with cold wet weather, so that in the autumn on the bishopric of Winchester estates, it was necessary to buy in corn for seed. A chronicler noted that in 1261 the fruits of the earth returned after many years of high mortality from hunger.[16] The harvest of that year may have been the first adequate one since 1255. The recorded pattern in Germany and Central Europe largely agrees with that for England, except that 1253 and 1254 were noted

---

[15]   Based on Farmer, 'Prices and Wages'. The next earliest price in this series is for 1236–7. The price for 1257–8 was ninety-two per cent higher than that of the mean of the previous twenty-five annual prices in the series, of which the earliest is for 1211–12. Analysis of the Hampshire prices, listed in J. Z. Titow, *English Rural Society 1200–1350* (London, 1969), produces similar results.

[16]   *Chronica Johannis de Oxenedes*, ed. H. Ellis (Rolls Series, 1859), 215, 218; *Matthaei Parisiensis monachi Sancti Albani Chronica Majora*, ed. H. Richards Luard (7 vols., Rolls Series, 1872–83), v, 561, 600, 607, 630, 660, 673–5, 690, 701–2, 706, 710–11, 724, 728, 746–7; *Annales Monastici*, i, 160–2 (*Annales de Theokesburia*); *Annales Monastici*, iii, 199, 204–8, 210–15 (*Annales de Dunstaplia*); *Annales Monastici*, iv, 118, 120 (*Annales de Oseneia*) and 118, 127 (*Chronicon Thomae Wykes*); *Annales Monastici*, ii, 351 (*Annales de Waverleia*); *Chronicles of the Reigns of Edward I and Edward II*, ed. W. Stubbs (2 vols., Rolls Series, 1882–3), i, 51, 56 (*Annales Londonienses*); *The Chronicle of Bury St Edmunds, 1212–1301*, ed. A. Gransden (London, 1964), 22–23; *Calendar of Liberate Rolls, 1251–60* (London, 1960), 57. The reference in the later and chronologically unreliable compilation *Annales Monastici*, iii, 462 (*Annales de Bermundeseia*), to wheat being sold in London for 24*s*. a quarter in 1261–2 may be fiction or a misdated annal for 1258, 1259 or 1260.

Table 3.2: Winchester bishopric manors with high sale prices for wheat, 1256–63

County	Manor	Sale price in shillings per quarter					
		1256–7		1257–8		1262–3	
		min	max	min	max	min	max
Berks	Harwell*	6.66	7.5	8	10.5	3.66	4.33
	Brightwell*	7	7.66	8.33	10.5	4	4.66
	Wargrave*		7.33	9	9.3	4	4.33
Bucks	Ivinghoe	6	6.66	8	11	3.66	4
	Morton	6.66	7.66		10	3.66	4
	West Wycombe*	4.66	8	6.66	9	3.83	4
Hants	Bishops Sutton	6.66	8	6.66	9		
	Bishopstoke			8	9		
	Bitterne	7	8		9		
	Burghclere			7.5	9.5	4	5
	Crawley	6.66	8	6.66	9.5	4	5
	Fareham		8		9		
	Merdon	6.66	7	7	10	4	5
	North Waltham	7	8	7.6	10	4	5
	Overton		8	6.5	10	4	5
Oxon	Adderbury			6	10	2.66	3.66
	Witney	6	6.66	6.6	9	3	4
Wilts	Fonthill Bishop	6	6.66	7	9	3	4.33

Source: Hampshire Record Office, Pipe Rolls of the Bishopric of Winchester, s.a.

Notes: High sale prices are defined as those of 9s. or more per quarter in 1257–8. With the exception of Fonthill Bishop, prices recorded for Wiltshire and Somerset manors were no higher than 7.5s. in 1257–8.

* manors which appear to have been within London's 'normal' supply zone (see Campbell et al., *Medieval Capital*, figures 5 and 7). Burghclere, Ivinghoe, Morton and Witney were just outside it.

as years of cold, shortages, hunger and high mortality, followed by more localised shortages in 1255 and 1256.[17]

Prices for wheat sold from the bishop of Winchester's manors between 1256 and 1258 suggest regional variations in intensity of demand (Table 3.2), the highest prices in both years being for sales from manors with access to the river Thames and thence to the London market. Some manors just outside that zone appear to have been drawn into it, while Adderbury in north Oxfordshire may have been influenced by high prices at Northampton. The prices suggest that a peak of 15s. or more in London was not unlikely. Prices for the Hampshire manors of Bishops Sutton, Crawley and Merdon may have been influenced by

[17] Curschmann, *Hungersnöte*, 178–81.

demand in Winchester, where the king was for part of the critical time, while just outside Winchester, at Crawley, exceptional alms payments of 1½d. per day between 10 April and 7 July 1258 were made on the order of the bishop elect, the half-brother of the king.[18]

The crisis of 1258 appears to have arisen from a world-wide climatic disaster, caused by the effects of an immense volcanic explosion, of a scale with a frequency below one in 5,000 years. To put that in perspective, the Tambora eruption in 1815 and that of Krakatau in 1883 were around one-in-500 and one-in-100 year events, respectively. The sulphurous and glassy dust deposits arising from the dispersal of volcanic debris in the atmosphere have been identified in Africa and both Polar Regions. Writers in Europe and in the Middle East noted thick clouds, a discoloured atmosphere, frequent and violent storms, thunder and lightning, heavy rains, extreme cold, failure of crops, high prices and outbreaks of disease among men and animals, especially for the years 1258 and 1259. After a mild winter it became cold again in the spring and summer of 1260, after which there was a harsh winter. Such cycles, often purely atmospheric but sometimes associated with successive eruptions, are typical of the aftermath of major volcanic events.[19] The crises and high mortality were especially apparent in major cities. Bologna and Italy generally suffered from high prices and a shortage of seed in 1258. Near Parma, a Franciscan friar noted how in 1259 people died in church during Vespers and that across the whole of the province of Bologna the Franciscans not could say the office of Palm Sunday (9 April) since they were all sick as a result of the cold; he then wrote a moralising 'Book of Pestilences'. At about the same time many thousands died in Florence, Milan and Paris.[20] The location of the volcanic event remains uncertain. Ice-core evidence dates it to the mid thirteenth century. Suggestions that it took place in 1257 or early in 1258 may not be correct, however, since in England the disturbed weather patterns accounting for poor harvests

---

[18] N. S. B. Gras and E. C. Gras, *The Economic and Social History of an English Village (Crawley, Hampshire) A.D. 909–1928* (Cambridge, Mass., 1930), 225–6; *Annales Monastici*, ii, 97 (*Annales de Wintonia*); Curschmann, *Hungersnöte*, 178–9.

[19] R. B. Stothers, 'Climatic and Demographic Consequences of the Massive Volcanic Ruption of 1258', *Climatic Change*, 45 (2004), 361–74; C. Oppenheimer, 'Ice Core and Palaeoclimatic Evidence for the Timing and Nature of the Great Mid-13th century Volcanic Eruption', *International Journal of Climatology*, 23 (2003), 417–26; C. Oppenheimer, 'Climatic, Environmental and Human Consequences of the Largest Known Historic Eruption: Tambora volcano (Indonesia), 1815', *Progress in Physical Geography*, 27 (2003), 230–59; J. Emile-Geay, R. Seager, M.A. Cane, E. R. Cook and G. H. Haug, 'Volcanoes and ENSO over the Past Millennium', *Journal of Climate*, 21 (2008), 313–48; I am grateful to Clive Oppenheimer and Robert Myhill for advice on this topic.

[20] Salimbene, *Chronicle*, 473–4; *Corpus Chronicorum Bononiensium*, ed. A. Sorbelli (4 vols., Rerum Italicarum Scriptores 18.1, 1905–48), ii, 146; *Matthaei Parisiensis*, v, 746–7; *Notae Constantienses*, in *Recueil des historiens des Gaules et de la France*, xxiii, ed. [N.] de Wailly, [L.] Delisle, [C.-M.-G. Bréchillet] Jourdain (Paris, 1844), 543–6 at 543.

seem first to have appeared in July 1255, when the Tewkesbury annalist recorded very dreadful thunder, or in July 1257, when he noted a great terror of thunder and lightning, followed by tumultuous wind in October.[21] This suggests the possibility that there were five successive phases of disturbed weather arising from volcanic eruption: late in 1254 or early in 1255, late in 1256 or early in 1257, late in 1257 or early in 1258, late in 1258 and late in 1259 or early in 1260. Alternatively, the poor harvest of 1255 and even that of 1257 may have arisen from a 'normal' pattern of bad weather and the successive atmospheric events of 1258–60 from a single eruption in 1257.

English chroniclers provide graphic accounts of famine in London during 1258–9. Their statistics may be exaggerated but, unlike some writers on the famine of 1315–17, they do not recycle biblical episodes by way of rhetorical embellishment.[22] The incipient disaster was revealed about March 1258, when it was apparent that corn was not growing in three counties, probably close to London. As usual in periods of grain shortage, speculators accumulated food in the city. Men flowed from the countryside to the city in search of food and died there in large numbers of hunger and disease: one writer mentions 15,000 dead in London and another 20,000. They were to be found everywhere, in the muddy streets, in doorways and on dunghills. Trenches were dug in cemeteries for use as mass graves. The greatest mortality appears to have been in early summer, when there was an outbreak of disease. Much of the harvest was lost on account of bad weather. The citizens of London and many people elsewhere participated in solemn fasts and processions in the hope of a good harvest. Attempting to cope with shortage, people sold their possessions and reduced their households. These conditions continued through 1259, when in April and May there was an unexpected outbreak of disease and high mortality, to which the bishop of London succumbed. Storms in October sank much of the Yarmouth herring fleet, adding to London's problems. The wealthy were still able to buy what they needed, thereby denying supplies to the less well off, nicely illustrated by the canons of Dunstable, who had to buy their own food and ale rather than live off the produce of their estates and who, at the same time, bought land and rents from the unfortunate. The supposed poisonings of some leading magnates in this period may have resulted from the outbreaks of disease arising from famine or perhaps from atmospheric pollution.[23]

During the first half of 1258 the nation was in a state of political crisis,

[21]   *Annales Monastici*, I, 156–7 (*Annales de Theokesburia*).

[22]   J. Marvin, 'Cannibalism as an Aspect of Famine in Two English Chronicles', in *Food and Eating in Medieval Europe*, ed. M. Carlin and J. T. Rosenthal (London, 1998), 73–86.

[23]   *Annales Monastici*, I, 166 (*Annales de Teokesburia*); *Matthaei Parisiensi*, v, 673, 690, 693, 701, 710–12, 738, 746–7; *Liber de Antiquis Legibus*, 37; *Chronicles Edward I and Edward II*, I, 51, 53 (*Annales Londonienses*); *Annales Monastici*, III, 204–12 (*Annales de Dunstaplia*); R. F. Treharne, *The Baronial Plan of Reform, 1258–1263* (Manchester, 1932), 80–1.

culminating in the most radical baronial assault yet made on the prerogatives of the crown. In the city of London there was a deep divide, which the crown attempted to exploit, between its aldermanic and mercantile rulers and the populace. The king's position weakened decisively in April as famine emerged. At the Oxford parliament in June, as famine neared a peak, the king accepted the baronial proposals for reform.[24] The natural disasters probably enhanced these confrontations, adding to widespread perceptions of crisis. That in turn presumably limited the city authorities' capacity to take concerted action to deal with problems of food supply. The assize of bread was apparently neglected, so that later in November or December the royal justiciar, recently appointed as a result of representations by the barons, held an assize of bread at Guildhall, where he was accompanied by the earl of Gloucester, one of the baronial leaders. Bakers found guilty of having infringed the assize were punished by a higher degree of shaming than had been customary in the city for this offence.[25]

Contemporaries noted with reference to March or April 1258 that many more thousands would have died had not corn and bread been sent for sale in London in large quantities from Germany and Holland, especially in at least fifty great ships procured by Richard of Cornwall, brother of King Henry III, and there may have been similar imports later in the year. Richard had been crowned king of Germany in 1257 and during 1258 remained in Germany, which was itself seriously affected by famine. Anticipating that merchants would attempt to corner these newly-arrived supplies, a royal edict prohibited the citizens from buying up and reselling the corn.[26] Richard was a man of formidable power and wealth and, given his imperial ambitions, this public display of generosity may have been informed specifically by knowledge of imperial practice in ancient Rome, one purpose of such euergetism having been to avert disorder.[27] Similar ideas concerning the duties of rulers, including bishops, were widespread in medieval Europe and had been expressed in the life of Charles the Good. Henry III himself had pursued them in London during the 1240s when he sponsored many thousands of free meals for the poor at Westminster and St Paul's.[28] In 1258 Henry had lost the initiative and so depended upon his brother Richard for such action, although Henry himself may have persuaded his half-brother to be modestly generous to the villagers of Crawley. When Richard returned to England early in 1259, a splendid

[24] Treharne, *Baronial Plan*, 64–81; J. R. Maddicott, *Simon de Montfort* (Cambridge, 1994), 152–65; G. A. Williams, *Medieval London, from Commune to Capital* (London, 1963), 204–13.

[25] *Liber de Antiquis Legibus*, 40–1.

[26] *Liber de Antiquis Legibus*, 37; *Matthaei Parisiensis*, v, 673, 701, 710–11; Curschmann, *Hungersnöte*, 179–80.

[27] Garnsey, *Famine*, 176–97, 218–43.

[28] R. C. Stacey, *Politics, Policy and Finance under Henry III, 1216–1245* (Oxford, 1987), 240.

and joyous entry to London was staged for him, perhaps to celebrate his support of the city as much as his recent elevation.[29]

One London response to the crisis has been dramatically revealed by the recent discovery of two successive sets of grave pits in the cemetery of the sub-urban hospital of St Mary without Bishopsgate (Spitalfields), datable with some precision to about 1260. Together they account for several thousand individuals, almost certainly victims of the famine. The first set of pits probably accommo-dates victims from 1258. The second set was dug only a year or two later, since it cut through some of the earlier pits, thereby removing from the earlier corpses limbs still articulated which were redeposited with the bodies of the second set of victims, who were probably buried in 1259.[30] The initiative in establishing this emergency burial site may have been taken by the bishop of London as patron of the hospital, but prominent Londoners, of the same rank as those citizens who had founded and had continued to support the hospital, may also have been involved in some sort of civic action to bury the dead. Much later, the hospital cemetery had a distinct association with the mayoralty.[31]

Much less is known about the events in London during the famine of 1315–17, noted at the time as the worst dearth for a century,[32] and now often called the Great Famine. The crisis was precipitated rapidly by bad weather in the spring of 1315 and appears to have affected much of northern Europe, but no further afield.[33] Daily prices in the city (Figure 3.2) indicate a midsummer peak, followed by an inad-equate harvest which only briefly halted a continuing rise to an even higher peak in the summer of 1316. After the harvest of that year conditions began to improve, but a similar though more extended pattern of cumulative shortage, typical of severe famines, appeared during the years 1321–3. Many people died of starvation and disease. Population totals in districts near London fell sharply, and there are similar, though less readily quantifiable, indications for the city itself.[34] The crown was maintaining armies against the Scots and Welsh and was encouraged by the flow of food into London to purchase supplies for them there and in the surround-ing region.[35] In February 1316 the king, who needed honey and wheat to supply his castles in Wales, ordered an official to buy all the honey in London and 1,000

29 *Matthaei Parisiensis*, v, 736; *Liber de Antiquis Legibus*, 41; *Annales Monastici*, iv, 122 (*Chroni-con Thomas Wykes*).

30 Information from Chris Thomas, Museum of London Archaeology Service.

31 C. Thomas, B. Sloane and C. Phillpotts, *Excavations at the Priory and Hospital of St Mary Spital, London* (London, 1997), 19–21, 26, 127.

32 *Vita Edwardi Secundi Monachi cuiusdam Malmesburiensis*, ed. N. Denholme-Young (Lon-don, 1957), 69–70.

33 W. Chester Jordan, *The Great Famine: Northern Europe in the Early Fourteenth Century* (Princeton, 1996).

34 L. R. Poos, 'The Rural Population of Essex in the Later Middle Ages', *EcHR* 38 (1985), 515–30; D. Keene, *Cheapside before the Great Fire* (London, 1985), 19–20.

35 *CPR, 1313–17*, 370–71, 373, 386.

quarters of wheat there, since he understood that these commodities had lately come into London in great quantity.[36] Such demands presumably drove up prices in the city, but perhaps not by much since even 1,000 quarters of grain represented less than one per cent of London's annual needs. London's cornmongers benefited from the famine and the extra trade: tax assessments reveal that in 1319 they were significantly wealthier in relation to other Londoners than in the 1290s.[37]

However serious the famine, Londoners could be sure of at least some supplies, so long as the price of food was higher there than elsewhere. In this way London, presumably unintentionally, inflicted hunger on the territory round about and encouraged the immigration of the starving. This was recognised in 1375, when the city authorities fined a citizen who offered too high a price for corn at Henley, a market town which routinely supplied the city. At a later date, Venice during times of shortage routinely posted guaranteed high prices for grain which were supported out of public funds, while attempts to keep city prices down in times of shortage ended in disaster, as was the case at Cordoba in 1502–3.[38] London dealers also gathered in foodstuffs so as to supply them to the territory round about. Thus in a crisis the city probably contained more than its actual needs. In April 1325, a time of relatively high prices, for example, London merchants were stockpiling grain shipped in from Flanders in expectation of supplying districts outside London as well as the city itself. In response to a royal order to prevent a rise in prices, the city authorities attempted to prevent corn being carried out through the city gates. In other years when prices were similarly high, the city authorities, in pursuit of royal orders concerning the kingdom as a whole, issued proclamations against the export of corn from London, while in 1432 the 'commonalty' of London, fearing a scarcity, asked the ruling elite to urge the royal government to restrict exports from the city itself.[39] Thus as the city became ever more a site of national wealth, its leaders could employ their influence with the crown to help secure the food supply.

State intervention during the Great Famine was largely directed at national needs. Royal proclamations fixing the prices of livestock were issued in March 1315, in response to pressure from parliament earlier in the year. For some items London prices were set higher than those for elsewhere, but the overall effect of the measures was to drive goods out of the market place, and they were repealed a year later. After the poor harvest of 1315 exports of corn and other victuals were forbidden. Attempts were made to encourage the flow of supplies within the kingdom. In spring 1316 the king granted protection to London merchants who were

---

[36]   CCR, 1313–1318, 267.

[37]   Campbell et al., Medieval Capital, 35, 82–3.

[38]   Calendar of the Plea and Memoranda Rolls of the City of London, II: 1364–1381, ed. A. H. Thomas (Cambridge, 1929), 192; Lane, Venice, 306; J. Edwards, Christian Córdoba: The City and its Region in the Late Middle Ages (Cambridge, 1982), 112–13.

[39]   Letter-Book E, 196–7; Letter-Book K, 146–7.

seeking supplies for the city in Cornwall, which was relatively unaffected by the crisis and lay far outside London's normal supply zone.[40] In 1317 the trade in food-stuffs was facilitated by removing the customs dues on the import and export of corn, salt and fish at London and other ports, and the price of ale was fixed, so that brewing would not withdraw wheat and barley from the supply of grain for bread, the latter being a policy similar to that pursued by Charles the Good in 1124.[41] Overall, the crisis in London was addressed by such essentially national measures as these, and by the crown's diplomatic efforts to secure permission for English merchants to purchase supplies overseas. In December 1315 those efforts were addressed to Ponthieu, Normandy and Brittany, but a year later corn was being brought from more distant sources in Gascony and Spain, parts of Europe where the harvests had not failed.[42] Developments in commerce and shipping since 1258 perhaps favoured this longer-distance trade. In particular, the highly-capitalised Italian merchants were now much better established in London and England than formerly, and so, as prices rose in northern Europe, they began to invest in grain from Gascony and the south. The king extended his special protection to alien merchants supplying corn, including those of Sicily, Spain and Genoa.[43] The port of Sandwich assumed particular significance as a site for stockpiling this grain since it was strategically situated for transferring supplies to London, to the royal garrisons in the north or, if the export ban could be evaded, to hungry Flemish towns.[44] The international market in grain which focused in the southern part of the North Sea probably achieved an unprecedented level of intensity and specula-tion, and at Liège it was noted that supplies were being carried toward the Flemish coast.[45]

In marked contrast to 1258, the city authorities also took concerted action. In August 1317 they prohibited the London brewers from making malt, presumably so that barley and other grains would be available for bread. They maintained the assize of bread and during the year 1315–16 issued the first known comprehensive account of the customary regulations governing the city corn market.[46] These rules were primarily concerned to ensure the openness of the market and the vis-ibility of the grain for sale. Only the four accustomed market places for grain were

[40] *Rotuli Parliamentorum* (6 vols., London, 1783), I, 295.

[41] *CCR, 1313–1318*, 308, 449, 498; J. Hatcher, *Rural Economy and Society in the Duchy of Cornwall, 1300–1500* (Cambridge, 1970), 85; M. Kowaleski, 'The Grain Trade of Fourteenth-Century Exeter', in *The Salt of Common Life: Individuality and Choice in the Medieval Town, Countryside and Church: Studies presented to J. Ambrose Raftis*, ed. E. B. DeWindt (Kalama-zoo, Mich., 1995), 1–52. Cf. *Murder of Charles the Good*, 88.

[42] *CCR, 1313–1318*, 318, 385, 452; Jordan, *Famine*, 173–74.

[43] *CCR, 1313–1318*, 425.

[44] *CCR, 1313–1318*, 291, 341, 380, 385, 522; *CPR, 1313–1317*, 466, 501–2.

[45] I. Kershaw, 'The Great Famine and the Agrarian Crisis in England, 1315–1322', *P&P* 59 (1973), 3–50.

[46] *Letter-Book E*, 56–7, 77.

to be used. The operations of middlemen and buying and selling between dealers, rather than directly to consumers, were prohibited, as was sale by sample. In several instances the code contains the first surviving formulation of rules or ideals which continued to be applied throughout the Middle Ages and beyond. While in the aftermath of the Great Famine Ghent appears to have established its famous grain staple,[47] the most enduring legacy of that episode in London was the code of rules governing its corn trade.

During the late thirteenth, fourteenth and fifteenth centuries most English towns, with London in the lead, developed more coherent and stable systems of internal government which, per head of population, controlled greater financial resources than had been the case formerly. This found expression in public building, in the role of civic authorities as trustees for charitable and religious endeavours, and in attitudes towards food supply. In 1391, for example, when corn was scarce, the London authorities used the money that they held on behalf of orphans to buy corn for the 'commonalty'. In 1429, a year of similar shortage, the city ordered persons to be sent abroad to buy corn at the city's risk of any loss by sea or otherwise.[48] The more serious shortage of 1439, which according to one chronicler drove the 'poor commons' of London to make bread of barley, beans and peas rather than wheat,[49] prompted more drastic action, including the first establishment of a public granary. Civic funds were used to pay for at least a substantial part of the new building, erected on a property known as Leadenhall that it already owned. Donations from wealthy individuals assisted the project. The work was being planned in March 1440 and was substantially complete about six years later.[50] In 1443 John Rainwell, a wealthy citizen whose knowledge of Prussia suggests that his commercial interests included the Baltic grain trade, left funds for stocking the city's granary with wheat when needed by the *communitas*.[51] The outcome of this effort was one of the most architecturally sophisticated and ambitious civic buildings ever erected in London.[52] The granary occupied part of the upper storey of a quadrangular structure, which in its central space and ground floor galleries provided accommodation for a market in other foodstuffs. In addition, the complex included an elegant chapel, a college of priests and a school.

[47]   D. Nicholas, *The Metamorphosis of a Medieval City: Ghent in the Age of the Arteveldes, 1302–1390* (Lincoln, Neb., 1987), 241–4; Stabel, *Dwarfs among Giants*, 168–70.

[48]   *Calendar of the Plea and Memoranda Rolls of the City of London*, III: *1381–1412*, ed. A. H. Thomas (Cambridge, 1932), 174–5; *Letter-Book H*, 361–2; *Letter-Book K*, 92.

[49]   *Great Chronicle*, 174.

[50]   A. H. Thomas, 'Notes on the History of the Leadenhall, A.D. 1195–1488', *London Topographical Record* 13 (1923), 1–22.

[51]   Public Record Office, *Report on the Foedera, Appendix C* (London, 1869), 22–7.

[52]   M. Samuel, 'The Fifteenth-Century Garner at Leadenhall, London', *The Antiquaries Journal* 69 (1989), 118–53; C. M. Barron, *London in the Later Middle Ages: Government and People* (Oxford, 2004), 54–6.

This investment appears out of all proportion to the scale of the crisis which prompted it. Moreover, the building was not long used as a granary, and in the sixteenth century, when the maintenance of grain stocks became a routine element in city policy, those stocks were usually kept elsewhere.[53] Several more general explanations for the building of a granary are possible. Perhaps by this date there had emerged in the city a clearer appreciation, characteristic of a more commercialised economy, of the value of maintaining a grain stock so as to even out price fluctuations from year to year. Or perhaps since the London market was now less dynamic by comparison with those of its nearest continental rivals, and because the internal corn market was less integrated than it had been in 1300,[54] the risk of grain being diverted to overseas consumers in times of scarcity was greater than it had been in the past, especially now that Baltic grain made a significant contribution to the needs of cities on both sides of the North Sea. Probably more important than these purely economic considerations, however, was what seems to have been an increasingly common policy in English towns during the fifteenth century to provide buildings to house the commercial activities of unenfranchised traders who brought in foodstuffs and other goods from outside, and who in earlier times would have traded in the street.[55] The food traders in the new buildings at Leadenhall appear previously to have stood in the street outside, while later the complex also accommodated markets in cloth, lead, nails, and hides, all supplied by outsiders. The granary may thus from the beginning have been part of a larger plan for organising the trade of the city and for enhancing the dignity of public space by removing traders from the street and erecting an impressive multi-purpose civic structure, at a key site where one of the pageants that formed part of royal entries to the city was staged.[56] Moreover, the years 1438–44 were a period of artisanal unrest in opposition to the ruling elite,[57] whose members perhaps envisaged the project as an expression of their good ordering of the city as a whole and as a reassurance to the populace that their food supply was provided for.

At Florence, where the public provision of grain dated from at least as early as 1139, there had been a similar expression of reassurance in the aftermath of the Tuscan famine of 1328–30, when in 1336 the commune proposed to build a palace in the corn market of San Michele in Orto where the Virgin Mary could be venerated and the communal stock of grain safely kept, thereby assuring a supply for the *popolo*. The result was the Orsanmichele, one of the most imposing public

---

53   Gras, *Evolution of the English Corn Market*, 80–2.

54   Galloway, 'One Market or Many?'.

55   D. Keene, *Survey of Medieval Winchester* (Oxford, 1985), 258.

56   *Great Chronicle*, 162.

57   C. M. Barron, 'Ralph Holland and the London Radicals, 1438–1444', in *The Medieval Town: A Reader in English Urban History, 1200–1540*, ed. R. Holt and G. Rosser (Harrow, 1990), 160–83.

structures in the city, which, building on earlier associations of the site, became a major expression of guild, civic, charitable and artistic culture, although the granary was not completed until 1377.[58] A century later the citizens of London had the political, financial and cultural capacity to make a similar gesture. Their building was completed quite quickly. While it soon ceased to be used as a granary, its cultural and other economic functions endured.

This examination of three crisis episodes in London's food supply offers useful insights into the city's position within the realm and into the evolution of a sense of the public good in the city's affairs. In the mid thirteenth century there was perhaps a sense, not dissimilar to that in the Roman empire, that in a crisis it was the monarch's duty to see to the food needs of a potentially disordered and threatening capital city. This would have been especially the case in a city such as London whose autonomy was severely limited and which was internally divided on class lines. Earlier in the Middle Ages the bishop of London would probably have assumed such a responsibility for the city on behalf of the king,[59] but by the thirteenth century the bishop to a large extent had been marginalised from direct involvement in civic affairs, although he may have played a role in London in 1258. During the Great Famine of the early fourteenth century, following a further strengthening of royal authority, the monarch acted primarily in the interests of the realm as a whole, but the Londoners, conscious of the strength of their market for food, coherently articulated perhaps for the first time their customary practices for regulating it. Subsequently the citizens appear to have developed their collective capacity to take remedial action during food crises. So far as the organisation of markets was concerned, that capacity ultimately found an expression in the construction of a major public building, part of a wider development in the provision of civic buildings in English towns apparent from about 1400 onwards and in some respects following models established by cities overseas. Whether or not the food crisis of 1439 was the immediate impulse behind the building of Leadenhall, the provision of the facilities it contained expressed a wider concern for the standing of the city and for the ordering of its trade and public space. As in our own day, it seems that investment in public infrastructure is often driven as much by civic pride, a sense of cultural identity and sometimes by a desire to resolve or gloss over political problems, as by purely utilitarian objectives.

[58] C.-M. de La Roncière, *Prix et salaires à Florence au xive siècle (1280–1380)* (Rome, 1982), 18, 126–27, 523–38, 569–86; *Orsanmichele a Firenze*, ed. D. Finiello Zervas (2 vols., Modena, 1996); D. Finiello Zervas, *Orsanmichele: Documenti, 1336–1452* (Ferrara, 1996), esp. nos. 1–5.

[59] R. Doehaerd, *The Early Middle Ages in the West: Economy and Society*, trans. W. G. Deakin (Amsterdam, 1978), 152–3, 158, citing the case of St Didier of Cahors; K. J. Leyser, 'The Tenth-Century Condition', in idem, *Medieval Germany and its Neighbours, 900–1250* (London, 1982), 1–11; P. Wormald, *The Making of English Law: King Alfred to the Tenth Century*, 1: *Legislation and its Limits* (Oxford, 1999), 451–4.

4

Grain Shortages in Late Medieval Towns
....
John S. Lee

He that withholdeth corn, the people shall curse him: but blessing shall
be upon the head of him that selleth it.[1]

THIS ARTICLE EXAMINES the impact upon English towns of shortages of grain
during periods of harvest failure in the later Middle Ages. It explores the reactions of civic and central governments at times of shortage, looking in detail at
the census of people, grain, bakers and brewers drawn up in Coventry during the
dearth of 1520. This census seems to have formed more than simply a headcount,
and it is argued here that its purpose was to ensure that resident traders did
not retain surpluses of grain beyond their immediate production needs, and to
provide a means by which the city government could demonstrate to its citizens
that immoral behaviour was being curtailed. As this census formed one of the
key pieces of evidence which Charles Phythian-Adams used to identify a 'crisis'
period in Coventry between 1518 and 1525, which 'decisively sounded the knell of
the medieval city', this study also questions whether grain shortages contributed
in any way to the significant challenges faced by many towns in this period, which
have been collectively labelled as 'urban decline'.[2] The marketing patterns, regulation and economic development of late medieval towns, and the social and economic policies of urban and central governments, are all areas which have been
illuminated by Richard Britnell's wide-ranging and detailed research.

The outcome of each harvest was of fundamental importance in a pre-
industrial economy: 'no other aspect of economic life was consistently of such

The idea for this article came from my exercise in bibliographical method, 'The 1520 Dearth
in Coventry: The Census and Related Entries from the Coventry Leet Book', supervised by
Richard Britnell, which formed part of my M.A. in Medieval History at the University of
Durham in 1997. I am most grateful to Richard for his support and encouragement over
many years. This article has benefitted from the advice of James Davis and Catherine Casson.

[1]   Proverbs 11:26.

[2]   C. Phythian-Adams, *Desolation of a City: Coventry and the Urban Crisis of the Late Middle
Ages* (Cambridge, 1979), 50–67.

great concern to private individuals and to public authorities alike'.[3] Many groups in English society enjoyed improved standards of living, from rising real wages and greater availability of land, in the two centuries that followed the Black Death of 1348–9. Many consumers obtained a wider range and better quality of food-stuffs, eating bread made from wheat rather than barley or rye, although it was observed in 1521 that bread made from oats was still a staple in Wales, northern England and Scotland.[4] Yet despite rising living standards, poor harvest yields continued to have a significant impact. The decade of the 1430s saw three ex-tremely bad harvests which were accompanied by increased livestock mortality.[5] Wheat price data suggest clusters of bad harvests occurred in 1481–3, 1500–3, 1519–21, and 1527–9, with 1482, 1520 and 1527 being years of dearth.[6] Grain shortages in the fifteenth and sixteenth centuries rarely resulted in starvation, but there were exceptional cases, such as in the remote pastoral region of late-sixteenth-century Westmorland, and the burial entries relating to 'famine' at St Margaret's Westminster in 1557 and the 'poore man' who 'by famishment was buried' at York in 1587.[7] Dodds found a clear coincidence of poor harvests and epidemic disease in north-eastern England between 1390 and 1402, during the 1430s, and other possible correlations in the 1480s and early sixteenth century, while similar patterns have been discerned in the later sixteenth century. It seems

[3] E. A. Wrigley, *People, Cities and Wealth. The Transformation of Traditional Society* (Oxford, 1987), 116–17.

[4] R. H. Britnell, *Britain and Ireland, 1050–1530: Economy and Society* (Oxford, 2004), 388, 396–7, 510.

[5] C. Dyer, *Standards of Living in the Later Middle Ages: Social Change in England c. 1200–1520* (Cambridge, 1989), 261–8; B. Dodds, *Peasants and Production in the Medieval North-East: The Evidence from Tithes, 1270–1536* (Woodbridge, 2007), 111.

[6] W. G. Hoskins, 'Harvest Fluctuations and English Economic History, 1480–1619', *AgHR* 12 (1964), 28–46. A harvest judged 'bad' was a twenty-five to fifty per cent deviation in the wheat price above a thirty-one-year moving average, and 'dearth' > fifty per cent. An al-ternative series, based on the average price of all grains, produces broadly similar results for these decades: C. J. Harrison, 'Grain Price Analysis and Harvest Qualities 1465–1634', *AgHR* 19 (1971), 135–55. A direct and consistent link between price and yield has, however, been questioned, particularly due to the impact of grain carried over from one harvest to the next: P. R. Schofield, 'Regional Price Differentials and Local Economies in North-East England, c.1350–c.1520', in *Agriculture and Rural Society after the Black Death: Common Themes and Regional Variations*, ed. B. Dodds and R. H. Britnell (Hatfield, 2008), 40–2.

[7] Dyer, *Standards of Living*, 261–73; J. Walter and R. Schofield, 'Famine, Disease and Crisis Mortality in Early Modern Society,' in *Famine, Disease and the Social Order in Early Mod-ern Society*, ed. idem (Cambridge, 1989), 29–30; A. B. Appleby, *Famine in Tudor and Stuart England* (Stanford, 1978); P. Laslett, *The World We Have Lost* (2nd edn, London, 1971), 123; C. Galley, *The Demography of Early Modern Towns: York in the Sixteenth and Seventeenth Centuries* (Liverpool, 1998), 87.

that while dearth and disease operated independently, they could have greater impact when they coincided.[8]

As towns relied on the surrounding countryside for their food supplies and raw materials, they were particularly vulnerable at times of shortage. Even the consumption needs of small towns could rarely have been satisfied by the produce cultivated by the townspeople themselves. A town of 1,000 inhabitants would probably consume the surplus produce from a dozen villages in the vicinity.[9] The comparatively limited size of English medieval towns meant that the area that was needed to supply larger towns was relatively restricted. Colchester, for example, with a population of between 3,000 and 4,000 in the early fourteenth century, received foodstuffs from within an eight-mile radius of the town. When the town's population grew and its living standards increased during the later fourteenth century, stimulated largely by its expanding cloth industry, these supplies were supplemented by grain from the Norfolk coast. Cambridge, with probably fewer than 4,000 inhabitants in the 1520s, drew wheat and malt barley from up to 10 miles away.[10] Coventry's hinterland for grain was particularly restricted by geography, communications and competition, and this may have increased the city's vulnerability in periods of dearth. To the west of the city was the Forest of Arden, where relatively little wheat was cultivated, while elsewhere the city had to compete with demand from Stratford-upon-Avon, Warwick, Bristol and Leicester.[11] Coventry was not situated on a navigable river, which made the transportation of grain more expensive: corn could be carried by water at between one-half and one-eighth of the cost of land carriage.[12] Inland markets like Coventry that were dependent on the higher costs of overland transport experienced more volatile grain prices, because it was less likely that deficiencies would be compensated by supplies from elsewhere.[13]

It may have been partly in recognition of the geographical vulnerability of Coventry at times of shortage, that following the wet summer of 1520, with a very

---

[8]   Dodds, *Peasants*, 96–100, 111–12, 115; P. Slack, 'Mortality Crises and Epidemic Disease in England, 1485–1610', in *Health, Medicine and Mortality in the late Sixteenth Century*, ed. C. Webster (Cambridge, 1979), 9–39.

[9]   C. Dyer, 'Small Places with Large Consequences: The Importance of Small Towns in England, 1000–1540', *Historical Research*, 75 (2002), 17.

[10] R. H. Britnell, *Growth and Decline in Colchester, 1300–1525* (Cambridge, 1986), 41–7, 132, 141–2, 246–7; J. S. Lee, 'Feeding the Colleges: Cambridge's Food and Fuel Supplies, 1450–1560', *EcHR* 56 (2003), 243–64; J. S. Lee, *Cambridge and its Economic Region, 1450–1560* (Hatfield, 2005), 29, 152–9.

[11] Phythian-Adams, *Desolation*, 58.

[12] P. J. Bowden, 'Agricultural Prices, Farm Profits and Rents', in *AHEW* IV, 612; J. Masschaele, 'Transport Costs in Medieval England', *EcHR* 46 (1993), 266–79.

[13] J. A. Galloway, 'One Market or Many? London and the Grain Trade of England', in *Trade, Urban Hinterlands and Market Integration, c.1300–1600*, ed. J. A. Galloway (London, 2000), 34–5.

poor harvest and rising grain prices, the city government ordered a census of the number of people and the quantities of grain available:

> Memorandum that the xth day of Octobre and in the yer of the raigne of Kyng Henry the Viij[th], then Maister John Bonde beyng Maier of the Cite of Coventre, the price of all maner of corne and graynes be-ganne to a-ryse, wheruppon a veu was takon by the said Maier and his brethren what stores of all maner of corne, and what nombre of people was then whithin the said Cite, men, women and children, etc.[14]

The Coventry census covered the city's ten wards, each containing an important main road and several side streets, which were the principal administrative divisions within a city of only two ecclesiastical parishes.[15] The census reveals which wards were most seriously affected by the dearth of 1520, while four other contemporaneous documents help to show the social and economic characteristics of these areas. These documents are the muster roll of 1522, a 'numbering' of the people, probably made in 1523, and lay subsidy assessments from 1524 and 1525.[16]

As Table 4.1 shows, the greatest shortages of breadcorn (wheat and rye) were in Broadgate, Spon Street and Jordan Well, while the largest per capita stocks were in Earl Street, Smithford Street and Bayley Lane wards. The wards with the greatest shortages tended to have the largest number of households assessed at less than £2 in goods or wages, a high proportion of textile workers, and to be suburban. Conversely, wards with the largest per capita stocks of breadcorn possessed, on average, wealthier households and a lower proportion of textile workers, and were centrally located within the city. When a similar survey was made in the Hinckford hundred of Essex in 1527, villages with a greater proportion of higher rate taxpayers also tended to have larger stocks of breadcorn, although there were exceptions.[17] There was no apparent link in Coventry between the number of empty houses in each ward and the quantities of breadcorn available.

The survey made by William Clopton for Hinckford in Essex in 1527 assumed that six persons needed one bushel (or strike) of breadcorn and one and a half bushels of drinkcorn per week.[18] On this basis, the Coventry census of 1520

---

[14] Coventry History Centre, BA/E/6/37/1: Coventry Leet Book 1420–1555, fol. 330[r-v], published in *The Coventry Leet Book*, ed. M. D. Harris (Early English Text Society, 134–5, 138, 146, 1907–13), 674–5, and reprinted in *Tudor Economic Documents*, 1, ed. R. H. Tawney and E. Power (London, 1924), 141–3.

[15] Phythian-Adams, *Desolation*, 158. The wards were used for the assessment and collection of taxes, murage, loans and the organisation of policing by constables, fire-fighting, and ale-tasting. For a map of the wards see *Coventry and its People in the 1520s*, ed. M. Hulton (Publications of the Dugdale Society, 38, 1999), endpapers.

[16] *Coventry*, ed. Hulton.

[17] D. Dymond, 'The Famine of 1527 in Essex', *Local Population Studies*, 26 (1981), 37.

[18] Ibid., 40.

Table 4.1: Coventry wards in the dearth of 1520

Ward	No. of people	Breadcorn (quarters)	Breadcorn per person (bushels)	Taxpayers <£2	Taxpayers >£20	Empty houses	Textile workers	Character
Broadgate	552	3.0	0.04	88.4%	3.3%	25	13.2%	suburb
Spon Street	627	3.9	0.05	84.0%	3.2%	107	30.5%	suburb
Jordan Well	354	3.0	0.07	86.1%	4.0%	61	40.0%	suburb
Gosford Street	875	16.0	0.15	67.6%	4.9%	62	53.2%	suburb
Much Park Street	719	14.6	0.16	78.8%	4.2%	28	32.5%	suburb
Cross Cheaping	884	19.5	0.18	56.5%	11.3%	59	9.0%	central, marketing
Bishop Street	1,018	26.0	0.20	81.6%	3.4%	127	31.4%	central & suburb
Earl Street	707	21.8	0.25	66.9%	11.0%	38	34.1%	wool/cloth marketing
Smithford Street	406	17.8	0.35	56.0%	6.7%	38	15.4%	central, trading, victualling
Bayley Lane	459	20.8	0.36	59.1%	14.8%	16	33.9%	central
Total	6,601	146.3	0.18	73.7%	6.3%	561	27.7%	

Sources: No. of people and breadcorn (wheat and rye) from *Coventry Leet Book*, 674–5; other columns from *Coventry*, ed. Hulton, 6–10, 21, 23, 30–2. A quarter was a grain measure, comprising eight bushels (or strikes).

Note: The sum of the total breadcorn in each ward (146.3 quarters) differs slightly from the total wheat and rye stated at the end of the document (147.1 quarters).

indicates that five wards had less than a week's supply of breadcorn, while even those wards with the largest per capita stocks, Smithford Street and Bayley Lane, had only just over two weeks' supply. The Coventry census also records,

> Memorandum that ther was at that tyme xliij bakers within the Cyte, the which dyd bake wekly amongest all vj[xx] quarter of whet & xij besydes pese and rye.[19]

It has been suggested that the great mass of country people and the poorer inhabitants of towns baked their own bread.[20] But if we accept William Clopton's estimates, the 132 quarters of wheat consumed by the Coventry bakers would have supplied 6,336 people, or all those enumerated in the 1520 census. Even if this figure is read as 120 quarters '& xij [strikes]' this would still supply 5,832 people.[21] Add to this the bread made from peas and rye, and bread sold by country bakers who were permitted to enter the city, and it would appear that most of the townspeople relied on the bakers for their bread. Indeed when the bakers had abandoned Coventry in 1484 during a dispute with the mayor, it was claimed that the city was left 'destitute of bred'.[22]

This history of uneasy relationships between the borough government and the bakers in Coventry may have prompted the census in 1520. The bakers had asked for a statement of prices and weights under the assize of bread in 1379, suggesting that this was not being set properly, and disputes over the assize in 1374 and 1387 had led the commons to rise and throw loaves at the mayor. In 1477 the mayor had punished bakers for making and selling underweight bread, and in 1484 the bakers had gone on strike and temporarily left Coventry.[23]

In conducting the census of 1520, it is not clear whether the borough government had any direct precedent within the city on which to draw. An earlier survey of a similar, if less comprehensive, nature may have been undertaken when crowds arrived in Coventry during the visit of the Benedictine Chapter in 1498, as the mayor ordered an enquiry of the price of all victuals to be set on the minster door.[24] The city government may have repeated the exercise undertaken in 1520 as 'a veue of the wardes' was drawn up in June 1523. By providing totals of the people in each ward and the names of each householder, this may have been the initial work for a similar survey. However, the purpose of the 1523 'numbering' is not clear: drawn up at a time of better harvests, it may have been 'an elaborate

[19] Coventry Leet Book 1420–1550, fol. 330[v]; Coventry Leet Book, 675.
[20] W. Ashley, Bread of our Forefathers (Oxford, 1928), 154–5.
[21] Dymond, 'Famine', 40.
[22] Coventry Leet Book, 518–19.
[23] P. Willcox, The Bakers' Company of Coventry (Coventry, 1992), 6–7.
[24] Coventry Leet Book, 588–9.

and unnecessary anticipation of shortage', a survey for local economic planning, or evidence to support a request for a trade or tax concession from the crown.[25]

The crown, however, ordered a national survey of grain stocks after a disastrous harvest in 1527, which was very similar to the census conducted in Coventry in 1520. Commissioners were appointed in every English county

> to visit and search the barns, garners, ricks, and stacks of all and every such person and persons which is or be supposed to have more corn than shall be thought convenient by their discretions for the use of their households and seed; and to compel the owners therof to bring the same unto the markets.[26]

The names of those who refused to release their surpluses were to be presented in Star Chamber before 21 January.[27] Records of the searches survive for some of the hundreds or wapentakes of Essex, Kent, Middlesex, Nottinghamshire, Wiltshire and the North Riding of Yorkshire.[28] Ashley suggested that 'the Tudor Government did but take over, and make more general, a practice which had grown up in some of the larger towns', although he quoted only the Coventry census of 1520 as a precedent.[29] The crown may have arranged some searches the following year. Lincoln corporation notified a member of the privy council on 10 February 1521 that certain men in Lindsey had complained that corn which they intended to bring to Lincoln market was stopped by the sheriff and his officers, and asked by what authority this was being carried out.[30] The earl of Arundel informed Cardinal Wolsey in March that 'those who made the search reported that in the space of twenty miles there was not more than 412 quarters, besides what the farmers have for their houses and for seed'.[31]

The Coventry census of 1520, and the national searches conducted in 1527–8, emerged from a context of wider social and economic discourse, in which the scarcity of grain was a key concern for the government, alongside manpower, employment and social order. High grain prices in 1512 and 1513 had led to anxieties that the conversion of arable land to pasture and parkland, and its enclosure, was causing landlessness and depopulation. This found expression in a royal

---

[25] *Coventry*, ed. Hulton, 17–18; Phythian-Adams, *Desolation*, 291–305.

[26] *Tudor Royal Proclamations*, 1: *The Early Tudors, 1485–1553*, ed. P. L. Hughes and J. F. Larkin (London, 1964), 173.

[27] P. Gwyn, *The King's Cardinal: The Rise and Fall of Thomas Wolsey* (London, 1990), 457.

[28] Summarised in Ashley, *Bread*, 187–8, though he omits the returns for Hinckford, Essex, selectively transcribed in Dymond, 'Famine'. See also E. P. H. Pugh, 'A Grain Shortage of the 1520s', *Local Historian* [Ealing Local History Society], 2 (1962), 20–3, 33–7.

[29] Ashley, *Bread*, 42.

[30] J. W. F. Hill, *Medieval Lincoln* (Cambridge, 1948), 30.

[31] *Letters and Papers, Foreign and Domestic, of the Reign of Henry VIII*, ed. J. S. Brewer, J. Gardiner and R. H. Brodie (21 vols and *Addenda*, London, 1862–1932), III, pt. 2, appendix no. 23, p. 1578.

ordinance of 1514 or 1515, which attributed the scarcity of grain, unemployment and crime, to the engrossment of farms and the growth of pasture farming. This ordinance was followed by commissions of enquiry to investigate illegal enclosures.[32] In describing the scarcity and dearness of corn in 1528, Sir Edward Guildford noted that Romney Marsh, where corn and cattle had been plentiful, was in decay, and many farms were held by graziers, rather than those who tilled the land or bred cattle.[33] Enclosures were particularly prevalent in the Midlands, and these may have reduced Coventry's chances of procuring grain supplies by 1520. The antiquarian John Rous had presented a petition against enclosure in Warwickshire to the Coventry parliament of 1459.[34] In response to a 'great darthe and scarsenes of corne' in 1534, it was reported that many common pastures around Coventry had been recently ploughed up.[35]

Commissioners in 1527 also investigated cases of persons who were refusing to sell their corn in the local market, or were attempting to increase the price that they obtained for it. James Newby of Oundle was charged under this proclamation with failing to bring his grain to Oundle market, but selling it 'unto Strawngers dwelyng in owt shyers'. Newby was also allegedly enhancing the price of grain in Oundle market through buying grain in Cambridgeshire, and making men from that county buy grain in Northamptonshire, thus keeping up the price.[36] Such complaints were repeated at times of scarcity. York city council wrote to the privy council in 1586 about the 'great scarcities and dearthe' caused 'chiefly by the gredynes of the famors and others having sufficient provision of corne in their barnes and grayners and yet of purpose to enhance and rise the prices do forbeare to serve and furnishe the markette of such convenient quantities'.[37]

Vagrancy formed another aspect of contemporary political debate about the common weal, and at times of grain shortage, local and central governments increased their efforts to ensure that relief was targeted at the 'deserving poor' and migrants were dissuaded from flooding into towns for food and charity.[38] Coinciding therefore with the surveys of grain supplies was the introduction of legislation controlling begging and vagrancy. At Coventry, the Easter leet of 1521 instructed every alderman to search his ward for impotent and needy beggars, who were to carry a bag bearing the city arms. Those without a bag were to leave

---

[32] *Tudor Royal Proclamations*, I, 122–3; R. H. Britnell, *The Closing of the Middle Ages? England, 1471–1529* (Oxford, 1997), 204.

[33] *Letters and Papers*, IV, pt. 2, no. 4414, p. 1933.

[34] Phythian-Adams, *Desolation*, 57; J. Thirsk, 'Enclosing and Engrossing' in *AHEW* IV, 240; *English Historical Documents*, IV: 1327–1485, ed. A. R. Myers (London, 1969), 1014.

[35] *Coventry Leet Book*, 719.

[36] *Select Cases Before the King's Council in the Star Chamber*, II: 1509–44, ed. I. S. Leadam (Selden Society 25, 1910), 168–78.

[37] Galley, *Demography*, 88.

[38] Ibid., 89.

the city.[39] In 1524 beggars were forbidden to beg within the city's parish churches at service times.[40] The number of beggars probably increased during years of dearth as the rural poor migrated to the city seeking food, and payments made by the Corpus Christi guild in Coventry to 'mendifaunts in money' between 1516 and 1526 peaked in 1520.[41] London, York, Shrewsbury, Bristol and Norwich also introduced licensing procedures or officials responsible for beggars in this period.[42] This concentration of activities in towns between 1517 and 1522, which included orders to expel vagrants, badge beggars, and clean streets, led Slack to suggest that Cardinal Wolsey personally prompted the compilation of the Coventry census, as part of his attention to the common weal.[43] Certainly the commissioners ordered to search barns and stacks for corn in 1527 were also instructed to enforce statutes for beggars. The commissioners in the North Riding of Yorkshire certified that they had 'punished divers valiant beggars with scourges to be beat'.[44]

Legislation regulating alehouses, brewers, and unlawful games also emerged at times of grain shortage, to ensure that grain was not diverted unnecessarily from the market place into making ale, and to prevent alehouses from becoming centres of social unrest. Unlawful games were thought to impoverish players, who would then resort to crime.[45] When the cloth industry in Coventry experienced a downturn between 1518 and 1521, it was reported that under-employed craftsmen were playing bowls or quoits and 'levyng ther besynes at home that they shuld lyve by'.[46] The national commission issued in 1527 to search for grain ordered the execution of statutes concerning alehouses and unlawful games.[47] In Middlesex, the commissioners reported that they had caused all tables, cards, dice and bowls to be burnt.[48] The case brought against James Newby of Oundle in 1528 for refusing to sell grain in the market also included the charge that he was 'a commen gamener with Tabull play and dyse and Cards'.[49]

The responses that local and central government made to grain shortages in the early sixteenth century were built upon much older foundations. Medieval town governments exerted considerable control over the supply and marketing of foodstuffs, and Richard Britnell has argued that authorities intervened more

---

[39]   *Coventry Leet Book*, 677.

[40]   Ibid., 687.

[41]   Phythian-Adams, *Desolation*, 196 n. 4.

[42]   C. Phythian-Adams, 'Urban Decay in Late Medieval England', in *Towns in Societies*, ed. P. Abrams and E. A. Wrigley (Cambridge, 1978), 181–2.

[43]   P. Slack, *From Reformation to Improvement: Public Welfare in Early Modern England* (Oxford, 1999), 15.

[44]   *Tudor Royal Proclamations*, I, 172–4; *Letters and Papers*, IV, no. 3822, pp. 1701–2.

[45]   Galley, *Demography*, 89; Britnell, *Closing*, 205.

[46]   Phythian-Adams, *Desolation*, 54–5.

[47]   *Tudor Royal Proclamations*, I, 172–4.

[48]   Pugh, 'Grain Shortage', 37.

[49]   *Select Cases Before the King's Council*, 174.

actively during the later Middle Ages than before.[50] The assize of bread specified different weights for a loaf of bread in inverse proportion to the price of wheat. By ensuring that a loaf costing a farthing would always be available (although consumers received less bread when wheat prices were high), and fixing the profit and allowances that bakers could receive for each loaf, the assize recognised that grain prices would fluctuate but helped to protect poorer consumers as well as guaranteeing that producers received a consistent return. Similarly, the assize of ale regulated the price of ale according to the prices of different grains.[51] Authorities also restricted access to the market, so that consumers were given priority over producers. In Coventry, bakers were not permitted to buy corn in the Monday or Friday markets under an ordinance of 1445, and in 1473 they were restricted from buying before 2 pm.[52] Traders from outside the town were also closely regulated. Country bakers were permitted to sell bread in Coventry on specified days and had to leave their unsold bread for 'sale to the comen people'.[53] These regulations by urban authorities sought to ensure that an even supply of grain was available, which met the needs of the whole community and avoided excessive profiteering by individuals.[54]

Several towns reviewed or reissued legislation relating to baking and brewing around 1520, which may reflect the dearth of that year. Leicester council ordered rye bread for the poor to be wholesome and made according to the statute in 1520.[55] Bristol ordinances of 1519–20 specified that bakers were not to buy corn within ten miles of the town, bakers were not to mix rye or maslin (mixed grain) in their bread, bakers' wives were not permitted to buy corn in the market, country bakers were to bring wheat bread only into the town, and town bakers were not to send wheat or bread into Wales or elsewhere in the country without a licence.[56] In response to a complaint addressed to Wolsey from the bakers of London, the city's common council decreed in 1521 that the bakers should bake all the wheat remaining in the garners of the Bridgehouse at the price set by the mayor.[57] The bakers' guild in Lincoln was overhauled after the price rises of the early 1520s, with bakers' marks allotted in 1522 and a new charter sealed in 1523.

---

[50] R. H. Britnell, 'The Economy of British Towns 1300–1540', in *The Cambridge Urban History of Britain, 1: 600–1540*, ed. D. M. Palliser (Cambridge, 2000), 331; R. H. Britnell, *The Commercialisation of English Society, 1000–1500* (2nd edn, Manchester, 1996), 173–5.

[51] J. Davis, 'Baking for the Common Good: A Reassessment of the Assize of Bread in Medieval England', *EcHR* 57 (2004), 465–502.

[52] *Coventry Leet Book*, 223, 385.

[53] *Coventry Leet Book*, 23–4, 29, 32, 717.

[54] E. Gemmill, 'Town and Region: The Corn Market in Aberdeen, c.1398–c.1468', in *Agriculture and Rural Society*, ed. Dodds and Britnell, 69.

[55] Hoskins, 'Harvest Fluctuations', 34.

[56] *Ordinances of Bristol, 1506–1598*, ed. M. Stanford (Bristol Record Society 41, 1990), 13.

[57] *Letters and Papers*, III, nos. 1528–9, pp. 630–1.

In 1524 a member of the guild acknowledged deficiencies in serving bread to the commons of the city, and on behalf of the fellowship he submitted to correction.[58]

Urban governments also claimed to act in the interests of consumers when preventing the commercial practices that allegedly cornered the market for excessive profit. Forestalling was the offence of intercepting goods on their way to market and buying them up to resell in the market at a higher price. The term was further used to include the offence of buying produce in the market before the official opening time with the intention to resell later at a profit, also described as regrating.[59] Such offences became prominent at times of rising prices, when local officials reacted with hostility to the idea that the local price should be determined in other markets rather than their own. Engrossing, the monopolising of a market through buying large quantities of merchandise, was also unacceptable, particularly in a time of scarcity.[60]

There were many parallels between market regulations and the ideas promoted in sermons and moral texts. Writers condemned those who stored grain in the hope of profiting during periods of scarcity, on the basis that the act of hoarding could create a shortage and that offenders were profiting from the misery of fellow human beings and were wasting resources when corn rotted in barns.[61] James Newby of Oundle was also charged in 1528 with throwing twenty or thirty quarters of malt, which contained weevils, out of his garners into ditches: 'he kept it so long that nother best nor folle wold ett of it whych myght have bene better applyed to the sustynauns of gods pepull yff it had bene browght to the market in tyme'.[62] Such criticisms could draw on biblical references such as the text from Proverbs quoted at the head of this chapter. Nonetheless, it was also recognised that middlemen had a role in supply and distribution so long as they were socially responsible in their actions. There was indeed the biblical parallel of Joseph storing grain during years of plenty to feed the people of Egypt during years of famine.[63]

The responses of Cardinal Wolsey and his contemporaries during the periods of dearth in the early sixteenth century also reflected earlier attempts by central government to exercise control over the grain market. From the early fourteenth century, the most common response at times of scarcity was to prohibit grain exports.[64] In reaction to rising labour costs, royal statutes had been introduced

[58] Hill, *Lincoln*, 30.

[59] R. H. Britnell, 'Forstall, Forestalling and the Statute of Forestallers', *EHR* 102 (1987), 89–102.

[60] R. H. Britnell, 'Price-Setting in English Borough Markets, 1349–1500', *Canadian Journal of History*, 31 (1996), 11–15.

[61] J. Davis, *Medieval Market Morality: Life, Law and Ethics in the English Marketplace, c.1200–c.1500* (forthcoming).

[62] *Select Cases Before the King's Council*, 174.

[63] Genesis 41:29–36, 41:53–7, 47:13–26; Davis, *Market Morality*.

[64] B. Sharp, 'The Food Riots of 1347 and the Medieval Market Economy', in *Moral Economy and*

during the second half of the fourteenth century concerning the treatment of beg-gars, victuallers' profits and the prices of foodstuffs.[65] Commissions to enquire into forestalling had been established following reports of scarcity in Exeter in 1347 and across eight counties in 1370, while in 1375 justices of the peace in thir-teen counties were instructed to examine the activities of merchants and their grain exports, which were reported to be causing a dearth. Enquiries ordered by the king at Tamworth and Winchester in 1391 into the amount of hoarded grain in private houses and granaries may have been the forerunner of the searches undertaken in Coventry in 1520 and nationally in 1527. Hoarders were to be pun-ished and the grain sold in local markets.[66] These surveys may in turn have been derived from the assessments of surplus grain, livestock and goods compiled for taxation purposes in the thirteenth and early fourteenth centuries.[67]

Arrangements were also made during the shortages of the 1520s, and at ear-lier periods of dearth, to secure additional grain supplies for certain cities. John Bond, mayor of Coventry, brought to the city nearly one hundred quarters of wheat during the shortage of 1520.[68] Similarly, Stephen Brown, mayor of London, had sent ships at his own expense to Danzig to bring rye to relieve the wants of the poorer citizens during the dearth of 1438. Mayor Roger Acheley personally bought grain and stored it at Leadenhall and other granaries in London in 1511. In 1522 the mayor of Exeter bought a large store of corn and distributed it to the poor, and the mayor of Bristol authorised Mr Ware and others to provide grain for the city from Worcestershire.[69] The corporation of Worcester bought rye at Bristol during shortages in the winter of 1556–7.[70] Central government attempted to import corn from France, the Low Countries and Prussia in 1527–8.[71] Bequests helped to fund some of the purchases of grain made by urban governments. Mark William of Bristol left one hundred marks in 1434 to be kept in a common chest for the town government to buy corn at times of scarcity.[72] In 1520–1 Alderman Stephen Genyns left more than £62 for corn to be bought annually and stored at the Bridgehouse garner in London, which had been established in 1514. Contribu-

Popular Protest: Crowds, Conflict and Authority, ed. A. Randall and A. Charlesworth (Basing-stoke, 2000), 45–8.

[65] Britnell, *Growth and Decline*, 134–5.

[66] Sharp, 'Food Riots', 49.

[67] M. Jurkowski, C. Smith and D. Crook, *Lay Taxes in England and Wales 1188–1688* (Kew, 1998), p. xxx.

[68] *Coventry Leet Book*, 675.

[69] Ashley, *Bread*, 45; *The Maire of Bristowe is Kalendar*, ed. L. Toulmin Smith (Camden Society 5, 1872), 49; W. G. Hoskins, *Two Thousand Years in Exeter* (Chichester, 1960), 54.

[70] A. Dyer, *The City of Worcester in the Sixteenth Century* (Leicester, 1973), 167.

[71] *Letters and Papers*, iv, no. 3542, p. 1597; no. 4147, p. 1832; appendix 1, no. 216, p. 3173; E. Hall, *The Union of the Two Noble and Illustre Famelies of York and Lancaster*, ed. H. Ellis (London, 1809), 736.

[72] Davis, *Market Morality*.

tions towards the provision of corn were levied from the London crafts in 1520 and in subsequent years of shortage.[73]

Earlier schemes to construct garners in London at Leadenhall and the Stocks appear to have been prompted by the famines of the late 1430s. The scheme at the Stocks was shelved, but Leadenhall was completed in 1455, largely through the efforts of Simon Eyre, a rich draper and mayor in 1445–6. The complex comprised four ranges around a courtyard, with a common market on the ground floor and granary on two floors above, and a chapel. Excavations in the 1980s have shown that the first and second floors of the building were well designed for grain storage, with solid masonry construction and elevation which deterred rodents, windows giving ventilation, and stairs at each end of open galleries allowing grain to be moved flexibly. The design also included defensive features such as wall walks, parapets, an absence of windows at the ground-floor level, and turrets which could be used as look-out posts, to protect stockpiles of grain from both casual theft and civil unrest. Eyre intended to encourage market traders 'to resort to the said city to victual the same', improving the supply while keeping prices lower through greater competition. Eyre envisaged that the garner would maintain permanent stockpiles of grain which could be sold to citizens at times of shortage.[74] However, the purposes for which Eyre had envisaged Leadenhall were not fully achieved, and the complex was generally put to other uses, suggesting that successive civic officials were not often persuaded of the need to address grain shortages in the way that Eyre had intended.

Grain shortages could create unrest, as was reflected in the design of the Leadenhall granary, and one particular flashpoint was the sight of grain being loaded on to ships at times of scarcity. This sparked disturbances in Bristol, Lynn, Thetford, Boston and Kent in 1347, Yarmouth in 1375, Norfolk and Suffolk in 1410–11, Ipswich and Southwold in 1438, and Gloucester in the early fifteenth century.[75] There was another rising in Yarmouth following the harvest failure of 1527 when men sought to prevent the export of corn. The villagers of Yaxley in Huntingdonshire challenged a merchant of Lynn who brought a boat to export peas in 1528 following the dearth of the previous year, and claimed 'You men of Lynn did carry our peas into Scotland last year, and pined us for hunger here, for lack of sustenance'.[76] Although grain was regularly carried from Cambridge to London, complaints were voiced in years of harvest failure that this trade created shortages for the town and university. In 1439, shortly after the worst dearth of the fifteenth century, a brewer named William Bodevyle showed testimonial

---

[73] N. S. B. Gras, *The Evolution of the English Corn Market from the Twelfth to the Eighteenth Century* (Harvard, 1915), 80–2, 421–2.

[74] M. Samuel, 'The Fifteenth-Century Garner at Leadenhall, London', *Antiquities Journal*, 69 (1989), 119–53.

[75] Sharp, 'Food Riots', 33–54.

[76] Hoskins, 'Harvest Fluctuations', 34–5.

letters to the mayor and aldermen of London, from the chancellor of Cambridge University, stating that William had 'been defamed by a malicious and false story that he had engrossed and bought at an excessive price 8,000 quarters of malt and other grains in Cambridge and surrounding townships' to the harm of both the university and the inhabitants of the town and country.[77] In June 1565, shortly before a harvest that Hoskins rated as 'bad', the university asked the privy council to halt the transport of corn from Cambridge to Lynn, protesting that it was 'to the pinching of poor scholars' bellies', but the council replied that the county had been accustomed to convey grain to Lynn for supplies to London.[78] While coastal ports were particularly likely sites of unrest at times of food shortage, as they were in the early modern period, towns on navigable waterways, which collected grain from surrounding hinterlands, were also susceptible to complaints and disturbances.

Another group of communities that were particularly vulnerable at times of grain shortage were those where specialisation in pastoral farming or industrial production had led to a move away from arable cultivation, making the population more dependent on the market and creating exceptional risks in years of shortage. Schofield's recent analysis of wheat prices from Durham between 1350 and 1520 suggested that the north east may have experienced this vulnerability.[79] Cloth-making areas were similarly exposed to food shortages: 'Since others would always, when the pinch came, put food ahead of clothing in their domestic budgets, demand for the products of the textile industry, and hence employment within it, fell back just when it was most vital to those who made a living from it.'[80] In the late 1590s parts of Westmorland, Essex and Devon, where the population were largely dependent on by-employment in the cloth industry, were hit particularly severely by harvest failure.[81] Coventry's grain shortage in 1520 was similarly exacerbated by difficulties in its cloth industry. Phythian-Adams identified a local slump in 1518 arising from the long-term decay of the textile industry together with three years of soaring wool prices. The council enacted a series of measures relating to cloth making.[82] English cloth exports fell by more than 15,000 cloths between 1519–20 and 1520–1, a greater fall than during the slump of 1526–7.[83] This was because demand across Europe contracted with high grain

[77]   *Calendar of the Plea and Memoranda Rolls of the City of London*, v: 1437–1457, ed. P. E. Jones (Cambridge, 1954), 8–9.

[78]   CUL, University Archives, Collect. Admin. 5, fol. 163; Gras, *Corn Market*, 109 n. 1.

[79]   Schofield, 'Regional Price Differentials'.

[80]   Wrigley, *People, Cities and Wealth*, 103.

[81]   Slack, 'Mortality Crises', 53–4.

[82]   Phythian-Adams, *Desolation*, 54–5.

[83]   E. Carus-Wilson and O. Coleman, *England's Export Trade 1275–1547* (Oxford, 1963), 115–16, 139.

prices in Flanders, famine in Castile and Portugal, and the diversion of huge sums of money from trade to warfare by Francis I and Charles V.[84]

A combination of food shortages and disruption to overseas cloth markets created fears of trouble in East Anglia and Kent during the later 1520s. In 1526 there were grain shortages in Suffolk, and following disturbances in Stowmarket, the duke of Norfolk sought reassurance from the wealthier inhabitants of Lavenham that there was no similar unrest there. The dukes of Norfolk and Suffolk pleaded with Wolsey to ease the ban on food exports other than grain so that cash could be raised to purchase grain in the Low Countries.[85] Hinckford hundred lay in the centre of the Essex cloth-making area and opposite the Suffolk textile towns of Clare, Melford and Sudbury. In 1527 the shortage of grain within the hundred was particularly severe in Ballingdon, a poor suburb of the cloth-manufacturing town of Sudbury.[86] In April 1528 Archbishop Wareham of Canterbury received a petition from the inhabitants of Kent praying him to repay the tax known as the Amicable Grant as they were 'so impoverished by the great dearth of corn', and by May there were reports of seditious behaviour by textile workers in Goudhurst and Cranbrook, two prominent centres of cloth making.[87] Around the same time, the duke of Norfolk controlled grain prices and enforced the sale of grain stored at Colchester, as well as begging clothiers not to lay off clothworkers. Norwich and Yarmouth also experienced disturbances.[88] While these disturbances were not on the scale of protests that had occurred in Lavenham and Sudbury in 1525 (at a time of relatively low food prices) against the Amicable Grant, the shortages had clearly created a fear of unrest.[89] As Britnell has noted, many rural families in this area were experiencing unpredictable changes of fortune through their reliance on export markets.[90]

In a seminal article arguing the case for widespread urban decline in the later Middle Ages, Phythian-Adams identifed harvest failure as a factor contributing to a general urban malaise. Setting harvest failure alongside other challenges including the cost of urban residence, threats to the industrial and marketing functions of towns, and crises in overseas trade, he saw the period between 1520

---

[84] Phythian-Adams, *Desolation*, 61.

[85] D. MacCulloch, *Suffolk and the Tudors: Politics and Religion in an English County 1500–1600* (Oxford, 1986), 298. MacCulloch dates this shortage to 1526 rather than 1527 as dated in *Letters and Papers*.

[86] L. R. Poos, *A Rural Society after the Black Death: Essex 1350–1525* (Cambridge, 1991), 59–60; Dymond, 'Famine', 33–4.

[87] *Letters and Papers*, IV, pt. 2, no. 4173, pp. 1843–4; no. 4310, pp. 1893–4; M. Zell, *Industry in the Countryside: Wealden Society in the Sixteenth Century* (Cambridge, 1994), 153–7.

[88] MacCulloch, *Suffolk*, 298; Hoskins, 'Harvest Fluctuations', 34.

[89] A. Fletcher and D. MacCulloch, *Tudor Rebellions* (5th edn, Harlow, 2008), 25–6, 140.

[90] R. H. Britnell, 'The Woollen Textile Industry of Suffolk in the Later Middle Ages', *The Ricardian* 13 (2003), 95; idem, 'Urban Demand in the English Economy, 1300–1600', in *Trade*, ed. Galloway, 17–18; idem, *Closing*, 226–7.

and 1570 as 'years of acute urban crisis' which expressed themselves in increasing urban poverty and social upheaval. Phythian-Adams identified increasing numbers of bad harvests in this period compared to the four decades before 1520 noting, 'it seems clear that the spiralling problem of restricted cereal supplies was a major factor in the urban crises of an age when conversion to pasture had been the trend, and a probably increasing rural population had first access to what *was* available'.[91] Goose, however, in questioning this argument for extensive urban decay, regarded the social discontent that arose from food shortages as 'only sporadic and usually on a very limited scale'. He noted the general lack of linkage between high food prices and urban mortality crises, and the co-operation between central government and urban authorities to ensure that food supplies were maintained.[92] The unrest identified in the port towns from grain shortages in the later fourteenth and early fifteenth century arose at specific times of shortage and is difficult to link to wider urban decline; while several east-coast ports were experiencing contracting economies, other ports such as Bristol were prospering at this time.[93]

In the specific case of Coventry, Phythian-Adams identified several components within the 'crisis' of 1518–25. The city experienced a slump in the cloth trade in 1518, followed by dearth and high food prices in 1520–1. The fiscal demands of the crown exacerbated the situation: between 1522 and 1525 Coventry contributed £2,044, or forty times the annual tax quota of £50.[94] In June 1523 a second census was made, counting the number of vacant houses in each ward. The precise purpose is not clear, but appears to have been comparable to the rationale behind the 1520 census, for the documents have a remarkably similar layout. Using the two censuses, Phythian-Adams claimed that the population fell by 1,500 in the space of three years, or a loss equivalent to the fall over the previous twenty years.[95] His estimates of depopulation assumed that all the houses vacant in 1523 were occupied in 1520, but there is no reason why this should be so, particularly if Coventry had been declining since the mid fifteenth century.

Recent research on the economy of late medieval Coventry is revealing a more complex assortment of experiences of growth and decline across different economic sectors and different decades, a trend which has also been found in studies of other towns.[96] Goddard has explored how Coventry experienced a period of

---

[91] Phythian-Adams, 'Urban Decay', 180–1.

[92] N. Goose, 'In Search of the Urban Variable: Towns and the English Economy, 1500–1650', *EcHR* 39 (1986), 180.

[93] A. Dyer, *Decline and Growth in English Towns 1400–1640* (2nd edn, Cambridge, 1995), 18, 22–3.

[94] Phythian-Adams, *Desolation*, 51–67.

[95] Ibid., 197, 291–305.

[96] For other studies, see J. Laughton and C. Dyer, 'Small Towns in the East and West Midlands in the Later Middle Ages: A Comparison', *Midland History*, 24 (1999), 24–52; J. S. Lee, 'The

decline between the 1440s and 1480s, as part of a widespread economic slump. Wealth and investment in Coventry was diverted to London markets, and properties in some parts of the city were abandoned.[97] Hoyle's analysis of the taxation levied between 1522 and 1525 found that the richest citizens of Coventry saw their declared wealth plummet by nearly half in a period of two and a half years, which he believes reflected a genuine reduction in wealth and the supply of credit, and was a widespread experience across the country.[98] Hulton's studies have suggested that the growth of the capping industry in Coventry compensated for the decline of broadcloth manufacture.[99] Leech has argued for a more complex mixture of decline, stability and growth in Coventry between 1450 and 1525, while acknowledging that grain shortages, as well as wars, plagues and high taxation, had a local and national impact during the 1520s. He identifies the existence of an active property market and ongoing civic reconstruction, and an adapting economy, exemplified by a growing number of tailors responding to local consumption demands.[100] Urban decline is a problematic concept that often lacks precise definition or chronology. Richard Britnell has noted that many of the problems facing towns which have been described as symptoms of urban decline were also affecting the countryside, and grain shortages were no exception.[101]

Grain shortages had the potential to cause massive disruption to medieval towns. Food riots occurred not just because people were hungry, but because of their anger at the failure of civic authorities to maintain an adequate supply of food. Local and central authorities in the Tudor period responded to grain shortages by enacting legislation to tackle marketing offences such as forestalling and regrating, as well as measures to limit vagrancy and suppress alehouses and unlawful games, and many of these responses would have been familiar to fourteenth-century legislators. The effectiveness of these regulations can be debated. The assizes kept prices low for consumers, while maintaining a profit for producers, and tried to prevent speculators raising prices at times of shortage. The same regulations may have deterred enterprise to seek out alternative supplies at such times, and if they had been systematically enforced, would have disrupted regional marketing networks for grain.[102] Most importantly, however, the authorities were seen to be responding to a crisis in ways which corresponded

Functions and Fortunes of English Small Towns at the Close of the Middle Ages: Evidence from John Leland's *Itinerary*, *Urban History*, 37 (2010), 3–25; Lee, *Cambridge*.

[97] R. Goddard, *Commercial Contraction and Urban Decline in Fifteenth-Century Coventry* (Stratford-upon-Avon, 2006).

[98] R. W. Hoyle, 'Taxation and the Mid-Tudor Crisis', *EcHR* 51 (1998), 649–75.

[99] *Coventry*, ed. Hulton, 51–4.

[100] D. Leech, 'Stability and Change at the End of the Middle Ages: Coventry, 1450–1525', *Midland History*, 34 (2009), 1–21.

[101] Britnell, 'Economy of British Towns', 330–1.

[102] Davis, *Market Morality*; Britnell, *Commercialisation*, 174.

to contemporary morality. Despite the severe shortages in October 1520 and the dislocation of trade and possible depopulation, Coventry appears to have avoided significant unrest. The Coventry census reveals that shortages of grain were felt most acutely in the poorest and suburban wards, and areas where cloth making predominated, trends also reflected in the returns of the Essex hundred of Hinckford. The census suggests that the city was approaching the dearth in a rational and comprehensive way, indeed in a way that was adopted across the country by the crown only a few years later, and repeated at times of shortage throughout the sixteenth century.[103] More regular searches were even advocated in 1586 as a means of increasing corn supplies in urban markets:

> if men's barns might be indifferently viewed immediately after harvest, and a note gathered by an estimate and kept by some appointed and trusty person for that purpose, we should have much more plenty of corn in our town crosses than as yet is commonly seen, because each one hideth and hoardeth what he may.[104]

The Coventry census was more than just a check on the quantities of grain remaining to feed the townspeople, as it sought to ensure that resident traders did not hoard grain beyond their immediate needs. In drawing up the census, the city government was probably mindful of its turbulent past relations with the bakers, a group of traders who were particularly likely to retain large stocks. The restricted nature of the city's hinterland, with no navigable river and competition from other major towns, was also likely to have been a consideration. At times of shortage, authorities in English towns did not usually develop town granaries but preferred to buy and import grain. Through the compilation of the 1520 census, the government of Coventry demonstrated to its citizens that grain was not being hoarded for profit, but was being made available in the marketplace. Like other regulations and administrative devices made by civic and central governments during the late Middle Ages, the census showed that Mayor John Bond and his brethren were acting at a time of shortage to restrict morally unacceptable behaviour and thereby to promote social order.

[103] R. B. Outhwaite, *Dearth, Public Policy and Social Disturbance in England, 1550–1800* (London, 1991), 39–40.

[104] W. Harrison, *Description of England*, ed. G. Edelen (New York, 1968), 252.

5

Market Regulation in Fifteenth-Century England

James Davis

Close supervision of price, quality, weights, measures and hygiene was an expectation in medieval English markets, both large and small, and this made them attractive venues for commerce.[1] Regulation engendered confidence in users of formal markets, tempering the risks involved in commercial transactions.[2] Admittedly, market regulations were often couched in paternal, moral and protective language, offering succour to poorer consumers but also aiding certain vested interests. Middleman activity was curtailed, prices were fixed according to a consensus about prevailing market conditions, and retail trade could be reserved to residents and burgesses through restrictions and tolls. To an extent, such laws dampened entrepreneurial speculation, but they also addressed the flaws of an immature market system. Many trade regulations, especially those promulgated and enforced across the realm, were intended to allay understandable concerns about asymmetrical information, lack of technical knowledge, trust, adverse selection and haphazard supply. In a developing commercial economy, the provision of national standards and common expectations was a vital foundation for market confidence and success.

The development of market regulation in medieval England was a multifaceted process, influenced by a variety of interested parties. The king, government officials, municipal authorities, lords and the church were just some of those who were active in developing market laws that served fiscal, political and social

I would like to thank John Hatcher, Richard Smith, Ben Dodds, Chris Briggs, Edward Meek, Kaele Stokes and Sinéad O'Sullivan for their comments and advice, and also the Institute of Historical Research, the Economic History Society, the British Academy and the AHRC. I would particularly like to thank Richard Britnell for all his support and inspiration throughout my research.

[1] R. H. Britnell, 'Town Life', in *A Social History of England 1200–1500*, ed. R. Horrox and W. M. Ormrod (Cambridge, 2006), 134–78.

[2] R. H. Britnell, 'Local Trade, Remote Trade: Institutions, Information and Market Integration, 1050–1330', in *Fiere e mercati nella integrazione delle economie europee, secc. XIII–XVIII*, ed. S. Cavaciocchi (Florence, 2001), 185–203.

purposes. However, such laws could not be enforced effectively at a local level unless there was a degree of consensus regarding their viability and utility among
general market users. Recent research into markets, parliamentary petitions, the
cloth trade, and the assizes of bread and ale has laid to rest the fallacy that certain
economic legislation was merely imposed from above and begrudgingly accepted
in the localities, or else consistently breached or subverted.[3] Indeed, it could be argued that laws governing medieval markets were influenced as much by the needs,
morals and practices of everyday traders as by the aims and edicts of the state. The
creation and revision of much economic legislation was the product of continuing
dialogue, both formal and informal, between a myriad of interested parties.

One set of common rules, or assizes, appears in a number of fifteenth-century
town records and was known to officials as the 'Statute of Winchester'.[4] British
Library, Lansdowne MS 796 contains a copy of this legislation, which outlines
'assizes' for sixteen different medieval trades.[5] These trades were not those of
wealthy mercantile enterprise, but rather those found throughout the markets of
medieval England: miller, baker, ale-brewer, fisher, butcher, cook, innkeeper, taverner, beer-brewer, tallow-chandler, spicer, weaver, tanner, cordwainer, currier,
and white-tawyer. For each, the assizes succinctly cover regulatory issues relating
to price, quality, fraud, weights and measures. In addition, the document includes
a specific section on forestalling and regrating and one on weights and measures.
This last section also briefly mentions the wholesalers of internal trade, such as
grocers, drapers and mercers. An examination of the origins and provisions of
this piece of legislation yields a fascinating insight into the priorities and the creation of medieval market regulation. Assizes were formulated and disseminated
via a combination of interested parties who had a stake in the continued prosperity of the market.

An 'assize' was a formal statement of previously customary or localised laws,
which had often been observed for some years, thereby providing a nationalised
standard supported by royal assent.[6] The fact that the Lansdowne MS 796 assizes

---

[3]   R. C. Palmer, *English Law in the Age of the Black Death, 1348–1381* (London, 1993); A. Mus-
      son, *Public Order and Law Enforcement: The Local Administration of Criminal Justice, 1294–
      1350* (Woodbridge, 1996); A. Musson and W. M. Ormrod, *The Evolution of English Justice:
      Law, Politics and Society in the Fourteenth Century* (Basingstoke, 1998); A. Musson, *Medieval
      Law in Context: The Growth of Legal Consciousness from Magna Carta to the Peasants' Revolt*
      (Manchester, 2001); G. Seabourne, *Royal Regulation of Loans and Sales in Medieval England*
      (Woodbridge, 2003); R. H. Britnell, 'Forstall, Forestalling and the Statute of Forestallers',
      EHR 102 (1987), 89–102; idem, *The Commercialisation of English Society, 1000–1500* (2nd
      edn, Manchester, 1996); idem, *Britain and Ireland 1050–1530: Economy and Society* (Oxford,
      2004), 356–8.
[4]   Britnell, 'Town Life', 167.
[5]   BL, Lansdowne MS 796, fols. 4ᵛ–7ᵛ.
[6]   Such assizes first appeared during the reign of Henry II: B. Lyon, *A Constitutional and Legal
      History of Medieval England* (2nd edn, London, 1980), 29.

were copied into several municipal muniments by town clerks suggests that this legislation was of general interest and even of some importance. However, the reason for such interest is not immediately apparent, since the legislation does not exist in this form in any collections of royal ordinances or parliamentary statutes, and many (though not all) of the listed assizes were previously promulgated in various forms at national and local level. The details provided in the Lansdowne assizes are also rather sparse and formulaic.[7] It may simply have been a document created in one town and then passed between interested town officials as another guide for devising their own municipal ordinances. However, it will be suggested here that this particular codification of assizes emanated from the royal household and particularly the clerk of the market. This document highlights the important, if somewhat haphazard, influence exerted by the royal clerk of the market in local market regulation and, by association, the influence of the king. These assizes may have represented the same quasi-statutory authority that the *Composicio ad puniendum infringentes assisam panis et cervisie, forestallarios, cocos, etc.* (also known as *Statutum de Pistoribus*) had in the late thirteenth century.[8] It will be contended that these assizes were a continuation of the *Composicio* and drew upon local customs to elucidate basic commercial regulations. This was not a simple case of imposition of control from above, and closer examination reveals evidence of a tangled and complicated provenance. It could be argued that much market regulation was slow to develop and was rarely innovative, being more of a hybrid of previous laws and customs. However, there was also a tacit acceptance by local officials of the need for a certain level of standardisation.

The aim of this essay is not to provide a detailed study of the activities of the royal clerk of the market, a figure who deserves more devoted attention. Instead, this is an exercise in examining a single legislative document, investigating its origins, antecedents, development and dissemination, and what this reveals about the nature of retail trade laws in medieval England. Fascinating complexities are underscored regarding the creation of retail legislation and the relationship between the king, his household, royal government, self-governing municipalities and local courts.

The manuscript of Lansdowne MS 796 is composed of seven folios of unknown authorship. It is possible that these leaves were either an extract from an urban record or else part of a larger commonplace book, perhaps belonging to a trader or official interested in commercial laws. An example of such a compilation is the fifteenth-century commonplace book of Robert Reynes of Acle (Norfolk), which included taxes and trading assizes, alongside devotional and folklore material,

---

[7] To facilitate the following discussion, the assizes from BL, Lansdowne MS 796 will be referred to as the 'Lansdowne assizes'.

[8] *SR* I, 202–4.

and was probably intended for use in his official duties within the village.[9] In part, he borrows from statutes such as the *Assisa Panis et Cervisie, Composicio, Judicium Pillorie* and *Assisa de Ponderibus et Mensuris*, as well as from the legal treatise *Britton*.[10] There are conflations and scribal errors, hinting at the difficulties involved in enforcing standards in medieval England, but the compilation also shows the dissemination of commercial law into small towns and villages. This may have included the Lansdowne assizes, since the wording of some sections is strikingly similar, such as: 'If the baker lakke an vnce in the wyght of a ferthyng loff, he be amercyed at xx*d*. And if he lakke an vnce et dimidium, he to be amercyed at iis. in alle maner of bred so lakkyng. And if he lakke past iis., he mote haue iugement to the pelory.'[11] Indeed, Reynes's version highlights a connection between these trade ordinances and the clerk of the market, in a section appended to a table of bread weights.[12] He also records a visit to Acle in 1475 by John Becwyth, clerk of the market, to check weights and measures. Reynes's commonplace book thus provides a tantalising hint as to the potential origin, provenance and dissemination of the Lansdowne assizes.

The notion that Lansdowne MS 796 was part of a commonplace book is reinforced by the other entry in the manuscript, which was a poem of obvious interest to a local merchant. The poem is comparable to *The Libelle of Englysche Polycye* on the English wool trade and begins 'Anglia propter tuas naves et lanas omnia regna te salutare deberent'.[13] The poem in Lansdowne MS 796 (fols. 1ʳ–4ʳ) reuses the opening four lines of the *Libelle* and similarly tackles the national and international wool trade. Yet, it is more than a basic redaction, for the poem omits much of the original *Libelle* and introduces new concepts. It draws public attention to various commercial grievances in the cloth and wool trades, and includes vitriol against the dishonest practices of clothiers who 'fleeced' their employees:

9   *The Commonplace Book of Robert Reynes of Acle*, ed. C. Louis (New York and London, 1980), esp. 121–5, 136–40, 315–18, 350–2.

10 *SR* I, 199–205; *Britton*, ed. F. M. Nichols (2 vols., Oxford, 1865), I, pp. xxi–xxix, 186–9, chap. 31.

11 *Commonplace Book*, 136, ll. 343–8. This is a slight variation on the formula found in the *Composicio*. See also 138, ll. 399–402, where there are similarities between a section on the assize of ale and the Lansdowne assizes: BL, Lansdowne MS 796, fol. 4ᵛ.

12 'Et omnes predicit articuli deliberat sunt per magistrum Robertum de Beluero et dominum Thomam de Pakesword, marescallum, domini Regis itinerantes per totam Angliam anno domini Edwardi, filii Regis Henrici quarto, et liberati clerico de mercato': *Commonplace Book*, 125, 318.

13 Printed in *Political Poems and Songs relating to English History*, ed. T. Wright (2 vols., Roll Series, rev. edn, 1965), II, 282–7. For the *Libelle*, see: *The Libelle of Englyshe Polycye: A Poem on the Use of Sea-Power, 1436*, ed. G. Warner (Oxford, 1926); J. Scattergood, 'The Libelle of Englyshe Polycye: The Nation and its Place', in *Nation, Court and Culture: New Essays on Fifteenth-Century English Prose*, ed. H. Cooney (Dublin, 2001), 28–49.

'þe pore pepyll' of spinners, carders and weavers.[14] For Rossell Robbins, these divergences led him to suggest an approximate dating for Lansdowne MS 796 of *c*.1463/4, based on wool legislation in those years which paralleled phrases and demands made by the poet. The preciseness of such dating is open to question, particularly given the difficulties involved in associating literary diatribe with actual events. Nevertheless, most would agree with a broad attribution of the poem to the late fifteenth century or, at the latest, the early sixteenth century.[15] This dating would apply to the remainder of the manuscript, namely the assizes on fols. 4ᵛ–7ᵛ, which are in the same hand. An approximate dating of the assizes to the reign of Edward ɪᴠ tallies with evidence from other compilations discovered in several urban records.

Lansdowne MS 796 provides us with a complete version of the assizes, but variants survive in four late medieval town custumals, namely those of Coventry, Northampton, Colchester and Cambridge.[16] The surviving redactions differ in the way in which they order occupations, omit certain trades, and use specific terms. The texts also vary to some extent, not least because of copying errors, clerical revisions and local circumstances.[17] They are, nevertheless, the same basic document. Christopher Markham, J. Charles Cox and William Gurney Benham cautiously attributed the texts for Northampton and Colchester to Edward ɪᴠ's reign. Likewise, the Coventry version was entered in the town's Leet Book in 1474. The Cambridge version is the latest identified, entered in the Junior Proctor's Book of Cambridge University in *c*.1563.

If all the texts derive, ultimately, from a common source, the first question is: where did the text originate? It could have been a compilation by a town official, who had an interest in providing a standardised list of assize regulations. However, there is a lack of detail and few references to either local circumstances

---

[14] For a discussion of this version of the *Libelle*, see R. H. Robbins, 'A Political Action Poem, 1463', *Modern Language Notes*, 71 (1956), 245–8, and *Historical Poems of the xivth and xvth Centuries*, ed. R. H. Robbins (New York, 1959), pp. xlii–iv, and also no. 70, pp. 168–73. See also V. J. Scattergood, *Politics and Poetry in the Fifteenth Century* (London, 1971), 370–1.

[15] C. M. Meale, 'The Libelle of Englyshe Polycye and Mercantile Literary Culture in Late-Medieval London', in *London and Europe in the Later Middle Ages*, ed. J. Boffey and P. King (London, 1995), 222. Meale argues that the manuscript could be dated to the early sixteenth century. She also notes the clear watermark on the paper (a sun divided into seven segments, with twelve rays emanating from it), but there are no parallels to this mark which might help with dating.

[16] *The Coventry Leet Book*, ed. M. D. Harris (Early English Text Society, 134–5, 138, 146; 1907–13), 397–401; *The Records of the Borough of Northampton*, ed. C. A. Markham and J. C. Cox (2 vols., Northampton, 1898), ɪ, 344–9; *The Red Paper Book of Colchester*, ed. W. G. Benham (Colchester, 1902), 18–20; C[ambridge] U[niversity] L[ibrary], U.A. Collect. Admin. (Junior Proctors' Book), fols. 105ᵛ–107ᵛ (with thanks to John Lee for this reference). It is possible that another copy might yet be uncovered.

[17] For instance, the Cambridge version replaces 'town' with 'Unyuersitee'.

or geography. There are also indications that the town clerks themselves thought the document was an ordinance, proclamation or statute issued by the royal government. The Coventry version refers to 'Statutes de Wynchestur de vitellers & de aliis hominibus et artificiis' at the head of the entry,[18] while the Northampton *Liber Custumarum* text was entitled 'Inquisition according to the Statute of Winchester'. Because of this heading, Markham and Cox suggested that the assizes were an extended version of earlier ordinances.[19] The only known 'Statute of Winchester' was enacted during the reign of Edward I in 1285, and it mostly concerned common-law enforcement (in essence, an update of the assize of arms), the safeguarding of the kingdom's highways, and the prohibition of the holding of fairs and markets in churchyards.[20] The *Statutes of the Realm* for the fifteenth century do not record any statutes or ordinances similar to the Lansdowne assizes, and certainly none designated as a Statute of Winchester. This is a reference as puzzling as when the 1381 rebels demanded that there should be no law but the 'law of Winchester'.[21]

The only central statutes or ordinances similar to the Lansdowne assizes in their form and content are the quasi-statutes promulgated in the mid thirteenth century: the *Assisa Panis et Cervisie, Composicio* and *Judicium Pillorie*.[22] Of these, the *Composicio* elicits the most parallels to the assizes. Richard Britnell has dated the *Composicio* to c.1274/5, and it begins with a statement of the assize of bread 'according to what is contained in a writing delivered to them from the lord king's Marshalsea'.[23] This is probably a reference to the *Assisa Panis et Cervisie*, which was first issued around 1256.[24] After the assize of bread, the *Composicio* outlines the customary toll of millers, the assize of wine, the assize of ale, the punishment of butchers selling unwholesome meat, standard weights and measures, the law against forestalling, and a warning regarding adulterated oats. Except for the section on oats, similarities to the relevant Lansdowne assizes are immediately apparent in terms of format and punishments. The *Composicio*'s section on bakers is a direct forerunner to the assizes, outlining the way in which loaves should change in weight as the price of corn increased or decreased by 6d.[25] It also de-

---

[18] *Coventry Leet Book,* 395–7. Also included, under the overall heading of 'Thies ben the Statutes of Wynchestur Ennakte & publisshed by the kyng and all his lordes Spirituall & Temporall thorough-out Ingelond vpon all maner vittellars and other diuerse men of Craft', was a detailed description of weights and measures, similar to the *Assisa de Ponderibus et Mensuris: SR* I, 204–5.

[19] *Borough of Northampton,* I, 344.

[20] *SR* I, 96–8.

[21] *The Anonimalle Chronicle, 1333 to 1381,* ed. V. H. Galbraith (Manchester, 1927), 147.

[22] *SR* I, 199–204.

[23] Britnell, 'Forstall', 94–6.

[24] See J. Davis, 'Baking for the Common Good: A Reassessment of the Assize of Bread in Medieval England', *EcHR* 57 (2004), 465–502, for dating the *Assisa* to c.1256.

[25] BL, Lansdowne MS 796, fol. 4ᵛ.

lineates a tolerance level for weight defaults, though the level was halved from two ounces to one by the time of the Lansdowne assizes. Both texts complain of forestallers who are harmful to the poor. The *Composicio* goes into a much higher degree of detail and vilification, stating that forestallers are 'an open oppressor of poor people', while the Lansdowne assizes complain that 'the power comynnys [are] gretly hurte' by such trading practices.[26] In all other cases, the Lansdowne assizes are more specific in detail, but the punishments are generally more lenient. For instance, fraudulent butchers and forestallers in the *Composicio* were to be punished firstly by amercement, then pillory, then imprisonment, and finally by abjuring the town. In the Lansdowne assizes, the equivalent punishments were escalating fines for the first three offences, with the pillory only applied for the fourth. The *Composicio* was also more limited in its range of trades, and omits specific references to the cloth trade, leather workers, spicers, chandlers, fishmongers, cooks and innkeepers, but this is connected to the commercial circumstances of the thirteenth century and the comparatively greater opportunities for these trades after the Black Death.

Comparisons between these sets of laws, promulgated two hundred years apart, are instructive. In effect, the *Composicio* was an early set of market assizes dealing with trade at the lowest level, where the retailer met the consumer. It was also a significant extension of thirteenth-century royal government into the life of the community, since the legislation rapidly assumed a wider role beyond its apparent origins within the king's household. The *Composicio, Assisa de Panis et Cervisie* and *Judicium Pillorie* all began in a quasi-statute form and were initially developed as Marshalsea rules for royal household clerks before being disseminated more widely. Britnell has noted that Marshalsea rules dealing with trading matters were copied into legal handbooks and identified as 'Statutes' alongside recognized statutes of the realm.[27] *Assisa* was created by the 'royal bakers', but because of its continual use by lawyers and local officials it soon achieved national significance and became invested with full statutory authority. The *Composicio* came to be widely regarded as an official statute by the early fourteenth century and was expected to be delivered to mayors, bailiffs and lawful men of towns throughout the realm, along with standard bushels, gallons, yards, and stones.

The precedents for the elevation of the *Composicio* to the status of a quasi-statute were laid by actions of royal household officials. From May 1273, officers of the Marshalsea were ordered to hold one-off inquests in the shires and towns regarding the regulation of markets, including a national scrutiny of weights and measures. Britnell has discussed a set of instructions used by two royal Marshalsea officials, Robert de Belvero and John de Swyneford, which was sent to the

---

[26] Ibid., fol. 7ᵛ.
[27] W. L. Warren, *The Governance of Norman and Angevin England 1086–1272* (London, 1987), 133–4; Britnell, 'Forstall', 100–1.

mayors and bailiffs of Suffolk from 29 August 1275.[28] This document was entitled *Statutum Mareshaucie*, but was effectively the same as the *Composicio*, with the *Assisa Panis et Cervisie* appended.[29] All of the clauses in the *Statutum Mareshaucie* were expected to be observed *ex parte regis*, and any who contravened them could be punished for being in contempt of the mandates of the king. Copies were also handed over to the mayor, bailiffs, and six loyal and sworn men from the town, 'so that when necessary they can be informed by this document'. Versions of the *Composicio* were thus sent out to sheriffs and urban officials as a guide to their duties and, in time, it acquired the status of a royal statute.[30] The use of such rules by local authorities is vividly illustrated in York, where the civic ordinances of 1301 paraphrased passages from the *Composicio* in constructing a list of trading regulations.[31]

It is possible that the Lansdowne assizes had a similar origin to the *Composico* in the royal Marshalsea, and were perhaps subsequently invested with quasi-statutory status by municipal and legal authorities. From the 1440s to the 1470s, an unprecedented number of ordinances and treatises appeared which sought to define the structures, functions and membership of the royal household.[32] The Lansdowne assizes may have been created as part of this expanding household literature and been intended as an extended version of the *Composicio*. The link between the assizes and a notional 'Statute of Winchester' is perhaps also explained by the assizes' association with the *Composicio* and the *Assisa*. One possibility is that these were household ordinances emanating from when the royal court sat at Winchester, before the better-known Statute of Winchester was promulgated in 1285.[33] Alternatively, the Statute of Winchester of 1285 became

---

[28] *CPR, 1272–81*, 16, 31, 73, 136. Similar inquests by the officers of the Marshalsea had taken place in 1255, 1257 and 1270: *CPR, 1247–58*, 427, 488, 502, 569; *CPR, 1258–72*, 454. Cf. Britnell, 'Forstall', 95–6. Robert de Belvero and John de Swyneford were 'assigned to the pleas of the Marshalsea'. They were referred to as serjeants of the market or king's clerks, not specifically clerks of the market, but these were later to become synonymous.

[29] BL, Stowe MS 386, fols. 50ʳ–51ʳ. Other copies can be found in CUL, Dd.15.12, fols. 163ʳ–164ᵛ, and CUL, Ii.6.25, fols. 121ʳ–122ʳ.

[30] Britnell, 'Forstall', 94–6; idem, 'Morals, Laws and Ale in Medieval England', in *Le Droit et sa perception dans la littérature et les mentalités médiévales*, ed. D. Buschinger (Göppingen, 1993), 26–7.

[31] *York Civic Ordinances, 1301*, ed. M. Prestwich (Borthwick Papers 49, 1976).

[32] D. A. L. Morgan, 'The House of Policy: the Political Role of the Late Plantagenet Household', in *The English Court from the Wars of the Roses to the Civil War*, ed. D. Starkey (Harlow, 1987), 25–70, at 27–8.

[33] The assize of bread is specifically linked to a so-called 'Statute of Winchester' in an Oxford municipal document of c.1450 and in Robert Wyer's sixteenth-century account. The latter also reinforces the link with the 'Marshalsie of our soueraygne lorde the kynge': *Mediaeval Archives of the University of Oxford*, ed. H. E. Salter (2 vols., Oxford, 1921), II, 135–6; Robert Wyer, *The Assyse of Breade (c.1540)*, in *Occasional Facsimile Reprints*, ed. E. W. Ashbee (London, 1868–71), fasc. VII, pp. Aii–Aiii.

entwined with the *Composicio* and the *Assisa* through repeated proclamations of royal commissions. Indeed, on 24 December 1307, the crown appointed royal commissioners in various counties 'to make proclamation throughout the county that the king's peace and the Statute of Winchester are to be observed inviolate, to take all necessary precautions and to announce that the currency is to be of the same value and weight, and that no wares or merchandizes are to be sold at a higher price than their true value in the time of the late king.'[34] Anthony Musson has noted that the Statute of Winchester was frequently reiterated in peace commissions alongside the Statutes of Northampton and Westminster.[35] It is possible that the enforcement of the Statute of Winchester and certain economic regulations became linked together in the common consciousness through the activities of royal commissions and later through the justices of the peace.

Overall, some of the late fifteenth-century assizes in Lansdowne MS 796 are similar to the *Composicio* in form and purpose. It is likely that they were regarded as an extension of the *Composicio*, with further assimilations from central and local sources. The *Composicio* thus provides an important antecedent and illustrates that some national economic legislation originated in the royal household. Yet, what was the actual purpose in developing another centralised list of assizes? Was this simply an extension and assertion of royal authority in trading standards or were there other influences at work? The answer may lie in the aims and role of the royal household, and particularly the Marshalsea, which was apparently instrumental in the creation of the *Composicio* and may have also drawn up the Lansdowne assizes.

The Marshalsea was one of three domestic offices in the royal household, alongside the pantry/buttery and the kitchen, and dealt with the preparation of the king's food and lodging. One of the main servants of the marshal of the household was the royal clerk of the market.[36] The clerk rode ahead of the king to warn people to bake, brew and make ready victuals for the king's household.[37] The thirteenth-century legal treatise, *Britton*, described the clerk's authority to examine the assizes of bread, wine and ale, and to investigate other retail trades,

---

[34]   *CPR, 1307–13*, 29–31, cf. Britnell, 'Forstall', 100.

[35]   Musson, *Medieval Law*, 250; idem, *Public Order and Law Enforcement*, 26–30.

[36]   The clerk is mentioned in several household ordinances: T. F. Tout, *The Place of the Reign of Edward II in English History* (2nd edn, Manchester, 1936), 252; *A Collection of Ordinances and Regulations for the Government of the Royal Household, Made in Divers Reigns, From King Edward III to King William and Queen Mary*, Society of Antiquaries (pr. J. Nichols, London, 1790), 53; *The Household of Edward IV: The Black Book and the Ordinance of 1478*, ed. A. R. Myers (Manchester, 1959), 140–1.

[37]   Assistants accompanied the clerk to undertake minor tasks of surveillance and administration, and they stayed at the expense of local communities. C. Given-Wilson, *The Royal Household and the King's Affinity: Service, Politics and Finance in England 1360–1413* (London, 1986), 32, 44; *Records of the Wardrobe and Household 1285–1286*, ed. B. F. and C. R. Byerly (London, 1977), pp. xxv–xxvi; *CPR, 1343–5*, 42.

such as cloth-makers, cooks, middlemen, butchers and taverners. He also had the right to seal weights and measures in the localities and to destroy those which did not conform to royal standards, as well as the power to punish any who infringed the assizes.[38] In each market, the clerk would charge twelve of the 'saddest men of dwellers' to assess the assizes of 'brede, wyne, ale, mannes mete and horse mete and othyr stuffe'.[39]

The primary duty of the clerk pertained to the domestic provision of the household, and he was theoretically not meant to be involved in wider governmental matters. The 'verge' determined the extent of the clerk's jurisdiction and stretched up to a radius of twelve miles from wherever the household and the sovereign were located.[40] The clerk's main purpose was to make preparations for the royal purveyors and ensure that local victuallers served the household well with no unreasonable prices or substandard measures. However, so long as the king had a personal role in government, then his household also had a place in government, and the distinction between the private and public role of such offices could become blurred.[41] By examining the role of the clerk of the market, the intimate relationship between the royal household and assize regulations becomes clear.

There is specific evidence linking the Lansdowne assizes with the jurisdiction of the royal clerk of the market. A later copy of the assizes was printed by John Strype in *A Survey of the Cities of London and Westminster, by John Stow (1633)* in 1720. This version contained the same trade categories as Lansdowne MS 796, except for the beer-brewers, and was very similar in both content and wording, although the English was updated. Strype claimed to have extracted the assizes 'that concerned provisions of meat and drink, and apparel . . . out of an ancient Book of the Clerk of the Market'. At the end of the section that lists the assizes it states: 'Here endeth the Assize of dyvers Artificers, aftyr the Book of Henry Brooke Esquire, Clerk of the Market of our Sovereigne Lord King Edward the

---

[38]   *Britton*, I, 189–93, ch. 31. See also: TNA, E101/257/2, II(1), 13, 15, 16; *SR* II, 62, 83. There have been few in-depth studies of the medieval clerk of the market. The best studies are: J. T. Rosenthal, 'The Assizes of Weights and Measures in Medieval England', *Western Political Quarterly*, 17 (1964), 409–22; N. Williams, 'Sessions of the Clerk of the Market of the Household in Middlesex', *Transactions of the London and Middlesex Archaeological Society*, 19 (1958), 76–89; J. H. Johnson, 'The King's Wardrobe and Household', in *The English Government at Work, 1327–1336*, I: *Central and Prerogative Administration*, ed. J. F. Willard and W. A. Morris (Cambridge, Mass., 1940), 245–8; R. D. Connor, *The Weights and Measures of England* (London, 1987), 325–8. See also J. Masschaele, *Peasants, Merchants, and Markets: Inland Trade in Medieval England, 1150–1350* (London, 1997), 168–70, for a study of the clerk in medieval Huntingdonshire.

[39]   *Household of Edward IV*, 140–1, and *A Collection of Ordinances*, 53.

[40]   *PROME*, parliament of June 1344, items 12.iiii, 12.xii, and parliament of April 1376, items 87, 152; *Britton*, I, 4, chap. I, items 5–6. If the king was abroad, the verge extended from the keeper of the realm. Williams, 'Sessions', 76; *CPR, 1340–3*, 562.

[41]   A. L. Brown, *The Governance of Late Medieval England 1272–1461* (London, 1989), 23.

ɪvth' in the year 1468.[42] The assizes allegedly appeared in the handbook of a royal clerk of the market.

The link between the assizes and the clerk is reinforced when one examines the municipal copies, most notably those for Northampton and Cambridge. The Cambridge version of the assizes was actually entitled *Officium Clerici Mercati*. The text of the Northampton version was followed closely by an oath to be made by the town's own clerk of the market, whereupon the mayor of Northampton was expected to undertake the offices of the royal clerk of the market. These duties were listed as inquiring into the pillory and tumbrel, as well as into the activities of certain occupations that replicate the concerns and phrasing of the Lansdowne assizes.[43]

In addition, the stipulations of the *Composicio* were basically the same articles that were assigned to the jurisdiction of the royal clerk of the market by the late-thirteenth-century law-books, *Fleta* and *Britton*.[44] Similarly, the *Liber Niger Domus Regis* (c.1471–3) of Edward ɪv stated that the clerk was enjoined to make examination of assizes and measures and of any excessive winnings in victuals and other merchandise. The clerk was to punish any trespasses caused by 'mysseuse of sises, ageynst the olde statutes or new of Englond, and agaynst the Kinge's proclamations'. For instance, in 1484, John Sibill, clerk of the market, was noted to have 'supervision of all artificers, labourers, victuallers, bakers and brewers, and power to imprison those accused or found guilty of fraud in the exercise of their crafts'.[45] The clerk was thus responsible for upholding the very laws subscribed by the Lansdowne assizes. Indeed, one of his deputies, the crier of the Marshalsea, had a duty to proclaim assizes in the markets visited, and one could imagine him using a document similar to Lansdowne MS 796.

The clerk's enforcement of 'assizes' is most clearly illustrated by the exchequer accounts for the Marshalsea of the household. The clerk of the market was expected to return estreats (lists of fines) to the exchequer twice a year, and after the 1350s these listed fines of individuals as well as a town's common fine. This was confirmed in a 1389 statute, whereby the clerk was forbidden from continuing to impose common fines on towns in general, and transgressors were instead to be

---

[42] *A Survey of the Cities of London and Westminster, by John Stow (1633)*, ed. J. Strype (2 vols., London, 1720), ɪɪ, bk v, pp. 341, 343–5. These assizes were not included in the original editions of Stow's *Survey* in 1598, 1603 or 1633. Cornelius Walford refers to the same manuscript book in his 'Early Laws and Customs in Great Britain Regarding Food', *TRHS* 8 (1880), 148–9, and his *The Famines of the World: Past and Present* (London, 1879), 140, but gives no manuscript reference. It is likely that he drew this information directly from Strype and that the actual manuscript is long lost.

[43] *Borough of Northampton*, ɪ, 373–6.

[44] *Britton*, ɪ, 189–93, chap. 31; *Fleta*, ed. H. G. Richardson and G. O. Sayles (2 vols., Selden Society 72, 89, 1953–72), ɪɪ, 117–20.

[45] *CPR, 1476–85*, 436; cf. Williams, 'Sessions', 78.

punished according to the severity of their individual infractions.[46] The estreats all begin with an accusation that a given town did not have a sufficient pillory or tumbrel and that the traders there used false weights and measures. Individuals were then named under certain offences. For instance, in 1406–7, Thomas Holgyll, clerk of the market, travelled through thirteen counties, surveying forty-one towns including Henley, Watford, Rugby, Barnet, Lutterworth, Southwark, Windsor, Lynn, Dunstable, Boston, Newark, Grantham and Newmarket. The common town fines ranged from 3s. 4d. for small towns like Coleshill and Southam, to 30s. and 34s. 8d. for the large ports of Boston and Lynn respectively.[47] In total, Holgyll prosecuted 126 bakers, 198 brewers, forty-nine butchers, thirty-five hostelers, nineteen tanners, eleven millers, eleven shoemakers, seven fishers, six cooks, six weavers, and two vintners, as well as twenty-eight traders for using unjust weights and measures.[48] The offences listed in the clerk's estreats provide evidence for his practical jurisdiction within market franchises. Indeed, by collating all the offences noted in various extant estreats during the late fourteenth and fifteenth centuries, we are presented with a very similar list to the Lansdowne assizes. The following is a summary of all the trades and associated offences that were included in a selection of thirteen estreats during the period 1353 to 1458:[49]

(a) Millers — for false measures and excessive toll;
(b) Bakers — for breaking the assize;
(c) Brewers — for breaking the assize and selling ale by the cup;
(d) Fishers — for selling corrupt fish, and for regrating and forestalling;
(e) Butchers — for unwholesome meat and forestalling;
(f) Cooks — for selling corrupt food and reheating victuals;
(g) Poulterers — for forestalling;
(h) Innkeepers and Hostelers — for selling victuals at excessive price and baking horsebread;
(i) Vintners and Taverners — for breaking the assize, false measures, and corrupt wine;
(j) Chandlers — for false weights;

---

[46] SR, II, 62; PROME, parliament of January 1390, items 34–5; R. E. Zupko, British Weights and Measures: A History from Antiquity to the Seventeenth Century (Madison, Wisc., 1977), 67–8; Given-Wilson, Royal Household, 50. Estreats were sent to the wardrobe in the thirteenth century, but an ordinance of May 1324 shows these lists being sent to the exchequer, together with a copy of an indenture by which he paid the money over to the wardrobe: Red Book of the Exchequer, ed. H. Hall (3 vols., Rolls Series, 1896), III, 922–3, 926–9; Johnson, 'The King's Wardrobe and Household', 246.

[47] This brought the clerk a total revenue of £26 2s. 2d. for the financial year 7–8 Hen IV: TNA, E101/258/2.

[48] Ibid. The counties were: Lincolnshire, Warwickshire, Hertfordshire, Middlesex, Essex, Suffolk, Norfolk, Cambridgeshire, Berkshire, Surrey, Bedfordshire, Nottinghamshire, Rutland.

[49] TNA, E101/256/14, 15, 25; E101/257/1, 11(2), 17; E101/258/1, 2; E101/259/12, 15, 18, 21, 25.

(k) Tanners — for leather badly tanned;

(l) Shoemakers — for using leather badly tanned;

(m) Tailors — for false ells and taking too much cloth;

(n) Skinners and Shoemakers — for cutting too much and using badly tanned leather;

(o) Smiths — for taking too much iron;

(p) Spicers — for using false weights;

(q) Buyers of grain and sellers of flour — for false bushels and measures;

(r) Forestallers.

Traders were regularly linked to particular concerns, so the above list does not prove conclusively a connection between the Lansdowne assizes and the clerk of the market. Nevertheless, the offences listed in the estreats are almost identical to those listed in Lansdowne MS 796, with the exception of poulterers (often conflated with cooks) and tailors. Beer-brewers, who became more prevalent in the late fifteenth century, are the only major omission in the list. Similarly, spicers only appear in estreats from the reign of Henry VI.

The royal clerk of the market should not be confused with those officials who were appointed by a lord or mayor to regulate the market on their behalf, and who were also referred to as 'clerks of the market'. Often a borough was granted the right, by charter, to exercise the assizes of bread, wine, beer and victuals, the assay of weights and measures, and 'all else that pertains to the office of the Clerk of the Market'.[50] In essence, they judged the same infringements and practices as the royal clerk of the market, but operated by virtue of a royal franchise. For instance, both Northampton and Cambridge burgesses were granted liberties normally held by the clerk of the market, with the mayor and other local officers acting *ex officio* as his deputies. Both towns could theoretically exclude the royal clerk from their jurisdiction.[51] However, the clerk still had authority in many large and small towns. It is recorded in the Coventry Leet Book that the royal clerk of the market visited the town in 1451 whilst the king was staying there. The clerk, Brooke, confirmed and sealed the town's standard strike of brass with the signet of his royal office, 'that is to sey the prynte ther of is a crowne'.[52] The royal clerk is also recorded in the Colchester Red Paper Book as visiting the town in *c.*1390, when transgressions were judged by twelve sworn men of the town and the clerk sealed

---

[50]   As seen in a charter for Southampton for 1401, in *The Charters of the Borough of Southampton*, ed. H. W. Gidden (Southampton Record Society 7, 1909), 50–1.

[51]   *Borough of Northampton*, I, 68–70; *The Charters of Borough of Cambridge*, ed. F. W. Maitland and M. Bateson (Cambridge, 1901), 32–9 (1385).

[52]   *Coventry Leet Book*, 267. It is unlikely that this was the same Brooke as mentioned by Stow.

weights and measures.[53] By contrast, in 1447, Henry VI granted to Norwich that 'the mayor and citizens may have assay and assize of bread, wine, beer, measures, flesh, fish and all things belonging to the office of the king's Clerk of the Market of his household'.[54] The subsequent presentment of misdemeanours is close to the Lansdowne assizes in its categories, order and wording.[55] Phrases such as 'not holsome for mannes body', 'bottelles of hay', 'kyll ther bulls unbayted', 'ffysshe not well wateryd', 'pottes unsyzed and sealyd', and 'do not sell a quart of the best ale or beare for a halfpenny' are often seen singularly in ordinances and court proceedings, but taken together they provide circumstantial evidence that the Norwich clerk was referring to a similar list as the assizes under discussion.

The evidence suggests that the Lansdowne assizes were originally intended for use by the clerk of the market in his duties, but were later copied into several town custumals. It is possible that local officials recognised the utility of a standardised list of assize laws, even if this potentially impeded their autonomy. There was a practical need to prepare for potential visits by the clerk when the royal household was nearby. It could, however, be argued that the clerk was a haphazard instrument of royal control. Exemptions were provided in the charters of many medieval boroughs, such as Northampton and Cambridge.[56] The fact that the clerk rarely operated beyond the verge of the royal household also meant that he achieved an uneven coverage of the country. The clerk's activities were theoretically limited by the extent of the royal itinerary, both geographically and chronologically. An examination of the clerk's estreats suggests a bias towards southern counties and, although the travels of the household could be quite extensive at times, significant areas were left untouched.

It is certainly possible that the king and government had little ambition beyond the verge and the needs of the household. Gwen Seabourne has, however, argued that self-interest was not the only relevant motivation for royal intervention.[57] She has posited that many actions by the king and government did not

---

[53] The king's household at this time was located at Chelmsford: *Red Paper Book of Colchester*, 157–8.

[54] *The Records of the City of Norwich*, ed. W. Hudson and J. C. Tingey (2 vols., Norwich, 1906), I, 121; see also 285.

[55] Ibid., II, 181–2.

[56] See also: *CChR, 1300–1326*, 487–8 (Bury St Edmunds); *The Little Red Book of Bristol*, ed. F. B. Bickley (2 vols., Bristol, 1900), I, pp. xvi, 122–3; C. Platt, *Medieval Southampton: The Port and Trading Community, AD 1000–1600* (London, 1973), 166; *City of Norwich*, I, 26, 33, 121, 285; *Records of the Borough of Nottingham, 1155–1485*, ed. W. H. Stevenson (2 vols., London, 1882–3), II, 6–7; *Munimenta Gildhallae Londoniensis: Liber Albus, Liber Custumarum et Liber Horn*, ed. H. T. Riley (3 vols., Rolls Series, 1859–62), II. ii (*Liber Custumarum*), 434–5. Such exemptions were reinforced by Parliament: *PROME*, parliament of April 1376, item 87.

[57] G. Seabourne, 'Laws, Morals and Money: Royal Regulations of the Substance of Subjects' Sales and Loans in England, 1272–1399', in *Expectations of the Law in the Middle Ages*, ed. A. Musson (Woodbridge, 2001), 117–34.

affect royal dealings in an obvious way and that there were examples of a desire to act even when the profits of jurisdiction were granted away. The ideas underlying these actions were moral duty, prevention of abuses in commercial transactions, and due punishment of wrongdoers. Could a similar disinterest have influenced the clerk of the market, beyond his practical household and provisioning duties?

A by-product of the clerk's duties was his inspection of the activities of trades-men for the protection of consumers in general. He represented the king and his supreme law, which superseded all others, and by the fifteenth century he was referred to as the clerk of the market of the king's household *and throughout the whole realm* ('et infra et per totum regnum nostrum Anglie').[58] Indeed, the powers of the clerk of the market appear to have blossomed during the fifteenth and six-teenth centuries, especially in relation to purveyance. Henry viii tried to ensure that the clerk could exercise his power wherever he was within the verge, regard-less of exemptions.[59] Similarly, the concept of the verge, or the jurisdiction of the clerk of the market, could be more extensive in reality than in theory. In a com-mission of 1257, the verge was regarded as comprising the entire county of Berk-shire which the king had 'passed through'.[60] The clerk personified the unwritten and prescriptive authority of the king's prerogative in the same way as purveyors, butlers and aulnagers.[61] However, the notion of disinterested communal concern was secondary to protecting the king's rights. Even in towns where the clerk was formally excluded, their liberties were still based on an adequate upkeep of the franchise and laws. In turn, the clerk's powers were founded upon the king's claim to all market franchises, as well as royal jurisdiction over the assizes through view of frankpledge and leet courts.[62] These royal franchises could be forfeited if a market-holder failed to assist the clerk or, more generally, uphold market-ing laws. The clerk was not only a guardian of immediate provisioning costs and quality, but also of the market charters and certain legal franchises that were the prerogative of the king.

This relationship between the king, clerk and market franchise can be seen in medieval law-books, which outlined the standard procedure undertaken by the clerk and his deputies. The clerk would go to a market within the verge and sum-mon the bailiff, who would collect all the bushels, half bushels, quarts, gallons, and half gallons to check against the royal standards, as well as a loaf of every sort

---

[58] Rosenthal argues that other clerks could work beyond the verge, armed with royal writs 'to remind villagers of the long arm of royal government'. Such clerks were sent out by Edward iv to inspect weights and measures 'throughout the realm': Rosenthal, 'Assizes', 412; *CPR, 1476–85*, 19, 436.

[59] *SR* iii, 556–7 (27 Hen. viii, item 24, 1535–6); iii, 772 (32 Hen. viii, item 20, 1540).

[60] *CPR, 1247–58*, 569; Seabourne, *Royal Regulation*, 90.

[61] *Select Cases Concerning the Law Merchant, AD 1239–1633, vol. 2: Central Courts*, ed. H. Hall (Selden Society 46, 1930), pp. xlvi–xlviii.

[62] Seabourne, *Royal Regulation*, 96–8.

from the bakers. All the traders were then gathered and twelve of the 'most law-ful householders' were sworn to present on various articles. This was effectively a court, presided over by the clerk of the market, under the jurisdiction of the court of the verge or Marshalsea court. This latter body was a household tribunal, usually held under the auspices of the steward and marshal, which was available for the punishment of persons who usurped the prerogatives of household offi-cials or defrauded the household. Violations of the assizes within the verge were also cognisable by this court, with jurisdictional power delegated to the clerk of the market.[63] *Britton* and *Fleta* list the articles that the court was expected to ad-dress: whether the lord had set up a market by the king's warrant; whether he had the franchise of view of frankpledge; whether he had correction of assizes and how he enforced these; and whether he had the necessary and well-kept instru-ments (gallows, pillory and tumbrel) to carry out due punishments. If the lord was found wanting in any of these articles the franchise could be seized into the king's hands.[64] In a similar way, the king's greatest check on chartered towns was through visiting justices and royal officials, and his sanctions included a fine or revocation of the town's privileges.[65] On this basis, the king had the right to inter-vene, even in places with chartered privileges, if there were complaints of a failure to enforce trade regulations.

An entry in the *Little Red Book* of Bristol from 1283 demonstrates a town's anxiety about the king's authority over their liberty: 'the Mayor and Commonalty of the town of Bristol fear that they will be severely punished unless the assize in the town aforesaid be strictly observed by the same Mayor and Commonalty'.[66] In 1331 Lincoln was upbraided for not making assay of the assizes as often as was necessary and for being too lenient in punishment by remitting corporal meth-ods.[67] Records for the clerk of the market suggest that local remittance of corporal punishment for fines was widespread and that the upkeep of penal apparatus was often considered to be insufficient.[68] There were also examples of franchises being taken into the king's hands when local officials failed to punish adequately offend-ers against the assizes, such as at Bodmin (Cornwall) in 1284 and at Winchcombe (Gloucestershire) in 1287, though franchises were often swiftly returned upon

---

63   W. R. Jones, 'The Court of the Verge: the Jurisdiction of the Steward and Marshal of the Household in Later Medieval England', *Journal of British Studies*, 10 (1970), 1–29; *Select Cases Concerning the Law Merchants*, pp. cix–cx; Given-Wilson, *Royal Household*, 48–50.

64   *Britton*, I, 186–9, chap. 31; *Fleta*, II, 117–8.

65   Brown, *Governance of Late Medieval England*, 155.

66   *Little Red Book of Bristol*, II, 222–3.

67   *CIM, 1307–49*, 294–5, no. 1201. Cambridge was similarly chastised in 1327: *CChR, 1327–1341*, 57–8.

68   TNA, E101/256/14, 15, 25; E101/257/1, 11 (2), 17; E101/258/1, 2; see also *Borough of North-ampton*, I, 373. A statute of 1389–90 ordered that no corporal punishments should be remit-ted for the assizes of bread and ale: *SR* II, 63.

a payment to the crown.[69] Nevertheless, local officials recognised that the clerk of the market had a wider and more anomalous role as a guardian of market and assize franchises. In essence, the clerk acted in the short term by punishing offenders in the verge and in the long term by checking that local policing was carried out properly.[70] Royal commissions could be sent out under the same remit if a particular problem occurred beyond the verge. It was important to local officials to know what articles and questions would be raised.

Consequently, although the Lansdowne assizes were apparently prepared by the royal clerk of the market primarily for his own use and in the interests of the king, they also became widely influential in towns both within and beyond his jurisdiction. The clerk of the market represented royal surveillance upon the activities of local markets and lords, ensuring that they were running their franchises correctly and following the law. Although this was not the primary intent of the clerk's jurisdiction, it was the ultimate effect, and the clerk's duties were to monitor an amalgam of statute and quasi-statute laws, encompassing a wide variety of manufacturing and retail trades. In the role of the clerk of the market we see a strong reason for the formulation of both the *Composicio* in the thirteenth century and the Lansdowne assizes in the fifteenth century.

The Lansdowne assizes themselves can be characterised as issues to be addressed rather than ordinances *per se*, providing a standard pro-forma as to how clerks should conduct inquiries into local trading malpractices. They were also a set of articles for which twelve 'worthy men' were expected to provide sworn answers. Such commercial regulation had parallels in local venues. For instance, the *Modus Tenendi Curias* included comparable articles of inquisition, which were intended for use in leet courts and the view of frankpledge.[71] The significance of manorial courts and municipal customs in contributing to the form of the assizes, and to centralised commercial laws in general, provides another perspective on this legislation. Market authorities looked to comply with statutory provisions, with scribes often including national promulgations in their own custumals and ordinances as a practical guide for officials and courts.[72] Chartered privileges did not

---

[69] Seabourne, *Royal Regulation*, 92–5. For a similar dispute in Bury St Edmunds, 1285–90, where the royal clerk of the market was ordered to investigate, see *The Letter-Book of William of Hoo, Sacrist of Bury St Edmunds, 1280–1294*, ed. A. Gransden (Suffolk Records Society 5, 1963), 16, 40 (no. 26), 81 (no. 148), 125–30 (appx 7), 136 (appx 9).

[70] Britnell, *Commercialisation*, 96.

[71] *The Court Baron*, ed. F. W. Maitland and W. P. Baildon (Selden Society 4, 1891): 'De Placitis et Curiis Tenendis', 71–8, 'Modus Tenendi Curias, c.1307', 79–92, 'Modus Tenendi Curias, c.1342', 93–106. See also: BL, Harleian MS 773, fol. 39ʳ (c.1440); *Historia et Cartularium Monasterii Sancti Petri Gloucestriae*, ed. W. M. Hart (3 vols., Roll Series, 1863–7), III, 221–2; *The Stoneleigh Leger Book*, ed. R. H. Hilton (Dugdale Society 24, 1960), 98–100.

[72] For instance, the Northampton *Liber Custumarum* includes copies of the statutes *Assisa*

mean that borough authorities were undertaking entirely new regulatory procedures nor that they were shunning laws that the clerk had previously enforced.
However, many towns certainly issued their own by-laws and ordinances, which
tackled the minutiae of trading practices and the repercussions of local circumstances.[73] Many of them did so before certain trading concerns became a matter
for national legislation, from the early town laws concerning ale and bread to later
concerns regarding leather-sellers and innkeepers.

A brief overview of the Lansdowne assizes demonstrates how they synthe-
sised various commercial customs and laws. The assizes were part of a general
medieval response to commercial concerns, namely: quality standards; foodstuffs
which were fit for human consumption; control of weights and measures; the
prevention of forestalling and regrating; and a limitation on excessive profit.
Many of the stipulations in the assizes sought to protect consumers against potentially fraudulent tradesmen, particularly those sections concerning reasonable
profit. The Lansdowne assizes for bread follow the basic formula outlined in the
c.1256 quasi-statute, the *Assisa Panis et Cervisie*, whereby for every rise by 6*d.*
in the price of wheat the weight of the farthing loaf would fall by a stipulated
amount.[74] For ale, as the price of a quarter of barley or malt increased by 12*d.*,
a gallon would cost a farthing more, which is a simplified version of the *Assisa*
and the *Composicio*.[75] Other price considerations in the Lansdowne assizes could
be quite specific. For instance, a miller was to 'haue a busshell of malte a pynte for
the gryndyng' and for every bushel of wheat a quart;[76] fishers and butchers were
to take no more profit than a penny in the shilling;[77] an innkeeper was to 'haue of
euery busshell provandire a peny wynnyng';[78] a taverner was allowed 2*d.* in every

Panis et Cervisie, Assisa de Ponderibus et Mensuris, Judicium Pillorie, and the majority of the
Composicio: Borough of Northampton, I, 314–29.

[73] Craft guilds also issued ordinances specific to their craft and local community: H. Swanson,
Medieval Artisans: An Urban Class in Late Medieval England (Oxford, 1989).

[74] BL, Lansdowne MS 796, fol. 4ᵛ; *SR* I, 199–200; Davis, 'Baking for the Common Good'.

[75] BL, Lansdowne MS 796, fols. 4ᵛ–5ʳ. A quarter of malt is used in the *Composicio*. The national
formulae for the assizes of bread and ale were incorporated into town ordinances, e.g. *Records of the Borough of Leicester 1103–1688*, ed. M. Bateson (4 vols., London, 1899–1923), II,
20–2; *Little Red Book of Bristol*, II, 217.

[76] BL, Lansdowne MS 796, fol. 4ᵛ: equivalent to 1/32 and 1/64 respectively. The *Composicio*
allowed the miller either 1/20 or 1/24 of the corn: *SR* I, 203. For regulations concerning
millers who take excessive toll, see: *Calendar of Letter-Books of the City of London*, ed. R.
R. Sharpe (12 vols., London, 1899–1912), II, 217; J. Langdon, *Mills in the Medieval Economy:
England 1300–1540* (Oxford, 2004), 139–40, 244–8, 261–2.

[77] BL, Lansdowne MS 796, fol. 5ʳ. Most statutes and town ordinances were vague in terms of
a 'reasonable profit', as opposed to a fixed price, for fish and meat: Seabourne, *Royal Regulation*, 77; *SR* I, 353–6; *York Civic Ordinances*, 13; *Borough of Northampton*, I, 264; *Little Red
Book of Bristol*, II, 72–4; *Coventry Leet Book*, 25; *Borough of Leicester*, II, 289.

[78] BL, Lansdowne MS 796, fol. 5ᵛ. An ordinance for Coventry in 1421 stated that an innkeeper

gallon of white and red wine and 4*d.* for sweet wine;[79] and a tallow-chandler was ordered that when 'he beyith a li of talowe for an ob than shall he sell a li of candill for a peny'.[80] The notion of a reasonable and calculable profit was upheld throughout the assizes.

Similarly, quality standards were continually reiterated, if only in vague terms, such that products should be 'of goode stuffe' or 'abill for mannys body'.[81] Fishmongers were specifically warned not to water their fish to make it look fresher than it was.[82] The butchers were also targeted when it came to the quality of their goods and the hygiene of their practices. The stipulation that 'he shall sel no bullys fflesche but yf it be baytyd' is repeated in town ordinances, where it was believed that baiting made the flesh more tender.[83] Anxieties about corrupted and diseased foodstuffs, particularly meat, are found in thirteenth-century statutes as well as municipal ordinances, but the controls upon skins, tallow and offal, as well as upon where in the marketplace such goods should be sold, were traditionally a local concern.[84] Towns also put down strict guidelines as to where fish could be sold, similar to the Lansdowne assizes' broader statement that sales should take place 'in the playne market place'.[85]

The very language and form of the Lansdowne assizes display a cumulative

---

could make one penny profit on every shilling's worth of oats, beans or peas sold: *Coventry Leet Book*, 24.

[79] BL, Lansdowne MS 796, fol. 6ʳ. A profit margin is unusual since most statutes and town ordinances set a fixed price: *SR* I, 203; II, 18–20; *Borough of Leicester*, II, 20–2; *Coventry Leet Book*, 24–5; *Little Red Book of Bristol*, II, 218.

[80] BL, Lansdowne MS 796, fol. 6ᵛ. This was similar to London regulations: *Memorials of London and London Life in the xiiith, xivth, and xvth Centuries*, ed. H. T. Riley (London, 1868), 358–60. See also *Borough of Leicester*, II, 294; *City of Norwich*, II, 162.

[81] BL, Lansdowne MS 796, fols. 5ʳ–7ʳ. Similar language is found in statutes and town ordinances, e.g. *SR* I, 199–204; *Borough of Leicester*, I, 180–1; II, 288–9; *Monumenta Juridica: The Black Book of the Admiralty*, ed. T. Twiss (4 vols., Rolls Series, 1871–6), II, 104–5 (item 30), 144–7 (item 67), 146–7 (item 58), 176–7 (item 79); *York Civic Ordinances*, 12–13; *Little Red Book of Bristol*, II, 218; *Coventry Leet Book*, 25–6, 29; *Borough of Northampton*, I, 227, 230; *Beverley Town Documents*, ed. A. F. Leach (Selden Society 14, 1900), 28–9.

[82] BL, Lansdowne MS 796, fol. 5ʳ. See also *The Great Red Book of Bristol*, ed. E. W. W. Veale (Bristol Record Society 2, 4, 8, 16, 18, 1931–53), III, 115.

[83] BL, Lansdowne MS 796, fol. 5ʳ. *The Early Records of Medieval Coventry*, ed. P. R. Coss (London, 1986), 42; *The Regulations of the City of Hereford*, ed. F. C. Morgan (Hereford, 1945), 3–4; *Borough of Leicester*, II, 289; West Suffolk Record Office, Petworth House Archives (PHA) 6766 (1440), with thanks to Maria Osowiecki for this reference.

[84] *Black Book*, II, 142–5, item 56; *The Oak Book of Southampton*, ed. P. Studer (2 vols., Southampton Record Society 10–11, 1910), I, 68–9; *Munimenta Gildhallae*, I, 274, 279; *Borough of Leicester*, II, 288–9.

[85] BL, Lansdowne MS 796, fol. 5ʳ; *Black Book*, II, 102–3, items 28–9; *Oak Book*, I, 64–7, items 64–5; *Munimenta Gildhallae*, I, 373–82; *Little Red Book of Bristol*, I, 35–6; *Borough of Northampton*, I, 264, 307–9.

effect of (at least) two hundred years of retail regulations and connections between the centre and localities. As such, it should not be assumed that royal officials clumsily lumped together a number of differing customs and ideas. There is an internal logic to much of the regulation and a number of specific issues that outlined the preoccupations of central government and the clerk of the market. Many of the regulations had direct antecedents in thirteenth-century statute law, particularly those on baking, brewing, milling, forestalling, and weights and measures, though it must be remembered that the statutes themselves were often drawn from local customs. For instance, the stipulation that no innkeepers were to bake bread appears to have originated in Oxford, London and Northampton, before becoming enshrined in statute law in 1389–90 in response to municipal petitions.[86] However, the demand that no inn should house a bawdry is found regularly in local laws but not in central legislation.[87] In another example, the legal delineation between the cordwaining trade and tanning was first entered into statute law in 1389–90,[88] but such controls separating shoemakers from tanners were already in place in Beverley in 1375. This, in turn, probably drew upon a vague desire for craft demarcation outlined in a royal ordinance of 1363.[89] This all led to new rules regarding craft responsibilities, and the Lansdowne assizes clearly outline a demarcation between the types of leather that a tanner or tawyer could work.[90]

The regulations concerning the chandlers, spicers, weavers and leatherworkers all have precedents in previous local and national laws, though it is surprising that trades such as tailors, fullers and dyers were omitted from these assizes. Cloth had long been regulated by a national assize that inquired into both quality and measurements, but the Lansdowne assize for weavers concentrates mostly on weights, measures and 'thrumys'.[91] Thrums were the waste ends of warp after the cloth was woven and many municipal ordinances stipulated that cloth made from thrums was to be forfeited and burnt.[92] The assizes for tanners, cordwainers, curriers and tawyers also focus on quality issues, ensuring that the

---

[86]   BL, Lansdowne MS 796, fol. 5ᵛ; *SR*, II, 63, 140; *Munimenta Civitatis Oxonie*, ed. H. E. Salter (Devizes, 1920), 136–7 (Oxford, 1355); *Memorials of London*, 323–4 (London); *CIM, 1377–88*, 143 (Northampton); *Borough of Northampton*, I, 249 (1383). See also: *Beverley Town Documents*, p. lvii; *Henley Borough Records: Assembly Books i–iv, 1395–1543*, ed. P. M. Briers (Oxfordshire Record Society 41, London, 1960), 108.

[87]   *York Civic Ordinances*, 16–17; *Beverley Town Documents*, 15; *Munimenta Gildhallae*, I, 476; *Coventry Leet Book*, 545; *The Making of King's Lynn: A Documentary Survey*, ed. D. M. Owen (London, 1984), 268, no. 325.

[88]   *SR* II, 65. This was repealed in 1402 and reimposed in 1423: *SR* II, 142, 220.

[89]   *Beverley Town Documents*, 31; *SR* I, 379–80.

[90]   BL, Lansdowne MS 796, fol. 7ʳ.

[91]   Ibid., fol. 6ᵛ.

[92]   *Coventry Leet Book*, 400; *Little Red Book of Bristol*, II, 2–6, 40–1, 117–27; *Borough of Leicester*, II, 195–6.

work was carried out thoroughly and that the materials were sufficient.[93] Quality, fraud, weights, measures and price were thus the primary concerns for the Lansdowne assizes, just as they were for the clerk of the market. In this vein, two concluding sections outline the need for all weights and measures to be sealed according to the king's standard and insist that there should be no forestalling or regrating that might raise prices to the hurt of the poor commons.[94]

Another notable aspect of the Lansdowne assizes concerns their system of an escalating scale of punishments. Many of the penalties outlined were conspicuously uniform, and in the last few entries the clerk merely states that offenders will be 'jugyd acordyng vnto the reformor statute', which could be either referring to the previous entry or some unnamed statute law. For most traders the schedule of punishments was 12*d.* for the first offence, 2*s.* for the second, 40*d.* for the third, and the pillory for the fourth. The scale was similar to that prescribed by the *Assisa Panis et Cervisie*, which stated that bakers or brewers were to be punished by amercement for the first three offences and the pillory for the fourth.[95] However, in comparison to those who used unsealed measures or charged excessive prices, those who sold corrupt food or committed frauds were liable to much harsher penalties. Millers, spicers and cooks were given fewer warnings for their adulterations and were expected to be amerced 40*d.* for every offence, and at the third time they were sentenced to the pillory. Tanners who tanned leather badly or cordwainers who made shoes from insufficient leather faced fines of 6*s.* 8*d.* every time.[96]

The system of escalating punishments had a long heritage in both statute law and town customs. It was usually the fraudulent and corrupt who were subject to the severest penalties. The schedules of punishments in fourteenth-century Bristol were similar to the Lansdowne assizes. Brewers had to sell their ale at a certain price or else face a 20*d.* fine for the first offence, 40*d.* for the second, half a mark for the third, and conviction (presumably corporal punishment) for the fourth.[97] Butchers and cooks selling diseased meat faced the most severe fiscal penalties and these were followed by the pillory, imprisonment and abjuration of the town. Next in severity came forestallers and sellers of adulterated flour, who faced the pillory at their third offence and then forswearing of their trade.[98] Whether these

---

93   BL, Lansdowne MS 796, fol. 7ʳ. See also *SR* II, 220 (1423); *Little Red Book of Bristol*, II, 101–17, 167–70; *Munimenta Gildhallae*, II, i, 83, 94.

94   BL, Lansdowne MS 796, fol. 7ᵛ. These again draw upon both statutes and local customs: Britnell, 'Forstall'; Connor, *Weights and Measures*.

95   *SR* I, 199–200 ('Assisa Panis et Cervisie'). See also *SR* I, 201–2 ('Judicium Pillorie'). The use of the pillory, a type of upright stocks, was the stipulated punishment not only for recidivists but also for serious malpractice.

96   This was a remnant of earlier statute law: *SR* II, 220 (1423).

97   *Little Red Book of Bristol*, II, 36–7. See also *Borough of Leicester*, II, 288.

98   *Little Red Book of Bristol*, I, 38–9, and II, 30, 36–8, 218, 221.

schemes of punishment were followed in practice is another matter, and the assizes are imprecise about the details of everyday enforcement. It is likely that the minutiae of marketing enforcement remained largely in local hands, and there would have been an element of discretion and flexibility in how officials interpreted national laws, quality assessment criteria, and pricing practices. However, the royal government did not expect to be entirely ignored in such matters.

There were many influences upon the Lansdowne assizes. Central legislation was significant, but certain elements of the assizes appear to have either begun or developed locally, within town ordinances. The assize for beer-brewers is particularly interesting, for it appears to be one of the first laws specifically laid down for this trade in England, though it obviously draws upon long-established regulations for ale.[99] In general, the Lansdowne assizes were the culmination of a complex, 'organic' interplay between local and central jurisdictions. Musson has noted that central legislation encouraged local communities to make and record their own laws, while local legislation and practice could provide the inspiration and example for national legislation.[100] Similarly, Seabourne has suggested that the creation of national commercial law usually derived from an interplay, overlap and cross-fertilisation between local, urban and royal sources.[101] These views encapsulate the lineage and influence of this particular set of medieval assizes.

This brief survey of the Lansdowne assizes shows how the creation of national trade legislation was the product of a mixture of royal and local influences. Pressure from central government also shaped the character of many commercial customs in towns, shires and hundreds and lent a growing level of uniformity. Borough and market charters allowed authorities to accommodate local needs, and there were vagaries in their enforcement of market regulations.[102] Nevertheless, certain commercial laws became increasingly uniform within towns and mirrored legislation initiated by parliament or emanating from the royal household. The Lansdowne assizes could be an important guide for local authorities concerning how to carry out commercial regulation according to royal stipulations.

Indeed, a number of historians have argued that commercial issues were subject to increasing codification in statutory law from the thirteenth to the fifteenth centuries.[103] We have already seen that in the thirteenth century there were various royal proclamations concerning bread, ale and meat. These certainly had their

---

[99] BL, Lansdowne MS 796, fol. 6ʳ. Other regulations for beer appear in Norwich in 1498: *City of Norwich*, ɪɪ, 155–6.

[100] Musson, *Medieval Law in Context*, 208.

[101] Seabourne, *Royal Regulation*, 166–7.

[102] Ibid., 165–6; Britnell, *Commercialisation*, 90.

[103] R. H. Britnell, 'Urban Economic Regulation and Economic Morality in Medieval England', in *Markets, Trade and Economic Development in England and Europe, 1050–1550*, ed. idem (Farnham, 2009); W. Holdsworth, *A History of English Law* (10 vols., 7th edn, London,

origin in local customs but were subsequently collated and unified into national legislation from the reign of Henry II and, more coherently, in the *Assisa* and the *Composicio* under Henry III.[104] Weights and measures, wine, and cloth were also subject to greater 'assize' stipulations from the thirteenth century, a period in which commercial and industrial expansion drove regulatory development.[105] Medieval kings had long insisted upon the uniformity of measures and trading standards throughout the realm, but by the late Middle Ages national legislation came to supersede, or at least to supplement, much municipal regulation.[106]

Robert Palmer has gone further and suggested that after the Black Death there was a qualitative change in economic laws, which established parameters for governmental concerns and new directions for legal development. Seabourne has argued, in contrast to Palmer's thesis, that there was not a sudden and unprecedented degree of royal intervention in subjects' economic affairs after the Black Death. The burst of activity after 1349 represented more a change in degree than in the nature of legislation; little was innovative.[107] Central government certainly took an increasing responsibility for mundane commercial and social regulation, including social and labour relationships.[108] By the fourteenth century, older local laws were supplemented by parliamentary statutes, which governed aspects of economic life ranging from employment, wages and manufactures, to standards of hygiene and prices of foodstuffs.[109] This trend towards broader legislation was mirrored in the new areas covered by the Lansdowne assizes, but ignored in the *Composicio*. This was driven partly by the diversification of the economy and partly by a self-confident monarchy.

However, Seabourne is perhaps right to indicate that little in retail trade measures was really innovative after the Black Death. Older customs and regulations prefigured much of what occurred in the assizes, with national or local laws from the thirteenth and fourteenth centuries being merely revised or updated. The London authorities had pre-empted the ordinance of labourers (1349) with some of their municipal laws of the early fourteenth century.[110] No new statutes

1956), II, 466–7; Britnell, 'Forstall', 90. For instance, legislation concerning forestalling was gradually elaborated to cover a number of specific cases: *SR* I, 315 (1351), 354 (1357).

[104] Davis, 'Baking for the Common Good', 465–502.

[105] R. H. Britnell, 'Economy of British Towns 600–1300', in *The Cambridge Urban History of Britain*, I: *600–1540*, ed. D. M. Palliser (Cambridge, 2000), 125.

[106] E. Lipson, *The Economic History of England* (12th edn, London, 1959), I, 294. Older regulations concerning standard measures were continually renewed, e.g. *SR* I, 365–6 (1361), II, 63–4 (1389–90), though even in the late fifteenth century there were local discrepancies: Britnell, *Commercialisation*, 173–4.

[107] Palmer, *English Law*, 140–1; Seabourne, *Royal Regulation*, 160–2.

[108] Palmer, *English Law*, 1–2, 14–16, 24.

[109] *SR* II, 307–8 (1349), 311–12 (1351).

[110] A. Musson, 'New Labour Laws, New Remedies? Legal Reaction to the Black Death Crisis', in *Fourteenth Century England I*, ed. N. Saul (Woodbridge, 2000), 73–88.

on prices were promulgated during the reigns of Henry IV or Henry V, though there were efforts to enforce existing laws. Similarly, a statute from the reign of Edward IV simply stated that the chief officers of every municipal corporation should have 'the searching and surveying of victual'.[111] The Lansdowne assizes were another attempt to coalesce existing laws rather than establish new ones. The main policy of central government was to provide coherence to traditional and local custom, while also reinforcing royal authority and policing methods. Nevertheless, as Britnell has asserted, the extension of royal authority through national commercial regulations also meant that urban officials had to attend more to the interests of non-burgesses.[112] The fact that the assizes were entered into several town custumals, even in those boroughs which had gained liberty from the clerk of the market, implies that local urban authorities had to recognise and acquiesce to the development of codified legislation.

The assizes in Lansdowne MS 796 can be viewed as part of a continual readjustment and restatement of assize legislation, which began in earnest in the thirteenth century with the creation of the *Assisa, Composicio* and *Judicium Pillorie*. They were also part of a long-term, and sometimes uneven, process of standardisation and conformity in commercial practices across medieval England. For instance, Lansdowne MS 796 provides us with central assizes for commodities such as meat and fish, which are otherwise missing from the documentary record but which proliferated in courtly presentments after the Black Death. The way in which such codifications were created was complex in both origins and aims, as reflected in the two-way interaction between local and national influences. In particular, the Lansdowne assizes were part of the apparatus of the king's household and the royal clerk of the market, but they also affirmed and consolidated laws that had often originally emanated from the localities. Enforcement remained primarily a local affair, but the supervisory and extensive influence of the clerk of the market and royal commissions should not be underestimated, especially given the threat that a market or borough franchise could be seized back into the king's hands. The actions and surveillance of royal household officials remained important throughout the fifteenth century, even for enfranchised boroughs. On the one hand, municipal officials simply viewed the assizes as a suitable national framework upon which to hang local variations, but on the other they were also responding to the pervasive demands of royal government.

The laws of trade developed through a long and complex process of assimilation, drawing extensively upon local examples and enforcement. This symbiotic and hybrid process for creating trade legislation was perhaps more acceptable to the officials who had to enforce it, and the traders and consumers who had to live

---

[111]   *SR* II, 442–3 (1472).
[112]   Britnell, 'Urban Economic Regulation'.

by it, than laws that were regarded as imposed arbitrarily through royal officials. Consensus was important and bred confidence in the marketplace. This seems to be the case with the Lansdowne assizes, which exude the scent of centuries of customs, petitions, local by-laws and royal concerns. A seemingly innocuous and unprovenanced set of assizes raises many intriguing issues concerning the relationship between centre and locality and the formulation of market regulation.

6

Self-Government in the Small Towns of Late Medieval England
····················
Mark Bailey

AFTER DECADES IN WHICH research into the largest and greatest towns dominated the agenda of urban historians, they now recognise the important economic role played by the small towns of medieval England. Richard Britnell's research has been influential in effecting this change in emphasis, because one of his first publications considered the foundation and early development of the small market town of Witham (Essex), and his later, magisterial, work on the commercialisation of the economy sketched the background to the expansion of small boroughs, markets and fairs in the twelfth and thirteenth centuries.[1] Rodney Hilton and Chris Dyer also championed these 'small places with large consequences', emphasising their importance both as barometers for economic and social change, and in shaping regional differences across England.[2] Their published works have inspired others to research small-town life in late medieval England, the cumulative effect of which has been to counterbalance the excessive concentration upon the largest — and best-documented — English towns and cities.[3] As Dyer rightly states, 'the concern for the top ranks of the urban hierarchy

---

[1] R. H. Britnell, 'The Making of Witham', *History Studies*, 1 (1968), 13–21; idem, *The Commercialisation of English Society* (Cambridge, 1993). Having first introduced this undergraduate to medieval history at the University of Durham, later Richard kindly directed me to the court rolls of the towns of Clare (Suffolk) and Sudbury (Suffolk).

[2] R. Hilton, *The English Peasantry in the Later Middle Ages* (Oxford, 1975), 76–94; C. Dyer, 'Small Places with Large Consequences: The Importance of Small Towns in England, 1000–1540', *Historical Research*, 75 (2002), 1–24.

[3] The explosion in such studies over the past thirty years is readily apparent in the examples cited by Dyer in his two important surveys: Dyer, 'Small Places', 1–24, and idem, 'Small Towns 1270–1540', in *The Cambridge Urban History of Britain*, 1: *600–1540*, ed. D. M. Palliser (Cambridge, 2000), 305–40. See also C. Dyer, 'Market Towns and the Countryside in Late–Medieval England', *Canadian Journal of History*, 31 (1996), 18–35. For a more recent example of the work in a single county, see the three medieval chapters in *A County of Small Towns: The Development of Hertfordshire's Urban Landscape to 1800*, ed. T. Slater and N. Goose (Hatfield, 2008).

can be readily understood ... [yet] small towns were not optional additions to the economy, but formed the crucial means of communication between the country-side and the higher reaches of the world of commerce'.[4]

Around 1300 there were perhaps 650 urban foundations in England, of which around 600 might reasonably be described as 'small'. 'Small towns' are defined as those with a population of between 300 and 2,000 people, a weekly market, and a distinctive occupational structure and topography.[5] The majority of English towns were boroughs, and the remainder were manorial market towns. Boroughs were places where some tenants enjoyed burgage tenure, and a variety of other trading privileges, and thus they were institutionally distinct from manorial mar-ket towns, which possessed no separate legal identity and were simply subsumed within the manorial holdings of landlords.[6] For example, in 1199 the Templars acquired a market charter and set aside forty-five acres of their rural manor of Witham to establish a new marketplace and a tightly-packed trading settlement. Late medieval Witham was undoubtedly urban, but legally it retained many 'ar-chaic' tenurial features typical of the rural manor.[7] It is difficult to be certain about the exact split between boroughs and market towns, because the calculation de-pends upon the definition of a town and the date chosen, but between sixty per cent and seventy-five per cent of all medieval English towns were boroughs.[8] The largest and wealthiest towns — those ranked in the top fifty by size and wealth — were almost exclusively boroughs, whereas a larger proportion of small towns were market towns.

The institutional and legal standing of a town was an important determinant of how it was governed, and, in particular, the extent to which the leading resi-dents were able to manage their own affairs. This aspect of small-town life has received less attention from historians, yet it comprises the central theme of this essay.[9] The relative neglect of this subject is entirely understandable, because ex-tant urban archives from the largest and greatest towns are much more informa-tive and plentiful than from the smaller ones. Urban historians have tended to be dismissive about the scope for self-government in the latter as a consequence,

---

[4]   Dyer, 'Small Places', 3.

[5]   Dyer, 'Small Towns', 505–6.

[6]   Hilton, English Peasantry, 77–8, 82–3; J. Laughton and C. Dyer, 'Small Towns in the East and West Midlands in the Later Middle Ages: A Comparison', Midland History, 24 (1999), 28–9.

[7]   Britnell, 'Witham', 13–15.

[8]   The higher figure is inferred from Dyer, 'Small Towns', 505–6. The lower figure is derived from Heather Swanson's estimate of 500 English towns, coupled with Donkin's observation that just under 300 boroughs were created in England before 1334: H. Swanson, British Me-dieval Towns (Basingstoke, 1999), 14; R. Donkin, 'Changes in the Later Middle Ages', in An Historical Geography of England before 1600, ed. H. C. Darby (Cambridge, 1977), 121–9.

[9]   The best introduction to small-town governance is Dyer, 'Small Towns', 526–32. The general indifference to the subject is exemplified by its complete omission from K. D. Lilley, Urban Life in the Middle Ages 1000–1450 (Basingstoke, 2002), which is otherwise exemplary.

ignoring the possibility that a lack of archival material is not necessarily indicative of the absence of self-government. Many would concur with Rodney Hilton's statement that 'small towns still had institutional structures which in many ways resembled those of the villages'. However, his subsequent assertion that small towns therefore lay in a state of limbo — they had 'lost the mutual solidarity of the peasant communities, without yet having acquired to replace it the apparatus of social control exercised by the rulers of the bigger boroughs' — is more contentious and unproven.[10]

The precise package of privileges enjoyed by boroughs varied from place to place, as did the extent to which the burgesses — its leading residents — were permitted to act as a corporate body: the grant of a charter enshrined the privileges of an individual borough. The range and extent of personal privileges, and the degree of corporate freedom from seigniorial authority, tended to be greatest in the larger towns.[11] This was especially true of royal boroughs, many of which were able to run their affairs with little or no interference from their feudal overlord, the crown. Burgesses in royal boroughs usually enjoyed a wide range of personal and trading privileges, together with collective privileges allowing them to administer the borough themselves, all in return for an annual rent, or 'fee farm'. Hence they enjoyed the freedom to collect the borough rents, tolls and perquisites, and to raise additional levies on the townsfolk; to run the market, fairs and courts belonging to the borough; to determine how to expend this burghal income; and to elect their own officials, including a town council to serve as an executive body.[12] In short, they exercised genuine and formal fiscal, judicial and administrative power as a corporate body. Royal boroughs constituted around thirty per cent of all borough foundations in medieval England.[13]

In contrast, burgesses in seigniorial (or 'mesne') boroughs tended to possess fewer personal privileges and no legal standing as a corporate body. They 'generally could not aspire to [the] independence' enjoyed by royal boroughs, and so, according to Whittle and Rigby, 'in seigniorial boroughs the townsmen were far less likely to achieve the administrative independence enjoyed by the burgesses of the royal towns'.[14] This is because the institutions of the mesne borough belonged to

---

[10]   Hilton, *English Peasantry*, 90–1.

[11]   Dyer, 'Small Towns', 526.

[12]   S. H. Rigby and E. Ewan, 'Government, Power and Authority 1300–1540', in *Cambridge Urban History*, ed. Palliser, 292–3.

[13]   P. T. H. Unwin, 'Towns and Trade 1066–1500', in *An Historical Geography of England and Wales*, ed. R. A. Dodgshon and R. A. Butlin (2nd edn, London, 1990), 129.

[14]   R. H. Hilton, 'Small Town Society in England before the Black Death', in *The Medieval Town: A Reader in English Urban History 1200–1500*, ed. R. Holt and G. Rosser (London, 1990), 87; Swanson, *Medieval British Towns*, 83; J. Whittle and S. H. Rigby, 'England: Popular Politics and Social Conflict', in *A Companion to Britain in the later Middle Ages*, ed. S. H. Rigby (Oxford, 2003), 78–9.

the lord as feudal overlord, not to the burgesses as a corporate body, and the lord directly ran them through his local officials. Hence there was no reason for the burgesses to meet or govern formally though a town council, because the borough was not theirs to administer. Lords, and especially monastic and resident lords, retained a close control over the administrative structures of their towns, appointing their own officials to run the key institutions of the borough court and market, and to collect all the burghal revenues.[15] Seigniorial boroughs were operated by lords for the townsfolk, for which reason they have been labelled 'towns without authority' when viewed from the perspective of the burgesses.[16] Indeed, the first historian of monastic boroughs laments 'the failure of the monastic corporations to recognise the growing corporate spirit of the townsmen and to concede to them rights of self government'.[17] Around seventy per cent of all medieval borough foundations were seigniorial.[18] Among mesne boroughs, more were founded by secular lords (sixty-one per cent) than ecclesiastical lords (thirty-nine per cent).[19]

Scholars have carefully explored the institutional arrangements prevailing within many of the largest seigniorial boroughs, not least because these represented some of the most important towns in England (such as Boston, Bury St Edmunds, Leicester, Southwark and Wells). In almost every case, the feudal overlord retained direct control over the key administrative functions within the borough, although the seigniorial desire to retain and exercise control was often at odds with the burgesses' desire for greater autonomy, which resulted in notoriously fractious relationships.[20] However, the burgesses still found informal ways to act as a corporate body and to influence the town's affairs, despite their lack of formal legal standing. For example, they often assumed responsibility for some public works, and they usually held some land as a community, both of which involved collective organisation and action. Furthermore, the burgesses often belonged to a particular religious fraternity within their town, whose meetings

---

[15] Dyer, 'Small Towns', 527; Swanson, *Medieval British Towns*, 78–9. Appointing seigniorial officers to run the market and the borough is regarded as a key element in retaining power over the burgesses: N. M. Trenholme, *The English Monastic Boroughs: A Study in Medieval History* (Columbia, Mo., 1927), 84–5; R. H. Hilton, 'Low Level Urbanisation: The Seigniorial Borough of Thornbury in the Later Middle Ages', in *The Medieval Manor Court*, ed. Z. Razi and R. M. Smith (Oxford, 1996), 484.

[16] S. Reynolds, *An Introduction to English Medieval Towns* (Oxford, 1977), 114–15.

[17] Trenholme, *Monastic Boroughs*, 1.

[18] Unwin, 'Towns and Trade', 129; Laughton and Dyer, 'Small Towns in the Midlands', 35. Dyer, 'Small Towns', 509–10.

[19] Unwin, 'Towns and Trade', 129.

[20] See, for example, Trenholme, *Monastic Boroughs*; S. H. Rigby, 'Boston and Grimsby in the Middle Ages: An Administrative Contrast', *Journal of Medieval History*, 10 (1984), 57–62; D. G. Shaw, *The Creation of a Community. The City of Wells in the Middle Ages* (Oxford, 1993); and M. Carlin, *Medieval Southwark* (London, 1996).

served as an informal and shadow council to discuss corporate issues, and as a court to resolve disputes: hence the device of the guild was craftily deployed 'as a surrogate government and a focus of urban identity'.[21]

Some of the practices adopted by the townsfolk of the greatest seigniorial boroughs were replicated in smaller ones. For example, the burgesses of modest towns such as Clare (Suffolk), Manchester (Lancashire) and Sheffield (Yorkshire) acquired and managed parcels of land and property on behalf of their fellow townsfolk. The quantity of land involved, and its local significance, could be considerable. Sidney and Beatrice Webb showed how the townsfolk of Beccles (Suffolk) held a 1,400-acre fen on a long-term lease from their overlord, and elected four fen reeves from the body of burgesses annually to administer it. The election and meetings of the fen reeves provided a legitimate forum through which the burgesses could appoint leaders and representatives, and thus discuss informally a much wider range of issues relating to the life of the town.[22] Similarly, the burgesses of some small mesne boroughs were answerable directly to the crown for a restricted range of responsibilities on its behalf: the 'bailiffs and commonalty' of Lymington (Hampshire) had to respond to royal demands for naval shipping, and in the 1320s the crown granted the burgesses of Burford (Oxfordshire) the right to collect tolls to pay for the upkeep of the town bridge.[23] Again, such responsibilities required the burgesses to act as a corporate body, which in turn helped to foster their sense of urban identity. Finally, the use of a religious fraternity as a front for organising urban affairs was also known among these smaller boroughs.[24] Chris Dyer cites the example of the Holy Cross guild in Stratford-upon-Avon (Warwickshire), and Richard Holt detects a similar arrangement in nearby Birmingham (Warwickshire).[25]

Hence the burgesses of small mesne boroughs could act as a collective group, and extend their influence over the corporate life of their town, in a variety of subtle and restricted ways, despite the formal legal restrictions upon them: in this sense, they followed the example of the greatest seigniorial boroughs. In every other sense, however, it has been assumed that the residents of small towns

---

[21] R. Holt and G. Rosser, 'Introduction: The English Town in the Middle Ages', in *Medieval Town*, ed. Holt and Rosser, 12–13; Rigby and Ewan, 'Government, Power and Authority', 292–5.

[22] S. and B. Webb, *The Manor and the Borough*, 1 (London, 1908), 134–6.

[23] 'Lymington Borough', in *Victoria County History of Hampshire and the Isle of Wight*, IV, ed. W. Page (London, 1911), 641; *The Burford Records: A Study in Minor Town Government*, ed. R. H. Gretton (Oxford, 1920), 18; G. A. Thornton, *A History of Clare, Suffolk* (Cambridge, 1928), 40.

[24] Dyer, 'Small Towns', 528; idem, 'Small Places', 10–11.

[25] C. Dyer, 'Medieval Stratford: A Successful Small Town', in *The History of an English Borough: Stratford upon Avon 1196–1996*, ed. R. Bearman (Stroud, 1997), 55–8; R. Holt, 'The Early History of the Town of Birmingham, 1166–1600', *Dugdale Society Occasional Papers*, 30 (1985), 13.

exercised no power over their affairs. If the wealthiest burgesses in the greatest seigniorial boroughs could only obtain some informal powers of self-government after decades of pressing and challenging, then it is reasonably assumed that the lowly burgesses of the smaller seigniorial boroughs achieved far less, because they lacked the economic muscle to wrestle any concessions from their lords. Similarly, it is assumed that the residents of manorial market towns enjoyed no autonomy, because they were mere local traders and craftsmen, subject to the feudal overlordship of their manorial lord, without any separate urban institutions. For these reasons it is widely held that, 'in general, the greater the size of the town, the more independent would be its system of government, and the majority of small towns were ruled by lords . . . some lords conceded rights of self-government to their towns . . . but most lords kept clear control'.[26]

This essay challenges the accepted wisdom that residents of small towns enjoyed little or no autonomy to run their affairs, and that they had no control mechanisms as an urban community. By considering more closely the institutional arrangements in small towns, and especially in mesne boroughs, it contends that their leading residents often wielded significant informal control over their towns. Indeed, it also goes much further to argue that the burgesses in many small mesne boroughs were able to attain direct and *formal* control over the key institutions of their towns, especially after the mid fourteenth century, in stark contrast to the larger seigniorial boroughs where such control was seldom obtained. Historians have long recognised that the residents of small towns in the seventeenth and eighteenth centuries could wrestle free of seigniorial control by taking over the rudimentary institutions of their borough, but the contention that this practice was widespread in the Middle Ages is novel.[27]

How might the burgesses of small mesne boroughs acquire formal control of the institutions of their towns? The principal sources of burghal revenue were the rents due from land and property, notably burgage plots, shops and stalls; the tolls payable on transactions in the weekly market and seasonal fairs; and the profits of jurisdiction from the borough (and perhaps also the market and fair) courts. The principal levers of power were the rights to collect and utilise these revenues; to exercise control over the borough court and the running of the market, both of which shaped the commercial effectiveness of the town; and the creation of an executive function to administer the town's affairs on behalf of the burgesses.

Historians have usually assumed that lords exploited all of these institutions directly for the purposes of both profit and power. Seigniorial officials are assumed to have collected the burghal rents, the tolls from markets and fairs, and

[26] Dyer, 'Small Towns', 526–7.
[27] Webb, *Manor and Borough*, I, 148–60.

run the market and borough courts on behalf of the lord. However, a landlord could choose to lease any or all of these key privileges and tasks to a third party for a fixed cash sum on a stipulated term, and, in so doing, would be effectively relinquishing control over them for the duration of the lease. Leasing some or all of a landlord's assets or privileges was an established and acceptable practice in medieval estate management, and it bestowed upon the lessee(s) considerable scope for private initiative and discretion in the exploitation of such assets.

It follows from these simple observations that the decision whether to lease burghal privileges or to exploit them directly carried great significance for the management of the borough and, by extension, the relations between landlord and burgesses, and for the trading conditions within the town. It also follows that the identity of the lessee(s), and the length of the lease, added further significance. The decision to lease the different components of the borough to different lessees, on successive short terms of a year or two, risked administrative discontinuity and internal dispute. On the other hand, leasing them all to the burgesses themselves for an extended period would confer extensive and formal (although not perpetual) rights of self-government and self-determination.

Hence it was entirely possible for the burgesses of seigniorial boroughs to obtain formal corporate autonomy by leasing their town from their lords for a term of years. This is not a contentious statement, yet it would be contentious to state that this arrangement was commonplace. After all, landlords did not lease the largest and wealthiest seigniorial boroughs, so why adopt a different policy with the smaller ones? Furthermore, urban historians have not previously identified or commented upon a widespread tendency to lease out any mesne boroughs: on the contrary, Edward Miller and John Hatcher concluded that before 1348 landlords exploited their small boroughs in a direct manner, thus retaining complete control over their management.[28] Unfortunately, few published studies of small towns make any comment on their management, concentrating instead upon their economic, social and topographical characteristics. However, a reworking of the published studies, supplemented by original research into a random sample of around twenty-five mesne boroughs for which documentation survives, reveals that landlords regarded their small towns in much the same way as they regarded any other asset on their estates: although they generally preferred to exploit them directly during the thirteenth and early fourteenth centuries, thereafter they shifted by degrees to rentier management.

There is ample evidence from the thirteenth and early fourteenth centuries to support Miller and Hatcher's view that landlords controlled their small mesne boroughs directly. Burford, Manchester, Salford (Lancashire) and Sheffield were

---

[28] E. Miller and J. Hatcher, *Medieval England: Towns, Commerce and Crafts, 1066–1348* (London, 1995), 287.

all directly run by their lords.[29] In 1282–3 the reeve of the manor of Bungay (Suffolk) rendered account for the collection of the borough rents (73s.), the tolls and perquisites of two fairs (55s.), and of the market (115s. 10d.), and also for the income of the borough court (small tolls, 60s.).[30] In 1265–6 the constable of Skipton (Yorkshire) organised and collected all the miscellaneous rents, tolls and perquisites generated from the two fledging boroughs of Howton and Plumpton, and recorded the income in his annual account.[31] In 1269–70 Beaulieu abbey ran its small borough of Great Faringdon (Berkshire) directly.[32]

There is, however, some evidence before 1348 of a mixed managerial approach, whereby a landlord exploited most of the components of the mesne borough, but leased one component — usually the market tolls — each year. In 1287–8 the reeve of the borough of Lymington (Hampshire) managed the borough rents, court and fair tolls directly on behalf of the earl of Devon, but the market tolls were leased for 30s., and a similar arrangement prevailed at Brading (Isle of Wight) on the same estate.[33] In 1285 the market and fair of Oakham (Rutland) were leased at farm.[34] Between 1268 and 1271 the borough court of Skipton was run and exploited directly by the lord, but the tolls and stallage of its weekly market, and of its two fairs, were leased for £16 13s. 4d. per annum.[35] The earliest surviving account (1350–1) for the manor of Thetford (Norfolk) records that the tolls from the weekly market, seasonal fairs and passage over the main bridge and ford through the town generated income of £8 3s. 4d., but previously they had generated £13 6s. 8d. per annum. Such rounded sums (in marks) are strongly indicative of leasing.[36] Seigniorial officials collected all of the rents and curial perquisites due from the borough of Sudbury (Suffolk), indicating that the borough court was administered directly, but the tolls of the weekly market and annual fairs were leased to an unnamed lessee for £10; similarly, the market of nearby Clare was routinely farmed for £6 per annum throughout the early fourteenth century.[37] In all of the above examples, a mixed approach to the exploitation of the main institutions of the borough was a sustained managerial policy.[38]

29   *Burford Records*, ed. Gretton, 16–18; J. Tait, *Medieval Manchester and the Beginnings of Lancashire* (Manchester, 1904), 51, 54–5, 57.
30   TNA, SC6/991/20.
31   TNA, SC6/1087/6.
32   *The Account Book of Beaulieu Abbey*, ed. S. F. Hockey (Camden Society, 4th ser. 16, 1975), 84.
33   TNA, SC6/984/11.
34   TNA, SC6/964/1 (Oakham), where the heading states 'Farms . . . of the market and fair', but fire damage to the account means that the detail is lost.
35   TNA, SC6/1087/6.
36   TNA, DL29/288/4719; A. Crosby, *A History of Thetford* (Chichester, 1986), 33.
37   TNA, SC6/1006/16 (Sudbury); for Clare, see, for example, TNA, SC6/992/9, 14, 18, 23, and SC6/993/5–9.
38   In a few cases, this approach appears to have been a temporary expedient, created by circumstances that are not apparent. For example, although the honor of Gloucester directly

The decision to lease the market — i.e. effectively handing over the running of the core function of a market town to a third party — carried significant implications for the governance and commercial effectiveness of a small town. Unfortunately, before c.1348 the identity of the lessee is seldom stated.

Finally, in a small number of cases, there is some evidence before c.1348 that a few boroughs were leased entirely. Sometimes, this policy appears to have been a temporary expedient, a short-term change to the standard practice of direct exploitation for unexplained reasons. So, although at the end of the thirteenth century the borough of Bungay was usually exploited directly, in 1291, and then again in 1306, it was wholly leased for a rent of £20.[39] In 1287–8 both the tolls of the market and the perquisites of the borough court of Newport (Isle of Wight) were bundled into a single lease for £13 6s. 8d., when other boroughs on the same estate were directly exploited.[40] Yet, elsewhere, leasing was the predominant, deliberate and sustained policy. The earldom (from 1337 the duchy) of Cornwall routinely leased the boroughs of Grampound, Helston and Launceston (Cornwall), while retaining other Cornish boroughs in direct management (see Table 6.1).[41] The boroughs of Hitchin and Standon (both Hertfordshire) were routinely leased, and in 1346 John son of Robert paid 25s. 'for the farm of the market, tolls and rents of stallage' at Lidgate (Suffolk).[42] In the 1160s the entire manor of Doncaster (Yorkshire), including the borough, was farmed to a consortium of local men. In the 1270s the manor was back in direct exploitation, but the market tolls were still leased to locals.[43] The borough of Leeds (Yorkshire) was leased throughout the early fourteenth century, even when other components of the manor were exploited directly. 'The farm of the borough of Leeds' entitled the lessee to collect the income from the land rents owed by all the burgesses; the tolls from the weekly (Monday) market, including stallage; the perquisites of the borough court; and the tolls from two fairs held on 29 June and 28 October each year. In addition, it usually included the common oven and the manorial water mills, and in 1322–3 it was valued at a sizeable £42 per annum. This extensive

exploited Burford most of the time, its records note that in 1231, 54s. 4d. was received 'for the *farm* of the borough mill and market' (my italics): *Burford Records*, ed. Gretton, 18. Similarly, in 1282 the tolls of the market and fairs at Manchester generated £6 13s. 4d., a rounded sum which either must be a valuation or is strongly indicative of leasing: Tait, *Medieval Manchester*, 45.

39   TNA, SC6/991/25 and 28.
40   TNA, SC6/984/11.
41   For the background to the Cornish estates, see J. Hatcher, *Rural Economy and Society in the Duchy of Cornwall 1300 to 1500* (Cambridge, 1970), 18–28.
42   M. Bailey, 'The Economy of Towns and Markets 1100 to 1500', in *A County of Small Towns*, ed. Slater and Goose, 49–50. For Lidgate, see TNA SC6/1002/16 and M. Bailey, *Medieval Suffolk: An Economic and Social History c.1200 to c.1500* (Woodbridge, 2007), 120–1.
43   P. J. P. Goldberg, 'From Conquest to Corporation', in *Doncaster: A Borough and its Charters*, ed. G. H. Martin (Doncaster, 1995), 49–50.

package provided the lessee with the autonomy to run the borough of Leeds free of any seigniorial interference. Indeed, the manorial lord (the aristocratic and non-resident de Lacy family) had no interest in administering the borough directly even in one year (1326–7) when a lessee could not be found, preferring instead to parcel out the individual components on an ad hoc basis to the highest bidders (recorded in the account as *de exitus* payments).[44]

Overall, then, this evidence reveals approaches to the management of seigniorial boroughs before 1348 a good deal more varied than historians had previously assumed. Many components of small seigniorial boroughs were exploited directly, just like in the larger seigniorial boroughs. However, in a number of places the tolls of the weekly market were leased separately. It would have been administratively irksome for landlords and their officials to run a market directly, given the modest size of many of them, and the variable volumes of trade transacted there each week, so that leasing for a fixed annual rent made good sense. Of course, the lessees of a market franchise were required to uphold statutes, local customs and privileges, and to render the agreed rental each year, but otherwise they were free to run things as they saw fit. Finally, in a minority of places, there is clear evidence that the whole of the borough was leased to a third party. This approach was not a characteristic of the management of larger mesne boroughs in this period, and therefore it represents a deliberate and particular administrative choice for smaller ones. Unfortunately, and frustratingly, the sources dating from this period seldom state the identity of the lessee of either the market or the borough, although the task of running them would have been convenient enough for any local burgess or resident who was commercially active.

Whatever the extent of leasing of small mesne boroughs before the middle of the fourteenth century, the practice became widespread thereafter. Increasingly, the key components of the borough (market and fair tolls, and the borough court) were leased together as a single package, and the documents also become more explicit about the identity of the lessee(s), an invaluable piece of evidence if we are to understand fully the governance of these places. The evidence for leasing in the fifteenth century is so compelling and commonplace from the random sample of around twenty-five boroughs that it is remarkable that urban historians up to now have neither commented upon the tendency nor highlighted its significance. The following discussion provides examples to support this statement, but also to outline the permutations in leasing strategies and their implications for the government of small seigniorial boroughs.

The shift to widespread leasing was pronounced by the 1460s on the estate of the duchy of Cornwall (Table 6.2), where the only boroughs not to be leased —

44 'Documents Relating to the Manor and Borough of Leeds 1066–1400', ed. J. le Patourel (Thoresby Society 45, 1956), 15–16, 31, 33.

Table 6.1: Exploitation of some boroughs on the estate of the duchy of Cornwall in 1338–9

Borough	Rents	Tolls	Borough court	Fee farm	Lessee
Bossiney	£9 11s. 8d.	2s. 4d.	22s. 7d.		
Camelford	£4 7s. 8d.	8s. 6d.	29s. 8d.		
Grampound				£26 13s. 4d.	Not stated
Helston				£12 11s. 4d.	Not stated
Launceston				£5	Not stated

Source: TNA, SC6/816/11

Table 6.2: Exploitation of some boroughs on the estate of the duchy of Cornwall in 1461–2

Borough	Rents	Tolls	Borough court	Fee farm	Lessee
Bossiney	£9 9s. 17d.				
Bradnich	£7 4s. 5d.		21s.		
Camelford				£4 5s. 4d.	Burgesses
Crampound				£12 11s. 4d.	Not stated
Helston				£6 13s. 4d.	Burgesses
Launceston				£5	Burgesses
Liskeard				£13 1s. 6d.	Not stated
Lydford	31s. 3d.		2s. 6d.		
Saltash				£18	Burgesses

Source: TNA, SC6/821/11

Bossiney, Bradnich and Lydford — had probably ceased to exist as active trading centres by that date. Significantly, four of the six boroughs at farm were leased in their entirety to the burgesses of each town, and the rental payments were described as a 'fee farm'. Burgesses were obvious candidates to become lessees of their mesne borough, and after c.1350 this is a familiar pattern. For example, from 1422 the identity of the lessees of the market and fair at Sudbury is revealed explicitly as 'the burgesses of the vill', and, additionally, a large area of town pasture, and the borough fishery, were farmed to the 'commoners of the vill'.[45] It follows from these arrangements that the townsfolk of Sudbury were actively, directly and corporately responsible for the administration of major assets within their borough.

Standon (Hertfordshire) provides one of the finest and clearest examples of

[45] TNA, SC6/1006/27.

the high degree of autonomy that could be obtained by the burgesses of a small mesne borough. In the 1320s 'the borough of Standon, [its] tolls, markets, stallage, fairs and six acres of land' were leased to its burgesses for £6 13s. 8d., payable at four annual terms, and the proceeds of the borough court were split equally between the manor and the burgesses.[46] This arrangement provided the community of burgesses with extensive control over the borough, directly comparable to that enjoyed in royal boroughs. They collected all the rents of the borough; they ran every aspect of the market and fairs, from regulating the traders, and collecting rents from stalls and booths. The inclusion within the lease of 'six acres of land' suggests that they also controlled the land upon which the small borough was situated, including the market place and fairground.

Subsequent manorial account rolls for Standon are neither plentiful nor evenly distributed, but every surviving account from the fourteenth and fifteenth centuries confirms that the burgesses continued to lease, and therefore control, the borough. Economic decline meant that they paid progressively less for the privilege: in 1471–2, for example, the burgesses paid 66s. 8d. 'for the fee farm of the borough'.[47] There is no evidence that the lord of the manor — who was a distant, non-resident, aristocrat — or his officials involved themselves in the daily affairs of the town, other than collecting the annual farm. The only exception to this occurred in 1367, when the landlord petitioned Edward III to close a successful neighbouring market, which he claimed was damaging the trade of his borough of Standon: this petition, which was unsuccessful, must have been instigated by the burgesses.[48]

Thus it is probable that the small seigniorial borough of Standon was leased in its entirety and continuously to its own burgesses for at least two centuries. We have no way of knowing how they organised themselves internally to run their borough, because none of their own records — assuming they kept any — have survived. Yet the longevity with which they ran its affairs must have resulted in the establishment of certain fixed structures for administration, and set procedures for conducting business, presumably along the lines of those established in royal boroughs. It is therefore probable that they elected a bailiff and other lesser officials annually, to take executive action on behalf of all the burgesses, and they probably elected their own town council: given that they were legitimately in control of their own affairs, they would have no obvious need for the device of a religious guild to act as a surrogate council. The burgesses certainly had to make some decisions of importance as a collective body. For example, it is unlikely that the decision in 1367 to make representations to their manorial lord

---

[46]   TNA, SC6/868/19.

[47]   TNA, SC6/870/8.

[48]   M. Bailey, 'A Tale of Two Towns: Buntingford and Standon in the Later Middle Ages', *Journal of Medieval History*, 19 (1993), 360–2.

about the commercial threat posed by the emergence of a local market was made by a single burgess acting unilaterally. Similarly, the financial management of the annual lease of the borough would throw up issues annually which affected the whole body of burgesses: how to dispose of any surplus cash remaining after the annual farm had been paid to the manor (to be spent collectively on behalf of the burgesses, or divided between them as a form of profit share) or how to fund any shortfall.

In contrast to the example of Standon, not all small town burgesses were successful in acquiring direct and unobstructed control over all the components of their borough. For example, throughout the fourteenth and fifteenth centuries the landed rents of the borough of Clare were collected directly by the lord's officials, who also ran, and collected the perquisites from, the borough court, although after 1425 the burgesses are explicitly named as the lessees 'of the fee farm of the market', and they obtained episodic remission from their rent due to their collective poverty. They also came to acquire *de facto* control over the borough court, because from 1431 the borough bailiffs were elected through 'the advice and discretion of the burgesses'.[49] Hence the burgesses of Clare ran the borough market as lessees without interruption for most of the fifteenth century, and had probably done so throughout much of the fourteenth century too; they exercised *de facto* control over the borough and market courts; and after the 1430s they even appointed the borough bailiffs (responsibility for which had previously been invested in the lord). Consequently, the lord of Clare had little say over the running of his borough.

The identity of the borough lessees is usually stated in fifteenth-century account rolls. If not leased to the body of burgesses, the borough was leased to named individuals, although in such cases it is not easy to establish their status or background. For example, in 1375–6 the market, fair and borough court (portmoot) of Oakham were leased for £23 to William Chamberlain and John Wappelode, with only the rents from the burgage plots paid directly to the lord. Chamberlain was a certainly a local man, because he was also renting pastures for his animals from the demesne, but we learn nothing else about him.[50] In 1404 the mesne borough of Chesterfield (Derbyshire) was subsumed within the lease of the manor to five named men for £56 13s. 4d. per annum for a twenty-year term. One of the five was John Callow, a wealthy Chesterfield merchant and therefore a likely burgess. It might be instructive that, within four years of this grant, a royal commission was dispatched to Chesterfield to investigate allegations that a group of men had obstructed the bailiff from collecting market tolls. We have no more than these fragmentary details, but this looks suspiciously like a handful of

---

[49]   The market and fair had been routinely leased in the fourteenth century, but the lessees were not named. Thornton, *History of Clare*, 41–3; TNA, SC6/HenVII/1448 (1491–2).

[50]   TNA, SC6/964/5.

burgesses running the borough as lessees, in a manner which brought them into conflict with either other burgesses or townsfolk. In the 1470s the borough was back in the lord's hands.[51]

The difficulties in reconstructing the background of some of the individual lessees are illustrated by the example of Leeds. They are identified in only four out of ten extant accounts between 1322 and 1400, and there is insufficient incidental information to construct anything more than the most rudimentary profiles of those who are named. For example, in 1322–3 the lease was taken by William Paslew senior and John Godfrey. They were both burgesses, because an extent of 1341 lists two John Godfreys, both of whom were 'free burgesses' of Leeds, while Paslew was also listed as a free burgess 'for a term'.[52] In 1373–4 the lessee is named as John Maysard, who was a prominent and active local tradesman in the 1370s and 1380s, although his family had not been established burgesses in 1341.[53] In both these cases, we can be certain that the borough of Leeds was being run by local tradespeople. Whether they did so as enterprising individuals, or as the named senior representatives of the community of burgesses, is unknowable.

We can be certain that the profile of the lessees of the borough of Leeds changed significantly from the 1380s, after which date they were exclusively from gentry families: initially Sir Robert Neville (1382 and 1388) and then Sir Roger de Leeds (1388 to 1400).[54] Neither family was recorded as burgesses in the extent of 1341, nor can we find evidence of their involvement in commerce. Neville was a local landowner and active justice of the peace in the West Riding, while the de Leeds family held a small local manor and Sir Roger was active in leasing meadow locally and granting quarrying rights over his land.[55] In 1398 his son, William de Leeds, was accused of ambushing and murdering one William Passelow just outside the town 'with the assent of Roger'. The surname of the victim may be a coincidence, but, if not, it is suggestive of serious conflict between an unsympathetic lessee of the borough and the offspring of a long-established family of burgesses.[56] During the fifteenth century a succession of gentry landlords leased the borough, usually on terms of around twenty years. Some, such as Gilbert Leigh, were clearly enterprising and commercially orientated individuals.[57] Whatever the background or disposition of these lessees, the lord of Leeds — and its body

---

[51]   J. M. Bestall, *History of Chesterfield*, 1: *Early and Medieval Chesterfield* (Chesterfield, 1974), 69, 90–1.

[52]   'Manor and Borough', ed. Le Patourel, 15–16, 32–3.

[53]   Ibid., 32–3, 52, 54, 60, 71.

[54]   Ibid., 59, 70.

[55]   *CPR, 1388–92*, 343, 439; 'Manor and Borough', ed. Le Patourel, 32, 45, 61–2.

[56]   *CPR, 1396–99*, 465; *CPR, 1399–1401*, 310, 472.

[57]   *The Manor and Borough of Leeds 1425–1662: An Edition of Documents*, ed. J. W. Kirby (Thoresby Society 57, 1981), 4, 10, 19, 272–3, 276–7.

of burgesses — appear to have had no direct involvement in the running of this borough at any stage after the late fourteenth century.

If the violence recorded at Leeds in 1398, and at Chesterfield in 1409, was rooted in conflicting interests between lessee and burgesses over the running of the borough, then it is indicative of another potential source of social tension within urban society. It is easy to imagine how a non-commercial lessee, or one ruthlessly bent upon commercial self interest, could pursue policies contrary to those which suited the townsfolk, which could then readily flare into conflict. It is probably not coincidental that the accession of new lords to the manor of Doncaster in the 1360s resulted in a rise in tension within the town.[58] The practice of appointing members of the local gentry as lessees of their boroughs, presumably as an act of patronage, raised the likelihood of dispute. Indeed, some lessees might have had an irreconcilable conflict of interest: for example, in 1352–3 the borough of Trematon (Cornwall) was leased, remarkably, to the burgesses of nearby Saltash (Cornwall).[59]

The potential complexity of governance in mesne boroughs, and the historian's difficulties in reconstructing them, are exemplified at Thetford. Its burgesses had been active as a corporate body since the thirteenth century, when they were accustomed to electing a mayor annually as their most senior representative. However, the mayor remained answerable, and therefore subservient, to the landlord's most senior official, the bailiff of the manor of Thetford. Little else is recoverable about the day-to-day administration of the borough at this earlier date, but from the mid fourteenth century the burgesses began to wield greater formal influence over their borough. In part, this was a consequence of obtaining formal extensions to their privileges from their manorial lord. In 1373 the lord elevated the office of mayor to a status superior to that of the manorial bailiff, and by the late fifteenth century only a former mayor could occupy the office of coroner, which hitherto had been the pre-eminent royal appointment within the borough. Both of these changes presented the burgesses with formal opportunities to control the borough's affairs directly.[60] Their influence was probably extended further by holding and running their own borough court separately, free from manorial interference: there is no reference to any income from a borough court in the extant manorial accounts of Thetford, which suggests that it fell wholly within the jurisdiction of the burgesses.

---

[58]   Goldberg, 'Conquest to Corporation', 51–2.

[59]   TNA, SC6/817/3. A further source of tension might arise if a landlord granted the financial proceeds from the lease of a borough to a third party, such as when the Black Prince temporarily granted the fee farm of Liskeard to Sir William Danbeneye, because the recipient might seek to interfere in the running of the town: TNA, SC6/817/3 (Liskeard). This happened when the annual rent for the Buntingford market was granted to a third party, Bailey, 'Tale of Two Towns', 362.

[60]   Crosby, *History of Thetford*, 30–3, 65.

During the fifteenth century the lords of Thetford did not adopt a consistent managerial approach to the administration of the borough. Between the 1420s and mid 1430s the borough market and fairs were directly managed under the control of the three leading manorial officials, judging by the marked variation in annual revenues. After 1436 the tolls were once again leased for the fixed sum of £8, initially to John Lewys, who was bailiff of the manor in successive years between 1434 and 1438 and therefore a prominent local man and probably a burgess.[61] The tolls remained at farm continuously between the late 1430s and 1480, but unfortunately Lewys' successors are not identified in the accounts. While the tolls of the market were leased, its court continued under direct seigniorial control (perhaps as a means of exercising some residual control over the lessee). However, its income fell dramatically as soon as the market tolls were leased in 1436 (it had averaged 38s. 7d. between 1420 and 1435 [eight years], compared to 21s. 9d. between 1436 and 1461 [ten years]), and the number of market courts held each year declined, from around forty courts to twenty-two, between the 1430s and the 1450s. These snippets of evidence indicate a complex and shifting set of arrangements, although one suspects that from the late 1430s the burgesses were heavily involved as lessees of the market and fairs, and controlled their own borough court at the expense of the lord's market court.[62]

The above examples are all taken from lay estates, which is entirely appropriate given that the majority of mesne boroughs were founded by lay landlords. They demonstrate conclusively that most small mesne boroughs were leased in the later Middle Ages, and that the lessees tended to be either the body of burgesses or individual burgesses acting as representatives of the other burgesses or as independent agents. Ecclesiastical landlords were not as prolific founders of mesne boroughs, although, among ecclesiastics, Benedictines and bishoprics were the most active.[63] It is likely that Benedictine landlords were generally much less permissive in their approach to leasing, and therefore to the administration, of their small boroughs. They tended to be conservative estate managers, who displayed a stronger inclination to protect the rights and privileges of their houses, characteristics which made them less likely to alienate them and more likely to exploit their mesne boroughs directly. Unfortunately, the classic studies of monastic estates seldom discuss the ways in which their small mesne boroughs were

---

[61]   TNA, DL29/292/4793 (1434–5); DL29/292/4795 (1436–7); DL29/292/4797 (1437–8).

[62]   TNA, DL29/290/4773; DL29/290/4775; DL29/291/4778; DL29/291/4781; DL29/291/4787; DL29/291/4788; DL29/291/4791; DL29/292/4793; DL29/292/4795; DL29/292/4797; DL29/292/4805 (1438–9); DL29/292/4806 (1439–40); DL29/292/4808 (1440–1); DL29/293/4810 (1443–4); DL29/293/4811 (1444–5); DL29/293/4820 (1451–2); DL29/293/4828 (1452–3); DL29/294/4832 (1455–6); DL29/294/4836 (1459–60); DL29/294/4838 (1460–1); DL29/295/4847 (1479–80).

[63]   Laughton and Dyer, 'Small Towns in the Midlands', 35.

managed.[64] However, Hilton demonstrated how Evesham abbey exercised heavy control over its town, and Dyer has revealed how monastic lords retained firm and direct control over the boroughs of Cirencester (Gloucestershire) and Shipston-on-Stour, which led to local antagonism and conflict.[65] Likewise, the bishopric of Lincoln exploited Banbury (Oxfordshire) directly for most of the Middle Ages, which probably explains why the burgesses utilised a powerful guild to represent their interests in the absence of formal structures for self-government.[66]

Yet, for the most part, bishoprics tended to be run along the lines of lay estates, and they appear to have been more willing to lease their mesne boroughs. The bishopric of Worcester established the institutional and topographical framework of the borough of Stratford-upon-Avon (Warwickshire), but then left the residents 'to get on with their own business', and by the late fifteenth century its burgesses were leasing the tolls of the market and fairs.[67] Similarly, the bishopric of Winchester routinely leased the burghal institutions of Witney (Oxfordshire) to local burgesses.[68] By the late fifteenth century the bishopric of London was leasing many of its manors, and, within those leases, many of its boroughs. For example, in 1464–5 Maldon (Essex) was leased for £6 13s. 4d. to John Fuller and John Hosier, 'bailiffs of the vill there for their fee farm', phraseology which is strongly indicative of the lease of the borough to its burgesses. The manor of Chelmsford (Essex) was leased for the substantial sum of £40 to Thomas Tendering, who still held the lease in 1496, while the manor of Bishop's Stortford (Hertfordshire) was leased for £32: in both cases, the manorial lease almost certainly included the borough.[69] One of the lessees of Stortford, Thomas Rotor or Rutor, was a prominent townsman.[70]

At first glance, the prospect of the residents of manorial market towns obtaining any control over their affairs seems remote. After all, they were mere manorial tenants, who did not enjoy any of the benefits of burgage tenure, and their towns did not possess any separate urban institutions. Peculiarly urban issues — such

---

[64] See, for example, H. P. R. Finberg, *Tavistock Abbey: A Study in the Social and Economic History of Devon* (Newton Abbot, 1969), 74–5, 204–7.

[65] R. Hilton, *Crisis, Conflict and the Crisis of Feudalism* (London, 1990), 119–20; C. Dyer, 'Small Town Conflict in the Later Middle Ages: Events at Shipston-on-Stour', *Urban History*, 19 (1992), 183–210.

[66] 'Banbury: Introduction and Growth to 1554', in *Victoria County History of Oxfordshire*, x, ed. A. Crossley (London, 1972), 71–3.

[67] Dyer, 'Medieval Stratford', 51, 55; C. Dyer, *Lords and Peasants in a Changing Society: The Estates of the Bishopric of Worcester, 680–1540* (Cambridge, 1980), 185–6, 280.

[68] 'Witney Borough: Local Government', in *Victoria County History of Oxfordshire*, xiv, ed. S. Townley (London, 2004), 104, 111–12.

[69] TNA, SC6/1140/25, and SC6/Henvii/1107.

[70] *The Early Churchwardens' Accounts of Bishop's Stortford 1431–1558*, ed. S. R. Doree (Hertfordshire Record Publications 10, 1994), 128, 134, 142.

as the regulation of trade, and keeping the town clean and safe — were handled through a combination of three (manor, leet and market) courts, which were run directly by the landlord or his officials. These institutional arrangements enabled landlords to maintain their control over such places, as illustrated by the example of Mildenhall (Suffolk). Its landlord, the cellarer of the abbey of Bury St Edmunds, retained a close interest in the commercial activities of this sizeable market town, resulting in a succession of violent flashpoints and, ultimately, the stultification of its development.[71]

Yet, in the spirit and context of our reassessment of governance in small mesne boroughs, one might advance three good reasons for supposing that many other manorial towns obtained a good degree of *de facto* self-government. First, why should landlords bother themselves with an active and regular involvement in the running of the daily business of market towns? The benefits that might accrue to such a policy — either to their revenues or prestige — do not obviously outweigh the hassle of the routine administrative involvement in such modest markets and localised trade. Second, landlords could, and did, choose to hand over the effective running of the main manorial institutions to the residents. For example, fifteenth-century Newmarket (Suffolk) was efficiently and flexibly run by its leading inhabitants with little interference from its absentee landlord, and Romford (Essex) enjoyed similar autonomy.[72] This point applies particularly to the market franchise, which could be leased in exactly the same manner as in mesne boroughs: for example, in the early fourteenth century the markets of Forncett (Norfolk) and Needham (Suffolk) were at farm for small, rounded, sums.[73] Finally, innovative legal devices were sometimes deployed to enable the leading inhabitants to assume formal control of the operation of the weekly market. The lay landlord of Hadleigh (Suffolk) leased the market franchise to six local men, who in turn entrusted the lease, together with the land upon which the market square and hall were located, to nominated trustees on behalf of the townsfolk: the market was thus run without seigniorial involvement, and in the middle of the fifteenth century the trustees were sufficiently wealthy and organised to construct a magnificent new market and guild hall on the land.[74] Likewise,

---

[71]   C. Dyer, 'The Rising of 1381 in Suffolk and its Participants', *Proceedings of the Suffolk Institute of Archaeology and History*, 26 (1988), 225–8; M. Bailey, *A Marginal Economy? East Anglian Breckland in the Later Middle Ages* (Cambridge, 1989), 140, 304–7; J. Sears, 'Trade and Commerce in Mildenhall c.1350 to c.1500' (MStud. thesis, University of Cambridge, 2007), 11–17.

[72]   J. Davis, 'The Representation, Regulation and Behaviour of Petty Traders in Late Medieval England' (PhD thesis, University of Cambridge, 2001), 288–90; M. K. McIntosh, *Autonomy and Community: The Royal Manor of Havering 1200–1500* (Cambridge, 1986), 152–60, 201–15. Market towns located on ancient demesne probably enjoyed considerable autonomy: Hilton, *English Peasantry*, 76–87.

[73]   TNA SC6/1121/1 and SC6/995/14, m. 6.

[74]   S. Andrews and T. Springall, *Hadleigh and the Albaster Family* (Bildeston, 205), 7–8; Bailey, *Medieval Suffolk*, plate 13.

in 1367 the lady of the manor of Chipping (Hertfordshire) granted a market franchise to the inhabitants of the fledging town of Buntingford (Hertfordshire), who thereafter administered it through their own court and officials, and laid out a new market place. Consequently, the townsfolk acted as a self-governing body, fiercely resistant to any external interference in their affairs.[75] There are three reasonable grounds, then, for suggesting that the leading residents of manorial market towns could acquire a substantial role in the running of the institutions of trade within their communities.

Urban historians have long argued that the burgesses and residents of small towns found some informal ways to run their affairs and to nurture a sense of urban community, despite lacking formal legal powers or recognition. This essay has demonstrated that such townsfolk could also exercise formal control over their town by leasing some or all of the burghal and trading institutions from the lord. This simple device, which became widely utilised in the fourteenth and fifteenth centuries, possessed a formal status that transferred complete control of the nominated assets away from the landlord for a term. The number of small mesne boroughs leased to their burgesses, or to other local people, increased markedly during the course of the Middle Ages, so that by the fifteenth century it was the standard method of administration. This was especially true of lay and episcopal estates, less true of monastic ones.

It follows, therefore, that the decision whether to lease, what to lease, to whom and for how long were important, influential and potentially unpredictable variables in determining both the precise extent of self-government in small seigniorial boroughs, and its quality. Furthermore, control over those variables laid largely in the hands of the landlord or his estate officials. The landlord determined which, if any, of the range of borough institutions was to be offered at leasehold, and, as we have seen, the variety in this regard was considerable: in some boroughs, only the tolls of the market and fairs were leased and all other burghal elements remained directly managed by the landlord, while, in others, all the borough institutions were leased. The landlord might decide to lease these components at some times, and to exploit them directly at others. The landlord was also instrumental in determining the length of the lease(s), and/or the readiness with which it was renewed upon termination to the same lessee(s).

The outcome of this decision-making had a significant bearing upon the consequent degree of urban self-government. A decision to lease the whole borough to its body of burgesses continuously, or on a lengthy lease, bestowed upon that community significant corporate power, akin to that enjoyed by burgesses in royal boroughs. The example of Standon represents the ultimate expression of what was possible through this mechanism: the burgesses as a corporate body

---

[75] Bailey, 'Tale of Two Towns', 359, 361–3; idem, 'Economy of Towns', 51–2.

leased and ran all the institutions of their borough uninterrupted for at least two centuries, with no interference from their landlord. It is highly unlikely that such places failed to develop some permanent 'apparatus of social control', and stable institutions of government, as Hilton had once feared. Leasing to a single burgess, or to a consortium of burgesses, would have had a similar effect, as long as those burgesses were simply the nominated representative(s) of the corporate body: this policy might, however, cause division within the burgesses if the lessee(s) were operating as a private individual, or on behalf of a self-interested elite. Finally, leasing to an outsider, such as a local landlord, was more likely to cause administrative instability, because it increased the risk of a direct clash of interests with the townsfolk and thus the prospect of conflict. Social tensions within medieval towns are usually categorised in three ways: those generated from relations between the landlord and the townsfolk; those emanating from within the body of burgesses; and those between the burgesses and other townsfolk.[76] This study has identified another potential source of tension, namely from the relationship between the lessee and the townsfolk.

Although the leasing of boroughs presented real opportunities to small town burgesses for formal self-government, they could never be assured of the permanence of their arrangements. First, there was no certainty of renewal at the end of the term, and landlords deployed leases precisely because they represented no more than a *temporary* alienation of assets. Second, for most of the later Middle Ages, the tenant of a lease for a term of years was not permitted to defend the title under the common law, and, in this respect, leasehold enjoyed no more legal protection than tenures in villeinage. Leases were regarded in law as an economic, not tenurial, arrangement. In contrast, royal boroughs held their land and privileges through a fee farm, which was defensible in common law: it was regarded as a feudal tenure, because it was held heritably for a perpetual rent.[77]

Landlords do not appear to have shown any inclination to lease the institutions of the greater mesne boroughs. The prestige and symbolism attached to administering the larger towns directly, the substantial revenues involved, and, perhaps, the political influence it brought, persuaded lords to retain direct control of these places. Furthermore, resident monastic lords appeared determined to retain direct control over the town outside their walls. Smaller mesne boroughs were less important and lucrative, and so their exploitation was primarily a matter of administrative convenience: consequently, they were simply an asset which became swept along by the general drift towards rentier farming during the later Middle Ages. Perhaps awareness that the burgesses of lesser mesne boroughs often enjoyed formal control of their towns heightened the frustration felt by the burgesses of the greater mesne boroughs.

[76] Rigby and Ewan, 'Government, Power and Authority', 295.
[77] A. W. B. Simpson, *A History of the Land Law* (2nd edn, Oxford, 1986), 72–7.

Why did the managerial approach to small boroughs change so dramatically between the thirteenth and fifteenth centuries? The first reason is the change in trading conditions. The contracting volume of local trade and commercial transactions after *c*.1350 created enormous challenges for towns, and it made sense for landlords to hand over control of urban assets to local people who knew that trade intimately, and who had a vested interest in a successful outcome. Second, the growth of leasing also owed something to the general drift away from direct exploitation towards rentier management on the larger seigniorial estates. Indeed, landlords may have been keen to nurture boroughs directly when institutionally immature in the thirteenth century, but were probably less inclined to be protective about more mature institutions in the fifteenth century. Third, the general use of leases became more widespread after *c*.1350, and their security of tenure was gradually increasing: in the late fifteenth century, Littleton implied that lawyers now regarded leasehold as feudal tenures.[78] However, after 1440 the use of leasehold tenure to transfer urban assets was itself gradually overtaken by the legal device of incorporation, which enabled towns to hold land as a perpetual body and to issue by-laws (among other things) formally and securely.[79] The widespread experience of some form of self-government in the small towns of late medieval England must have created a context for the emergence of incorporation: one suspects that the townsfolk in places such as Woodstock (Oxfordshire, incorporated 1453) and Southwold (Suffolk, 1489) had already enjoyed a good deal of autonomy before their formal act of incorporation.[80]

Although the policy of leasing constituted a fillip to local self government for many bodies of burgesses, it is not clear whether it made any real difference to the economic competitiveness of a town. Did small seigniorial boroughs enjoy better economic fortunes when directly managed by their landlord, or did lessees run the markets, fairs and courts in a way which better suited the needs of traders and thus enhanced their effectiveness? Intuitively, the latter seems most likely. However, the example of Standon indicates the difficulty in finding a decisive answer to this question: the borough appears to have flourished when run by its burgesses in the early fourteenth century, despite an unfavourable geographical location, yet self-governing burgesses could not prevent its spiralling economic decline in the fifteenth century.[81]

Although the economic benefits of self-government are difficult to prove, its wider significance was considerable. It provides an example of the loosening of seigniorial control of the institutions of trade, which Larry Epstein envisaged

[78] Ibid., 74, 77–8.
[79] M. Weinbaum, *The Incorporation of Boroughs* (Manchester, 1936), 65–8; Reynolds, *Introduction*, 113; Rigby and Ewan, 'Government, Power and Authority', 298.
[80] Reynolds, *Introduction*, 114.
[81] Bailey, 'Tale of Two Towns', 366–8.

as the crucial element in the transition from feudalism to capitalism, and it also supports Dimmock's sense that the catalytic role of small towns in the English transition has been overlooked.[82] An observation made by Richard Britnell upon a different, but similar, issue seems an appropriate way to end: while it is doubtful whether the running of seigniorial boroughs by their burgesses brought a significant increase in average prosperity to these towns, the arrangement was — at the very least — important in building and developing civic society in Britain.[83]

---

[82] S. R. Epstein, 'Rodney Hilton, Marxism and the transition from feudalism to capitalism', in *Rodney Hilton's Middle Ages*, ed. P. Coss and C. Wickham (*P&P* Supplement 2 , 2007), 262–5; S. Dimmock, 'English Towns and the Transition, c.1450 to 1500', ibid., 284–5.

[83] Britnell, *Commercialisation*, 150.

7

Marketing and Trading Networks in Medieval Durham

....

Christine M. Newman

Almost one hundred years after the publication of Madeleine Hope Dodds's meticulously detailed essay on the subject, the history of the Durham 'bishop's boroughs' continues to attract historians.[1] There is little doubt that research into these small marketing centres is rewarding for it can serve to reveal much about the administrative, political, social and economic structures of the society in which these institutions operated. Of the six Durham boroughs over which the bishop enjoyed unmediated lordship, charters have survived for three: Durham, Gateshead and Wearmouth (Sunderland). These were all granted by Bishop Hugh du Puiset (1154–95) at various times in the later twelfth century. Darlington, too, was designated a borough by 1196 and had, almost certainly, received a similar grant of liberties, but no evidence of its charter has survived.[2] The aim of this discussion is to explore the nature and *raison d'être* of these early boroughs, in terms of their marketing and trading functions.

It is clear that the provisions of each charter served a different purpose. That granted to the borough of Durham provided a confirmation of existing rights rather than a conferral of new privileges since this was already an established town, which acted, predominantly, as the service centre for its twin 'ecclesiastical overlords', the bishop and prior of Durham, and their respective administrations. Margaret Bonney has made the point that, whilst in many respects medieval Durham was a typical, relatively small market town, it nevertheless possessed 'a significance and uniqueness unrelated to economic factors', purely because of its relationship with these two ecclesiastical institutions.[3] In view of Durham's 'special relationship' with these entities, it seems sensible to focus this exploration

My research on Darlington and Sunderland was undertaken as part of projects conducted under the auspices of the Victoria County History of Durham. See especially *A History of the County of Durham*, IV: *Darlington*, ed. G. Cookson (Woodbridge, 2005), and M. M. Meikle and C. M. Newman, *Sunderland and its Origins: Monks to Mariners* (Chichester, 2007).

[1] M. H. Dodds, 'The Bishops' Boroughs', *Archaeologia Aeliana*, 12 (1915), 81–185.

[2] Ibid., 91.

[3] M. Bonney, *Lordship and the Urban Community: Durham and its Overlords, 1250–1540*

rather upon the lesser boroughs of Gateshead, Darlington and Wearmouth, for in the case of each of these, the ambitious and enterprising Bishop du Puiset was almost certainly seeking to promote economic and commercial expansion in areas of growing potential.

It seems likely that Gateshead's emerging capacity for economic growth was linked to the rebuilding of the bridge over the river Tyne, which had taken place in the late eleventh or early twelfth century. The prospects of Gateshead, which, at this stage, was still a small agricultural settlement bounded by a large episcopal park, were thus transformed into those of a commercially viable trading centre, strategically placed on the main route into Newcastle.[4] The recently created borough of Darlington, too, was a settlement with considerable scope for further development, standing, as it did, on the main thoroughfare between the bishopric of Durham and the south.[5] Finally, there was the borough of Wearmouth, a small fishing port situated on the southern bank of the Wear. Directly across the river lay the ancient settlement of Monkwearmouth, the site of the Anglo-Saxon monastery founded by Benedict Biscop in 673. Its history is known to us through the writings of Bede.[6] This was a borough carved out of the larger settlement and parish centre of Bishopwearmouth.[7] Of all the grants of liberties, this charter was the most speculative in terms of expected commercial return, for the potential of Wearmouth rested wholly on the fact that it was the only harbour in the bishopric belonging to the bishop. Control of Hartlepool — by this time an established seaport and the only other harbour in the bishopric — resided firmly in the hands of the de Brus family.[8] Each borough was thus at a different stage of development and it can be argued that these differences served to impact upon their economic well-being and helped to shape their responses to the crises of the fourteenth century.

In drawing up his charters Bishop du Puiset followed the common practice of modelling the boroughs' privileges upon the customs of an existing borough, the 'mother' borough in this case being Newcastle-upon-Tyne, the customs of

(Cambridge, 1990), 7, 27–8; K. C. Bayley, 'City of Durham: Jurisdictions', in *Victoria County History of Durham*, ed. W. Page (3 vols., London, 1905–28), III, 54–5.

4   R. H. Britnell, 'Medieval Gateshead', in *Newcastle and Gateshead before 1700*, ed. D. Newton and A. J. Pollard (Chichester, 2009), 142–4; Dodds, 'The Bishops' Boroughs', 91–2.

5   C. M. Newman, 'Economy and Society in North-Eastern Market Towns: Darlington and Northallerton in the Later Middle Ages', in *North-East England in the Later Middle Ages*, ed. C. D. Liddy and R. H. Britnell (Woodbridge, 2005), 130.

6   See Bede's *Historia Abbatum* and the *Historia Abbatum Auctore Anonymo* in *Venerabilis Baedae Opera Historica*, I, ed. C. Plummer (Oxford, 1896), 364–87, 388–404.

7   Tradition held that Wearmouth stood on land belonging to but separated, or 'sundered' from the monastery by the river.

8   M. H. Dodds, 'Hartlepool', in *Victoria County History of Durham*, III, 270; Dodds, 'Bishops' Boroughs', 95.

which dated from the reign of Henry I. The bishop had no intention of allowing his boroughs to enjoy a real sense of independence; these were, after all, seigniorial boroughs with the lord retaining effective overall control. Nevertheless, as the Wearmouth charter (dated c.1180–3) demonstrates, burgesses were granted a number of legal and tenurial rights and privileges. These included the right to be sued only in the borough court, except in the case of crown pleas. Similarly, all lawsuits pertaining to the borough were to be dealt with there. Burgesses were also allowed to dispose, freely, of their lands and were exempted from various customary dues and impositions. Clauses such as those permitting townsmen the freedom to sell their corn and to acquire firewood and timber indicate that this was a largely agricultural community. In similar vein was the confirmation of the Wearmouth burgesses' rights to common pasture on the Town Moor, although the charter makes it clear that this was an acknowledgment of a longstanding privilege.[9] In addition, the burgesses were granted a number of economic privileges designed to encourage and regulate trade within the locality, especially that generated by shipping. Salt and herrings were amongst the commodities brought into the port and the fishing trade was, presumably, a lucrative enterprise since the bishop reserved for himself the same duty on the revenue from the sale of fish in Wearmouth as that enjoyed by Robert de Brus in Hartlepool.[10]

Newcastle was not just a model for Wearmouth. Du Puiset, seeing the potential for wealth creation through the promotion of trade, undoubtedly wanted the little borough to generate the same degree of commercial success as that enjoyed by Newcastle.[11] This raises the question whether the borough was economically viable at the time of its creation, perhaps having benefited from the general growth in commerce and trade which took place during the twelfth century.[12] On the other hand, it is possible that borough status may have been granted on the basis of Wearmouth's potential for economic growth, rather than any existing trading success. Until recently there was little evidence to support either of these hypotheses. Recent excavations in the port area of the town, however, have revealed quantities of good quality pottery, dating from the twelfth to the fourteenth centuries. Included amongst the finds were sherds of Scarborough ware and Tyneside-type ware, as well as a small quantity of Low Countries Greyware,

---

9   Durham Cathedral Muniments [hereafter DCM], Priory Register II, fols. 353ᵛ–354ʳ. A modern transcript of the charter appears in *English Episcopal Acta*, xxiv: *Durham, 1153–1195*, ed. M. Snape (Oxford, 2002), 133–5. The provisions of the charters are discussed in detail in Dodds, 'Bishops' Boroughs', 93–5 and (briefly) in F. Bradshaw, 'Social and Economic History', in *Victoria County History of Durham*, II, 253.

10   Dodds, 'Bishops' Boroughs', 95, 96.

11   Meikle and Newman, *Sunderland and its Origins*, 85.

12   R. H. Britnell, 'Boroughs, Markets and Trade in Northern England, 1000–1216', in *Progress and Problems in Medieval England: Essays in Honour of Edward Miller*, ed. R. H. Britnell and J. Hatcher (Cambridge, 1996), 46–67.

possibly of late-fourteenth-century origin, suggesting that the port may have had trading links more substantial than previously thought.[13]

The economic enterprises of Sunderland (as Wearmouth was now increasingly known) were, on the whole, either small-scale or based on local resources. The town developed trading links with other parts of the bishopric, some of which had been in existence from at least the twelfth century and probably earlier. Du Puiset's charter highlighted the importance of salt and herrings as part of the borough's staple trading commodities and such goods were undoubtedly carried inland through local trading routes. In c.1183, Darlington was acquiring both commodities, which were probably carried over from Sunderland.[14] In the fourteenth century the cellarer of Durham priory was also drawing fish supplies from Sunderland and the other Wearmouth settlements, including Southwick, from which it acquired salmon.[15] One priory account, that of 1307–8, reveals the purchase of salt fish, eels and haddock; another, dated 1333–4, records the purchase of five loads of whiting and other fish from the port.[16] A stable owned by William Rakwood was used as 'the fish house' wherein provisions were probably stored until they could be transported to the priory.[17] That other provisions were also acquired is evident from an account of 1438–9 which noted that the cellarer and his servants had journeyed to Sunderland to buy 'victuals'. The actual purchasing of goods was made by a *provisor*, or buyer, with a number of entries in the cellarer's account rolls referring to the payment of his stipend. In 1438–9, for instance, Geoffrey Mawer was paid 20s. for this role. A hundred years later, in 1536–7, the *provisor* of fish at Sunderland and Hartlepool was one John Cotysforth.[18] Analysis of the bursars' accounts from the 1490s through to the second decade of the sixteenth century reveals that Sunderland, together with a number of other local centres, continued to supply the priory throughout that period, with carriers transporting wine, iron, herring, salmon and other necessities from Newcastle, Shields and Sunderland.[19]

The shipping of small quantities of coal confirms the impression of Sunderland's essentially localised trade in the late Middle Ages. In 1394–6, for example, the account rolls of Whitby abbey (in the north riding of Yorkshire) noted a payment of 13s. 4d. to William Rede of Sunderland, who had supplied four chaldrons

[13] Meikle and Newman, *Sunderland and its Origins*, 85.

[14] G. T. Lapsley, 'Text of the Boldon Book', in *Victoria County History of Durham*, I, 338.

[15] M. Threlfall-Holmes, *Monks and Markets: Durham Cathedral Priory 1460–1520* (Oxford 2005), 156, 157–8, 182.

[16] *Extracts from the Account Rolls of the Abbey of Durham*, ed. J. T. Fowler (3 vols., Surtees Society 99, 100, 103, 1898–1900), I, 3, 20.

[17] Ibid., I, 3, 4, 14, 20, 72, 73, 79.

[18] Ibid., III, 666.

[19] DCM, Bursar's Accounts, 1492–3 to 1519–20; Threlfall-Holmes, *Monks and Markets*, 156, 157–8, 182.

of coal.[20] The transportation of coal through Sunderland probably continued, intermittently, throughout the fifteenth century. Mention of a coal staithe on the north bank of the Wear, known as Thrylstanhugh, appeared in the accounts of the medieval monastic cell of Wearmouth. In the years 1415–17 this was let for 3s. 4d. per annum, although an entry in 1418 noted that the farm of 'le staye' (unnamed, but presumably the same one) was only 1s. 8d.[21] A coal staithe was mentioned again in the accounts of the early 1450s, and in 1471–2 it was in the tenure of Michael Salter, who paid a yearly rent of 2s. 6d. In the following year the staithe was leased by William Lambton, who held it from 1472 to 1476.[22] The small rents paid for these assets contrast sharply with those of Gateshead, where, in the 1480s and 1490s, the bishop was charging rents of 10s. and 13s. 4d. respectively.[23] There is no way of calculating the amount of coal that was shipped, although whatever there was certainly came from beyond the locality since there is no evidence of mining activity in the immediate Sunderland area at this time.

In the 1440s, another small-scale industry, that of salt making, was set up by Wearmouth priory, with the monks seeking to make a profit whenever they were fortunate enough to find a tenant. Mention of a salt pan first appears in the accounts of the mid 1440s to the mid 1450s. In 1446–7 the monks received 9s. worth of salt, this being the price of the tithe of the salt pan. It continued to appear in subsequent accounts, drawn up between 1448–9 and 1453–4, thereafter vanishing from the records only to reappear in the early sixteenth century, when there was evidence of renewed investment with a new salt pan being built in 1503–4.[24] In 1506–7 a keel was constructed to carry coal to the salt pan with the costs for wood and for food and drink for the labourers totalling £6 13s. 4d. Repairs were also carried out to the salt pan itself, with the sum of 66s. 8d. expended upon materials and equipment and also upon a new anchor and cable. The salt pan continued to receive mention in the few surviving accounts for the years leading up to the dissolution of the Wearmouth cell, suggesting that it continued to function throughout this time.[25]

Information concerning Sunderland's medieval shipping trade is also scarce, although one significant piece of evidence does exist in the Hatfield Survey. This notes the lease of a parcel of exchequerland in 'Hynden' (Hendon) for the

[20] L. Charlton, *The History of Whitby, and of Whitby Abbey* (York, 1779), 263.

[21] *The Inventories and Account Rolls of the Benedictine Houses or Cells of Jarrow and Monkwearmouth*, ed. J. Raine (Surtees Society 22, 1850), 192, 213–5.

[22] Ibid., 206, 207, 213–5; J. W. Summers, *The History and Antiquities of Sunderland* (Sunderland, 1858), 296.

[23] Britnell, 'Medieval Gateshead', 169.

[24] *Jarrow and Monkwearmouth*, 203–8; Summers, *History and Antiquities*, 79–80, 225; *Sunderland: An Archaeological Assessment and Strategy* (Tyne and Wear Historic Towns Survey, 2004), 32.

[25] *Jarrow and Monkwearmouth*, 225, 227, 229, 230, 232.

mooring of ships.[26] The lease, granted to Thomas Menvill, farmer of the borough of Sunderland, for a yearly rent of 2s., was renewed for eight years in 1395.[27] The Wearmouth cell also received payments for anchorage from time to time during the later fifteenth century.[28] By the early 1500s, there is evidence of increased activity, such as that in 1502–3, when 4s. was received for anchorage and ground-age from the masters of three ships, these being Thomas Boyshay of Lynne, John Marriott of Rochester and Edward Baxter of Newcastle. In the next year John Younger of Sunderland paid 6d. for anchorage of a ship of Lynne.[29]

The picture of Sunderland, then, is of a town whose economic growth in the late Middle Ages was slow and whose trade was highly localised. The town may well have prospered in the short term. Certainly, for a while, the town did assume some of the administrative functions of a borough, indicating a height-ened awareness of its own potential for growth. This is evident from a surviving document of 1296 in which Stephen Gare, described as mayor of Sunderland, witnessed a charter concerning the grant of a burgage in the town. The document also provides a rare reference to the holding of a borough court in Sunderland.[30] No further references to a mayor appear in the medieval records, and it may have been that, as the town's economy failed to expand, so its aspirations lowered ac-cordingly. Other references to the town's chief official refer to him only as reeve (although he was, presumably, the bishop's steward). In 1319 and 1327, for in-stance, William, reeve of Sunderland, is mentioned in connection with a charter of John, his son.[31] Another reeve, Henry, appears in two undated early charters of Finchale priory, which held property in Sunderland.[32]

Trade within the smaller Durham boroughs developed during the course of the thirteenth century, and it was at this time that both Gateshead and Darling-ton began to hold markets and fairs. Darlington fair was first recorded in 1217 whilst mention of its market appeared in the *quo warranto* proceedings of 1293.[33] In Gateshead the market was mentioned in 1246, its fair being in evidence by 1334.[34] There is, however, no early evidence of a market being held in Sunderland. Indeed, first reference to its market and fairs came only in 1634, when Bishop Morton's charter granted Sunderland a weekly market to be held each Friday, and

[26]   Hendon lies to the south-east of Bishopwearmouth.

[27]   *Bishop Hatfield's Survey*, ed. W. Greenwell (Surtees Society 32, 1857), 132.

[28]   *Jarrow and Monkwearmouth*, 205, 215.

[29]   Ibid., 215, 224–5.

[30]   Tyne and Wear Archive Service, 838/56; Meikle and Newman, *Sunderland and its Origins*, 85–6.

[31]   *CPR, 1317–21*, 405; *CChR, 1327–41*, 323.

[32]   DCM, Finchalia, 2.3.3.Finc.4; 2.3.3.Finc 5.

[33]   *Feodarium Prioratus Dunelmensis*, ed. W. Greenwell (Surtees Society 58, 1872), 148; *Placita de Quo Warranto*, ed. W. Illingworth (London 1818), 604.

[34]   Britnell, 'Medieval Gateshead', 147.

fairs on the feasts of SS. Philip and James (1 May), and the feast of St Michael (29 September). This charter hints at a confirmation of fairs and markets anciently held but, sadly, there is little surviving evidence to confirm the existence of these early trading institutions.[35]

In contrast to Sunderland, Darlington's trading and marketing mechanisms extended beyond the confines of its own locality. As such, in the period before the Black Death, it could boast a flourishing economy. Indeed, it is suggested that, by the end of the twelfth century, it stood second only to Durham in terms of its commercial success.[36] As with Durham, Darlington had a number of craft-based industries.[37] Its dye works were so long-established that they had been mentioned in Boldon Book (an episcopal estate survey dating from the 1180s). Its thriving leather industry, a spin-off of the town's increasingly famous cattle trade, was situated in the town's Skinnergate. Documentary evidence of this exists from the beginning of the fourteenth century, although both the street and the trade were probably in existence from a much earlier stage.[38] Also, in company with Durham, Darlington had a number of wealthy merchants whose business and trading interests encompassed both national and international networks.[39] In the 1330s, for instance, the Darlington merchant William de Durham, who was later to make his name as an international wool trader, was a regular supplier to the bursar of Durham priory, dealing in a variety of commodities including cloth, cattle, foodstuffs and wine.[40] John of Kelloe, another Darlington merchant, was similarly engaged, although dealing primarily in grain. Both men were prepared — and could afford — to offer loans and credit facilities to the priory thereby securing, in return, options to acquire grants of the farms of the priory's grain and wool tithes at extremely favourable prices.[41]

From the late thirteenth century, the monks of Durham priory had regularly patronised Darlington fair for purchases of cloth. Further purchases were made over the following years, such as the £7. 19s. 11¾d. spent by the bursar in 1293. Records show that, almost a hundred years later, cloth from Darlington fair was still in demand, with the bursar buying up quantities of striped cloth, suitable for the priory's household livery.[42] Darlington fair was also noted for the quality of

---

[35] Dodds, 'Bishops' Boroughs', 108, 110; Meikle and Newman, *Sunderland and its Origins*, 88, 112.

[36] Dodds, 'Bishops' Boroughs', 84.

[37] Bonney, *Lordship and the Urban Community*, 153, 154–5.

[38] G. Cookson with contributions from C. M. Newman, 'Trade and Industry', in *Darlington*, ed. G. Cookson (Woodbridge, 2005), 110–11.

[39] Bonney, *Lordship and the Urban Community*, 157–8.

[40] Newman, 'Economy and Society', 135.

[41] C. M. Fraser, 'The Pattern of Trade in the North-East of England, 1265–1350', *NH* 4 (1969), 50, 51.

[42] *Account Rolls of the Abbey of Durham*, II, 492, 494; III, 577, 633; Bonney, *Lordship and the Urban Community*, 171.

its cattle and in the fourteenth century the bursar made regular purchases of live-stock. On two occasions in the late 1330s and early 1340s, for example, he bought a large number of oxen for ploughing. There are, however, few references to cat-tle purchasing in the fifteenth century. By this time, the demographic upheavals wrought by the Black Death had forced landlords to move towards pastoral rather than arable farming. Whilst the bulk of their land was let to tenants, both the priory and the bishop exploited suitable areas of their demesne for the raising of stock, both cattle and sheep, presumably obviating the need to buy livestock from other suppliers.[43] However, in the early years of the sixteenth century, Darlington was again appearing in the accounts. In 1507–8 details appear of the expenses of Anthony Thomson, Roland Busby and others, riding to Darlington and other towns to purchase animals. The bursar's household books for 1530–4 similarly show purchases of stock made in Darlington.[44]

The economic and demographic upheavals which followed in the wake of the Black Death inevitably wreaked havoc in the boroughs, as in the rest of the north east. This was a region already weakened by famine, agricultural crisis and the Scottish depredations of the early decades of the century. The Black Death arrived in the bishopric in the summer of 1349 and quickly spread throughout the Sun-derland region, with records of the halmote courts revealing that the plague had taken hold there before mid July. At the sitting of the court, held in Houghton-le-Spring on the fifteenth of the month, it was reported that four tenants from Bish-opwearmouth had already died. Across the Wear, in Monkwearmouth, eleven tenants died in the 1349 outbreak, with a further eight deaths recorded in South-wick and four in Fulwell, indicating an average tenant death rate of sixty per cent in these vills. In the borough of Sunderland, too, the impact of the *magna pesti-lencia* seems to have been equally as severe.[45] Indeed, Nicholas de Skelton, the farmer of the borough at the time of the outbreak, in 1349, was granted a rebate of four marks in respect of his payment of the annual farm.[46] Gateshead, too, was severely affected, with the nearby townships of Over Heworth and Nether Heworth experiencing death rates of thirty-six per cent and seventy-two per cent, respectively.[47] By September, the plague had reached the ward of Darlington, kill-ing four ploughmen in the vill of Coatham Mundeville, which lay close to the bor-

[43] A. J. Pollard, *North-East England During the Wars of the Roses: Lay Society, War and Politics, 1450–1500* (Oxford, 1990), 59–61.

[44] *The Durham Household Book; or, The Accounts of the Bursar of the Monastery of Durham from Pentecost 1530 to Pentecost 1534*, ed. J. Raine (Surtees Society 18, 1844), 71–2, 202, 301.

[45] Bradshaw, 'Social and Economic History', 210, 258–9; F. Bradshaw, 'The Black Death in the Palatinate of Durham', *Archaeologia Aeliana*, 3 (1907), 156–7, 159; R. A. Lomas, 'The Black Death in County Durham', *Journal of Medieval History*, 15 (1989), 127–40.

[46] Bradshaw, 'Black Death', 155–6; TNA, DURH 3/12, fol. 23ᵛ.

[47] Britnell, 'Medieval Gateshead', 157.

ough of Darlington.[48] The vill of West Thickley, in the western part of Darlington ward, lost all of its tenants.[49]

The effects of the Black Death and the subsequent outbreaks of plague undermined still further the shaky foundations of Sunderland's economy. Its borough farm, let for £20 in 1358 had decreased to £6 by the time of the Hatfield Survey (dating from the end of the episcopate of Thomas Hatfield, 1345–81).[50] Throughout the fifteenth century the little borough gradually sank into the long-term decline in which it was to remain until the late sixteenth century. For Darlington, the initial impact of the Black Death was not so immediate, as had been the case with Sunderland. Indeed the borough farm of Darlington actually increased in the latter part of the fourteenth century, from £86 13s. 4d. in 1351 to £93 6s. 8d. in 1395. By the 1470s, the profitability of the borough had declined considerably. In 1476–7, for instance, it was demised for only £40.[51] Nevertheless, the town's markets and fairs did not decline, remaining in operation throughout the period. The profits, which appeared in the borough bailiff's accounts, were not substantial, averaging around £4 to £5 a year, but they remained relatively stable.[52] John Leland's observation, whilst travelling through Durham in the late 1530s, that after Durham, Darlington was the best market town in the bishopric, lends weight to the theory that trade there, if not exactly flourishing, was certainly operating at an acceptable level.[53] This was not unique to Darlington, for a similar situation has been identified in fifteenth-century Gateshead. There, marketing and trading mechanisms continued to operate even though rents declined. Moreover, it is suggested that, whilst numbers of decayed or untenanted properties increased, standards of living there probably rose.[54] Gateshead, by this period, was beginning to revive its coal industry, although it was yet to expand into the major enterprise that it would later become. It was certainly well placed to grasp the opportunities that lay ahead.[55]

Darlington and Gateshead were, of course, well-established centres in their own right and sufficiently well positioned to take advantage of any potential commercial opportunities. Episcopal manor houses and been built in both townships and both boasted impressive churches. St Cuthbert's collegiate church in

[48] Bradshaw, 'Social and Economic History', 211; *Hatfield's Survey*, 247–8.

[49] Bradshaw, 'Black Death', 57; Cookson with Newman, 'Trade and Industry', 109.

[50] *Hatfield's Survey*, 137.

[51] C. M. Newman and G. Cookson, 'Town, Government and Politics', in *Darlington*, ed. Cookson, 75; DUL, Archives and Special Collections, Coroner's Account, Darlington Ward: CCB B/48/5 (190199).

[52] See for example, DUL, Archives and Special Collections, Accounts of the Bailiff of Darlington Borough: CCB B/68/1 (188916), CCB B/68/2 (188918), CCB B/68/9 (189513).

[53] *Itinerary of John Leland*, I, ed. L. Toulmin Smith (London, 1907), 69.

[54] Britnell, 'Medieval Gateshead', 159–60. See also the case of Northallerton in Newman, 'Economy and Society', 137–8.

[55] Britnell, 'Medieval Gateshead', 170.

Darlington, one of the most important churches in Durham, was begun in c.1192, in the later years of Bishop du Puiset's episcopate, possibly on the site of an earlier Anglo-Saxon church. St Mary's church in Gateshead dates from the same period.[56]

Of the three boroughs Sunderland was by far the least successful at the beginning of the sixteenth century. In terms of geographical position, it was also the least well situated of all the Durham boroughs. First, the medieval port of Sunderland was never sufficiently developed or resourced to compete with its near neighbour, Newcastle, which flourished during the twelfth and thirteenth centuries, expanding its trade in both national and international terms. Even after the ravages of the Black Death, which saw it fall into recession, its trade decline and its population halved, Newcastle survived to see its fortunes revived by the expanding coal trade of the later fifteenth century.[57] Secondly, from a local perspective, Sunderland was a minor settlement, comprising the port area of the larger township of Bishopwearmouth, out of which it had been carved. Bishopwearmouth was the central settlement of the medieval parish of the same name. Its church, dedicated to St Michael, was probably of twelfth-century origin, and it seems likely that this was built over an earlier Anglo-Saxon church, suggesting a long-established pattern of settlement pre-dating the Conquest. Bishopwearmouth also had a central position on a road network that connected the area with Newcastle and Chester-le-Street to the north and Durham and Stockton to the south. Thus it had a clear advantage over the smaller, more isolated Sunderland, which, by road, was only accessible through Bishopwearmouth. Indeed, the borough of Sunderland was to remain as part of the parish of Bishopwearmouth for several more centuries and it was only in 1719 that the parish of Sunderland was created.[58] Until the latter half of the sixteenth century, Sunderland remained a sparsely populated fishing town with a hinterland totally dependent upon agriculture. Indeed, in 1565, a royal survey of the 'havens, ports, creeks and landing places' in Durham described Sunderland as a fishing town and landing place, in great decay of building and inhabitants, with only thirty householders. As for its shipping industry, the report noted that whilst ships were permitted to load and unload their cargoes, by licence of the bishop, in fact there were no ships or boats there, apart from seven fishing cobles which employed twenty men.[59]

Ironically, perhaps, it was the decision, in the 1580s, to revive one of Sunderland's small-scale, localised industries, the salt-making trade, which was to

[56] C. M. Newman, D. J. Howlett and G. Cookson with contributions by E. A. Williamson, 'Religious and Cultural Life', in *Darlington*, ed. Cookson, 193; Britnell, 'Medieval Gateshead', 144–5.

[57] C. M. Fraser, 'The Economic Growth of Newcastle upon Tyne, 1150–1536', in *Newcastle and Gateshead*, ed. Newton and Pollard, 41–64.

[58] Meikle and Newman, *Sunderland and its Origins*, 45–7.

[59] *Calendar of State Papers Domestic: Elizabeth, 1601–3 with Addenda 1547–65*, 573; Meikle and Newman *Sunderland and its Origins*, 91

provide the catalyst for change that would transform the fortunes of this tiny borough so that, within little more than a century, it would become a populous town of some 6,000 people and a successful English trading port of the second rank. Thanks to the growing demand for salt, which from the 1560s had become a scarce and expensive commodity, and the entrepreneurial ingenuity of Robert Bowes, a local gentleman and the borough's leading officer, plans were drawn up to establish a salt-manufacturing business in Sunderland. Ultimately the salt-making venture was to fail, but the mine owners who supplied the low-grade coal that was necessary to fuel the furnaces of the salt pans began to realise Sunderland's potential as an export centre and started using the port to ship out their better-quality coal. As a result, by the end of the sixteenth century, increasing numbers of coal-carrying vessels, many from the Netherlands and Germany, were sailing into Sunderland, heralding the start of the port's rise to national prominence.[60]

[60] Meikle and Newman *Sunderland and its Origins*, 96–102, 176–82.

8

Peasant Opportunities in Rural Durham:
Land, Vills and Mills, 1400–1500

....

Peter L. Larson

PROBABLY UPWARDS OF HALF of County Durham's population died in 1349.[1] Upsetting the ratio of land to labour in an area where serfdom was tottering on the edge of irrelevancy might have opened the door to greater individualism and entrepreneurial activity.[2] Using tithe receipts, Ben Dodds has shown there was a 'rapid recovery in aggregate output' in the aftermath of the Black Death that fits A. R. Bridbury's 'Indian Summer', and rather than 'retreating into subsistence production, peasants adopted new techniques and expanded output to meet the demands of the market'.[3] Subsequently, aggregate production relative to pre-plague levels tailed off and there were a number of crises (in the 1390s, 1430s and 1490s); as A. J. Pollard has pointed out, 'The fifteenth century after 1440 was a bleak era' for the region, and the period preceding it was not strong either.[4] Nevertheless, producers — including peasants — were able to respond to

---

[1] R. A. Lomas, 'The Black Death in County Durham', *Journal of Medieval History* 15 (1989), 129; P. L. Larson, *Conflict and Compromise in the Late Medieval Countryside: Lords and Peasants in Durham, 1349–1400* (New York, 2006), 72–5.

[2] For the broader context of agricultural and economic change in this period, see *AHEW* III; R. H. Britnell, *The Commercialisation of English Society 1000–1500* (Cambridge, 1993, repr. Manchester, 1996), 155–64, 179–85; idem, *Britain and Ireland 1050–1500: Economy and Society* (Oxford, 2004), 268–450.

[3] B. Dodds, *Peasants and Production in the Medieval North-East: The Evidence from Tithes, 1270–1536* (Woodbridge, 2007), 74–80 at 74, 173; A. R. Bridbury, 'The Black Death', *EcHR* 26 (1973), 580–4.

[4] A. J. Pollard, *North-Eastern England During the Wars of the Roses: Lay Society, War, and Politics 1450–1500* (Oxford, 1990), 30–80 at 78. The economic trends can be broken up into smaller movements, both regional and national; see J. Hatcher, 'The Great Slump of the Mid-Fifteenth Century', in *Progress and Problems in Medieval England: Essays in Honour of Edward Miller*, ed. R. H. Britnell and J. Hatcher (Cambridge, 1996), 239; R. H. Britnell, 'English Agricultural Output and Prices, 1350–1450: National Trends and Regional Divergences', in *Agriculture and Rural Society After the Black Death: Common Themes and Regional Variations*, ed. B. Dodds and R. H. Britnell (Hatfield, 2008), 20–39.

the market.[5] Opportunities existed for peasants to take a chance to increase their fortunes. By 1500, there were individuals with sufficient resources to lease large parcels of land and even partial or whole vills. One such was John Hall, the son of William Hall, who took up lands in both Bishop Middleham and Sedgefield in 1500; his father had leased the demesne of Bishop Middleham and various parcels, with works, in 1485. In turn, John passed these holdings to his son, another William, in 1537.[6] John Halyman, whose father had amassed sixty acres of customary lands in Norton before his death, took a share in the mill at Norton, leased demesne lands in Stockton, and with another man leased the entire village of Hardwick.[7] Men such as these could afford other ventures, such as buying tithes to sell for a profit.[8]

These developments are characteristic of the transformations taking place throughout the country. Since Durham had a relatively low population and settlement density, with mixed agriculture and the potential for industrial production (namely coal), a variety of opportunities were available to enterprising souls. For that reason, then, those who came forward to farm for the market and accumulate holdings or to engage in non-agricultural work are, in many ways, less of an enigma than those who did not do so. In Durham, initial findings on the patterns in accumulation of land suggest a cautious or even non-entrepreneurial approach to these opportunities, with small syndicates and even entire villages becoming involved alongside enterprising individuals. The economy was changing, but most peasants still planted their crops with an eye to consumption, not specialisation.[9] While they increasingly did so alongside men with substantial holdings who were producing for the market, strong communities persisted and took advantage of the opportunities for economic development, or, at least, self-determination.

Source and Methodology

The bishopric of Durham contained approximately sixty-eight villages in County Durham under direct administration.[10] These villages contained a mix of tenures; the largest single category was customary land, where the original rents, a mixture of labour services and renders in kind, underwent commutation into a money rent by the middle of the fourteenth century. Prominent in the Survey

---

[5] Dodds, *Peasants and Production*, 74–118.

[6] TNA, DURH 3/18, fol. 21^r (William Hall I); 3/19, fol. 160^v (John Hall); 3/23, fol. 117^r (William Hall II). For regional examples, see Pollard, *North-Eastern England*, 64–7. The holdings of William Hall II would pass to his widow, who married into the gentry, and to his nephew.

[7] TNA, DURH 3/13, fol. 349^v; 3/14, fols. 144^r, 271^r; 3/15, fols. 70^r, 403^r; 3/16, fol. 5^v.

[8] Dodds, *Peasants and Production*, 165–7.

[9] Ibid., 157–8.

[10] Larson, *Conflict and Compromise*, 51–2.

made by Bishop Hatfield in the early 1380s are intact holdings, generally cotlands of less than twelve acres, fifteen-acre bovates and thirty-acre husbandlands.[11] Some of these tenures, such as mallands and dringage tenures, were quasi-free although still regulated by the bishop's halmote court and thus considered here alongside more traditional customary lands. There was considerable demesne land either associated with a village or found within a *manerium*: not a manor as found elsewhere, but more of a demesne farm, drawing works from neighbouring villages but with no jurisdictional rights. Most tenants were personally free, and by the fifteenth century the bishop's officials largely had ceased to keep track of the few serfs by blood (*nativi*).[12]

These customary and demesne lands were regulated by the bishop's halmote court, which met thrice yearly during most of the late Middle Ages. The halmote court was similar to the manor court with leet jurisdiction elsewhere in England; its primary purpose was to regulate the estate through recording conveyances and extracting or protecting seigniorial rights, while providing a forum for the settlement of tenant disputes. By the end of the fifteenth century, the business of the court was limited to conveyance of land and enforcement of village by-laws. While most of those appearing were customary tenants, free tenants and even gentry could be found doing business at the court. The halmote books provide data not only on acquisition of land and other assets, but on the role of debt, capitalisation and tradition in shaping economic activities.[13]

Historians have focused more on the lands of Durham priory, and for good reason; the priory left far more records suited for economic analysis. However, the bishopric has the advantage of a richer archive for its halmote court after 1400. This archive is massive, despite gaps at critical periods (most notably from 1362 to 1388 and from 1425 to 1438).[14] This has dictated a mixed approach, and with greater focus on the fifteenth century. The records for the entire estate were scrutinised for activity regarding mills, fishing and mining rights, market- or production-oriented activities (such as smithing, brewing and renting of market spaces) and leases of large parcels of land (sixty or more acres) or entire manors and villages.[15] These represent opportunities for increased production and profit rather than family-oriented subsistence and a potential disruption to traditional agricultural and cultural practices. The acquisition of such holdings by the peasantry could require changes in outlook and technique from more traditional activities, while the leasing of lands and villages (in particular by outsiders) could

---

[11]   *Bishop Hatfield's Survey*, ed. W. Greenwell (Surtees Society 32, 1857).

[12]   Larson, *Conflict and Compromise*, 50–3, 63–7.

[13]   On the halmote court and books, see P. L. Larson, 'Local Law Courts in Late Medieval Durham', in *North-East England in the Later Middle Ages*, ed. C. D. Liddy and R. H. Britnell (Woodbridge, 2005), 97–109.

[14]   TNA, DURH 3/12–19.

[15]   Only lands transferred in the halmotes are included, thus omitting most free tenures.

cause conflict and change with or within those communities. The number of such entries was relatively low, limiting much of this evidence to anecdotal usage, but data on rent levels and other data have been extracted when possible.

Entrepreneurial engagement in these activities must be measured alongside the accumulation of traditional tenures for use in production for the market, and the study of the land market has provided a window onto the motivations and mentalities at work before and after this period. Work on the medieval land market has thrived in recent decades, both in regional, national and international contexts. In much of England, population growth in the thirteenth century had fragmented many holdings and promoted an active market in small parcels of customary land; population decline in the later Middle Ages coupled with the introduction of leasing and the release of demesne land into the market led to a polarisation, with some large amalgamated tenures and many smallholdings.[16] As has been made very clear, however, local customs had a powerful influence on the mechanisms of the land market, with variations even between nearby villages. For County Durham, Timothy Lomas has already established some general trends from an examination of twelve villages in the south-eastern part of the county.[17] A study of regional variations within the county would be valuable but is beyond the scope of the present essay; instead, three neighbouring villages (Bishop Middleham, Sedgefield and Cornforth) are used here to investigate the role of customary law and to reconstruct some of the constraints on economic activities and the cultural impact of these transitions. All three villages were in the same medieval parish and lay from six to ten miles south-east from the city of Durham, representing a mix of soil types and geography (spreading across parts of the Tees Lowlands, the East Durham Plateau and the Wear Lowlands); there was a variety of tenures in the three villages, and Sedgefield was the site of a Friday market.[18] As such, when placed alongside Lomas's work and the present

---

[16]   See P. D. A. Harvey, 'The Peasant Land Market in Medieval England — and Beyond', in *Medieval Society and the Manor Court*, ed. Z. Razi and R. M. Smith (Oxford, 1996), 392–407. Two major collections were published in 1984: *The Peasant Land Market in Medieval England*, ed. P. D. A. Harvey (Oxford, 1984); *Land, Kinship and Life-Cycle*, ed. R. M. Smith (Cambridge, 1984). For a recent study of the land market of an estate and its variations, see J. Mullan and R. H. Britnell, *Land and Family: Trends and Local Variations in the Peasant Land Market on the Winchester Bishopric Estates, 1263–1415* (Hatfield, 2010).

[17]   T. Lomas, 'South-East Durham: Late Fourteenth and Fifteenth Centuries', in *Peasant Land Market*, ed. Harvey, 252–327.

[18]   On the geography and soil of the parish, see S. J. Harris, 'Wastes, the Margins and the Abandonment of Land: The Bishop of Durham's Estate, 1350–1480', in *North-East England in the Later Middle Ages*, ed. Liddy and Britnell, 200, map 13.1; B. K. Roberts, H. Dunsford and S. J. Harris, 'Framing Medieval Landscapes: Region and Place in County Durham', in *North-East England in the Late Middle Ages*, ed. Liddy and Britnell, 225, 230. The vitality of the market is in question, as there later was trading on Sunday instead: S. Letters, *Online Gazetteer of Markets and Fairs in England Wales to 1516*, http://www.history.ac.uk/cmh/gaz/gazweb2.

examination of mills and other industrial or commercial activities, the parish makes a good in-depth case study. Consequently, data on landholding (including subletting when available) were extracted from the court books to construct trends in rents and entry fines, volume of activity and accumulation of holdings at ten-year intervals; for 1400 to 1420 and 1480 to 1500, all landholding data were extracted to focus on the specific nature of the land market at the beginning and end of the century. More broadly, the entries in the court books were used to explore the mentalities active in this period. Although the villages of Bishop Middleham parish form the core of the land-market portion of the study, additional evidence has been used from other villages to present a broader picture of the peasants' landholding mentality.

The scope of this essay is admittedly limited as the records omit landholding, production and commercialisation that occurred outside the remit of the halmote court. The focus is on customary (later copyhold) and demesne land; most of the actors are peasants or those who were actively involved in that rural, agricultural world. Yet, although primarily agricultural, the bishopric halmote books do record echoes of commercial activities otherwise unregulated by the court, which suggest avenues for further research. Fully understanding the themes addressed here requires integration of other bishopric and county records. Despite the drawbacks, however, this rural world was a key site for economic expansion, and how this did or did not happen is one of many keys to understanding the broader changes between the medieval and the modern worlds.

Engrossment and Accumulation of Village Lands

The shift of the agrarian focus from subsistence to market, driven by the accumulation of lands, is one of the foundations of the transition from the medieval manorial system to a more modern commercialised economy. If the pattern holds true for Durham, despite contraction in agriculture, there should be increasing accumulation of holdings by wealthier peasants and outsiders.[19] While tracing

---

html: [County Durham] (last updated 23 July 2007; accessed 11 December 2009). Spaces in the market were being leased as late as 1410 for butchers' stalls (*fleshamills*), although the day of the market was not specified: TNA, DURH 3/14, fols. 185^v–186^r. By 1423, however, these stalls were back in the lord's hand for want of tenants: TNA, DURH 3/14, fol. 619^r.

[19] Britnell, *Commercialisation*, 199–203; C. Dyer, *An Age of Transition? Economy and Society in England in the Later Middle Ages* (Oxford, 2005), 194–210. In Holywell-cum-Needingworth, the tenurial structure was transformed with the emergence of 'proto-yeomen,' but it was not only villagers but outsiders who took advantage: E. B. DeWindt, *Land and People in Holywell-cum-Needingworth: Structures of Tenure and Patterns of Social Organization in an East Midlands Village, 1252–1457* (Toronto, 1971), 107–61. See also P. R. Schofield, 'Tenurial Developments and the Availability of Customary Land in a Later Medieval Community', *EcHR* 49 (1996), 260–4.

the full development of such a pattern is beyond the scope of this essay, it is clear that Durham did see the rise of independent farmers, but at the same time many village communities remained strong.[20]

The land market

Lomas used twelve villages from three different estates (about six to eight miles south and east of Bishop Middleham parish) to sketch the basics of rural life and the land market in south-east Durham. This was an area akin to southern England in rural economic and agrarian organisation, and he concluded that despite some exceptions the region 'does not appear very different from other parts of England' in terms of experience in the later Middle Ages.[21] The economic situation was in the tenantry's favour, but the land market itself was not very active and had little subletting. Few peasants left their home village or went far beyond it, though in some places outsiders were major actors in the market. Nevertheless, enterprising individuals were beginning to accumulate holdings, and while most families that did so immediately after the Black Death came to nought, those that rose closer to 1400 continued to play active roles in their villages for the rest of the century.[22]

Examining Durham as a whole through the bishopric estate, and examining the role of groups and villages in the land market rather than only individuals and families, modifies certain of those conclusions by placing the sub-region into a broader context. Greater attention can be paid to the cultural and institutional factors that shaped the market, as some aspects of rural society changed little. There was accumulation of holdings by individuals, although the large farms were built on demesne lands rather than composite holdings of customary lands; in many villages, individuals rarely acquired more than forty-five to sixty acres of customary land in a single village.[23] The village community played a powerful role, and villages themselves became the lessees of significant property, building

---

[20] R. H. Britnell, 'Feudal Reaction After the Black Death in the Palatinate of Durham', *P&P* 128 (1990), 28–47; Larson, *Conflict and Compromise*. On the transformation of the medieval village, see R. M. Smith, '"Modernization" and the Corporate Medieval Village Community in England: Some Sceptical Reflections', in *Explorations in Historical Geography: Interpretive Essays*, ed. A. R. H. Baker and D. Gregory (Cambridge, 1984), 140–79.

[21] Lomas, 'South-East Durham', 326. See also J. A. Tuck, 'Tenant Farming and Tenant Farmers: The Northern Borders', in *AHEW* III, 587–96.

[22] Lomas, 'South-East Durham', 289–316. Rosamund Faith, 'Berkshire: Fourteenth and Fifteenth Centuries', in *Peasant Land Market*, ed. Harvey, 157–77, uncovered a similar pattern of wealthy peasant families that could not survive.

[23] The average holding among jurors in the period 1349 to 1424 was fifty per cent higher in Norton than in the priory village of Billingham: P. L. Larson, 'Village Voice or Village Oligarchy: The Jurors of the Durham Halmote Court, 1349 to 1424', *Law and History Review* 28 (2010), 698–9.

on (sometimes fragile) traditions of community and solidarity that emerged in the period immediately following the Black Death.

In Durham the population was declining before the Black Death struck, and there was little 'surplus' population available to take up the empty lands.[24] In the immediate aftermath of the epidemic there was too much vacant land, and the bishop's steward had to take strong measures to find tenants. Richard Britnell has described the process whereby the steward collaborated with village juries to impose vacant lands on men judged able to work them, while other lands were let at special rates.[25] The halmote court records from time to time included lists of lands *in manu domini* for lack of tenants, even to the end of this period; for example, in Sedgefield there were still two thirty-acre tenures, a parcel of land and a dovecote in hand in 1485.[26] There were smaller parcels of land available from exchequerland and demesne, but whereas fragmented holdings were common in parts of England, the old tenurial categories were preserved intact in Durham even when this meant more than one person held a tenure.[27] This made subletting common, and in the late 1350s the bishop's steward first tried to regulate the practice and then began issuing licences to sublet as a matter of course when a tenant took up lands.[28] In many cases, that sixpence licence was the only payment the tenant made on entering a holding.

The death of so many men and the dearth of willing tenants did more than shift the land market in the tenants' favour; it made the lords desperate to find anyone to take the land, and when not imposing vacant lands on unwilling tenants, the steward tried to cut deals.[29] The entry fines tell the story. In 1349 forty per cent of entry fines on the estate were 20s. or more, with less than twenty per cent at 2s. or less; by 1400 that pattern had reversed, with 5.5 per cent of fines at or greater than 20s. and nearly sixty-three per cent 2s. or less.[30] Even late in the fifteenth century, entry fines were low; in 1486, four bovates of malland incurred

---

[24] Dodds, *Peasants and Production*, 28, 55–70; R. A. Lomas, 'Durham Cathedral Priory as a Landowner and a Landlord, 1290–1540' (Ph.D. thesis, University of Durham, 1973), 29–30; Lomas, 'Black Death in County Durham'.

[25] Britnell, 'Feudal Reaction,' 35–45.

[26] TNA, DURH 3/18, fol. 21ʳ.

[27] *Bishop Hatfield's Survey*. For the priory estate, see *Durham Cathedral Priory Rentals, 1: Bursars Rentals*, ed. R. A. Lomas and A. J. Piper (Surtees Society 198, 1989). On north-eastern England in general, see R. A. Lomas, *North-East England in the Middle Ages* (Edinburgh, 1992), 151–2; Tuck, 'Northern Borders', 591. On fragmentation in England, see P. D. A. Harvey, 'Introduction', in *Peasant Land Market*, ed. idem, 7–19; J. Williamson, 'Norfolk: Thirteenth Century', in *Peasant Land Market*, ed. Harvey, 31–105; P. R. Schofield, *Peasant and Community in Medieval England, 1200–1500* (New York, 2003), 25, 55–6, 65–70; B. F. Harvey, *Westminster Abbey and its Estates in the Middle Ages* (Oxford, 1977), 264–6.

[28] Cf. Lomas, who did not find much evidence of subletting; 'South-East Durham', 239.

[29] Britnell, 'Feudal Reaction'.

[30] Larson, *Conflict and Compromise*, 202.

an entry fine of only 6s. 8d.[31] Durham priory reacted to this situation by offering leases, so that by the 1380s most customary land would be held that way, and entry fines disappeared early in the fifteenth century.[32] Leases appeared on the bishopric estate, and the numbers slowly but steadily increased, further eroding entry fines. Still, many bishopric tenants preferred to hold their lands in the usual manner, for life.[33]

Overall, the market for customary land in Durham was weak, although it varied by time and location. Lomas found a land-transfer rate of 1.9 holdings per year for the bishopric vills he studied, with a slight increase in the early fifteenth century.[34] This number is skewed by the very low numbers of transfers later in the fifteenth century and by the packaging of multiple holdings, but even at its height the market was not very active. Figure 8.1 shows the land market in Bishop Middleham, Sedgefield and Cornforth, sampled every tenth year. The figures include all transactions that the halmote books recorded as demises or as new or increased rents, plus some conveyances not labelled as such; thus these include demesne lands and some village or manorial buildings but not leases of land for herbage. There was an initial burst after the Black Death and a second but smaller peak early in the fifteenth century. John Hatcher's 'Great Slump' is apparent in the 1450s and 1460s, and the land market had not recovered by the end of the century.[35] Unfortunately, the loss of nearly all bishopric halmote records from 1362 to 1391 hides what likely was a period of intense internal disruption, judging by events in the priory villages.[36]

Closer examination of the apparent peak in the early 1400s shows a fairly steady market overall, with peaks in 1409–10 and 1416, as shown in Figure 8.2. There was an average of 5.8 transactions per year, just over half what Jane Whittle

[31] TNA, DURH 3/18, fol. 37ʳ. Faith, 'Berkshire', 116–17, found similar low entry fines and a lack of tenants.

[32] Lomas, 'South-East Durham', 307, 311–12, and Lomas, 'Durham Cathedral Priory', 32–3. The priory's conversion to leasehold would cost the tenants in the long run by eliminating heritable right: R. B. Dobson, *Durham Priory, 1400–1450* (Cambridge, 1973), 283–4. Northern lords struggled to find tenants: Pollard, *North-Eastern England*, 67–9. See also P. D. A. Harvey, 'Conclusions', in *Peasant Land Market*, ed. idem, 333–4.

[33] Cf. Lomas, 'South-East Durham', 311.

[34] Ibid., 304–5.

[35] The middle of the century was hard in England and Durham: J. Hatcher, *Plague, Population and the English Economy, 1348–1530* (London, 1977), 36–44; Pollard, *North-Eastern England*, 47–54; A. J. Pollard, 'The North-Eastern Economy and the Agrarian Crisis of 1438–40', NH 25 (1989), 88–105. See also Dodds, *Peasants and Production*, 103–5; Dobson, *Durham Priory*, 250–96.

[36] Larson, *Conflict and Compromise*, 143–92; P. L. Larson, 'Rural Transformation in Northern England: Village Communities of Durham, 1340–1400', in *Agriculture and Rural Society*, ed. Dodds and Britnell, 199–214; Dodds, *Peasants and Production*, 94.

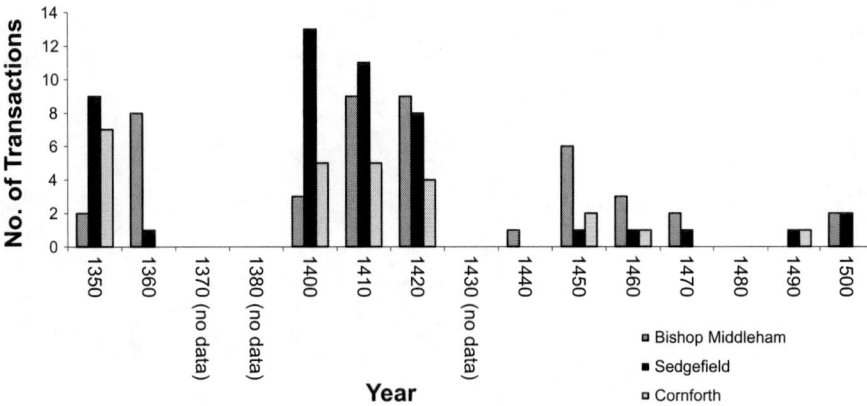

Fig. 8.1: Bishop Middleham parish land market, 1350–1500

Sources: TNA, DURH 3/12, fols. 3ᵛ–45ᵛ, 225ᵛ–265ᵛ; 3/13, fols. 266ʳ–326ʳ; 3/14, fols. 174ʳ–186ᵛ, 522ᵛ–556ʳ; 3/15, fols. 44ʳ–57ᵛ, 252ᵛ–268ʳ; 3/16, fols. 56ᵛ–72ʳ, 218ʳ–233ʳ; 3/17, fols. 62ʳ–70ᵛ; 3/18, fols. 122ᵛ–135ʳ; 3/19, fols. 154ʳ–168ᵛ. Halmote records for those years marked 'no data' do not survive.

Note: records sampled every ten years.

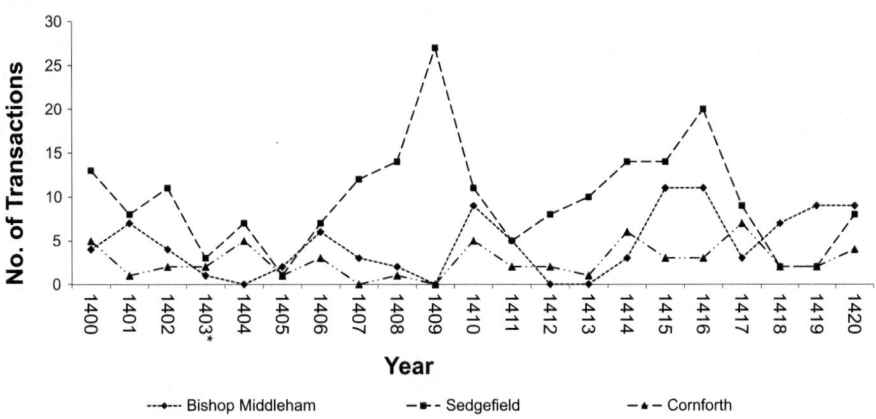

Fig. 8.2: Bishop Middleham parish land market, 1400–1420

Sources: TNA, DURH 3/13, fols. 266ʳ–446ʳ; 3/14, fols. 8ᵛ–556ʳ.

Note: These rates do not differentiate between new leases and renewals.

* = Incomplete data: one or more halmote tourns missing in the Halmote Books.

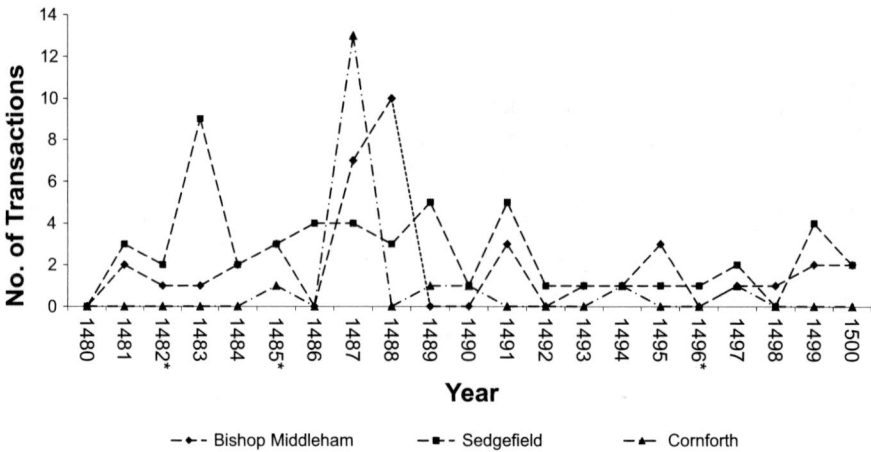

Fig. 8.3: Bishop Middleham parish land market, 1480–1500

Sources: TNA, DURH 3/17–18, *passim*; 3/19, fols. 5ᵛ–168ᵛ.

Note: These rates do not differentiate between new leases and renewals.

* = Incomplete data: one or more halmote tourns missing in the Halmote Books.

found for Hevingham (Norfolk) for the latter half of the century.[37] Despite the activity of the market, there are fewer examples of accumulation of customary lands in this sub-period compared to the decades following the Black Death, but as Rosamond Faith noted, 'a particularly active land market . . . was not by itself an index of local prosperity,' and that may well be the case here.[38] Conveyances of single holdings predominated and few tenants took more than one holding. Looking at Sedgefield from 1409 to 1418 in order to investigate the two peaks of activity in this sub-period, sixty-four people (including fourteen widows) took land a total of seventy-seven times. Of the holdings taken, twenty-six were cottages (including seven cottages leased together), twenty-one were for a bovate or half husbandland, and twelve were for two bovates or a whole husbandland, with the remaining demises mostly for small parcels of a few acres. The largest holding was forty-nine acres taken by Agnes, widow of John Addy, in widow-right.[39] That holdings of fifteen or fewer acres figure strongly here could indicate economic promotion, with villagers adding to their existing lands, but with few people taking more than one holding, it is difficult to speak of accumulation. The true accumulation of large holdings had already taken place (as in the case of John and

37   J. Whittle, 'Individualism and the Family–Land Bond: A Reassessment of Land Transfer Patterns Among the English Peasantry, *c*.1270–1580', *P&P* 160 (1998), 29.
38   Faith, 'Berkshire,' 156.
39   TNA, DURH 3/14, fols. 143ᵛ–456ᵛ; for Agnes Addy's lands, see fol. 288ʳ.

Agnes Addy), and with these instances of promotion, the general pattern for the rest of the century had set, before the problems in mid-century.[40]

By the end of the century, the land market was minimal, as shown in Figure 8.3. There was relatively brisker activity in certain years, especially 1487–8, but the volume had fallen and the average yearly rate was only 1.7 transfers. For Cornforth, only one year had more than one conveyance, and even Sedgefield, which usually had a more active market, climbed above two transfers in a year only twice in the 1490s. The decline in land transfers is matched by a decline in court business; this correlates with Dodds's findings on agricultural output, where recovery in the 1450s to 1470s crumbled in the 1480s and 1490s, as well as with Pollard's analysis of the bishops' and priory's income for that period.[41] The land market, court activity and production generally marched in lockstep throughout the late medieval bishopric.

Engrossment and accumulation

Looking at the bishopric estate, particularly before 1424, there was a clear potential for engrossment of customary lands.[42] The bishop's stewards were willing to let land at rates lower than the 'old rent' (*antiquam firmam*), and entry fines were low. The deterioration of tenures led to incentives for new tenants to repair the tenure and keep it in good state, often with building materials or an allocation provided by the lord. As noted above, serfdom was weak; most customary land was held for life, and few lands were held insecurely 'at the will of the lord'.[43] There was no taint to preclude taking up the vacant lands and no tenure 'at will' to frighten off potential tenants; tenure was cheap and secure.[44] One would expect

[40]   See Larson, 'Rural Transformation in Northern England', 199–214; idem, *Conflict and Compromise*. DeWindt found a similar pattern of readjustment from the 1370s to the early fifteenth century: *Land and People*, 112–13.

[41]   Dodds, *Peasants and Production*, 110–13; Pollard, *North-Eastern England*, 53–5. Christine Newman, *Late Medieval Northallerton: A Small Market Town and its Hinterland, c.1470–1540* (Stamford, 1999), 67–92, found economic stagnation and troubles collecting rent in one of the bishop's Yorkshire liberties.

[42]   This was a broad trend in England, and led to contraction and desertion of settlements as well: Britnell, *Commercialisation*, 198–200; Britnell, *Britain and Ireland*, 468–74, 389–95. There was a retreat from marginal lands in Durham too: Lomas, 'Durham Cathedral Priory', 34–6; Harris, 'Wastes, the Margins and the Abandonment of Land', 197–219.

[43]   On the effects of the decline of serfdom on the land market, see J. Whittle, *The Development of Agrarian Capitalism: Land and Labour in Norfolk 1440–1580* (Oxford, 2000); M. Mate, 'The East Sussex Land Market and Agrarian Class Structure in the Late Middle Ages', *P&P* 139 (1993), 65; Schofield, 'Tenurial Developments'; J. A. Raftis, *Tenure and Mobility: Studies in the Social History of the Mediaeval English Village* (Toronto, 1964, repr. 1981) 190–204.

[44]   The scattered references to a copy (*copiam* or *recordam*) indicate tenants received a record of their conveyance, which they held 'in right' (*in iure*): Larson, *Conflict and Compromise*, 50–67, 147, 197. As Faith, 'Berkshire,' 139 ff., rightly points out, 'Legal security, however, did not mean economic security'.

that in such a situation, a few enterprising tenants or outsiders would snap up the land, especially if they had managerial experience or authority in the village.

In the parish of Bishop Middleham, the early results were mixed. In Sedgefield, of the eighty-one malmen, husbandmen and cottagers recorded in the 1380s, only eight had acquired a second holding (excluding exchequerland) in the village, and four shared that second holding with another tenant. Many tenants had picked up a small parcel of exchequerland, usually of four to six acres, so it is possible to talk about small-scale promotion and improvement but not real accumulation.[45] In Bishop Middleham, fourteen of the thirty-five tenants had acquired a second holding, although the sizes varied considerably. Yet in Cornforth, seven of the fifteen husbandmen held sixty acres, and two more held forty-five acres.[46] Looking at the parish as a whole, some men held land in more than one village. John Atthegate held two husbandlands in Cornforth and two cottages and forty-one acres and half a rood of demesne land in Bishop Middleham, a total of 101 acres; William Todde held a husbandland in Sedgefield, two husbandlands in Cornforth and three acres of demesne in Bishop Middleham, a total of ninety-three acres. Judging by the surnames of tenants in the three villages, several families were dispersed throughout the parish.[47] The variation in the parish reflects the estate itself, with some villages displaying little engrossment while in others multiple holdings were common.

Promotion and accumulation can be seen elsewhere on the bishopric. Robert Jonson of Norton held fifteen acres as a free tenant in addition to forty-five acres of customary land; fellow juror Gilbert Spurnhare, by the early 1380s, had accumulated more than 150 acres, including sixteen cottages, and he continued to add more, leasing thirty acres of malland in 1401.[48] A third juror, Thomas Halyman, held only a cottage and three roods of land in Bishop Hatfield's Survey.[49] However, in 1401, he acquired a messuage, two bovates of malland and four other acres of land, then eight years later he obtained another messuage and thirty acres of husbandland, and in 1413 another cottage and three roods.[50] A study of

45 Exchequerland, apparently, was created after the twelfth century as a category for lands that that did not fit into the existing divisions of customary, free and demesne lands; some owed rent and court attendance in the same way as customary lands, while others were treated much the same as free lands except for being conveyed in the halmotes. Some of these lands clearly had once been customary lands, while Helen Dunsford and Simon Harris, 'Colonization of the Wasteland in County Durham, 1100–1400', EcHR 56 (2003), 41–6, have demonstrated that others were assarts.

46 Bishop Hatfield's Survey, 180–92. Free tenures are excluded. Two more tenants held 'wasted' messuages. Harvey, Westminster Abbey and its Estates, 266–7, found few tenants with large holdings before 1391.

47 Bishop Hatfield's Survey, 180–92. Judging by surnames in the court records — which is perilous — families could be found in multiple vills; cf. Lomas, 'South-East Durham', 314.

48 Bishop Hatfield's Survey, 172–7; TNA, DURH 3/13, fol. 349ᵛ.

49 TNA, DURH 3/14, fol. 578ᵛ.

50 TNA, DURH 3/13, fol. 349ᵛ; 3/14, fols. 144ʳ, 271ʳ.

the halmote court juries indicates that jurors from Norton had holdings averaging forty-five acres, with a third of them holding more than sixty acres.[51] In many instances, it was halmote jurors such as these who were building up their holdings and developing into what Faith termed a 'peasant aristocracy'.[52] Throughout Durham, many men were acquiring second holdings and some far more, but the tendency of the halmote clerks to refer to a 'total tenure' prevents easy identification of how large this group had become.

Engrossment and accumulation continued early in the fifteenth century, though not on the previous scale. Some holdings taken were composite holdings, so it was not necessary to start from scratch. Based on Sedgefield, new accumulation was modest; Peter Kay took up a cottage in 1412 that he surrendered after acquiring a husbandland in 1413, surrendered one bovate of land in 1414, and acquired six acres in 1416.[53] The patterns in the land market for the parish match the evidence for the jurors of Norton. Moreover, men were more likely to acquire a composite tenure rather than to build one up. The availability of vacant tenures made this easier. For example, in 1409 John Gebon, reeve of Sedgefield, took seven vacant cottages at 2s. per annum, while five years later Thomas Watson came forward and took all the vacant cottages in Shotton.[54] Tenants appear again and again to renew their leases, but few ever took additional holdings; of those who took a second holding in the parish, a handful acquired a third and none in the early fifteenth century took four. Men received a composite holding from their parents or through marriage, or else leased a large parcel all at once; there was little accumulation of customary land and holdings. Those who aspired to be what we might call 'proto-yeomen' had to look beyond customary lands and think in terms larger than husbandlands.

The roles of custom and context in shaping the land market

There were many factors in play hindering the continued accumulation and development of composite holdings.[55] One was the continued emphasis on the integrity of tenures. In the transfers recorded in the bishopric halmote books, integral holdings predominated, even near 1500, as in Cornforth in 1487, when all

---

[51] Larson, 'Village Voice or Village Oligarchy', 698–9. See also Lomas, 'South-East Durham', 315–16; DeWindt, *Land and People*, 124–8.

[52] Faith, 'Berkshire', 173–7.

[53] TNA, DURH 3/14, fols. 257ʳ, 288ʳ, 294ʳ, 314ʳ, 399ʳ. Lomas, 'South-East Durham,' 309, found that no bishopric tenant in south-eastern Durham took part in more than six land transactions. One of the few gentlemen active in the customary land market was the steward himself, Sir Ralph Eure, who acquired various customary lands in vills around Stanhope and Bishop Auckland, usually at the old rent: TNA, DURH 3/14, fols. 92ʳ –497ʳ. On the Eures' accumulation of free lands in Durham, see C. D. Liddy, *The Bishopric of Durham in the Late Middle Ages: Lordship, Community and the Cult of St Cuthbert* (Woodbridge, 2008), 47–51.

[54] TNA, DURH 3/14, fols. 143ᵛ, 310ᵛ.

[55] See R. M. Smith, 'Some Issues Concerning Families and their Property in Rural England', in *Land, Kinship and Life-Cycle*, ed. idem, 6–21.

thirteen transactions were leases for husbandlands (in multiples of two, three or four).[56] Partial holdings (for example, a fourth part of a husbandland) do appear in the fifteenth century, but both divided and composite holdings were reckoned as portions or collections of whole tenures rather than a lot measured in acres.[57] The straightforward approach to subletting must have eased the need for smaller lots of land for shorter terms, as would any market in small parcels of freehold land. If the community or bishop were pressuring tenants to keep holdings together, this would have dampened the land market as a whole by limiting the opportunity for more gradual accumulation, a few acres at a time. Subletting may have complicated the circumstances; a lively market for sublets may have satisfied the needs of tenants at all levels. Yet subletting would have done little for those wishing to expand their holdings more significantly, especially as the rents on sublet land must have been higher. While subletting may hide the 'promotion' of tenants and families or adaptations to changing needs, it should not do so for men looking to build up more substantial holdings.

Inheritance customs shaped the market by encouraging large holdings to move outside the family or be broken up. On the bishopric estate, the deceased's lands went to his widow for her life; only if she refused them did the sons and then daughters have right to the lands.[58] Such widows became sought after, and many frequently remarried; this happened so much that in the wake of the Black Death the bishops imposed a special marriage licence on these 'bishop's widows' (*vidua domini*), which persisted into the early fifteenth century.[59] Presumably younger men married these widows and then acquired the rights to the land, or at least profited from them while the widow was alive. This meant that heirs had to wait longer for their lands; alternatively, they could find their own holdings, either taking up vacant lands (especially in the later fourteenth century) or by marrying a 'bishop's widow' of their own, both of which could mean leaving the village. John Varty of Blackwell was lucky that his father's widow, Isabella, declined to take up her husband's four messuages, five cottages and 195 acres in Blackwell and Darlington in 1449.[60] Much more common were situations such as when Julianna, widow of Peter Cornforth of Middridge, took up his lands of one and half husbandlands, four acres of demesne and a cottage with five acres,

[56] TNA, DURH 3/18, fol. 51ʳ⁻ᵛ.
[57] On the priory estate, there were more small and irregularly-sized parcels: Lomas, 'South-East Durham', 308–9.
[58] Cf. ibid., 300–1. See also Lomas, 'Durham Cathedral Priory', 25.
[59] On the bishop's widows, see Larson, *Conflict and Compromise*, 94–7. This is the opposite of Halesowen: Z. Razi, *Life, Marriage and Death in a Medieval Parish: Economy, Society and Demography in Halesowen 1270–1400* (Cambridge, 1980), 138. The distinction could be the right of a Durham widow to her deceased husband's full holding; while widows of cottagers may have not had many suitors, those of men with thirty acres or more of land may have been far more attractive.
[60] TNA, DURH 3/15, fol. 42ʳ.

leaving Peter's son Robert to take up other lands.[61] The aforementioned Thomas Halyman provides another example. In 1416 his widow, Alice, took up his entire holding and soon married John of Wolsingham, and Thomas's son John had to wait a further five years for the lands.[62] Not all men and women remained connected to their home village, and many did not return even when they stood to inherit lands.[63]

When the father's lands became available, the heir could have many reasons not to take the land, perhaps having moved to another village, or already possessing a holding and being unwilling to take more; the availability of land meant a son did not have to wait for his inheritance. If no man had the means to take the entire tenure when it became available, it would go into the lord's hand or be broken up into its component parts if that was what it took to find a tenant. Widows also could break up composite tenures, choosing one holding for their widow-right and refusing the rest, leaving it to be demised separately. This pattern weakened the family–land bond, if it ever really existed. On the bishopric, half or more of the land transfers were to people outside the family, whether before or after death.[64] The description of lands in the halmote books confirms this assessment, with demises recording the previous tenant and sometimes the tenant before that, and whether the lands spent time in the lord's hand.[65] Between remarriage, migration and extinction of lines, there could have been little sustained connection between a family and land.

The poor state of the economy compounded the effects of custom and fertility.[66] After the Black Death, tenants refused holdings because of poverty, and heirs refused lands or simply did not show up to answer the proclamations.[67]

---

[61] TNA, DURH 3/14, fol. 169^r.

[62] TNA, DURH 3/14, fols. 256^r, 406^v, 429^r, 578^v.

[63] Heirs failed to come forward in many instances recorded in the halmote books, even when known to the court; cf. Lomas, 'South-East Durham', 288–301.

[64] Lomas, 'South-East Durham', 295–301. Many studies have addressed the willingness of peasants to part with land; specific treatments include Whittle, 'Individualism and the Family–Land Bond', 32–3; Z. Razi, 'The Myth of the Immutable English Family', *P&P* 140 (1993), 3–44; Schofield, 'Tenurial Developments'; R. W. Hoyle, 'The Land–Family Bond in England', *P&P* 146 (1995), 151–73.

[65] For example, in 1415 Robert Eure took the 'total tenure' of Adam Cowherd, which after Cowherd's death had been held by his widow, then his daughter, and then was taken by Thomas de Egilston, who surrendered it to Robert: TNA, DURH 3/14, fol. 357^v. See note 53 above.

[66] Hatcher, 'Great Slump', 261–2. In Durham, many old debts were pursued in the halmote courts in the early fifteenth century: TNA, DURH 3/14, fol. 398^r. Lack of currency could have been a factor: Pollard, 'North-Eastern England', 77; Dyer, *An Age of Transition?*, 175. Some of the larger Durham bishopric leases specified payments in coin; for example, see TNA, DURH 3/13, fol. 101^r; 3/14, fols. 294^v, 303^r. By 1496, rents from priory holdings were paid in a mix of cash (*in pecunia*) and kind: *Bursars Rentals*, 129–97.

[67] Britnell, 'Feudal Reaction', 34–8, 42–4; Larson, *Conflict and Compromise*, 75–86, 126–7; Lomas, 'Durham Cathedral Priory', 121; Lomas, 'South-East Durham', 307–8.

Numerous holdings were demised 'at his own risk' (*suo periculo*) or deteriorated and were left that way when vacated. Even with low entry fines, the rents may still have been high enough to discourage people from taking additional lands. In 1407 the executors of Bishop Walter Skirlaw litigated sixty-seven debts in the halmote courts. Most defendants were peasants, particularly village officers, and while the records do not say, these may have been arrears for rents and dues. The debts, ranging from sixpence to £70 0s. 9¼d., amounted to £323 9s. 3d.[68] Perhaps this was a holdover from the crisis of the 1390s and the particularly poor harvest of 1401; if so, recovery and stability were not enough to regain lost ground.[69] If tenants were in arrears for existing lands, there may have been little motivation to take on additional holdings. If this was the case at a time of a relatively brisk land market, the situation later in the century would have been grave.

Such a calculus is to be expected. Ben Dodds and David Stone have argued persuasively for producers, and particularly peasants, being able to react to the market and control their production.[70] If peasants could do this, they could speculate on the success of cultivating more land. Scarcity of labour could have influenced their decisions. With the general decline of the population throughout this period, tenants may have been hard pressed to work their own lands. Difficulty in capitalisation may have been another factor.[71] The availability of moorland and other pastures could have decreased pressure to acquire customary land for conversion to pasture, as did the pressure to maintain buildings or purchase a licence for not doing so.[72] Despite the attractiveness (to us) of lands with low rents and low entry fines, there were many reasons why few persons were accumulating sizeable holdings of customary land. With the stagnant land market, further polarisation of village society was limited.

Demesnes and Villages

The next step from conglomerate holdings and large parcels was the lease of entire demesnes and even villages. The bishops of Durham, like so many other lords

---

[68] TNA, DURH 3/14, fols. 60ᵛ–70ʳ.

[69] Dodds, *Peasants and Production*, 73.

[70] Ibid., esp. 136–44; D. J. Stone, *Decision-Making in Medieval Agriculture* (Oxford, 2005). See also J. A, Raftis, *Peasant Economic Development Within the Manorial System* (Montreal, 1996).

[71] See E. Miller, 'Introduction: Land and People' in *AHEW* III, 25; Pollard, *North-Eastern England*, 48–9. Lomas suggests that population had not recovered by 1400: 'Black Death in County Durham', 129–35. There was a wave of mortality in the 1390s: Larson, *Conflict and Compromise*, 219–22; Dodds, *Peasants and Production*, 98.

[72] Pollard, *North-Eastern England*, 58–9. Some village lands were turned over to pasture; for example, Robert Cronde took forty acres in Cornforth for this use: TNA, DURH 3/15, fol. 76ᵛ. The first licences to *not* rebuild structures on a tenure appear in the early 1450s, at 20d. per tenure: for example, see TNA, DURH 3/15, fol. 278ʳ.

in England, moved away from direct cultivation of the demesne, offering many manorial lands and buildings to tenants. Leasing of elements of the demesnes had begun before the Black Death, and troubles with paying rents for demesne lands and meadows occurred alongside general tenant distress in the early 1350s. While the bishop continued to retain some lands and even exact some work services (usually mowing meadows and carriage), most demesnes were let by the 1380s.[73]

The leasing of bundles of customary holdings followed the leasing of demesne and other manorial elements. Often vacant customary holdings would be let collectively to a single tenant or to a group, such as in Blackwell, when 'twenty bond tenants, in addition to their own holdings, held jointly five bovates' of customary land.[74] Enterprising individuals also took such lands; for example, in 1408 Thomas Redmershill took up twelve and a half messuages and twenty-five bovates of land, nearly half the husbandlands of Carlton.[75] Vacant lands and demesne would be enclosed, presumably for conversion to grazing, as when Richard Osbernne took two closes of demesne at Stockton and some other parcels with the associated works on an annual basis at £25.[76] The four men leasing the *utercourt* in Stockton received an allocation of one mark to their rent annually to cover the cost and maintenance of enclosure.[77] Some individuals and groups took both demesne and customary lands, as in 1406 when five men leased the demesne at Bishop Middleham for six years at £10 per annum and four husbandlands and a meadow at the usual rent.[78] This was where the greatest opportunities lay. Richard Denom took the grange of Middridge with various lands and works along with certain rents from Bolam for nine years at £25 14s. 4d.; the lease included a clause that should a war or a 'common pestilence' damage his profits, the bishop's council would deliberate on an allocation to his rent.[79] Later, with Robert Denom, he took two granges in Heighington along with several closes, 210 acres of demesne and sixty acres of pasture with associated works for twenty years at £14 9s.[80] The leasing of holdings in this way reduced the opportunity for

---

[73] *Bishop Hatfield's Survey*, 1–199; Larson, *Conflict and Compromise*, 151, 202–3, 207; see also Britnell, 'Feudal Reaction', 45–7. Most priory demesnes had been leased by 1416: Lomas, 'The Priory of Durham and its Demesnes in the Fourteenth and Fifteenth Centuries', *EcHR* 31 (1978), 339–53; E. M. Halcrow, 'The Decline of Demesne Farming on the Estates of Durham Cathedral Priory', *EcHR* 7 (1954), 345–56; *Bursars Rentals*, 199–227.

[74] Britnell, 'Feudal Reaction,' 44–45, referring to *Bishop Hatfield's Survey*, 12–13. There are many other examples of collective holdings in the Survey.

[75] TNA, DURH 3/14, fol. 118^r; *Bishop Hatfield's Survey*, 177–8.

[76] TNA, DURH 3/14, fol. 457^v ff. Members of the Osbernne family would renew the lease, annually, for several decades.

[77] TNA, DURH 3/16, fol. 5^r.

[78] TNA, DURH 3/14, fol. 43^r.

[79] TNA, DURH 3/14, fols. 154^v–155^r. He renewed the lease for twenty years at £25 12s. 4d.: DURH 3/14, fol. 426^r.

[80] TNA, DURH 3/14, fol. 414^v.

piecemeal accumulation, driving a cycle that took options away from all but the wealthier peasants, or groups.

In the fourteenth century, although village communities often leased parts of their vill or the local manor, leasing of hamlets and villages generally was limited to the gentry.[81] Ricknall was the first of the core of bishopric villages to be let, but it had been turned into a grange by the 1380s on account of depopulation.[82] In the fifteenth century, however, populated villages were turned over to lessees. By 1419, Cassop, Wardon and Moreton had been let.[83] Up to this point, the leases were taken by one or two men, usually for terms of twelve or sixteen years. The loss of the halmote books for much of the second quarter of the century deprives us of an exact chronology, but the leasing of vills had increased by the 1440s. West Thickley, Killerby, Heighington, Shaldforth, Hardwick, Ryhope and Tunstall had all been let in the 1440s, while Sherburn, Coundon, Shotton and Bishop Middleham were leased in the following decade.[84] The leases increasingly went to syndicates (often including jurors from the village) or the tenants themselves.[85] The terms of these leases were shorter than those granted to individuals, usually lasting from three to six years. The leases included most of the customary lands (with exceptions noted) with demesne, pasture, buildings and dues, and often including the ovens, forges and fishing and brewing rights; sometimes perquisites of the courts were included. When jurors Robert Cronde, John Huchonson and John Garry along with Richard Fyndlawe took the village of Cornforth in 1459 for six years, the lease included not only the vill and lands but the oven, the dues of cornage, *metrith* and *wodlades*, carriage of wine, forty chickens and 200 eggs among other items; however, the brewing, mill and halmote perquisites were reserved to the bishop.[86] As with smaller parcels of land, it is difficult to talk of men or families building up holdings. After acquiring a large holding, those who did

---

[81]   For example, Lady Isabella de Horden took the hamlet of Little Thorpe (Easington) in 1394 for twenty years: TNA, DURH 3/13, fol. 137[v]. The farm of boroughs such as Darlington is not included here.

[82]   Britnell, 'Feudal Reaction', 40–1; *Bishop Hatfield's Survey*, 25. It had been enclosed by 1417: TNA, DURH 3/14, fol. 427[r].

[83]   TNA, DURH 3/14, fols. 184[v], 303[r], 310[r], 510[v].

[84]   TNA, DURH 3/15, fols. 51[v], 114[v], 122[v], 148[v], 149[r], 172[v], 274[r], 297[v], 363[v]; 3/16, fol. 56[v].

[85]   This was later than the formation of the first syndicates on the priory estate, which began forming by 1414 and contained from one to thirteen shares: *Bursars Rentals*, 201–17. Lomas, 'Durham Cathedral Priory', 38–9, 57; R. A. Lomas, 'Developments in Land Tenure on the Prior of Durham's Estates in the Later Middle Ages', *NH* 13 (1988), 35–9. Lomas identified a bishopric syndicate in the village of Boldon in Hatfield's Survey: ibid., 38–9. This arrangement was not the same as other village leases, as it did not contain the entire village, but it clearly was heading in that direction: *Bishop Hatfield's Survey*, 101.

[86]   TNA, DURH 3/16, fol. 56[v]. John Garry took the mill of Norton that same tourn, for three years at £17 13s. 4d. for the first year and £18 thereafter: TNA, DURH 3/16, fol. 57[r]. See also TNA, DURH 3/18, fols. 49[v]–50[r].

keep it tended to renew it on similar terms without adding significantly to it, or new men took up the lease; in some instances the lands reverted to direct control by the bishop.[87]

The collective approach to taking lands suggests that pooling resources was necessary to acquire these larger holdings, and that there was continuing co-operation among peasants. In some cases, where the syndicate was the village jury, this seems to have been the logical conclusion of earlier developments concentrating judicial power in the hands of a few men as well as the possible development of patron–client networks within the villages.[88] Many syndicates included or were comprised of jurors from that village. The motivation of an entire village taking the village on lease is more difficult to discern. The tenants of Tunstall received a considerable discount from the old rent; the rent in 1457 of £16 was less than half the value in the 1380s (£34 13s.), and in 1467 the rent was reduced even further, to £12 11s. 8d.[89] On the other hand, the above lease of Cornforth at £22 6s. 8d. for the first three years of the lease, and £22 13s. 4d. for the remainder, is almost the same as the value of all lands (excluding freeholds) recorded in Hatfield's Survey as £22 5s. 2½d.[90] Given the preference for charging the old rent, the tenants received scant savings. As the bishop normally reserved the perquisites of the court, they did not receive greater control over their village (unless they found a way to keep pleas out of court). They did gain more economic control; and perhaps the pooling of resources permitted easier cultivation. It is difficult to put a price on self-determination, and the greater freedom to direct their village independently of the lord may have been of considerable worth.[91] While difficult to place in context by itself, the taking of the village by the tenants fits into the estate's history. Village communities were leasing parcels of demesne and even vacant tenures in the aftermath of the Black Death.[92] Even multiple villages worked together, as when in 1397 eight men on behalf of the villages of Bishop Middleham, Sedgefield and Cornforth came to court to take two meadows (Newmedowe and Edmondesmedowe), with the works, for twelve years at 66s. 8d.[93] Strong communities persisted in the bishopric. The situation was not always

---

[87] Some men did acquire additional holdings; Richard Denom, frequent lessee of the demesnes at Heighington, also took the lease of six vacant cottages in 1440: TNA, DURH 3/15, fol. 43[r].

[88] Larson, 'Village Voice or Village Oligarchy'; Larson, *Conflict and Compromise*, 172–98, 212–23. On patron–client relationships: DeWindt, *Land and People*, 281.

[89] *Bishop Hatfield's Survey*, 135–6; TNA, DURH 3/16, fols. 10[r], 172[r].

[90] TNA, DURH 3/16, fol. 56[v]; *Bishop Hatfield's Survey*, 184–6. The total from *averpenys* was left blank in the Survey.

[91] Britnell, 'Feudal Reaction', 45.

[92] Ibid., 42–6.

[93] TNA, DURH 3/13, fol. 216[v].

harmonious; but it is still possible to talk of a communal spirit and identity in the same period where individuals are increasingly prominent.[94]

Mining, Mills and Other Activities

The sampling involved in exploring the land market above revealed other examples of economic opportunity on the bishopric estate, although the nature of the halmote books limits these to mere glimpses. Resource extraction, including coal mining, is one such area, although the nature of mining means that examples in the halmote books occurred infrequently.[95] For example, a coal pit was opened in one of the fields at Broom in 1415 and leased for three years to William Molat and William Barre (a monk of the priory) for 40s. per annum.[96] One other industry was mining lime in the village of Sherburn. Thomas Alanson leased a pit there in 1410 in return for sixty quarters of lime delivered to Durham castle (with a 10s. allocation for costs of carriage), which was redefined as 160 packhorse-loads (*summagia*) at the renewal of the lease.[97] In 1415 Thomas opened a new pit at 4s. per annum for five years, rising to a half mark in the sixth and final year of his lease. However, leases of pits for coal or lime, never frequent to begin with, all but disappear from the halmote records after 1420.

The halmote books provide greater information on mills, predominantly for milling grain but also for fulling. After 1350, lords throughout England increasingly leased out their mills, and Durham is no exception. At least twenty-three mills had been let by the 1380s, mostly to village communities, and in the first three-quarters of the fifteenth century leases for mills in fifteen bishopric villages and boroughs are found in the halmote books.[98] The rents for the mills tended to remain steady or decline in value. For example, the Swalwellmill in Hatfield's Survey was let for £20 although it used to fetch £38; it declined to £13 6s. 8d. in 1406 before rising briefly to £14 0s. 9d. in 1414 and then to £15 in 1419. It then

---

94 Britnell, 'Feudal Reaction'; Larson, *Conflict and Compromise*, esp. 212–38. On stresses in communities, see also Dyer, *An Age of Transition?*, 74–8.

95 See Pollard, *North-Eastern England*, 74–7.

96 TNA, DURH 3/14, fol. 370ᵛ.

97 TNA, DURH 3/14, fols. 164ᵛ, 266ʳ.

98 There were additional mills recorded in Hatfield's Survey without indication of whether they had been leased: *Bishop Hatfield's Survey*, 9, 39, 61, 73, 80, 92–3, 112, 114, 131, 133–4, 139, 155, 160–1, 175, 178, 186, 188; TNA, DURH 3/14, fols. 3ʳ, 15ʳ, 48ᵛ, 52ᵛ, 100ʳ, 101ʳ, 111ᵛ, 147ᵛ, 154ᵛ, 160ᵛ, 197ᵛ, 203ᵛ, 213ʳ, 251ʳ, 262ʳ, 267ᵛ, 300ʳ⁻ᵛ, 387ᵛ, 410ᵛ, 421ʳ, 443ᵛ, 455ᵛ, 477ᵛ, 505ᵛ; 3/15, fols. 5ᵛ, 10ᵛ, 12ᵛ, 32ᵛ, 41ʳ, 73ᵛ, 75ʳ, 86ʳ, 201ʳ; 3/16, fols. 5ᵛ, 7ᵛ, 304ᵛ, 309ᵛ. On milling in England, see J. Langdon, *Mills in the Medieval Economy: England 1300–1540* (Oxford, 2004), esp. 178–218 for the lease of demesne mills. The data on the bishopric mills fit most trends described by Langdon (who used fifteen priory mills in his sample). One exception is that length of leases for bishopric mills generally remained short, rather than increasing in length: ibid., 187–192.

fell to £10 by 1438, before rising to £12 6s. 8d. in 1455.[99] About a quarter of the lessees were named or described as millers.[100] Some were clearly peasants from the village, as when John Halyman and Thomas Wedow, tenants in Norton, took half the mill there with a Stockton man taking the other half.[101] A few years later, John Garry, juror of Cornforth, leased the Norton mill at a slightly increased rent.[102] Robert Cronde, another juror of Cornforth, leased the Cornforth mill for six years at £5 6s. 8d. in 1459.[103] More interesting is the situation in the villages of Bishopwearmouth, Tunstall, Ryhope and Burdon. In 1407 a dispute arose among two of the village collectors over payments of *milneferme*, which was distributed between the four vills and totalled £33 6s. 5d.[104] This was a collective rent for the mill(s) and brewing rights of the four villages that the tenants had negotiated with the bishop. For an individual, a mill meant profit; for a village community, it meant independence, as multure was an unpopular seigniorial due.[105] However, the lease of a mill by the village was rare; most leases went to a single man.

Independence as a motive may have been behind the acquisition of a monopoly on brewing within a village. Traditionally, the brewing of ale and then beer was an individual matter, and throughout the period it was common to see four to six tenants or their wives amerced sixpence in the halmote court for 'breaking' the assize of ale.[106] Yet there are instances where an individual leased the right to brew in a village, as in 1440 when John Cornforth of Cornforth leased the 'brewing' of the village for a year at forty pence.[107] These leases covered not only an oven for malt or brewhouse, but the sole right to brew for sale, as demonstrated by amercements for those who brewed without the permission of the licence holder. Such individual leases were not common, however, perhaps because few brewers were able to satisfy the needs of the village, or because the profit margin was too slim; such monopolies are more commonly found included in the lease of a village.[108]

In a similar vein, in those villages near rivers, taking the fishing rights for

99 *Bishop Hatfield's Survey*, 93; TNA, DURH 3/14, fols. 15ʳ, 300ʳ, 505ᵛ; 3/15, fols. 10ᵛ, 365ʳ; see Langdon, *Mills in the Medieval Economy*, 58.

100 Langdon, *Mills in the Medieval Economy*, 201–4.

101 TNA, DURH 3/16, fol. 5ᵛ.

102 TNA, DURH 3/16, fol. 57ʳ.

103 TNA, DURH 3/16, fol. 26ʳ.

104 TNA, DURH 3/14, fol. 52ᵛ; *Bishop Hatfield's Survey*, 133–4.

105 Disputes over multure rates, complicated by the varieties of tenures, were a problem on the bishopric estate: Larson, *Conflict and Compromise*, 91–2, 107, 118, 128.

106 On the assize of ale, see J. M. Bennett, *Ale, Beer, and Brewsters in England: Women's Work in a Changing World, 1300–1600* (Oxford, 1996), esp. 4, 99–106, 160–3, 173.

107 TNA, DURH 3/15, fol. 53ᵛ.

108 In *Bishop Hatfield's Survey* these often were leased to the village community, sometimes under the heading 'toll of ale' (*tolnetum cervisiae*).

a stretch of river was an option.[109] William Taillor and Hugh Ayer took fishing rights in the Wear at Ryton for 48s. 8d., a rise from the previous rent of 36s. 8d.; by 1418, the rent had risen to 71s. 6d. and in 1438 the villagers of Ryton collectively leased the rights for £5.[110] Not all locations were as lucrative; the lease in 1410 of the rights in Bondgate-in-Darlington to three men for 2s. a year, or in Stockton, where the rate was raised from 40d. to 5s. in 1413 and then to half a mark in 1439, are more representative.[111] The extent of the right was limited geographically, often bounded on one side by the mill. As with brewing monopolies, this right often was included with other leases, in this case with the local mill or sometimes the ferry.[112] The rent levels suggest this may have been more of an economic opportunity for villages rather than an exercise in self-determination. Judging by the increase in many of these rents, there was some opportunity to make money in riverine fishing; this appears to be one of few sectors where the rural economy in Durham expanded.[113]

Conclusions: Understanding Economic Activity

The bishopric halmote books record few entrepreneurial activities open to the peasantry that were not related to land, although there are tantalising instances.[114] Evidence of non-agricultural activities dries up from the middle of the fifteenth century, as litigation (including debts, broken contracts and failure to pay salaries) began to disappear from the halmote books. By the end of the century, such information is hit-or-miss, and for some villages it is nearly impossible to tell even if peasants were poor because the records only contain a list of village jurors. What the records do preserve consistently is information on land, and this depicts broad trends but also numerous variations throughout the estate. The years after the Black Death saw peasants amass larger holdings, often of demesne, some of whom could even be thought of as farmers in the early modern or modern sense. As Dodds has pointed out, the stereotypical 'peasant psychology' does not appear to have constrained decision-making in Durham.[115] However, custom, community and the economic situation shaped attempts at accumulation and

[109] Dodds, *Peasants and Production*, 174.
[110] TNA, DURH 3/14, fols. 99ᵛ, 464ᵛ; 3/15, fol. 10ʳ.
[111] TNA, DURH 3/14, fols. 99ᵛ, 168ᵛ, 289ᵛ; 3/15, fol. 7ʳ.
[112] For an example of fishing rights included with other leases, see TNA, DURH 3/14, fol. 341ᵛ.
[113] Sea fishing also expanded and was far more profitable: Dodds, *Peasants and Production*, 89–92.
[114] Some priory tenants got into trouble rendering fish oil: Larson, *Conflict and Compromise*, 181. Dodds, *Peasants and Production*, 173, commented that 'for many, the benefits of the non-agricultural sectors must have been confined to the occasional chance find of a porpoise on the beach or an illegal but remunerative expedition with the dogs to the lord's rabbit warren'.
[115] Dodds, *Peasants and Production*, 174.

entrepreneurship.[116] Some villages remained intact and retained stable, consistent leadership by the same families for decades. The land market in Bishop Middleham, as in the south-eastern part of the county, was very sluggish and tenurial practices precluded piecemeal accumulation of acres.

Stability does not preclude change, of course, and the social and economic ordering of those villages was not the same as it had been at the time of the Black Death or even of Bishop Hatfield's Survey. By 1500, and in many places much earlier, there was considerable variation in the accumulation of lands and consequently in the social and economic stratification among tenants in the villages. The bishopric villages generally contained a mix of tenants: true smallholders, husbandmen and men with two or perhaps three husbandlands. The divide between the haves and the have-nots had increased, but the collective and communal possession of land may have softened the effects of such polarisation in some villages.[117] The most significant transformation was in some senses greater than or external to the village, as copyhold or proto-yeoman farmers, if we can call them either at this point, leased demesnes or held lands in more than one village. The wealth of men like John Halyman, John Hall and Robert Cronde was more truly measured in their acquisition or leasing of large closes, demesnes, mills and villages, not in the piecemeal accumulation of customary land; they and their families had made the leap from holding thirty acres to sixty to farming on a far larger scale. Syndicates and village communities acquired control over villages and demesnes, adding another stratum between lord and peasant.[118] The transformation of the bishop from lord to landlord and the insertion of a new layer of lessees between lord and peasants, begun in the 1350s, was largely completed by the middle of the fifteenth century.

This new social order demonstrates the slow evolution of two trends evident even in the aftermath of the Black Death. Many villages came together, to take land, to resist Bishop Hatfield's feudal reaction, and even to direct their own affairs.[119] Simultaneously, a small group within each village, of which the jury was

---

[116] Of course, tradition changed with the times, so care is needed when using it as an explanation; the same is true of the village community. Sherri Olson, *A Chronicle of All That Happens: Voices from the Village Court in Medieval England* (Toronto, 1996), 162–227, argued that the conservatism of late medieval villages came from the villages themselves, as they tried to grapple with the changes of the fifteenth century. See also Schofield, *Peasant and Community*, 75–6; Larson, 'Rural Transformation in Northern England'.

[117] Similar trends have been found elsewhere; see Harvey, 'Conclusions', 340–3; J. Mullan, 'Accumulation and Polarisation in Two Bailiwicks of the Winchester Bishopric Estates, 1350–1410: Regional Similarities and Contrasts', in *Agriculture and Rural Society*, ed. Dodds and Britnell, 188–93; Dyer, *An Age of Transition?*, 208–9. Cf. Whittle, *Development of Agrarian Capitalism*, 97–8.

[118] See Britnell, *Commercialisation*, 201.

[119] The reeve and jurors often represented the village in dealing with the lord and outsiders: Larson, *Conflict and Compromise*, 58–61, 217–19. During the crisis of the 1390s, bishopric

a significant part, took larger amounts of land and exercised considerable authority.[120] In some villages, these peasant oligarchies (sometimes joined or supplanted by outsiders) took even greater control over the village by leasing it from the lord; elsewhere, communal spirit saw the village take a stronger corporate form. In both cases, control of lands and control of people shifted away from the bishop. The patterns set early, and there was little change in the overall village socio-economic structure in the fifteenth century; it appears that what was true for Bishop Middleham, Sedgefield and Cornforth was broadly true for many other villages in the estate. While there is need for further work both on the regional variations in Durham and on the increasing differences between the priory and bishopric estates, it is again clear that the decline of lordship saw the increasing power of individuals *and* communities in agrarian affairs in the fifteenth century, both in entrepreneurial advancement and in protective self-determination.

villages held their own meetings to set their own bylaws: ibid., 216–17. In 1412 the reeve of Easington called a meeting to settle quarrels in the village before the court, to avoid amercements; their meeting was discovered, and they were fined half a mark: TNA, DURH 3/14, fol. 248ᵛ.

[120] Larson, 'Village Voice or Village Oligarchy', esp. 697–706.

9

The Shipmaster as Entrepreneur in Medieval England
....
Maryanne Kowaleski

THE SUCCESSFUL SHIPMASTER or *magister* of a medieval ship possessed many skills: navigational expertise to guide the vessel to its destination; commercial acumen to dispose of cargoes in his charge; management ability to employ, victual and direct a crew of men who were often of disparate backgrounds and ethnicities; business savvy to cope with wily seamen, shore-side workers and merchants in foreign ports; initiative to handle the dangers and risks that pervaded life at sea; and a basic understanding of law and international politics to steer his ship, cargo and crew through the dangerous waters of the medieval seas.[1] This essay focuses on the entrepreneurial skills that medieval English shipmasters needed to be successful, particularly in terms of shipowning, naval service, remuneration, trade, managerial skills and the hazy border between privateering and piracy. Shipmasters often had an important stake in individual trading voyages, particularly when they owned all or part of the ship or had some share of the cargo. Even when their ownership stake was small, their ability to react quickly to ever-changing circumstances — whether a shift in the wind that kept them in a foreign port for weeks on end, or the loss of cargo in a storm, attacks by pirates, a shortage of the goods customers wanted or the loss of crewmen to illness or death — was essential since they were most responsible for the ultimate profit or loss of the voyage. In a period when trust and reputation were crucial, the shipmaster's pivotal role as fast-thinking and experienced middleman between crew and the shipowners, merchants, shore-side workers and local port residents is worth investigating further.

The most entrepreneurial shipmasters were those who also owned the ship they skippered, since they had to split their time between the navigational and managerial role of mastering a ship and the commercial activities of an owner responsible for upkeep, arranging for freight, dealing with merchants and often

---

[1]   A good introduction to these skills, particularly in terms of maritime law and seamanship, is in R. Ward, *The World of the Medieval Shipmaster: Law, Business and the Sea c.1350–c.1450* (Woodbridge, 2009).

selling cargoes himself. If the vessel was primarily involved in fishing, the ship-master/shipowner had to be knowledgeable about the art of fishing, as well as supervising his crew and selling the catch. This dual managerial/commercial function was most suited to smaller boats of under twenty tons, which cost less to build, run and crew. A very high percentage of this category of shipmasters owned small passenger vessels or fishing boats, both of which could be pressed into coastal trade when necessary.[2] We should not underestimate the labour involved in even the smaller vessels, however; twenty-ton boats were usually manned by a crew of four to five, while thirty-ton ships required a crew of six.[3]

Shipmasters who also owned their boats were most common in the fishing industry, in which small craft of less than twenty tons were the norm. A 1336 royal inquisition to discover vessels suitable for naval transport in Norfolk, for instance, recorded nine fishing boats in Holkham and twelve in Wells-next-the-Sea; two were of twenty tons burthen, but the rest were mostly twelve tons.[4] All were owned by their own shipmaster, two of whom owned three vessels and three of whom had two. Similarly, three of the seven small boats and 'scaffs' in the fishing hamlet of Cokton in Dawlish (Devon) in the early fifteenth century were owned by their shipmasters; the other four were co-owned by two men who were said to be both possessors and masters, except for the boat owned by a father and son, which was skippered by the father.[5] In larger ports such as Dunwich, the fish-ing boats were also small and sometimes owned by their skippers, but were more often owned by the wealthier burgesses — most of them merchants — who hired masters and crew to work during the fishing seasons.[6]

Shipmaster/shipowners in the fishing industry resided mostly in rural com-munities or small coastal towns where they often ranked among the wealthier residents. These men tended to be relatively prosperous landowners; of the four shipmaster/shipowners at Holkham taxed in the 1332 lay subsidy, all ranked in the top ten taxpayers in the village, paying sums indicative of solid middling wealth.[7] The picture was much the same in Dawlish, where the shipmaster/ship-

[2] See, for example, A. J. F. Dulley, 'The Early History of the Rye Fishing Industry', *Sussex Archaeological Collections* 108 (1969), 46–7; D. Woodward, 'Ships, Masters and Shipowners in the Wirral 1550–1650,' *Mariner's Mirror* 63 (1977), 233–47; P. Hyde, *Faversham Ships and Seamen in the Sixteenth Century* (Faversham Papers 45, 1997), 6–8, 22–4, 49. Medieval naval service normally required ships of forty tons or more, but when the standard fell to twenty tons in times of great need, many fishing craft were pressed into service.

[3] Woodward, 'Ships, Masters, and Shipowners in the Wirral,' 235, and n. 5 below.

[4] TNA, C47/2/25; printed in *Lordship and Landscape in Norfolk 1250–1350: The Early Records of Holkham*, ed. W. Hassall and J. Beauroy (Oxford, 1993), 451–2.

[5] ECL, Dean and Chapter Archives [hereafter D&C] 957. The small size of the fishing boats is indicated by their crews, which ranged from two to five men.

[6] M. Bailey, 'Introduction,' in *The Bailiffs' Minute Book of Dunwich 1404–1430*, ed. idem (Suffolk Records Society 34, 1992), 17–18.

[7] They were John Bilney (taxed 10s., second highest in the community of fifty-three taxpay-

owners were also fisher-farmers and sometimes even villeins. Edward atte Berne, for instance, was a tenant who had a fishing boat with a crew of five; this may have been the *Nicholas* of Kenton (the manor next to Dawlish) which he mastered on a coastal voyage to ship wine to Exeter.[8] In port towns, shipmaster/owners ranked above hired shipmasters in terms of wealth and political status, but the latter were still of above-average means. In Dunwich, for example, the twenty-five fishing skippers working the herring and sprat fisheries in 1419 paid an average lay subsidy tax of 27.6*d.* compared to the overall town average of 17.9*d.*[9] Yet the wealthier shipowner/shipmasters like Robert Genew paid higher taxes (6*s.* 6*d.* in Robert's case) and also served in municipal office, a position that the hired skippers rarely attained. Evidence from other small port towns such as Hythe in Kent and Scarborough in Yorkshire also points to the ubiquity of fishing shipmaster/shipowners who took on the occasional coastal voyage and engaged in other activities (such as farming) on the side.[10] They tended to rank in the upper quarter of their home communities in terms of wealth, a reflection of the cost of building even a small, twenty-ton ship, which in the 1460s would have required an outlay of at least £40, to which should be added the significant costs of upkeep, wages and victuals for the crew and a multitude of other expenses.[11]

ers), William Daulin/Dollow (8*s.*), Walter Osbern (4*s.*), and John Speller (6*s.* 8*d.*); for their taxes and farming activities, see *Lordship and Landscape in Norfolk*, 449–50, 462, 474, 492, 500, 508, 516. The remaining shipmaster/shipowner, Richard Silk, may have been related to John Silk, taxed at only 8*d.*

[8]   ECL, D&C 957, 946 and 959 (residence and lands at Cokton), 955 (lands at Estdoune owing rent of 9*s.* 4½*d.*; DRO, Exeter Local Port Customs Accounts [hereafter Exeter PCA], 1449/50. The situation was similar in Walberswick and Thorpe in Suffolk; see M. Bailey, 'Coastal Fishing off South East Suffolk in the Century after the Black Death', *Proceedings of the Suffolk Instiute of Archaeology and History* 37 (1990), 102–14.

[9]   Bailey, 'Introduction', 18. The fishing masters working the summer fisheries, however, paid on average only 21.1*d.* in tax.

[10] About twenty-five per cent of 207 wills from Hythe before 1520 include bequests of maritime items, mostly fishing equipment; about one-quarter of the maritime bequests were for boats or shares in boats. See A. Hussey, 'Hythe Wills, First Part: A to F', *Archaeologia Cantiana* 49 (1937), 27–56; idem, 'Hythe Wills, Second Part: G to M', *Archaeologia Cantiana* 50 (1938), 87–121; idem, 'Hythe Wills, Third and Final Part,' *Archaeologia Cantiana* 51 (1939), 27–65. Initial analysis of the officeholders and local taxes assessed at Hythe (East Kent Record Office, H1052, H1055, H1068) indicates that the shipmaster/shipowners ranked in the top twenty per cent of the population in terms of wealth and political office. See also P. Heath, 'North Sea Fishing in the Fifteenth Century: The Scarborough Fleet', *NH* 3 (1968), 53–69.

[11] G. V. Scammell, 'Shipowning in England, *c.*1450–1550', *TRHS* 12 (1962), 112. In the Hanse towns of Germany, shipmaster/shipowners of large cogs were often wealthy citizens who were chosen as aldermen and even mayor; see K.-P. Kiedel, 'The Life of a Sailor in the Hanse Period', in *The Hanse Cog of 1380*, ed. K.-P. Kiedel and U. Schnall, trans. Norma Wieland (Bremerhaven, 1985), 74. In England, however, there was always a significant social gap between merchant oligarchs and shipmasters, even if the latter owned their own ship.

Shipmasters who owned their own sailing craft were also often engaged in the coastal carrying trade, which, although poorly documented for the Middle Ages, probably represented some three-quarters of all trading voyages.[12] The local port customs accounts of fifteenth-century Southampton, for instance, show that the majority of ship movements were by smaller vessels of twenty to thirty tons that seem to have been largely owned by their master, who also was the ship's chief merchant.[13] One such shipmaster was John Shepard, who in 1469–70 alone was involved in 83 separate journeys, almost all of them between Southampton and the Isle of Wight, suggesting he was following a very regular route in which he transported kerseys from the Isle of Wight in exchange for goods transshipped to Southampton from English coastal towns (primarily fish but also slate and grain) or from overseas. Other Southampton shipmasters/shipowners oriented their coastal trade more towards Sussex, while the fish trade was largely handled by master/owners from Cornwall and Devon.[14]

Shipmasters less often owned the larger ocean-going ships, which were usually attached to major seaports. In a sample of 174 English merchant vessels seeking royal license to carry pilgrims to Santiago de Compostela in the period 1390 to 1460, for example, only twelve per cent of the vessels with known owners included a shipmaster among the owners.[15] Their ships, moreover, tended to be smaller than the average vessel on the pilgrimage route, which suggests the lower capital at their disposal compared to the merchant shipowners who predominated among ocean-going ships of over fifty tons.[16] A sample of vessels called up for naval service between 1300 and 1498 shows much the same trend; just over thirteen per cent were owned wholly or in part by shipmasters.[17] Of sixty-three ships

---

[12] M. Kowaleski, *Local Markets and Regional Trade in Medieval Exeter* (Cambridge, 1995), 223–31. For fishing skippers involved in the carrying trade by coast, see Bailey, 'Introduction', 18.

[13] See S. Rose, 'The Port of Southampton in the Fifteenth Century: Shipping and Ships Masters', *Proceedings of the Hampshire Field Club Archaeological Society* 61 (2006), 177–9, for this and the following.

[14] *The Port Books of Southampton*, ed. P. Studer (Southampton Record Society 15, 1913), pp. xvii–xxii. For the transport of fish by coastal trade, see also M. Kowaleski, 'The Expansion of the South-Western Fisheries in Late Medieval England', *EcHR* 53 (2000), 429–54.

[15] This list is based on the licences tabulated in C. M. Storrs, *Jacobean Pilgrims from England to St. James of Compostela from the Early Twelfth to the Late Fifteenth Century* (Santiago de Compostela, 1994), 173–89, but checked and augmented by reference to the original documents, primarily TNA, C76 Treasury Rolls, *CPR*, and *Foedera, conventiones, litterae, et cujuscumque generis acta publica inter reges Angliae*, comp. T. Rymer (10 vols., The Hague, 1739–45).

[16] Note too that the pilgrim ships owned by shipmasters carried an average of fifty-three pilgrims compared to the overall average of sixty-one pilgrims.

[17] This sample is taken from a database of 1,393 records for 1,118 ships; shipowners could be identified for 683 ships, 169 of which were called for naval service in this period (an attempt was made to count each ship only once). The naval references were drawn from a variety

mustered at Plymouth in 1450 and 1451 for service to the crown, about twenty-one per cent listed a shipmaster as one of the owners, including the very large 300-ton *Barry* of Fowey, skippered and owned by Julian Hicke of Fowey.[18] This example, however, represents an exception. Most of the information at our disposal suggests that around fifteen per cent of larger ocean-going ships in the late Middle Ages had a shipmaster as an owner or co-owner, in contrast with smaller fishing, coastal and passenger craft of twenty tons or less, well over half of which were owned and operated by shipmasters. In terms of shipowning, therefore, it was small-scale shipmaster/shipowners, many of them captains of fishing craft, who had the edge in entrepreneurial investment and management. Their tendency to be involved in other income-generating activities, such as farming and the coastal carrying trade, could have been part of an overall strategy to mute the risks that ship ownership could entail.[19]

Shipmasters of vessels over fifty tons were sometimes co-owners with merchants or gentry, an arrangement that had advantages for both parties. Shipmasters were able to draw on the capital provided by their richer partners, while the latter had a trustworthy managing partner to keep a close eye on trading ventures. We know little of the financial arrangements entailed in such agreements, but having a knowledgeable co-owner along to manage the ship and its crew surely must have benefited the merchant owner and given the voyage a greater chance of success.[20] What little we do know often comes from disputes that made their way to the courts. In 1388, for instance, a dispute between the co-owners of *la Cristofre* of London — the shipmaster Nicholas Horne and the merchant John Burwell — reveals that John had clearly invested more than Nicholas in their wine cargo, since he claimed five-eighths and the shipmaster Nicholas three-eighths from the profits of selling the wine. John also noted his contributions towards the expenses of equipping the ship with appropriate tackle and the victuals and wages of the crew, although we do not learn the exact amount of his investment.[21] The law of the sea, as codified in the Rolls of Oléron and its associated judgments and additions, also refers to one distinct advantage of a shipmaster co-owner: the

---

of sources, but primarily from TNA, E101 and C47 naval ship calls, and references to naval service in the *CPR* and *CCR*. The 13.6 per cent figure includes a small number of shipmasters who were known to have owned another ship which they presumably must have mastered at some point.

[18] I. Friel, *The Good Ship: Ships, Shipbuilding and Technology in England 1200–1520* (London, 1995), 30.

[19] See also Woodward, 'Ships, Masters, and Shipowners in the Wirral', 243.

[20] See the discussion by Ward, *World of the Medieval Shipmaster*, 51–62; Scammell, 'Shipowning in England', 115.

[21] *Calendar of the Plea and Memoranda Rolls of the City of London*, III: 1381–1412, ed. A. H. Thomas (Cambridge, 1932), 136; Ward (*World of the Medieval Shipmaster*, 55–6) interprets Horne as the shipmaster.

right to pledge his ship and its goods as surety for a loan or recognisance when in dire need of cash while away from home.[22] Shipmasters who were not co-owners first had to gain the consent of the crew and could not include the ship's hull in the surety. Shipmaster co-owners might also sell their share of a ship, although they had to give right of first refusal to the other co-owner. Such arrangements could become fraught if the shipmaster was a foreigner, as in the case of Flemish and Portuguese shipmasters in partnership with London merchants.[23]

Although the scholarly literature tends to assume that the shipmaster who owned his own vessel was the norm in the twelfth and thirteenth centuries, there is in fact little concrete evidence for this assumption.[24] The crucial factor here was size: the larger the ship, the more expensive it was, and therefore the less likely it was to be solely owned by shipmasters, most of whom lacked the substantial capital needed to buy and maintain a ship over forty or fifty tons. Ships tended to be smaller in the twelfth and thirteenth centuries, hence more of them had shipmaster owners, although we have no idea of the percentage actually owned by shipmasters. As ships grew in size in the later Middle Ages, it appears that shipmasters who had sole ownership of their ship decreased in number, but they still predominated as owners of ships of twenty tons or less.[25] The growing size of ocean-going ships and the mounting dangers of sea travel during the war-torn centuries of the fourteenth and fifteenth century also encouraged the distribution of risk over multiple shipowners, which could include a shipmaster but frequently did not.[26] Even as employees, however, shipmasters took on a very large range of responsibilities and had to exercise a variety of entrepreneurial skills to ensure a successful voyage.

It is important to remember that most shipmasters did not run their own

---

[22] For this and the following, see *Monumenta Juridica: The Black Book of the Admiralty*, ed. T. Twiss (4 vols., Rolls Series 1871–6), I, 88–9; III, 5–6; Ward, *World of the Medieval Shipmaster*, 57, 62, 220–4.

[23] *Calendar of Letters from the Mayor and Corporation of the City of London, c.1350–1370*, ed. R. R. Sharpe (London, 1885), 81; *CPR, 1452–61*, 61, 166.

[24] For example, S. Rose, *The Medieval Sea* (London, 2007), 151–2; Ward, *World of the Medieval Shipmaster*, 50; I. J. Brugmans, 'Les Sources de l'évolution quantitative du traffic maritime des Pays-Bas (XIIe–XVIIIe siècles)', in *Les Sources de l'histoire maritime en Europe, du Moyen Âge au XVIIIe siècle*, ed. M. Mollat (Paris, 1962), 421, 426.

[25] See the examples cited for Holkham and Dawlish, nn. 4–5, 7–8 above. In Newcastle in 1544, ten of the twenty-eight shipowners had experience at sea, usually as a shipmaster; see G. V. Scammell, 'War at Sea under the Early Tudors, Part II', *Archaeologia Aeliana* 39 (1961), 116.

[26] The growing size and risks of ocean travel in the late Middle Ages was also reflected in the proliferation of investment partners called 'victuallers' who fronted the cash necessary to outfit, victual, and pay the crew for risky, non-coastal voyages. This proliferation of victuallers as silent investment partners is especially evident in privateering and piracy accusations; see, for example, *A Calendar of Early Chancery Proceedings relating to West Country Shipping 1388–1493*, ed. D. A. Gardiner (Devon and Cornwall Record Society, new ser. 21, 1976).

operation but were hired by owners for a specific voyage, although they held no less authority over the crew or responsibilities than shipmaster-owners. Indeed, the value placed on their skills is evident in the wages they received, which were at least twice that of other seamen, an arrangement that can be traced back to the twelfth century in naval accounts.[27] Most late medieval shipmasters of vessels over forty tons would have served in the navy for at least several months, since the medieval English kings relied on impressed commercial ships rather than maintaining their own permanent fleet. From the thirteenth through the fifteenth century, shipmasters in naval service earned 6*d.* a day compared to 3*d.* a day for their crew; master and crew also received room and board when in service, although shipowners — often working through their shipmasters — usually had to front the funds for the naval voyage and wait for repayment from the crown.[28] Labour shortages after the Black Death did not change the standard wage rate, but most naval seamen began to receive a bonus (called a *regard*) of 6*d.* a week, and there is evidence that their share of prize money grew as well.[29] Some shipmasters worked often enough on the king's own ships that they received regular salaries, which could be quite substantial. During the 1420s, for example, William Richman and other royal shipmasters were paid ten marks a year in lieu of daily or weekly wages, a more stable situation since wages when the ship was in port

[27] *Publications of the Pipe Roll Society* (94 vols., Pipe Roll Society, 1884–2007), xxxix, 9; N. A. M. Rodger, *The Safeguard of the Sea: A Naval History of Britain 660–1649* (New York, 1997), 498.

[28] These arrangements are spelled out in the large number of surviving naval accounts in TNA; see, for example, *The Navy of the Lancastrian Kings: Accounts and Inventories of William Soper, Keeper of the King's Ships, 1422–1427*, ed. S. Rose (Navy Records Society 123, 1982).

[29] There were more experiments in pay rates and bonuses in the post-plague period as the crown tried to find ways to economise while also dealing with demands for higher pay; see N. H. Nicolas, *A History of the Royal Navy* (2 vols., London, 1847), ii, 177; D. Burwash, *English Merchant Shipping 1460–1540* (Toronto, 1947), 54–5; Rodger, *Safeguard of the Sea*, 498–9. Rodger notes that the unchanging pay rates over more than two centuries might have worsened the condition of naval crewmen even if they received a *regard*, but this issue needs further investigation, since there appears to have been an increasing number of ways that late medieval naval crews (including masters) could augment their wages, such as fees for unloading goods or rigging, or a larger share of prize as privateering soared. On this latter point, see C. J. Ford, 'Piracy or Policy: The Crisis in the Channel, 1400–1403', *TRHS* 29 (1979), 63–77; S. Pistono, 'Henry iv and the English Privateers', *EHR* 90 (1975), 322–30; D. A. Gardiner, 'The History of Belligerent Rights on the High Seas in the Fourteenth Century', *Law Quarterly Review* 48 (1932), 521–46. There is little evidence, moreover, that the English crown had as much difficulty recruiting seamen for naval service in the later Middle Ages as they did in the early-modern period. The wages of shipmasters on occasional naval service also seem to have risen faster than that for mariners; see H. Kleineke, 'English Shipping to Guyenne in the Mid-Fifteenth Century: Edward Hull's Gascon Voyage of 1441', *Mariner's Mirror* 85 (1999), 473. See also below for a discussion of the role of shipmasters in privateering and piracy.

were far less than when out at sea.[30] Others received even greater rewards. John Mayhew's annual salary of ten marks in 1389 grew to forty marks ten years later, a reflection of his value to the new king, Henry IV, who also granted him a royal ship.[31] Some of the crown's own shipmasters took advantage of their position by buying captured ships (or shares in them) from the king, while others augmented their income by receiving grants of customs offices, supervising the construction of ships, trading goods overseas and selling prizes they had taken at sea.

Whether working temporarily or permanently for the crown, naval shipmasters' duties were notably varied, including mustering crews, assisting at sieges, transporting goods and men to garrisons overseas, patrolling the coasts, fighting at sea, protecting fishing fleets from enemy attacks, ship-keeping when the vessel was laid up in port, supervising rigging and repairs, shuttling ambassadors and other important passengers (such as the king) back and forth across the Channel and navigating the ship on both commercial and naval ventures ordered by the crown. This busy life, however, did not come without problems, as indicated by the difficulties some naval shipmasters had securing their wages, the occasional mutiny threatened by impressed seamen, the loss of cargo during enemy attacks, the round-the-clock effort to save a ship in danger of sinking during a storm and the laying off of virtually all of Henry v's royal shipmasters when his ships were sold after his death to pay his debts.[32] Yet even the petitions that unpaid shipmasters filed seeking back pay point to the legal savvy they had to cultivate in order to prosper.

Unlike the relative stability of naval pay, the remuneration offered to the majority of shipmasters who hired on for limited periods varied significantly. Some masters formed a temporary partnership with the shipowner, serving for a proportion of the profits, an arrangement that increased the master's personal investment in the successful outcome of the voyage. In Scarborough in the late 1390s, for instance, Thomas de Walpole promised the shipowner William Kawnce to serve him as shipmaster to sail westwards in return for a share of the profits, a bargain that went wrong when William sued him for leaving the ship prematurely, a charge that Thomas denied.[33] This appears to have been a service partnership in which the shipmaster contributed his labour and the shipowner the capital investment. Other partnerships were more commercial in nature, in which

---

30   *Navy of the Lancastrian Kings*, 71–2, 78, 231, 242, 244. For the wage rates at sea and when in port, see also *Naval Accounts and Inventories of the Reign of Henry VII 1485–8 and 1495–7*, ed. M. Oppenheim (Navy Records Society 8, 1896), pp. xl–xli and *passim*.

31   Rodger, *Safeguard of the Sea*, 498; Rose, 'Introduction', 32.

32   *Navy of the Lancastrian Kings*, 22–3, 50, 52–5, 237–8, 241, 242, 243; TNA, SC8/55/2722; C. F. Richmond, 'The Keeping of the Seas during the Hundred Years War 1422–1440', *History* 49 (1964), 283–98.

33   North Yorkshire County Record Office, Scarborough Court Rolls, 1398/99, MIC 1355, frame 16.

the shipmaster agreed to trade on behalf of the shipowner (or merchants who had freighted the ship), a pact that involved a proportion of the profits.[34] Masters hired to skipper a fishing craft were usually paid with a share of the catch, often twice that given to a regular member of the crew, although they could also receive straight wages or wages plus a share of the fish caught.[35] Far less is known, however, about the simple hiring of a shipmaster for a set wage on a limited contract, perhaps because such bargains were more straightforward, rarely recorded and ended up in court less often.

Shipmasters paid only a wage for the duration of a voyage were almost certainly less well off and perhaps less entrepreneurial than masters who were able to handle the risks of shipowning and partnerships. The maritime law codes recognised the peculiar constraints on the hired shipmaster, but also gave him wide leeway to manage the crew and run the ship.[36] We know little about the remuneration offered to hired shipmasters since the accounts of shipowners rarely survive, but what little evidence there is suggests that wage rates varied by the shipmaster's skill and experience, by the size of the ship (and crew), by the distance and duration of the voyage and by the other perquisites that the master may have enjoyed, such as claims for portage or clothing or footwear given as payment in kind.[37] Those at the helm of commercial vessels were often paid substantially more than the double wage rates received by shipmasters impressed to work for the crown. The Cely brothers, for instance, paid their shipmasters three times what they paid their crews for journeys to Bordeaux and across the Channel in 1487–9.[38] The purser, who kept the accounts and handled many of the commercial negotiations in port, received about two-thirds of what the master was paid, an indication of the value put on the skill set offered by shipmasters. And unlike naval pay, wages for service on trading vessels did shoot up in response to postplague labour shortages. A 1390 petition to parliament, for example, complained that shipmasters were claiming 24s. and three tuns of wine as portage for the Bordeaux route, higher than the 16s.–20s. and one or two tuns of portage that shipmasters would have received under the arrangements promulgated by the

---

[34] Ward, *World of the Medieval Shipmaster*, 51–68, offers a thorough discussion of the various agreements that masters entered into with shipowners and merchants.

[35] J. Webb, *Great Tooley of Ipswich: Portrait of an Early Tudor Merchant* (Ipswich, 1962), 74–8; M. Kowaleski, 'Working at Sea: Maritime Recruitment and Remuneration in Medieval England', in *Ricchezza del mare, ricchezza dal mare: Secoli XIII–XVIII*, ed. S. Cavciocchi (Florence, 2006), 917–22.

[36] See the discussion and comments on particular articles in the Laws of Oléron in Ward, *World of the Medieval Shipmaster*, 50, 191–205.

[37] These factors were also key in determining the wages of mariners; see Kowaleski, 'Working at Sea', 922–30, 934.

[38] A. Hanham, *The Celys and Their World: An English Merchant Family of the Fifteenth Century* (Cambridge, 1985), 370, 379, 382, 392.

Inquisition of Queenborough in 1375.[39] The wages paid by the Celys for voyages to Bordeaux in the late 1480s averaged 18s. for mariners and 54s. for shipmasters (if we assume that they customarily received three times what the crew was paid), which was more than what the 1390 petition complained was too high, providing evidence for a significant rise in wages for hired shipmasters during this last century of the Middle Ages.[40]

In addition to wages, mariners and shipmasters on commercial vessels could request portage, an allowance of free cargo space as all or part of their pay.[41] Portage was most commonly claimed on the Bordeaux wine route, where mariners were allowed to carry one tun of wine without paying freightage. By custom in Exeter and elsewhere, shipmasters had twice the amount of portage, which amounted to a substantial profit considering the rising costs of freightage in the late Middle Ages and the one tun of wine that could be purchased in Gascony for considerably less than the price it sold for in an English port. This price was never less than £4 and often significantly more in the fifteenth century, when transport costs soared.[42] The mere claim of portage — which required the shipmaster to purchase goods in a foreign port, arrange for their transport and storage and then sell the cargo at the ship's destination — involved commercial acumen, initiative and a risk-taking mentality.

The local port customs accounts of Exeter in Devon provide an idea of the proportion of shipmasters which chose this option as part of their pay.[43] In a sample twelve-year period of accounts in the early fourteenth century, thirteen per cent

---

[39] PROME, parliament of November 1390, item 37; *Black Book of the Admiralty*, I, 135–45. The Inquisition of Queenborough rates, which awarded mariners 8s. for the voyage to Bordeaux, were probably an attempt to bring wages back to their early-fourteenth-century terms; see Kowaleski, 'Working at Sea', 922–8, 934.

[40] Hanham, *The Celys*, 372. They paid each mariner 10s. and the shipmaster 30s. for the voyage to and from Calais in 1486 (ibid., 368), about twice the rate dictated in the 1375 Inquisition of Queenborough; see Kowaleski, 'Working at Sea', 934.

[41] For the customs of the sea that allowed mariners such freightage in lieu of or in addition to wages, see *Laws of Oléron*, articles 8, 18, 20 and *Inquisition of Queenborough*, articles 3 to 14, available in an updated translation with commentary in Ward, *World of the Medieval Shipmaster*, 183–218. No portage was allowed on the lucrative but short-run trips across the Channel to Calais and Flanders. For this and the following, see also Kowaleski, 'Working at Sea', 922–8, 934.

[42] These were the wholesale prices in ports; they were higher in inland towns; M. K. James, *Studies in the Medieval Wine Trade* (Oxford, 1971), 64–6, 91.

[43] The sample included all extant accounts from 1302 to 1321 (DRO, Exeter PCA). Although these accounts record only incoming ships and cargoes, they are by far the most detailed series of port customs records extant for medieval England, surviving for almost seventy per cent of all years from 1266 to 1498. They are also unusual in that they record all importers and their cargoes, whether customed or not, as well as all instances of portage, since they were custom free; see *The Local Customs Accounts of the Port of Exeter 1266–1321*, ed. M. Kowaleski (Devon and Cornwall Record Society, new ser. 36, 1993).

of all the shipmasters claimed portage, compared to probably less than seven per cent of the mariners, whose portage was in any case also limited to half that of shipmasters.[44] Wine was by far the most popular cargo to ship as portage, accounting for eighty-six per cent of all portage claims by shipmasters, although they also brought in garlic and onions, herring and grain as portage. In 1487 the Celys' shipmaster claimed a tun of wine as portage, which represented 18s. of his pay, the remainder of which he took in cash.[45] This was probably the same arrangement followed by the shipmasters in early fourteenth-century Exeter who chose to be remunerated by portage. The Cely shipmaster's resort to portage was rather unusual in the late fifteenth century, however, since the system as a form of compensation had become much less common. In Exeter there was only one case of portage in a sample of twelve years of local customs accounts in the late fourteenth century, compared to 418 portage imports in a similar period in the first part of the century.[46] Skyrocketing freight rates in the war-torn later Middle Ages probably made shipowners reluctant to grant free cargo space as part of seamen's pay, while the high price of wine limited the number of seamen who chose this type of remuneration.[47]

Shipmasters who owned and traded cargoes, even if not a shipowner, were also highly entrepreneurial, given the business contacts and investment that purchasing such cargoes required as well as the commercial acumen necessary to sell the merchandise at a profit. In early fourteenth-century Exeter, fifty-one per cent of shipmasters imported goods outright (including portage imports); they represented eight per cent of all importers (of mostly coastal cargoes) but by the late fourteenth century their share had risen to fifteen per cent, although the

[44] The sample included the twelve extant accounts in 1302–21, when there were 639 ships and 3,506 cargoes. It is not possible to determine accurately the relative percentage of mariners claiming portage since mariners were only identified in the accounts if they claimed portage, but if we assume that each of the 639 ships docking at Exeter in this period had a crew of seven (the average for a fifty-ton cargo vessel), then there would have been a total of 4,473 mariners on these ships, 326 of whom claimed portage. In this period, twenty-eight per cent of all incoming English ships to Exeter had men on board who claimed portage; mariners accounted for seventy-eight per cent of the portage cargoes and merchants who purchased the right of portage from mariners were responsible for two per cent of the portage cargoes; see Kowaleski, 'Working at Sea', 925–7, 935.

[45] Hanham, *The Celys*, 372.

[46] The sample is taken from DRO, Exeter PCA 1381/2 to 1392/93; the sole portage claim was by mariners on a ship from Lyme in 1382/3.

[47] For the rising freightage rates on Bordeaux wine, see James, *Studies in the Medieval Wine Trade*, 25–6, 141–6, 151–3; by the late fourteenth century, the cost rose as high as 23s., which came to over twice the wage a mariner was to be paid according to the 1375 Inquisition of Queenborough. Other changes in maritime law in this period also reduced the potential profit from portage (Kowaleski, 'Working at Sea', 927–8), while the rising price of wine made it more difficult for seamen to find the cash advance needed to purchase wine in Gascony.

volume of trade they controlled was not that substantial.[48] For example, wine was the single most valuable import, representing about seventy-five per cent of the value of all imports at Exeter in 1381–91; shipmasters were responsible for nine per cent of all wine cargoes, but just under six per cent of the total tonnage imported. Shipmasters were considerably more active in importing some commodities than others; in this period they were responsible for bringing in sixty-three per cent of the grain cargoes and forty per cent of the grain by weight; forty-six per cent of the salt cargoes, albeit only nine per cent by weight; forty per cent of the linen-cloth cargoes (all traded by Breton shipmasters), but only nine and a half per cent of the cloth by yardage. They were also much more likely to pool their capital with mariners on their ships; seventy-five per cent of all importing partnerships involved a shipmaster and a partner, usually members of his crew.[49] In other words, shipmasters active in the coastal (and to some extent, overseas) trade could maintain a lively commercial profile, but commensurate with their lower means compared to the investment capacity and commercial dealings of full-time merchants.

The main exception was the import of fish, in which shipmasters were especially energetic, probably because by the late fourteenth century they were coming straight from fishing grounds with cargoes of fish lightly cured on board ship. As the south-western fishing industry expanded, so too did the role of shipmasters and their crews, who were responsible for only four per cent of fish cargoes at Exeter in 1315–20, but thirty-five per cent in 1386–91, and a whopping fifty per cent in 1460–5.[50] Especially prominent in this trade were shipmasters from Cornwall, south Devon and the Channel Islands. Shipmasters from other ports also stood out for their mercantile activities, most notably those from the south Devon port of Dartmouth, who owned eighteen per cent of all the Dartmouth cargoes carried into Exeter in the late fourteenth century.[51] Their dominating presence at Bor-

---

[48]   See nn. 43, 44, 46 above for these samples; see also Kowaleski, *Local Markets and Regional Trade*, 238–60, 262–3, for this and the following. About seventy-five per cent of this trade was by coast; the rest consisted of ships arriving from overseas. The shipmasters' increasing proportion of trade in the later Middle Ages was due partly to the fewer trips taken to Exeter by foreign merchants and partly to the decline of the portage option for mariners as freightage rates rose.

[49]   Kowaleski, *Local Markets and Regional Trade*, 210, 242; about twelve per cent of all cargoes coming into Exeter from 1381/2 to 1390/1 were owned by partners, the majority of which involved a shipmaster.

[50]   Kowaleski, 'The Expansion of the South-Western Fisheries', 429–54, esp. 431. Shipmasters also controlled sixty-three per cent of the grain cargoes and forty per cent of the amounts imported, although these imports were far fewer than fish imports.

[51]   DRO, Exeter PCA 1381/2–1390/1; M. Kowaleski, 'Shipping and the Carrying Trade in Medieval Dartmouth', in *Von Nowgorod bis London: Studien zu Handel, Wirtschaft und Gesellschaft im mittelalterlichen Europa; Festschrift für Stuart Jenks zum 60. Geburtstag*, ed. M.-L. Heckmann and J. Röhrkasten (Göttingen, 2008), 473–5.

deaux in the fifteenth century also helped to account for the increasing activity of British shipmasters as wine importers. But even the Dartmouth shipmasters were rarely involved in retailing their cargoes. Instead, they, like most shipmasters, sold their cargoes mainly to merchant middlemen. On the few occasions that they did sell cargoes, it was in their home ports.[52]

The Dartmouth shipmasters were unusual in their mercantile activity on overseas routes; in general, shipmasters were more likely to trade cargoes on coastal routes than on overseas routes.[53] Indeed, short-haul coastal voyages or quick overseas trips to the Low Countries or across the Irish Channel represented the bulk of most medieval English shipmasters' work. Even amongst shipmasters employed primarily on overseas routes, those regularly involved in long-distance routes were a minority. Wendy Childs found that forty-four per cent of the Bristol shipmasters recorded in the Bristol overseas customs accounts in the second half of the fifteenth century regularly sailed the long-distance routes to Iceland and Iberia (sixty-two per cent if Bordeaux is included); in Hull, forty-three per cent of the overseas shipmasters navigated the longer Atlantic routes.[54] And many of these skippers only occasionally took on such lengthy trips; only twenty-five per cent of the Bristol overseas shipmasters recorded in the national customs accounts sailed these routes and seventeen per cent of the Hull shipmasters, suggesting that they represented an elite core of particularly experienced shipmasters who were familiar with local conditions and able to meet shipowners' demands for fast turn-rounds and efficient management at any time of year. Royal inquisitions to determine maritime expertise in particular ports also made distinctions between masters who sailed the coastal routes and the smaller number of masters with the navigational skills to sail to more distant destinations.[55]

Although experience and familiarity with particular ports would have set some shipmasters apart in the eyes of shipowners, the high turnover rate of hired shipmasters suggest that they all enjoyed the same basic skill set. Employment for one or two years on the same ship or even for a single voyage was the norm, with turnover dictated by a variety of factors, including changes in ownership, an alteration in family circumstances, the growing experience of younger masters or the declining abilities of older men on the verge of retirement.[56] The mobility of shipmasters was also evident in their willingness to master ships outside their

[52]   Kowaleski, *Local Markets and Merchants*, 263.

[53]   See, for example, Rose, 'The Port of Southampton'; Kowaleski, *Local Markets and Regional Trade*, 224–7, 242, 244, 254–8, 262–3.

[54]   W. Childs, 'The Career of Shipmasters in Fifteenth-Century Port Towns', unpublished paper given at the 38th annual meeting of the International Congress of Medieval Studies, Western Michigan University, Kalamazoo, May 2003. I thank Professor Childs for allowing me to cite her unpublished work.

[55]   Burwash, *English Merchant Shipping*, 28.

[56]   Childs, 'Career of Shipmasters'. Service on different ships and leaves of absences for

home port: Walter Wace of Dartmouth, for example, mastered a Winchelsea ship in 1293, Hugh Richardesson of Southampton mastered a ship of Exeter around 1386, many Irish shipmasters skippered Bristol vessels, and it was not unusual for English masters to serve foreign shipowners.[57]

A few shipmasters worked on the same ship for years in a row, but this type of employment was more characteristic of shipmaster/owners. And even master/owners moved from ship to ship. Peter Godlok of the Exe Estuary manor of Kenton, for instance, worked for over twenty-four years as a shipmaster on at least four different vessels. He mastered the *Blithe* of Exmouth in 1302–03, then the *St Mary* cog — of which he was part owner with four Exeter merchants — for eleven years, from 1304–15.[58] In 1310, he and his ship were hired by the mayor of Exeter to fulfil the city's naval service to the crown for forty days. The ship was back on trading routes in 1316–18, but Godlok was no longer its master (perhaps because he sold his portion of the ship?). Instead, from 1316 to 1319 he was the skipper of the *Notre Dame* and in 1321 and 1326, the master of the *Michael*, during which he again served the king. During this period he imported twenty-one cargoes, thirteen of them when he was a shipmaster (and four of these as portage cargoes), but the rest as a simple merchant. He imported wine fourteen times, but never more than four tuns at one time; other imports included iron, grain, salt and potash woad (for the dying industry). His most significant imports were two cargoes totalling 370 quarters of grain in 1319/20, when an agricultural crisis in Devon prompted absolutely enormous cereal imports into Exeter. Both of his grain cargoes were carried on the *Michael* of Exmouth, which was mastered by Richard Harvest, not Godlok, who seems to have only begun mastering this ship two years later. This pattern of service and trade points to the flexibility of shipmasters — moving easily from mastering coastal, overseas and naval voyages — and to the way in which their involvement in trade could augment their income. In Godlok's case, his importing partnership with other shipmasters (such as Richard Harvest, who was one of his partners on the cargo of 300 quarters of grain) and his experience as a shipmaster on the route to Picardy, where the grain and dyestuffs originated, were crucial elements in his success.

---

shipmasters returning home on personal business were also noted in naval accounts: for example, *Navy of the Lancastrian Kings*, 79, 83, 233, 237, 238, 241–6.

[57] *CCR, 1288–96*, 324; *Calendar of Plea and Memoranda Rolls of London*, III, 136; W. R. Childs, 'Irish Merchants and Seamen in Late Medieval England', *Irish Historical Studies* 32 (2000), 31–7; M. Kowaleski, '"Alien" Encounters in the Maritime World of Medieval England', *Medieval Encounters* 13 (2007), 96–121.

[58] For this and the following, see *Local Port Customs of Exeter*, references in the index under 'Godlok'; M. Jones, 'Two Exeter Ship Agreements of 1303 and 1310', *Mariner's Mirror* 53 (1967), 315–19; *CCR, 1323–7*, 609; M. Kowaleski, 'The Grain Trade in Fourteenth-Century Exeter', in *The Salt of Common Life: Essays in Honor of J. Ambrose Raftis*, ed. E. DeWindt (Kalamazoo, 1996), 8–18.

When Godlok mastered the *St Mary* cog on a naval voyage to the Isle of Man and Scotland in 1310, he would probably have been enticed by the promise of receiving a share of prize taken by his ship while on the king's service. From the late fourteenth century onwards, opportunities for prize increased significantly, whether vessels were in naval service, licensed to exercise a letter of marque, or simply operating under the general privateering licences that kings such as Henry IV and Henry VI handed out to weaken their enemies at sea.[59] By the fifteenth century, the king was also granting away his share to prize taken by vessels on naval service, and even charter-parties for trading voyages began to include clauses on the division of prize, since the English kings tolerated and even encouraged attacks on enemy shipping.[60] Maritime law and various parliamentary petitions laid out the division of prize in some detail.[61] By the mid fifteenth century, the shipmaster, crew and soldiers on board received half of the prize, while the other half was divided into three, with shipowners receiving two-thirds and the chief captain and his sub-captains (usually high-ranking gentry or noble men) received the other third. In recognition of their important role in the enterprise, however, shipmasters received one-third of the half reserved for the crew and soldiers. Shipmasters such as Mark Mixtow of Fowey and Henry Paye of Poole became infamous for their privateering and piratical exploits in the late Middle Ages, when the line between legally sanctioned privateering and free-booting piracy became more blurred.[62] The notorious sea exploits of shipmasters and mariners from the West Country ports of Fowey, Plymouth and Dartmouth were even singled out in one of the most important English political tracts of the Middle Ages, *The Libelle of Englyshe Polycye*.[63]

The skills needed to succeed in privateering — quick decision making, experience on the high seas and the ability to manage men, equipment, cargoes, foreign contacts and international law — were the same skills needed by shipmasters when they pursued more peaceful trading routes. The trading and supervisory duties required of shipmasters on overseas routes were spelled out in extant

[59]   R. G. Marsden, 'Early Prize Jurisdiction and Prize Law in England', *EHR* 24 (1909), 675–97; Gardiner, 'History of Belligerent Rights'; Ford, 'Piracy or Policy'; Pistono, 'Henry IV and the English Privateers'.

[60]   *Documents Relating to the Law and Custom of the Sea*, 1: A.D. 1205–1648, ed. R.G. Marsden (Navy Records Society 49, 1915), 37; Ward, *World of the Medieval Shipmaster*, 81.

[61]   *PROME*, parliament of March 1406, item 22; parliament of April 1414, item 22; parliament of January 1442, item 30; Kowaleski, 'Working at Sea', 934; Ward, *World of the Medieval Shipmaster*, 33–5, 81, 213.

[62]   C. J. Kingsford, *Prejudice and Promise in Fifteenth-Century England* (Oxford, 1925), 84–7; F. W. Mathews, 'Henry Pay: The Story of a Noted Poole Worthy', *Proceedings of the Dorset Natural History and Archaeological Society* 61 (1989), 89–93.

[63]   *The Libelle of Englyshe Polycye*, ed. G. Warner (Oxford, 1926), 12. The role of shipmasters in these exploits is also evident in *A Calendar of Early Chancery Proceedings*; Kingsford, *Prejudice and Promise*, 78–106, 177–203.

charter-party contracts. Although the terms could vary, most shipmasters were responsible for arranging for the victualling and supply of the ship; finding, supervising and paying the crew, pilots, lighters and shore-side workers who unloaded the boat or provided towage; and navigating the ship unless a special pilot was on board.[64] Shipowners not infrequently delegated to shipmasters the task of negotiating the finer points of contracts with the merchants hiring their vessels. These agreements illuminate, moreover, the flexibility expected of shipmasters on a long voyage to and from a foreign port. The charter parties often named several possible final destinations (because freightage rates varied by distance), making it clear that the shipmaster had to be ready to change course on short notice. Masters were also usually given an advance in order to pay for victuals and the first part of the seamen's wages, pointing to the accounting skills they exercised. A shipmaster's ability to manage time effectively was evident in the contracts' stipulation about the exact amount of time to be spent in port and to reach the destination, as well as penalties for delays. Other responsibilities required of all skippers were spelled out in the Laws of Oléron and their amendments. Maritime laws in particular elucidate the disciplinary powers of the shipmaster over the crew, who needed to receive his permission to leave service early or even go ashore, and could be fined at the will of the shipmaster for a range of infractions.[65] Indeed, alterations in maritime law during the later Middle Ages appear to have raised the status of the shipmaster vis-à-vis the crew, largely because shipowners — who were becoming more powerful in a period when larger ships and longer and more dangerous routes required even greater investment and risk — increasingly employed hired shipmasters as their direct agents in dealings with the crew.[66]

The authority and respect which shipmasters commanded in maritime society is obvious not only in the maritime law codes and courts, but especially in moments of crisis, when the power to make instant and often life-saving decisions rested solely in the shipmaster. When ships were in dire need of repairs to make the voyage home, or delayed so long in a foreign port that the crew ran out of food and drink, or could not get home because of shipwreck or capture, it was the

---

[64] For these agreements, see Ward, *World of the Medieval Shipmaster*, 27, 52–3, 65, 78–93, 229–34. For examples of shipowners delegating responsibilities to their hired shipmasters, see *The Red Paper Book of Colchester*, ed. W. G. Benham (Colchester, 1902), 71–3.

[65] For discussions of the duties of shipmasters according to maritime law, see Ward, *World of the Medieval Shipmaster*, 15–46, 82–4, 100–9, 191–205; Rose, *The Medieval Sea*, 148–52; Rodger, *Safeguard of the Sea*, 141–2.

[66] Other evidence of the rising status of shipmasters in the late Middle Ages lies in the proliferation of mariners' guilds, which were generally restricted to shipmasters; see Kowaleski, 'Working at Sea', 928–30. For the growing stature of naval shipmasters and their widening powers of discipline, see also C. S. L. Davies, 'Naval Discipline in the Early Sixteenth Century', *Mariner's Mirror* 48 (1962), 223–4.

shipmaster who stepped in to negotiate repairs, find pledges to pay for the return voyage, or bargain for the release of the ship, cargo and crew.[67] Thorny legal problems involving maritime matters were often settled by a jury of shipmasters and expert mariners.[68] In privateering expeditions led by powerful nobles, the king urged the expedition leaders to be advised by their shipmasters, an unusual inversion of power.[69] When ships and their passengers were captured by the enemy, it was often the shipmaster who was sent to negotiate the ransom.[70] Recognition of the value of their expertise grew especially sharp during the Hundred Years' War, when the war at sea — in terms of naval blockades of enemy ports, coastal patrols to safeguard English shipping and thwart enemy raids on English ports, transportation of troops and supplies to the Continent and actual sea battles — was the most crucial aspect of English strategy in the later Middle Ages. Acknowledgment of their key expertise is evident in the invitations issued by the king, his council and parliament for shipmasters to appear before the council to offer advice about the conduct of the war at sea.[71] In 1374 the king's council went so far as to issue summons to nineteen named shipmasters from eleven ports to come to Westminster in order to give their expert advice. Indeed, no other occupational group was so often recognised or relied upon by the crown and parliament for their informed expertise as were shipmasters.

It is harder to get at the popular view of shipmasters, although literary sources do provide some hints. Chaucer's Shipman came from Dartmouth, known for the prowess and daring exploits of its shipmasters; the Shipman — a common term for a shipmaster — was a widely-travelled working man, experienced and wise, but also on the look-out for a chance to make a profit, whether in commerce or by using questionable practices that shaded into smuggling and piracy.[72] The business acumen of shipmasters is also highlighted in the character of the shipmaster

---

[67] For example, Jacques Bernard, *Navires et gens de mer à Bordeaux (vers 1400 – vers 1550)* (Paris, 1968), 841–4; TNA, E163/2/4/4; Burwash, *English Merchant Shipping*, 56–60; Ward, *World of the Medieval Shipmaster*, 55,65–7, 92–107, 158–67.

[68] For example, Burwash, *English Merchant Shipping*, 53; Ward, *World of the Medieval Shipmaster*, 23, 32, 44, 46.

[69] *CPR, 1399–1401*, 349–50.

[70] For example, *CPR, 1381–5*, 420; *CIM, 1348–77*, 76. In the reciprocal ransom agreement worked out between the men of New Romney and several Norman ports, a shipmaster's ransom was twice that of the common seaman; see Kent Record Office, NR/FAC.2, fol. 72ᵛ.

[71] For this and the following, see M. Kowaleski, 'Warfare, Shipping, and Crown Patronage: The Impact of the Hundred Years War on the English Port Towns', in *Money, Markets and Trade in Late Medieval Europe: Essays in Honour of John H. A. Munro*, ed. L. Armstrong, I. Elbl and M. M. Elbl (Leiden, 2007), 233–54.

[72] W. Sayers, 'Chaucer's Shipman and the Law Marine', *The Chaucer Review* 37 (2002), 145–8; S. King, 'A Shipman Ther Was, Wonyng Fer By Weste', in *Chaucer's Pilgrims: An Historical Guide to the Pilgrims in The Canterbury Tales*, ed. L. C. Lambdin and R. T. Lambdin (Westport, Ct., 1996), 210–19.

in the Digby play, who negotiates directly with the king to exchange services for money.[73] But the play also associates the shipmaster with the gentry and nobility, a social elevation that disrupts the recognised social hierarchy, an indication of the difficulties that the hierarchical world of the Middle Ages had with a working man whose responsibilities included command of men and valuable ships and goods. Other sources depict the pridefulness that such command could sometimes entail and the peculiar package of skills that shipmasters were expected to have.[74] These literary perceptions match the legal, social and economic evidence in historical records of the sharp dealings of shipmasters, their unusual measure of authority (even over men of considerably higher rank), their heavy responsibilities for the success of expensive and risky trading and naval ventures, the trust that bound them to those depending on their skills for survival and commercial success and their entrepreneurial flexibility to make informed but quick decisions in often life-threatening situations.

[73] See for this and the following: T. Coletti, 'Paupertas est donum Dei: Hagiography, Lay Religion, and the Economics of Salvation in the Digby Mary Magdalene,' Speculum 76 (2001), 353–6; J. Bennett, 'The Mary Magdalene of Bishop's Lynn', Studies in Philology 75 (1978), 1–9.

[74] Sayers, 'Chaucer's Shipman'; G. W. Coopland, 'A Glimpse of Late Fourteenth-Century Ships and Seamen from Le songe du vieil pelérin of Philippe de Mézières (1327–1405)', Mariner's Mirror 48 (1962), 186–92.

10

Cheating the Boss:
Robert Carpenter's Embezzlement Instructions (1261×1268) and Employee Fraud in Medieval England
....

Martha Carlin

THIS ESSAY WILL CONSIDER a negative aspect of market production: the losses caused by employee embezzlement or fraud. Between 1261 and 1268 Robert le Carpenter (Robert Carpenter II, 1230–1280), of 'Hareslade' (modern Haslett Farm) near Shorwell on the Isle of Wight, compiled a formulary, in Latin, containing a collection of form letters, legal texts and other model documents having to do with law and administration.[1] Carpenter, who was probably a freeholder and a former bailiff of William de Insula, lord of the manor of Shorwell, copied into his holograph formulary many texts from other collections.[2] However, he

The research for this essay was supported in part by funds provided by the University of Wisconsin–Milwaukee.

[1] Carpenter's holograph formulary is now Cambridge, Gonville and Caius College, MS 205/111 (hereafter Gonville & Caius 205/111). I am grateful to the Master and Fellows of the College for permission to publish a portion of the manuscript here. For the suggested date of 1261×1268, see P. R. Robinson, *Catalogue of Dated and Datable Manuscripts c. 737–1600 in Cambridge Libraries* (2 vols., Cambridge, 1988), no. 241 and pl. 115. M. R. James described the elder Carpenter's formulary, and noted its correspondence with the younger Carpenter's formulary, in *A Descriptive Catalogue of the Manuscripts in the Library of Gonville and Caius College, Cambridge*, 1 (Cambridge, 1907), 238–42. For Robert Carpenter II, his family, his career, and his formulary, see N. Denholm-Young, 'Robert Carpenter and the Provisions of Westminster', *EHR* 1 (1935), 22–35; idem, *Seignorial Administration in England* (London, 1937), 121–2; C. A. F. Meekings, 'More About Robert Carpenter of Hareslade', *EHR* 72 (1957), 260–9. See also D. Oschinsky, 'Medieval Treatises on Estate Accounting', *EcHR* 17 (1947), 54–6, 58; eadem, *Walter of Henley and Other Treatises on Estate Management and Accounting* (Oxford, 1971), 36–7, 39, 237–9; S. Brendler, 'Hareslade: A Note on Robert Carpenter's Place of Abode', *Notes and Queries* 49 (2002), 12–13.

[2] Noël Denholm-Young, 'Robert Carpenter and the Provisions of Westminster', 26, suggested the likelihood of Carpenter being a free-tenant of the manor of Shorwell, and formerly a bailiff of William de Insula. An earlier formulary with which Carpenter's formulary has material in common is BL, Additional MS 8167, fols. 88^r–135^v. See M. Carlin and D. Crouch, *English Society, 1200–1250: Lost Letters of Everyday Life* (Philadelphia, forthcoming 2012).

also added some original material, including detailed instructions for half a dozen ways in which a reeve, bailiff or shepherd could embezzle from his lord or commit some other kind of fraud.[3] Sometime after 1283 Carpenter's eldest son, Robert Carpenter III (b. 1258), compiled his own formulary and included within it a copy of his father's text.[4]

Carpenter's matter-of-fact instructions for how to commit fraud appear to be unique for medieval England. However, although both Noël Denholm-Young and Dorothea Oschinsky commented briefly on this portion of Carpenter's text, and Oschinsky published a transcription of it, to date no one has published a translation of these instructions or examined them in detail.[5] This essay will investigate Carpenter's text, and will also explore the subject of employee fraud more generally, as reflected in prescriptive texts such as household regulations, instructions for manorial officers and other advice manuals, and in accounts of embezzlement cases. It will conclude with a consideration of some of the broader implications of this evidence in the context of medieval market production.

Carpenter's Text

Carpenter's embezzlement instructions occur within a specimen reeve's account for the manor of Shorwell. The date of this account is given as the year beginning at Michaelmas, 42 Hen. III (29 September 1258). Dorothea Oschinsky noted that the account itself was probably copied from a genuine account for Shorwell, but that the date was unlikely to be correct because the initial of the reeve as given in the heading ('D.') differs from the initial of the reeve in the account ('J.').[6] The embezzlement instructions appear, without any rubric or other introduction, towards the end of the Shorwell account, following a brief note about accounting practices used at the bishop of Winchester's manor of Wolvesey. An English translation of the instructions begins on the next page; the Latin text is printed in the Appendix. Text enclosed in angle brackets (< >) represents contemporary marginal additions or interlineations, which are discussed in the notes to the Appendix.

---

[3] Gonville & Caius 205/111, pp. 384–8.

[4] The formulary by Carpenter's son is now CUL, MS Mm. 1. 27. For its date, see Robinson, *Catalogue of Dated and Datable Manuscripts*, no. 241. The embezzlement instructions are on fol. 85ᵛ.

[5] Denholm-Young, 'Robert Carpenter and the Provisions of Westminster', 26; Oschinsky, 'Medieval Treatises on Estate Accounting', 55; eadem, *Walter of Henley*, 461–2. Other scholars have also noted Carpenter's text without discussing the frauds. See, for example, M. J. Stephenson, 'Wool Yields in the Medieval Economy', *EcHR* 41 (1988), 373; M. B. Parkes, *Their Hands Before Our Eyes: A Closer Look at Scribes* (Aldershot, 2008), 107 n. 25.

[6] Oschinsky, *Walter of Henley*, 238.

Item, whoever shall have 150 (*CL*)[7] breeding ewes, some of them will be barren, some will die before giving birth, some will abort, and some of the lambs will come from maiden ewes (*de gercis*).[8] <Note that sometimes a ewe has two lambs in one year.> Item, when it is said (*dicitur*) that six were barren, it will be reported (*dicetur*) that nine were barren; and [when] four died before giving birth, it will be reported that six died before giving birth; and [when] three have aborted, it will be reported that five aborted; and when it is said that that ten were born of maiden ewes, it will be reported that five were born of maiden ewes.

And thus you will make a profit of twelve lambs or twelve skins.

Item, in order to render well an account of the lambs of 150 breeding ewes, <and to make a profit of twenty-five skins for a fur lining (*fururam*)>:

Let us say that (*Sit ita quod*) no ewe of the said 150 breeding ewes is barren, and that none dies before giving birth, and that none aborts, and that all the lambs that are born of maiden ewes are reported (*demonstrantur*), that ten are born of maiden ewes, and that there are 160 lambs; [and] let us say that they all die, [then] one must render an account of 160 lambskins. Let the accounts be rendered well, and one will have and make a profit of twenty-five skins for a fur lining thus: from the said skins, select fifty skins, partly from the better ones, and partly from the middling ones, so that twenty-five of the selected skins are worth 2*s*. 1*d*., and the other twenty-five are worth 20*d*., [i.e.,] three farthings each.[9] And then let those skins that are worth 2*s*. 1*d*. be sold for a penny each, and let fifty skins be bought for ½*d*. each with the said money. And let the twenty-five skins that are worth 20*d*. remain for the fur lining.

Item, that any ewe shall love a different lamb than her own:

Let him take blood from the nose of that ewe and anoint the lamb that she is to love.

Item, to make a sheepskin appear to be that of a ewe (*ovis*) that died of murrain: As soon as it is flayed, let the skin be placed in hot water (*in aquam calidam*), and then immediately dried, and it will become as if [the ewe] were dead of murrain.

Item, let us say that a shepherd is supposed to render 100 wethers (*multones*) that were entrusted to his care, and he is missing three wethers:

Let him go to a shepherd who is his confederate (*ad bercarium socium suum*) in the same pasture, who has wethers marked (*signatos*) in the same manner, and let [the latter] lend (*acomodet*) three wethers. And let [the latter] say that he must

---

[7] Paragraph four below makes it clear that in this text the 'hundred' evidently was the ordinary hundred of five score, rather than the 'long' hundred of six score. Only in the east of England north of the Thames was it common to count sheep by the 'long' hundred. See R. Lennard, 'Statistics of Sheep in Medieval England', *AgHR* 7 (1959), 75–81, esp. 75–7.

[8] A *gerca* or maiden ewe was also known as a jerk or gimmer: R. Trow-Smith, *British Livestock Husbandry, to 1700* (London, 1957), 149 n. 1.

[9] The correct value of twenty-five skins worth three farthings each is 18.75*d*.

render up his wethers, and let [the first shepherd] say to him that when the three wethers come into the common pasture they will go to the wethers that are their fellows (*ibunt ad multones sibi socios*).

Item, he who would like to injure a shepherd:

When you come to shearing, take the fleeces (*vellera*) that are not 'pilled' (*depillata*) [i.e., *bald*], and put them in one part by themselves, and the pilled fleeces in another part by themselves. And when all the sheep (*oves*) have been shorn, take the pilled fleeces and put them in the balance (*in statera*). And take the fleeces that are neither of the better nor the worse sort and put them in the other part of the balance. And thus perhaps (*forte*) five fleeces, neither of the better nor the worse sort, will weigh more than ten pilled fleeces, and then the shepherd is in mercy to his lord for the sheep that he has kept in such a manner, and he will render five fleeces to his lord if it happens thus.

Item, by rights (*de iure*), from 100 wethers (*de c multonibus*) will be had one wey (*i pondus*) of wool, and of 150 breeding ewes one wey of wool, <and of 200 hoggs (*de cc hogastris*)[10] one wey of wool>.

Item, to render well the account of cheeses that began to be made on Easter Sunday and stopped being made on Michaelmas, one cheese daily, including Easter Sunday and Michaelmas (*utroque die computato*), and yet (*ad huc*) to have each week one cheese as big as any other of the week:

Firstly, on the day when they begin to make cheeses, let the milk be divided equally into eight parts, and let the eighth part be kept until the following day, and from the other parts let one cheese be made immediately. And the next day, let the milk be divided in the same manner, and on that day let two parts be taken from the milk, and let the first part, which was taken first [i.e., *the portion reserved from the previous day*], be poured into the other milk, from which the cheese is made immediately. And thus every day let the milk be renewed [i.e., *continue to reserve increasing portions of the fresh milk, replacing them with milk from the previous day*]. And on the seventh day you will thus have eight portions of new milk and six portions from the previous day, and thus on the seventh day you will make two cheeses of the same size as the others.

The Frauds

In this text, Carpenter suggests five different schemes by which an unscrupulous reeve, bailiff or shepherd might defraud his lord, and one by which a reeve or bailiff might intentionally injure a shepherd. In the first, the reeve or bailiff misrepresents the mortality and fertility of a flock of ewes. He does this by exaggerating the number of ewes that were barren, or died before giving birth, or aborted,

---

10 Hoggasters or hoggs were sheep of either sex in their second year: Trow-Smith, *British Livestock Husbandry*, 149 n. 1.

and by under-reporting the number of lambs born to maiden ewes. In Carpenter's example, from a flock of 150 ewes, a corrupt reeve or bailiff could in this fashion steal a dozen lambs or lambskins. If each ewe produced one lamb, that would represent 8 per cent of the total.

The second scheme is for the reeve or bailiff to sell best-quality lambskins and use the money to buy twice that number of poor-quality lambskins. He can then steal for himself the same quantity of skins as those that he has illicitly sold. In Carpenter's example, a reeve or bailiff who must account for 160 lambskins sells twenty-five skins of the best quality for a penny each, and with the money buys fifty lambskins of poor quality at a halfpenny each. This enables him to steal twenty-five skins of medium quality (15.625 per cent of 160), which are enough to make a fur lining. They are worth three farthings each, or 20*d*. (*recte* 18.75*d*.) in all. In rendering his account, the twenty-five best-quality skins that he has sold and the twenty-five medium-quality skins that he has stolen, which together are worth 45*d*., are replaced by the fifty poor-quality skins worth only 25*d*. This represents a net loss to the lord of 20*d*., or almost forty-five per cent of the value of the fifty skins.

Next, Carpenter notes that a ewe can be persuaded to foster a lamb not her own by anointing it with blood drawn from her nose, because when she sniffs the lamb she will think it is hers. This was a useful trick of practical husbandry, enabling an orphan to be accepted and nursed by a ewe that had lost her own lamb. However, Carpenter's inclusion of this note at this point in his text suggests that he connected it with the third fraud, in which a ewe is killed (presumably leaving an orphaned lamb) and flayed. The flayed skin is then soaked in hot water and dried so that it will appear to be that of a ewe that had died of murrain. This will enable the corrupt reeve or bailiff to purloin the flesh, which (unlike the skin) could not be sold.[11]

In the fourth fraud, a shepherd who has lost or — more probably — stolen three sheep from the flock entrusted to him, borrows three sheep from a fellow-shepherd whose flock is marked with the same mark.[12] When it is time to account for the flocks, the borrower assures his confederate that when the sheep are turned into the common pasture, the three borrowed sheep will naturally return to their original flock. This evidently will enable them to be counted twice, so that the borrower's loss of three sheep is not discovered.

The fifth set of instructions does not concern a monetary fraud, but rather

---

[11] See, for example, the accounts of the manor of Crondal for 1248, which include 5*s*. 6½*d*. from the sale of hides of two oxen, one bull, two cows, and two calves that had died of murrain: F.J. Baigent, *A Collection of Records and Documents Relating to the Hundred and the Manor of Crondal in the County of Southampton*, Part 1: *Historical and Manorial* (London and Winchester, 1891), 52.

[12] On the marking of sheep in medieval England, see Trow-Smith, *British Livestock Husbandry*, 159.

a scheme whereby a reeve or bailiff can maliciously injure a shepherd. When the sheep are shorn, the reeve or bailiff is to keep the ordinary fleeces apart from the 'pilled' fleeces (*vellera depillata*). A pilled fleece was one from which a visible portion of the wool had fallen out, or had been pulled out, or had been rubbed away. After the shearing, the reeve or bailiff is to weigh five average fleeces against ten pilled fleeces. If the five average fleeces outweigh the ten pilled fleeces, the unlucky shepherd will be fined five fleeces, evidently because the loss of value from the pilled fleeces will be blamed on his mismanagement. The 'pilling' of the fleeces would have been attributed to poor nutrition or illness, to the pulling out of wool by human theft or by the sheep's own teeth, or to the sheep rubbing themselves on trees, walls, fences, hedges, or other abrasive surfaces.[13] In any of these cases, the shepherd would be held responsible. Carpenter follows these instructions with a list of fleece-weights and ratios, perhaps to enable the reeve or bailiff to weight the scales convincingly. According to Carpenter, 100 wethers (castrated adult sheep) should produce one wey of wool, as should 150 ewes, or 200 hoggs (two-year-old sheep). Since the wey is defined earlier in the Shorwell account as weighing 192 lb.,[14] this works out to mean fleece-weights of 1.92 lb. per wether, 1.28 lb. per ewe and 0.96 lb. per hogg.[15]

---

[13] On disease causing sheep to lose their wool, see *Seneschaucy*, c. 32, in Oschinsky, *Walter of Henley*, 275. On the theft of wool by pulling it from the sheep, cf. *Dictionary of Medieval Latin from British Sources*, ed. R. E. Latham and D. R. Howlett (Oxford, 1975–   ), s.v. 'depilatio', which quotes a gaol delivery of 1300: 'S. filius R. nocte captus pro depilatione ovium . . . et aliis latrociniis'.

[14] The wey (*pondus*) was a standard unit of weight, but its size varied widely. In Robert Carpenter's formulary (Gonville & Caius 205/III, p. 380) the wey was defined as sixteen stone, each of 12 lb., making a total of 192 lb. Carpenter does not define the weight of the pound, but a note in another hand (top of p. 364) states that the ounce weighed 20*d.*, and was one-sixteenth of a pound weighing 26*s.* 8*d.* ('Uncia est pondus viginti denariorum; et sexadecima pars libre. et sic pondus libre erit de viginti sex s' et octo denar'. et illud probatum est in omnibus regionibus ubi opus ponderis interest'). However, pounds of twelve or fifteen ounces were also in use. See, for example, *Select Tracts and Table Books Relating to English Weights and Measures (1100–1742)*, ed. H. Hall and F. J. Nicholas (Camden Miscellany 15, 1929), 9–11; W. H. Prior, 'Notes on the Weights and Measures of Medieval England', *Bulletin du Cange* 1 (1924), 86. In *Husbandry* the wey was defined as containing fourteen stone, each of 14 lb.; while in *Seneschaucy* the stone weighed 12½ lb.: Oschinsky, *Walter of Henley*, 155 n. 1, 272–3. In the reign of Edward III the stone weighed 14 lb., and this weight was made statutory in 13 Ric. II c. 9: Prior, 'Notes on the Weights and Measures of Medieval England', 86–7. In the reign of Henry VI the wey was fixed at 224 lb.: Trow-Smith, *British Livestock Husbandry*, 121. This represented sixteen stone, each of 14 lb. avoirdupois at 16 oz per pound: B. M. S. Campbell, *English Seigniorial Agriculture, 1250–1450* (Cambridge, 2000), p. xxv. On the variety of weights of the wey of wool, cf. J. P. Bischoff, '"I cannot do't without counters": Fleece Weights and Sheep Breeds in Late Thirteenth and Early Fourteenth Century England', *Agricultural History* 57 (1983), 153–4; and R. E. Zupko, *A Dictionary of English Weights and Measures from Anglo-Saxon Times to the Nineteenth Century* (Madison, Wisc., 1968), 180.

[15] These fit well within contemporary norms for fleece weights. See, for example, Bischoff,

It is just possible that the 'pilled' fleeces here represent a very early reference to sheep scab, which is otherwise not recorded in Britain until 1272. Scab is an infestation of mange and related mites (*Psoroptes communis var. ovis*), which cause severe skin irritation. A scabbed sheep nibbles, scratches and rubs its skin raw, and scab also leads to a 'breaking' of the fleece, which causes an infested sheep to cast its wool.[16] The result is a 'pilled' or bald sheep.[17]

The sixth fraud concerns the making of cheese, which was done daily from Easter Sunday to Michaelmas. On the first day of each week the reeve or bailiff is to divide the milk into eight parts. He is to keep one part for the next day, and have a cheese made of the remaining seven parts. The following day the milk is to be divided again into eight parts. Six parts, together with the part kept from the previous day, are to be used to make one cheese and two parts kept for the following day. This system is to continue for the remainder of the week, so that on the seventh day there will be eight parts of fresh milk plus six parts kept from the previous day. This will enable two cheeses to be made, one of which the reeve or bailiff will take. Thus, he diverts from the lord's cheese-making one-eighth (12.5 per cent) of the milk each day, which is enough to make one cheese each week for him. The lord's cheeses are thereby reduced in size but, because they all look and weigh the same, the fraud will go unnoticed.

The Intent of the Instructions

What was Carpenter's motive for including this curious text in his formulary? Noël Denholm-Young assumed that Carpenter was simply a rogue: 'There can be little doubt that Carpenter was an astute and dishonest fellow, who did not scruple to cheat his master. No doubt many others were like him, but no other medieval bailiff of whom we have any knowledge thought fit to put it in writing.'[18] Denholm-Young did not, however, provide any suggestion as to *why* Carpenter would have inserted these instructions into his specimen account. If they were meant to remind him how to cheat his employer or to record past crimes, including them in the formulary would surely have been an inconvenient and potentially dangerous form of *aide-mémoire*.

Dorothea Oschinsky took the opposite point of view from Denholm-Young, and believed that Carpenter's intent was honest. She considered that the

---

'"I cannot do't without counters"', 143–60 (esp. 144–5, 155–7); Stephenson, 'Wool Yields', 370–3.

[16] On scab and the baldness that it causes, see T. Spence, MRCVS, 'Control of Sheep Scab in Britain', *Australian Veterinary Journal*, 27 (1951), 136–45 (clinical description on 136); Trow-Smith, *British Livestock Husbandry*, 154–6; D. Stone, *Decision-Making in Medieval Agriculture* (Oxford, 2005), 151, 153, 182.

[17] Cf. *Middle English Dictionary* (2001), s.v. 'pilen' (v. 1:6).

[18] Denholm-Young, 'Robert Carpenter and the Provisions of Westminster', 26.

description of frauds was unlikely to have been included as genuine advice by 'a cunning bailiff . . . on how to defraud his lord', because 'it is difficult to believe' that a bailiff would collude with a dairymaid and shepherd.[19] Oschinsky also dismissed the possibility that Carpenter could have intended this text to be used by other dishonest bailiffs and reeves, because they would never have seen it. Rather, she thought, Carpenter must have written it to warn 'supervising officials' about potential 'loopholes' that could be exploited to the lord's disadvantage.[20] Oschinsky's argument seems unpersuasive on several grounds, however. In the first place, these instructions are embedded in a specimen reeve's account, and the unnamed manorial officer to whom they are addressed could as well be a reeve as a bailiff. In addition, even a bailiff might well collude with a dishonest shepherd and dairymaid, since collusion among servants, officers and other employees must have been far from unknown, as I shall argue below. Also, Oschinsky ignores the instructional tone of Carpenter's text ('And thus you will make a profit of twelve lambs or twelve skins'; 'When you come to shearing'; etc.), and the fact that it contains no suggestions for how an honest bailiff or steward might prevent or expose these frauds.

One possible motive that neither Denholm-Young nor Oschinsky considered was that Carpenter might have recorded these frauds — perhaps culled from his own experience or that of his colleagues, and supplemented by his own imagination — simply as a form of wry recollection or humour with which to entertain himself and his intimates. A parallel can be seen in the collections of instructions for 'magic' tricks that can be found in many medieval commonplace books, and which presumably were recorded by the compilers for their own private amusement and also to entertain others.[21]

In the end, however, the real significance of Carpenter's text is not whether Carpenter described his six frauds as a *vade mecum* for how to defraud a lord, as a gloating record of his own malfeasance, as a righteous warning to himself and his superiors or as a private joke. Rather, the significance of Carpenter's text, written in such a matter-of-fact, nonchalant tone, is its evident implication that such ingenious frauds were widespread and commonplace.

[19]   Oschinsky, *Walter of Henley*, 239.
[20]   Oschinsky, 'Medieval Treatises on Estate Accounting', 55; she recapitulates these arguments in *Walter of Henley*, 239.
[21]   See, for example, BL, Egerton MS 2852, fols. 19ʳ–23ʳ (beginning, '*Ad faciendum speculum in quo uno visu apparebit multe ymagines*'); BL, Royal MS 17 A. viii, fol. 67ᵛ ('To mak a ryng hoppe'); BL, Additional MS 12195, fols. 122ʳ–127ʳ (including, 'If that thu wylt ben in visible'), and fol. 150ᵛ ('For to cause the howsse for to seym full of byrdes'). Cf. B. Roy, 'The Household Encyclopedia as Magic Kit: Medieval Popular Interest in Pranks and Illusions', in *Popular Culture in the Middle Ages*, ed. J. P. Campbell (Bowling Green, Ohio, 1986), 29–38; and *Conjuring Spirits: Texts and Traditions of Medieval Ritual Magic*, ed. C. Fanger (University Park, Pa., 1998), esp. chap. 1, pp. 3–31 (F. Klaassen, 'English Manuscripts of Magic, 1300–1500: A Preliminary Survey'); chap. 3, pp. 76–109 (J. B. Friedman, 'Safe Magic and Invisible Writing in the *Secretum Philosophorum*').

Employee Fraud in Prescriptive Literature

Medieval prescriptive literature abounds in references to employee fraud, and accounting procedures and regulations for the administration of households and manors were designed to prevent or expose it.[22] For example, the Latin *Statuta* (*c*.1235×1242) devised by Bishop Robert Grosseteste for the governance of his own household stipulated that no officer was to accept any gifts, other than a modest offering of food and drink, from any inferior or from another officer.[23] This evidently reflected a concern over the potential for collusion, or demands for bribes or kickbacks, among the bishop's officers and between officers and their underlings. The *Rules* (*c*.1240×1242) for estate and household administration that were based on Grosseteste's *Statuta* and written in Anglo-Norman for the use of the widowed countess of Lincoln, also assumed the likelihood of employee fraud. They advised that, at the end of the financial year, after all the manorial accounts had been rendered, the countess should have one or two of her most faithful and discreet men compare the new account rolls 'in great secrecy' with the rolls containing estimates of corn and stock that had been compiled after the previous harvest, to check for any 'shortcomings' (*defaute*) among her servants and bailiffs.[24] The treatises known as *Seneschaucy* (*c*.1260×1276) and *Walter of Henley* (*c*.1276×1290; perhaps 1286) contain similar directives designed to expose and prevent embezzlement and fraud by manorial servants.[25] In *Seneschaucy*, for example, the steward is advised to familiarise himself with the amount of seed needed per acre so that he will know 'whether the reeve or the hayward charge more seed than necessary' (c. 5).

Some of these directives have strong parallels with the frauds described in Carpenter's text. In *Seneschaucy*, for example, the bailiff is forbidden to allow dead animals to be flayed before the carcasses have been inspected, so that he can ascertain whether they died of illness, accident, poor supervision, or mistreatment, and also to prevent illicit sale of the flesh (cc. 26–7). 'A shepherd', warned the anonymous author, 'who accounts before someone who knows little about such loopholes will have a good bargain if he can acquit himself of ten or twenty sound carcasses stolen or taken from the fold by merely returning the correct number of

---

[22]   Cf. Bruce Campbell's comment, 'The Agrarian Problem in the Early Fourteenth Century', *P&P* 188 (2005), 43, that accounting techniques were generally 'more concerned with preventing fraud and embezzlement than with calculating profits'.

[23]   'Quod nullus omnino in laicali sive spirituali officio constitutus accipiat munera a quocumque subiecto vel prepositis alterius officii domini sui, excepto esculento et potulento moderato': Oschinsky, *Walter of Henley*, 196 (date), 409 (text).

[24]   Ibid., 196 (date), 394–5 (text).

[25]   For the following discussion of *Seneschaucy* and *Walter of Henley*, see ibid., 75–81 (comparison of the two works), 261–305 (text of *Seneschaucy*), 307–85 (text of *Walter of Henley*). On p. 184 Oschinsky noted some parallels between frauds described in *Walter of Henley* and those described by Carpenter.

skins' (c. 27). The bailiff was also warned to check that the mark and wool of any sheepskins matched the mark and wool of the lord's sheep, in order to ensure that no illicit exchanges had taken place (c. 28). For any sheep that died after shearing, the shepherd was to answer for its fleece, skin and carcass; in the case of a dead ewe, he was to answer for her lamb as well (c. 64). Both the bailiff and the reeve were to keep a close eye on the dairy and the cheeses, so that they would know 'when they increase and decrease in number, what their weight is, and that no loss or theft occurs in the dairy whereby the weight might suffer.' They were also 'to know, find out and watch how many cows give a stone of cheese and butter and how many ewes yield a stone of the same' (c. 68). In *Walter of Henley*, the bailiff is warned that many servants and reeves and dairymaids squander and waste milk and give it away (c. 89). Detailed calculations of milk yields are provided so that he can monitor the output of the dairy (cc. 90–2).

Provisions of this kind are also found in other administrative texts and advice manuals. Edward I's household ordinance of 1279, for example, required that the ushers of the hall were to report how many portions of food were served each day, and the issues of the pantry, buttery and kitchen were to be checked against that tally. Similar checks were made on other household departments and their officers.[26] In 1318 the new ordinances devised for the better administration of Edward II's household required that the controller be present each day in the kitchen when the portions of meat or fish were cut up, so as to ensure that it was done as ordained. Every Monday he was to inspect the various household offices to see if their remaining supplies and the supplies used in the previous week tallied with their receipts for that week. The head of each household office was to keep detailed records, and each day the clerks were to account to the steward and the treasurer for all goods delivered to and expended by their offices.[27] Clerks and other officers were fined if their records were defective.[28]

Despite the checks and balances built into household regulations and accounting procedures, low-level pilfering by employees of all kinds was widespread. An English formulary of the late 1240s includes a model letter in which a tenant writes to his lord to report that the lord's bailiff is corrupt, 'for he is selling your stock behind your back, and keeping the proceeds and spending them on his own account'.[29] Across the Channel, Christine de Pisan's advice book, *The Treasure of the City of Ladies* (1405), advised ladies who lived on their manors to keep a close

---

[26] Household ordinance of Westminster, 13 November 1279, printed by T. F. Tout in *Chapters in the Administrative History of Mediaeval England* (6 vols., Manchester, 1920–33), II, 158–63.

[27] T. F. Tout, *The Place of the Reign of Edward II in English History* (2nd edn, Manchester, 1936), 245, 247–8. On the development of household accounts in medieval England, see *Household Accounts from Medieval England, Part 1*, ed. C. M. Woolgar (Oxford, 1992), 3–65.

[28] For some examples of such fines in the royal household c.1300 and 1302, see C. M. Woolgar, *The Great Household in Late Medieval England* (New Haven and London, 1999), 44.

[29] Carlin and Crouch, *English Society*, document 50; see also documents 51–3.

eye on the field-workers, 'for there are a good many workers who will gladly abstain from working the land and give it up for the day if they think no one is keeping an eye on them'. At harvest time, a prudent lady 'will be careful that they do not leave any wheat behind them or that they do not try any other tricks not mentioned before that such people are apt to get up to'.[30] Christine described in detail the kinds of embezzlement that were practised by dishonest maidservants. For example, she warned, 'there are some dishonest chambermaids who are given great responsibility because they know how to insinuate themselves into the great houses of the middle classes and of rich people by cleverly acting the part of good household managers. They get their position of buying the food and going to the butcher's, where they only too well "hit the fruit basket", which is a common expression meaning to claim that the thing costs more than it really does and then keep the change.' Such servants, Christine concluded, 'can pose a very great danger in a house, for because of the excellent service that they know how to give, and their flatteries, and by preparing meals well, keeping the house neat and clean, and speaking well and answering questions politely, they blind people so much that no one is on the look-out for their wicked deeds'.[31] Servants who pilfered from their employers often justified this as a perquisite or custom. The pastoral guide known as *A Myrour to Lewde Men and Wymmen* (c.1400) characterised embezzlements of these kinds as 'Litel thefte . . . when menis servantes or other steleth mete, drinke, polayle [i.e., poultry], sheves in hervest, or othre smale thinges, and thinketh it is noght to charge, for it is a custome.'[32]

Employee Fraud in Financial and Legal Records

Financial and legal records provide numerous examples of such employee frauds in both town and countryside, and among both officers and servants. A study of the later fourteenth-century court rolls of the marcher lordship of Dyffryn Clwyd or Ruthin, for example, has found clear evidence of 'negligence and embezzlement of officials in concealing debts and succession dues'.[33] Urban records document thefts by domestic servants, apprentices and journeymen. In 1385, for example,

---

[30] Christine de Pisan, *The Treasure of the City of Ladies, or The Book of the Three Virtues*, trans. S. Lawson (London and New York, 1985), 'How ladies and young women who live on their manors ought to manage their households and estates', 131–2.

[31] Ibid., 'Of servant women and chambermaids', 170–1.

[32] BL, Harley MS 45, fol. 65^v; printed in *A Myrour to Lewde Men and Wymmen: A Prose Version of the Speculum Vitae, ed. from B.L. MS Harley 45*, ed. V. Nelson (Heidelberg, 1981), 134, ll. 2–4. The *Myrour* was a prose redaction of the metrical *Speculum vitae* (1349×1384). For the respective dates of the *Myrour* and the *Speculum vitae*, see ibid., 24–5.

[33] A. D. M. Barrell et al., 'The Dyffryn Clwyd Court Roll Project, 1340–1352 and 1389–1399: A Methodology and Some Preliminary Findings', in *Medieval Society and the Manor Court*, ed. Z. Razi and R. Smith (Oxford, 1996), 289.

two London apprentices admitted to having stolen 205 marks in cash from their master, a vintner, with which they had been entrusted to trade on his behalf in Bordeaux.[34] In 1403–4 a London goldsmith's apprentice confessed to a range of frauds that included stealing silver and gold from customers' bullion and wrought objects; stealing money, bullion and other materials from his master; borrowing plate from a jeweller in his master's name and then stealing it; and making duplicate keys to his master's counter-room and chest, with the intention of stealing plate and then absconding abroad.[35] Similar evidence can be found for contemporary Paris, and Bronisław Geremek concluded that most cases of theft there 'were the work of domestic servants, wage-earners, or the employees of artisans'.[36] In England in 1455, an act of parliament (33 Hen. vi c. 1) alleged that household servants 'of lords and other persons of good degree' were embezzling their masters' goods after their death, and in response ordained a procedure for the investigation and punishment of offenders. Under Henry viii, the embezzlement by servants of goods entrusted to them by their masters and mistresses was made a felony (21 Hen. viii c. 7), and guilty servants were denied benefit of clergy and the privilege of sanctuary (27 Hen. viii c. 17 and 28 Hen. viii c. 2).[37]

Some Wider Implications

In the modern world, as in the past, employee fraud has represented a significant economic cost. In the 1990s the annual cost of employee theft in the United States alone was estimated to range between $40 billion and $400 billion, and the insurance industry attributed one-third of all business failures to it.[38] Employee fraud has also historically constituted a significant part of the 'shadow' (or 'grey' or 'informal') economy. This is the unofficial or sub-legal economic sector of unrecorded exchanges, under-reported earnings, inflated expenses and

[34] *Calendar of Pleas and Memoranda of the City of London, 1381–1412*, ed. A. H. Thomas (Cambridge, 1932), 89–90.

[35] In 1427–9 another goldsmith's apprentice was expelled from the mistery for having made a duplicate key to his master's till: *Wardens' Accounts and Court Minute Books of the Goldsmiths' Mistery of London, 1334–1446*, ed. L. Jefferson (Woodbridge, 2003), 282–7, 445.

[36] E. Cohen, 'Patterns of Crime in Fourteenth-Century Paris', *French Historical Studies* 11 (1980), 307–27, esp. 321–3, 325; B. Geremek, *The Margins of Society in Late Medieval Paris* (Cambridge, 1987), 97; cf. 118–19.

[37] SR, ii, 369–70 (33 Hen. vi [1455] c. 1); iii, 289 (21 Hen. viii [1529] c. 7), 549–50 (27 Hen. viii [1535–6] c. 17), 652 (28 Hen. viii [1536] c. 2). The act of 1529 excluded servants under the age of eighteen and apprentices, and stolen goods worth less than 40s.

[38] B. J. Oliphant and G. C. Oliphant, 'Using a Behavior-Based Method to Identify and Reduce Employee Theft', *International Journal of Retail and Distribution Management* 29 (2001), 442–51, available online at http://www.emeraldinsight.com/Insight/ViewContentServlet?Filename=Published/EmeraldFullTextArticle/Articles/0890291002.html [seen 11 March 2010].

unpaid taxes; of vanishing goods and bogus accounting; of the fiddle, the scam, the kickback and the pay-off. The shadow economy is very large, even in the most economically-developed countries. In the early 1990s, by one estimation, the shadow economy represented 13–76 per cent of Gross Domestic Product (GDP) in Africa, Latin America and Asia; 7–43 per cent of GDP in countries of the former Soviet bloc; and 8–30 per cent of GDP in Western Europe, Japan and the United States.[39] In 2006 the shadow economy represented 8 per cent of GDP in the United States and 10.9 per cent in the United Kingdom.[40]

Robert Carpenter's embezzlement instructions do not tell us anything new about moral compromise in medieval England, but they do offer an unusual window onto the practical logistics of employee fraud, and they make it clear that, like employee fraud today, systematic pilfering by corrupt manorial officers and other workers could well have siphoned off a significant fraction of medieval manorial output. In Carpenter's examples, a corrupt reeve or bailiff could purloin as much as 12.5 per cent or more of the annual value of a manor's flocks and dairy production. However, such thefts, if — like most modern employee thefts — they were successful and undetected, would never have been reflected in the manorial accounts.[41] This suggests that manorial accounts may often under-report the true volume and value of manorial produce, an important consideration for scholars who rely on these accounts in calculating the yields and productivity of arable and pastoral farming.[42] The evidence of employee theft among apprentices and other non-agricultural employees suggests that, as in the modern world, a similar caution should be applied to other records of medieval production.

[39] M. H. Fleming, J. Roman, and G. Farrell, 'The Shadow Economy', *Journal of International Affairs* 53:2 (2000), 387–409, available online at http://jia.sipa.columbia.edu/pdf/farrell_capstone_final.pdf [seen 11 March 2010]. The figures given above are extrapolated and simplified from tables 1–3.

[40] A. Buehn and F. Schneider, 'Shadow Economies and Corruption All Over the World: Revised Estimates for 120 Countries', *Economics: The Open-Access, Open-Assessment E-Journal* 1 (2007–9) (Version 2), Table 3.6.1, available online at http://www.economics-ejournal.org/economics/journalarticles/2007-9 [seen 11 March 2010].

[41] Studies cited by Oliphant and Oliphant (n. 38 above) estimate that 80 per cent of employee theft goes undetected, and that only 5 per cent of those who steal from their firm are apprehended.

[42] As Mark Page acknowledged gingerly in a recent assessment of the productivity of sheep farming in England before the Black Death, the accuracy of statistics derived from manorial accounts depends 'to some extent on the honesty of the reeves and the vigilance of the auditors who examined their accounts'. For example, in comparing his own figures for lamb mortality on the bishop of Winchester's manor of Crawley, Hants., with those of Christopher Thornton for the bishop's manor of Rimpton in Somerset, he included the caveat that 'it is assumed that reeves were being honest in the number of deaths they recorded': M. Page, 'The Technology of Medieval Sheep Farming: Some Evidence from Crawley, Hampshire, 1208–1349', *AgHR* 51 (2003), 144.

Appendix

This is the text of Robert Carpenter II's embezzlement instructions, from his own holograph formulary in Cambridge, Gonville and Caius College, MS 205/111 (pp. 384–8). I have collated it with the version copied by his son, Robert Carpenter III, into the formulary that is now Cambridge University Library, MS Mm. I. 27 (fol. 85ᵛ), and with the text printed by Dorothea Oschinsky in *Walter of Henley* (pp. 461–2). In the transcript below I have, like Oschinsky, silently extended standard abbreviations except those for money denominations (s., d., ob., q.). Unlike Oschinsky, I have retained the original spelling, capitalisation and punctuation.

[*p. 384*] Item qui habuerit .CL. matrices oves. Quedam erunt steriles. quedam mortue ante partum. quedam facient ab orsum. Et de Gercis quidam agni provenient. ¶Item cum dicitur. quia .vj. fuerunt [*p. 385*] steriles; dicetur .ix. fuerunt steriles. <¶Nota quod aliquando una ovis; habet duas agnos in uno an[no]>[1] Et .iiij. mortue ante partum; dicetur .vj. mortue ante partum. Et .iij. fecerunt ab orsum; dicetur .v. fecerunt ab orsum. Et cum dicitur .et .x. proventi fuerunt de Gercis. dicetur .v. proventi fuerunt de Gercis. Et sic lucraberis .xij. agnos vel .xij. pelles. ¶Item. ad bene reddendum compotum de agnis .CL. matricium ovium. <Et ad lucrandum .xxv. pelles ad unam fururam>[2] Sit Ita quod nulla ovis de dictis .CL. matricibus ovibus sit sterilis . nec aliqua mortua ante partum. nec aliqua faciet ab orsum. et omnes agni qui provenient de Gercis[3] demonstrantur. Sit quod .x. provenient de Gercis. Et habentur .Clx. agni. Sit Ita quod omnes moriantur. oportet reddere compotum de .Clx. pellibus agninis. bene reddantur compoti et ad huc habebit vel[4] lucraberis .xxv. pelles ad una fururam. Sic. Elige de dictis pellibus .L. pelles partim de melioribus et partim de mediocris. Ita ut .xxv. de hiis electis; valeant .ij. s'. j. d'. et alie .xxv; xx. d'. quelibet pelles ob' q'. Et tunc hee [*p. 386*] pelles que valent .ij. s'. j. d'. vendentur. quelibet pellis pro .j. d'. Et emantur .L. pelles pellis quelibet pro ob'. cum denariis predictis. Et .xxv. pelles que valent .xx. [d.][5] remaneant ad unam fururam.

¶Item. ut ovis quelibet amet alium agnum. quam suum proprium. ¶Extrahatur sanguis de naribus ovis illius. et ungetur agnus quem amare debet.

¶Item. ad faciendum pellem ovinam tanquam ovis esset mortua de morina. ponatur pellis tam cito quam excoriata fuerit in aquam calidam. et tunc statim siccatur. et deueniet tanquam mortua esset de morina.

---

[1] The sentence in angle brackets is inserted at the top of p. 385 and was not printed by Oschinsky in *Walter of Henley*, even though it appears to be in Carpenter's hand or in a similar hand. The last word (*an[no]*) was truncated by the trimming away of the right edge of the page here.

[2] The phrase in angle brackets is inserted above the line.

[3] *gerciis*, in *Walter of Henley*.

[4] *et*, in *Walter of Henley*.

[5] *d.* omitted in MS.

¶Item. Sit quod bercarius reddere debuerit .C. multones sibi traditos ad custo-diendum. et sibi deerint[6] .iiij. multones. ¶Eat ad bercarium socium suum in eadem pastura. qui habuerit multones eodem modo signatos; et acomodet .iiij. multones. et dicat quod reddere debet multones suos. et dicat ei quod cum dicti .iiij. multones venerint in pasturam comunem; ibunt ad multones sibi socios.

¶Item qui gravare voluerit bercarium. ¶Cum veneris ad tonsionem; Cape vel-lera que [*p. 387*] non sunt depillata et pone in una parte per se. et vellera depillata in alia parte per se. et cum omnes oves tonse fuerint; cape vellera depillata et pone in stateram. Et cape vellera nec de melioribus nec de peioribus et pone in alia parte statere. Et sic forte .v. vellera nec de melioribus nec de peioribus; ponderabunt plus; quam .x. vellera depillata. et tunc bercarius in misericordia domini sui est; de ovibus sic custoditis; et redditurus est .v. vellera domino suo si ita contingit.

¶Item habebitur de .C. multonibus de iure .j. pondus lane. Et de .CL. matrici-bus ouibus .j. pondus lane. Et <de .CC. hogastris .j. pondus lane>.[7]

¶Item ad bene reddendum compotum de caseis.[8] qui inceperunt fieri die pasche. et desierunt fieri die sancti michaelis cotidie unum caseum. utroque die computato. et ad huc ad habendum in qualibet ebdomoda[9] .j. caseum tam ma-gnus sicuti nullus alius de ebdomoda.[10] In primo die quando incipiunt ad caseos faciendos dividatur lac eque in octo partes. et octava pars reservetur usque in cra-stinum. et ex aliis partibus statim unus caseus efficiatur. Et in crastino lac eodem modo dividatur. et capiantur due partes illo die de lacte. Et prima [*p. 388*] pars que primo capiebatur effundetur in aliud lac de quo caseus statim efficitur. et sic qualibet[11] die renovabitur lac. Et septimo die habebis sic. octo partes lactis novi; et sex partes anterioris diei. et sic die septimo facies duos caseos de eadem forma de qua sunt alii.

---

6   *desint*, in CUL, MS Mm. 1. 27.

7   The phrase in angle brackets is inserted above the line. A similar calculation for the produc-tion of cheese, wool, and butter from sheep and cows, with a similar interlinear insertion, occurs on p. 380: 'Item, from 25 milking ewes in good pasture will be had 1 wey (*pondus*) of cheese. And of 4 cows, 1 wey of cheese. And the wey is of 16 stone, and the stone is of 12 lb. Item, of 100 wethers will be had 1 wey of wool. And of 150 breeding ewes, 1 wey of wool. <and of 200 hoggs, 1 wey of wool.> Item, he who will have 8 weys of cheese should have by rights (*de jure*) 1 wey of butter.' ('Item de .xxv. bidentibus lactricibus in bona pastura; habebi-tur .j. pondus casei. Et de .iiij. vaccis .j. pondus casei. Et est pondus. de .xvj. petris. et petra; de .xij. libris. ¶Item de .C. multonibus habebitur .j. pondus lane. Et de .CL. matricibus ovibus .j. pondus lane. <et de .cc. hog' .j. pondus lane.> ¶Item qui habuerit .viij. pondera casei habere debet de jure .j. pondus butiri.')

8   *caseo*, in CUL, MS Mm. 1. 27.

9   *Sic*; Oschinsky corrects this to *ebdomada* in *Walter of Henley*.

10   *Sic*; Oschinsky corrects this to *ebdomada* in *Walter of Henley*.

11   *Sic*; Oschinsky corrects this to *quolibet* in *Walter of Henley*.

11

The Public Life of the Private Charter in Thirteenth-Century England

....

James Masschaele

Over the course of his career, Richard Britnell has frequently used charter evidence to document major attributes of the economy and society of medieval England. One thinks immediately of his pioneering use of royal market charters to illustrate the spread of commercialisation, but other examples also come to mind, such as the role charters played in creating the trust in public norms and rules that underpinned economic growth in the period and the way in which charter use facilitated pragmatic literacy.[1] His work has demonstrated the value of looking at the medieval economy as something embedded within a larger social and political framework, such that changes in law or administrative proce-dures could have significant repercussions on economic activity and vice versa.

This essay on the use of charters in medieval England is offered in the same spirit. One of the primary manifestations of the entrepreneurial spirit of the period involved the commoditising of land and the formation of an increasingly active land market.[2] Beginning in the later twelfth century, people came increas-ingly to treat land as an economic asset rather than as a static source of consump-tion and marker of status. A host of other changes happened in conjunction with this development. Some were principally economic, such as rising monetisation and an increasing emphasis on producing commodities for sale. Others involved law and politics, such as the introduction and subsequent expansion of the pos-sessory assizes and the use of 'feet of fines' to record land transactions in royal court records. Charters were associated with many of these changes, not neces-sarily in a simple cause-and-effect way but as an important contributor to the growing sense of trust and security in the rule of law that made other changes

---

[1]   R. H. Britnell, 'King John's Early Grants of Markets and Fairs', *EHR* 370 (1979), 90–6; idem, 'The Proliferation of Markets in England, 1200–1349', *EcHR* 34 (1981), 209–21; idem, *The Commercialisation of English Society, 1100–1500* (2nd edn, Manchester, 1996); *Pragmatic Literacy East and West, 1200–1330*, ed. idem (Woodbridge, 1997).

[2]   P. R. Schofield, *Peasant and Community in Medieval England 1200–1500* (New York, 2003), part I.

possible. The growing use of charters thus reflects the growing scope for human initiative and decision making that characterised the high Middle Ages as well as the complex interplay between individual decisions and more general forces for historical change.

Although there is a substantial secondary literature on the formal character-istics of medieval charters, surprisingly little attention has been given to their use in resolving disputes, particularly disputes that did not involve the church. The value of having a charter as evidence documenting a transaction is not nearly as simple or as clear cut as might be assumed. Having a properly composed and properly sealed charter was certainly a useful tool in warding off disputes about the nature of a transaction, but it did not guarantee that the possessor of a charter would triumph if a dispute actually emerged. While charters were advantageous in disputes, their utility was due nearly as much to the process by which they were created as to their form as a written document that could be shown in court.[3] Me-dieval people were well aware that charters could be forged or otherwise falsified, and they also understood that a written document could be invalidated by the circumstances of composition or the circumstances under which a deal was struck. As the use of charters proliferated — to the point that even villein peasants began to rely on them — a host of practical procedures for verifying and authenticating transactions described in charters also came into being.[4] The role charters played in documenting and attesting to transactions thus needs to be seen as a dynamic process, part of which involved the written document available to historians, but part of which involved other acts, deeds, and oral communications that histori-ans can see only obliquely. Royal court records of the thirteenth century shed considerable light on this process, chiefly in the form of disputes centering upon the implementation or interpretation of the terms spelled out in a charter. This essay will explore the use of charters by considering three related issues. First, it will look at some of the more common situations in which charters could be chal-lenged. Secondly, it will consider how the circumstances of a charter's drafting affected its success as a form of evidence when the underlying transaction came into dispute. Thirdly, it will treat the role charter witnesses played in resolving disputes in which the validity or authenticity of a charter was called into question.

Challenges to Charters

By the end of the twelfth century, charters were commonly made whenever land was transferred from one individual to another by means other than inheritance.

---

[3]   P. R. Hyams, 'The Charter as a Source for the Early Common Law', *The Journal of Legal His-tory* 12 (1991), 173–89.

[4]   *Carte Nativorum: A Peterborough Abbey Cartulary of the Fourteenth Century*, ed. C. N. L. Brooke and M. M. Postan (Northamptonshire Record Society 22, 1960).

In legal theory, charters provided evidence of a grantor's decision to convey seisin to a grantee but were not themselves necessary for the transfer of seisin to take effect. Transfers of seisin could and often did take place without an accompanying charter, but because charters provided a kind of insurance to grantees that the underlying transaction was valid, they were very often drawn up to accompany a transaction. Charters were typically not treated as final or definitive proof of an underlying transfer, but they lent credibility to one side of an argument if the transfer was ever brought into question. Litigants thus frequently produced charters in court to substantiate their cases, and the courts typically accepted charters as adding considerable weight to one side of the argument over the other.

There were, however, many reasons why the validity of a charter could be challenged. Some had to do with the very nature of the charter itself. Modern research has shown that charters were often forged, particularly in the twelfth century and particularly by ecclesiastical institutions.[5] Many forgeries succeeded in their own day and have been uncovered only by the rigorous application of procedures developed by modern diplomatists. But medieval people understood that forgery was possible, and medieval courts were well versed in how to handle allegations of forgery. Charters that showed signs of having been recently made, for example, were unlikely to find favour when the underlying transaction took place many years earlier.[6] Charters with erasures were similarly suspect.[7] Writing about some charters presented in court by Alan de Belfou in the late 1160s, a chronicler of Battle abbey noted that 'it was plain to those who studied them carefully that those charters bore the mark of forgery'.[8] The possibility of forgery was so widely known by the later twelfth century that Glanvill included it in his exposition of English law.[9]

While the ink and parchment were often inspected when the authenticity of a charter came into question, the courts generally treated seals as the most important tests of validity, and thus allegations of forgery were more likely to focus on the nature of the seal than the nature of the written text. Seals could be forged or fraudulently replicated in a variety of ways. Simple forging was one, the test for which was a careful comparison with other charters promulgated by the same

[5] C. N. L. Brooke and A. Morey, *Gilbert Foliot and the Letters* (Cambridge, 1965), chap. 8; Z. Hunyadi, 'The Identification of a Forgery', in *Dating Undated Medieval Charters*, ed. M. Gervers (Woodbridge, 2000), 137–49; A. Hiatt, *The Making of Medieval Forgeries: False Documents in Fifteenth-Century England* (Toronto, 2004).

[6] *CRR* I, 296; II, 135–6; XI, 562, no. 2793.

[7] *Select Cases in the Court of the King's Bench*, ed. G. O. Sayles (7 vols., Selden Society 55–88, 1936–71), I, 61–3; II, 137–41.

[8] *English Lawsuits from the Reign of William I to Richard I*, ed. R. C. Van Caeneghem (2 vols., Selden Society 106–7, 1990–1), II, 494, no. 458.

[9] *The Treatise on the Laws and Customs of the Realm of England commonly called Glanvill*, ed. G. D. G. Hall (Oxford, 1965), 127 (discussing debt litigation), 176 (discussing forgery).

person and bearing authentic seals.[10] When Osbert of Daggewurth sought in 1242 to reclaim land once held by his grandfather from the abbey of St Benet's Hulme in Norfolk, for example, the abbot brought two of the grandfather's charters into court to negate Osbert's claim.[11] Osbert countered by bringing four other charters sealed by his grandfather to demonstrate to the court that the seals of the two damaging charters presented by the abbot were not made from the same matrix. The abbot dismissed Osbert's allegation, claiming that the grandfather could have easily possessed a greater and a lesser seal. To prove the point, the abbot brought in yet another of the grandfather's charters which bore the same seal as the four charters Osbert had presented.

Litigants sometimes also challenged the circumstances in which their seal was affixed to a charter. In such cases, they were willing to concede that the seal was genuine, but they argued that it had been applied to the charter in a fraudulent or deceptive manner. In an eyre court in Huntingdonshire in 1286, for example, Beatrice Waldeshef claimed that her seal had been taken from her while she was seriously ill and used against her wishes.[12] Two sisters fell out over an inheritance from a deceased brother in Northamptonshire in 1229, with one alleging that the other had fraudulently used the seal that her brother had left in her custody while he went on a pilgrimage.[13] In a similar case in Hampshire in 1242–3, a litigant claimed that he kept his seal with a friend who betrayed him by using it maliciously and against his interest.[14] A certain Agnes in Leicestershire told a remarkable variant tale of a seal and misplaced trust in a loved one.[15] She claimed that her brother had approached her with a certain document and asked her to affix her husband's seal to it. Agnes was understandably reluctant to accede to her brother's request, but he reassured her by calling on God and the saints to witness that his intentions were good. She proceeded to steal her husband's seal so that her brother could use it, only to discover later that the document he then sealed was a charter conveying to him the land that she and her husband held.

While forging, faking and dissimulation lay at the root of many challenges, litigation more commonly involved the legitimacy of the underlying grant attested by a charter. In such instances, the party whose interests were undermined by an adversary's possession of a charter sought to vitiate the document by claim-

---

[10] *CRR* xi, 257, no. 1280; xv, 105, no. 508; *Bracton's Note-Book: A Collection of Cases Decided in the King's Courts During the Reign of Henry the Third, Annotated by a Lawyer of that Time, Seemingly Henry of Bratton*, ed. F. W. Maitland (3 vols., London, 1887), ii, 1.

[11] *CRR* xvii, 46–7, no. 181.

[12] *Royal Justice and the Medieval English Countryside: The Huntingdonshire Eyre of 1286, the Ramsey Abbey Banlieu Court of 1287, and the Assizes of 1287–88*, ed. A. DeWindt and E. DeWindt (Toronto, 1981), 240–1.

[13] *Bracton's Note-Book*, ii, 277–9, no. 332.

[14] *CRR* xvii, 248, no. 1302.

[15] *CRR* xi, 326, no. 1630.

ing that the donor lacked the lawful capacity to make a charter or effect a grant or sale of property. Widows, for example, sometimes contested charters made by their deceased husbands on the grounds that they were unable to contradict them while their husbands were alive.[16] In an interesting case from Suffolk in 1223, a jury was asked to determine whether a grantor was a leper when he issued a charter; if he was, the charter could not be valid because lepers did not have legal standing.[17] Charters could also be undermined if the grantor did not enjoy seisin of the property when the charter was formalised.[18]

Contests over charters that were formally proper but none the less invalid often involved the age or mental capacity of a donor. Minors could not convey property, and so any charter made during a grantor's minority was *ipso facto* traversable. The basic principle was well understood, and pleading typically ended with a charge to a jury to determine if the grantor was still in his or her minority when the grant was made; if the verdict was yes the charter was invalid.[19] But the temptation for others with influence over a minor to make deals involving the minor's property was strong. In such instances, promulgating a charter to document a transaction was probably seen as particularly worthwhile because of the tenuous nature of the underlying grant. Thus, Helen de Boxwood and her sister Margaret contested a holding in Surrey in 1235 then in the possession of Edward of Winchester — for which he had a charter from each sister — with the argument that their mother had issued the charters while they were minors and under her guardianship.[20] Robert son of Peter told a similar tale a few years earlier when he claimed two bovates and a few other small holdings in Yorkshire from William le Oyselur, although Robert claimed that he had been sold out by his guardian rather than a parent.[21]

Charters authorised from a deathbed were also problematic, particularly if they were made as part of a conveyance to a religious establishment. The dynamic of grant and challenge is well illustrated in a Norfolk case of 1200 involving rights to an advowson. Peter de Altobosco claimed that his father conveyed the rights to a local priory while he was languishing in the bed in which he died.[22] The case is particularly interesting because, after describing his father's condition, Altobosco went on to add that grants of this nature were contrary to the custom of the realm. His claim appears to be accurate, judging by the willingness of the

[16] CRR xii, 173, no. 845; *Civil Pleas of the Wiltshire Eyre, 1249*, ed. M. T. Clanchy (Wiltshire Record Society 26, 1971), 103, no. 314.

[17] CRR xi, 204, no. 1016.

[18] *Bracton's Note-Book*, ii, 101–2, no. 114; CRR xvii, 342, no. 1738.

[19] CRR xiii, 234, no. 1081, 446–7, no. 2117; xiv, 422, no. 1961.

[20] *The 1235 Surrey Eyre*, ii, ed. C. A. F. Meekings and D. Crook (Surrey Record Society 32, 1983), 310–11, no. 152.

[21] CRR xiii, 73, no. 323.

[22] CRR i, 352–3.

courts to rest the outcome of similar cases on the timing of the grant relative to the final illness.[23] Indeed, the prior of Buckenham agreed to buy out John son of William's interest in an advowson that John's father had conveyed to the priory simply on the grounds that the charter had been made after John's father had retired to the priory.[24] The dynamic is readily understandable. People who knew their days were dwindling had obvious reasons for wanting to put their affairs in order as well as to provide for the welfare of their souls. Alienations by charter, no matter when they were made, took land out of the family circle, and the loss of patrimony would have been particularly galling when it took place so close to the moment of transfer between generations.

Preservation of patrimony was probably the main reason the courts took a hard line on deathbed transfers by charter, but they may also have been influenced by the principle that an individual who made a charter had to be of sound mind. Challenges to grants based on the mental state of the grantor who authorised a charter were surprisingly common. In some instances mental incapacity was associated with old age and the onset of a final illness, as in a case involving Osbert Dacus, described by his disinherited grandson as 'impotent and no longer having a memory' when he made out a charter to a local religious house.[25] Other cases, though, indicate that the charters of otherwise healthy people who were mentally ill were also invalid. Thus Alice de Wauton challenged her brother's charter because he was 'demented and beyond memory', traits that were publicly manifest because he had sought to stab himself with a knife when he was brought before the county court to determine his mental capacity.[26] When John Edws sought to prove his right to a mill in Kent in 1258 by virtue of a charter made in his favour by Saffridus son of Peter, the sheriff of Kent intervened in the proceedings to inform the justices that Saffridus was an 'ydiota'.[27] He went on to say that Edws, who was Saffridus's guardian, had actually made the charter so that he could acquire the mill himself. On the basis of the sheriff's claim, the justices examined Saffridus, verified that he was indeed mentally incompetent, and asked the leading men in court to confirm whether he had been that way from birth, which they duly did. Having unearthed these facts, the justices voided the charter, ordered imprisonment for the malevolent guardian, and arranged for Saffridus to have the mill under the care of a new guardian.

As this brief survey indicates, the range of circumstances that could lead the courts to reject properly redacted charters was quite extensive. It also illustrates the great value people attached to having charters as evidence of their transac-

---

23 *CRR* x, 320; xiv, 53, no. 266; xv, 356–7, no. 1394.
24 *CRR* xvii, 250–1, no. 1313.
25 *CRR* xii, 469–70, no. 2344.
26 *CRR* xii, 516–7, no. 2594.
27 *The 1258–9 Special Eyre of Surrey and Kent*, ed. A. H. Hershey (Woking, 2004), 152, no. 273.

tions. In most of the cases discussed above, charters served as the fulcrums around which cases revolved. Defendants typically brought their charters into court as the bulwark of their claim to enjoy a contested property, and plaintiffs typically sought to refute their opponent's claims by undermining the legitimacy of their charters. Both strategies were based on the recognition that showing a charter in court was hugely advantageous to one side of the dispute. Litigants understood very well that courts looked kindly on charters as effective instruments for moving cases to satisfactory resolutions. But with so many possible flaws in the creation of the documents, grantors often sought to supplement the written text with public performances and ceremonies designed to publicise the terms of their charters. Like the charter itself, public notice about the contents of a charter and the grantor's wishes for the transfer of property enhanced the security of the transfer, and in cases of conflict, the public act that accompanied a charter could be more important than the written document.

Charter Making as a Public Event

The popularity of charters in the twelfth and thirteenth centuries was clearly part of a larger cultural shift that made writing more central to the ordering of society.[28] Paradoxically, however, their growing popularity also served to emphasise the importance of oral communication and public performance in the conduct of public and private affairs; charters were, in effect, scripts for staged performances as well as vessels for conveying evidence through time.[29] Their script-like quality is discernible from their form, which typically adopted the guise of a public address ('Let all present and future people know . . .'). The relationship between writing, speech and gesture can be easily overlooked, however, because charters have come down to us as written documents, documents that are wearyingly formulaic and repetitive. Fortunately, some of the words and gestures that attended their original use have left traces in other sources. Disputes about the accuracy or veracity of charters, for example, occasionally provide accounts of the circumstances in which charters were drawn up or formally promulgated, bringing to light some of the words and deeds that accompanied the handing over of the sealed document. Laurent Morelle has drawn attention to some French evidence bearing on this question, but there is still more to be learned, particularly with respect to private charters.[30] A careful study of drafting and conveying reveals

---

[28]   M. Clanchy, *From Memory to Written Record: England 1066–1307* (2nd edn, Oxford, 1993).

[29]   B. Bedos-Rezak, 'Towards an Archaeology of the Medieval Charter: Textual Production and Reproduction in Northern French Cartularies', in *Charters, Cartularies and Archives: The Presentation and Transmission of Documents in the Medieval West*, ed. A. Kosto and A. Winroth (Toronto, 2002), 43–60.

[30]   L. Morelle, 'Les chartes dans la gestion des conflits (France du Nord, XIe–début XIIe siècle)', *Bibliothèque de l'École des Chartes* 155:1 (1997), 267–98.

how closely the written word of the charter was associated with the spoken word of public life. Indeed, the extraordinary popularity of charters was due in part to their ability to combine speech and text rather than to privilege one form of communication over the other.

Contemporary notions of how charters should be promulgated were deeply influenced by the practices of the church. Many of the charters that conveyed land to an ecclesiastical institution note that the grantor finalised or solidified a grant by depositing a charter on an altar.[31] Heirs who were losing out through parental grants to a church or monastery were sometimes also brought into the church and associated with the deposition. When recounting the circumstances surrounding a grant made by his father to the monastery of St Werburgh in Chester, for example, Ranulph, earl of Chester, stated that he remembered the grant because he had placed the charter recording it on the altar of the abbey church in the presence of his father's body.[32] Similarly, on the day that Jordan de Builli entered Blyth priory as a monk, his eldest son not only placed his father's charter on the priory's altar but even added his own seal to it in front of a large number of witnesses.[33] Rituals involving deposition on an altar were undoubtedly designed to reinforce the religious significance of grants made to the church, but their public nature also served to solidify the terms of a grant by drawing public notice to it; the written charter and the formal act of conveyance were two sides of a single coin. They were, in effect, a form of public liturgy, as Arnold Angenendt has recently suggested.[34]

The public reading of royal writs and charters also influenced contemporary notions of how private charters should be formalised.[35] The habit of public reading can be traced back to the late Anglo-Saxon period, as Richard Sharpe has recently shown.[36] In the eleventh and early twelfth centuries royal charters were routinely read at gatherings of the county court. In fact, they were drafted on the assumption that they would be read, and that the public reading would be

---

[31] E.g. *Two Cartularies of Abingdon Abbey*, ed. C. F. Slade and G. Lambrick (2 vols., Oxford Historical Society, new ser. 32–3, 1990–2), I, 239–40; *The Cartularies of Southwick Priory*, ed. K. A. Hanna (2 vols., Hampshire Record Series 9–10, 1988), I, 16, 33, 81; *The Lanercost Cartulary*, ed. J. M. Todd (Surtees Society 203, 1997), 132, 133.

[32] *CChR, 1257–1300*, 310.

[33] *The Cartulary of Blyth Priory*, ed. R. T. Timson (London, 1973), 213, no. 331.

[34] Arnold Angenendt, 'How Was a Confraternity Made? The Evidence of Charters', in *The Durham Liber Vitae and Its Context*, ed. D. Rollason, A. J. Piper, M. Harvey, and L. Rollason (Woodbridge, 2004), 217.

[35] A. Adamska, 'From Memory to Written Record in the Periphery of Medieval *Latinitas*: The Case of Poland in the Eleventh and Twelfth Centuries', in *Charters and the Use of the Written Word in Medieval Society*, ed. K. Heidecker (Turnhout, 2000), 95–6.

[36] R. Sharpe, 'Address and Delivery in Anglo-Norman Royal Charters', in *Charters and Charter Scholarship in Britain and Ireland*, ed. M. T. Flanagan and J. A. Green (Basingstoke, 2005), 32–52.

an instrumental part of their implementation. Sharpe describes these early royal mandates as 'writ-charters', designed both to charge local officials with a task, as writs would later routinely do, and to provide public notice of a royal grant or act, as charters would later do. The procedures for publicising them were well known and frequently used, forming what Sharpe described as 'a well-organized system of communication'.[37] Sharpe suggested that this early method of proclamation and publication lost its vitality over the course of the twelfth century, but there is plenty of evidence from later periods to indicate that it remained in vogue. J. R. Maddicott, for example, has described how kings of the thirteenth and fourteenth centuries used proclamations of royal documents such as charters and statutes to influence public opinion.[38] As in earlier periods, these later royal proclamations served a variety of purposes, all intended to emphasise the king's role as the guarantor of peace, security and good government.

The practice of using county courts as venues for publicising royal enactments was adaptable by the makers of private charters to draw public attention to their personal acts, even when they had no connection whatsoever to royal interests. In a dispute over a wardship in 1221, for example, Roger de Reimes based his claim on a charter made by the ward's principal lord, who had the charter read out loud in a full session of the county court as part of the ceremony by which he placed Roger in seisin.[39] Likewise in a case of *mort d'ancestor* that began in 1225, Alice, daughter of Waleran, earl of Warwick, laid claim to a major landholding formerly held by her father on the strength of a charter he had made on her behalf about a year before he died.[40] In the initial pleading of the case, Alice stated that her father had given her the land in a session of the county court, at which he took homage from her before requiring the free tenants occupying the lands to perform homage to her. At some later time, her father drew up a charter to record the terms of his conveyance, which he gave to three of his knights with instructions that they should take it to the county court to be read. In a similar case from 1223, Walter and Margery Cumin claimed that Margery's father had conveyed some of his land to her in a charter.[41] The grant reduced the inheritance that eventually came to her brother Ralph, who sought reinstatement following their father's death. To strengthen her case, Margery presented a second charter that had been made out by her brother at the time of their father's grant. Ralph's charter confirmed his father's grant, leading Margery to claim that Ralph was obliged to warrant her possession of the land rather than take it away. Ralph, however, told the

---

[37] Ibid., 45.
[38] J. R. Maddicott, 'The County Community and the Making of Public Opinion in Fourteenth-Century England', *TRHS* 28 (1978), 27–43; J. Ferster, *Fictions of Advice: The Literature and Politics of Counsel in Late Medieval England* (Philadelphia, 1996), 22–3.
[39] *CRR* x, 97.
[40] *CRR* xii, 282–3, no. 1380; xiii, 68, no. 307.
[41] *CRR* xi, 191–2, no. 952.

justices that his charter of confirmation was not legitimate, because he had been forced to make it by his mother. He went on to state that his mother had not only compelled him to make the charter but had also hauled him to the county court so that the charter could be formally read there.

The reading of private charters at county courts appears to have been a common event, but since attendance consisted mainly of men of relatively high status, it is likely that the announcements made there were relevant principally to the upper crust of county society. Similar publicising, however, took place in lower-level courts, including hundred courts and manor courts. For the bulk of society, these local courts must have provided the main public gatherings at which charters were broadcast. When William Luciel sought to substantiate his claim to a messuage in Essex in 1227, he showed the eyre justices a charter that had been made in his favour by Beatrice, widow of Stephen de Bononia, who was now claiming possession of it.[42] After showing the charter, he claimed that it had been made in the court of the hundred of Clavering, which immediately led to a challenge from Beatrice, who claimed that she had never in her life attended Clavering's hundred court. A Bedfordshire case of a few years later makes the importance of local courts in establishing the legitimacy of charters particularly evident.[43] Ralph of Eye brought suit against Henry of Nafford claiming that the latter 'broke' (*fregit*) the charter that established his right to a free tenement. Ralph alleged that Henry did the breaking in his court, when Ralph sought to show the charter to substantiate a claim. Ralph also noted that he took the charter to the local hundred court to have it read there. In Ralph's telling of events, his charter was both script and symbol of his title. Equally illuminating is the evidence provided by an assize of *mort d'ancestor* heard in an Oxfordshire eyre in 1241.[44] Once again, the assize turned on the validity of a charter made by a father to endow non-inheriting children. The jury's verdict describes the elaborate measures the father took to ensure the validity of his charter. He first had it drawn up at his lord's honor court and then afterwards took it to his local manor court, where it was read out. In spite of these precautions, however, his eldest son still filed suit, on the grounds that his father had not actually allowed his brothers to take control of the land after the charter was made and publicised.

Formal public gatherings such as manor courts and hundred courts were well suited for the promulgation of charters because they functioned both as judicial venues and as spaces for transacting a wide range of other public business.[45] But

---

[42] *Bracton's Note-Book*, III, 691–2, no. 1929.

[43] *CRR* xv, 270–1, no. 1128.

[44] *The Oxfordshire Eyre*, 1241, ed. J. Cooper (Oxfordshire Record Society 56, 1989), 100–1, no. 689.

[45] On the function of manor courts as public spaces shaping cultural norms, see S. Olson, *A Mute Gospel: The People and Culture of the Medieval English Common Fields* (Toronto, 2009).

the reading and publicising of charters also went on in less formal settings, such as simple gatherings of friends and neighbours. These informal modes of communication are rarely mentioned in the text of a charter, but once again court cases bearing on the validity of charters can provide some valuable insights. A jury verdict emanating from an assize of novel disseisin in Middlesex in 1233 is a good case in point.[46] The assize ultimately turned on whether delivery of seisin followed the making of a charter, but the circumstances in which the charter was made also came in for relatively full discussion. The jurors explained that the plaintiff, Roger son of Jordan, claimed the disputed land by virtue of a charter from his brother Simon, which charter had been read out loud to a group of neighbours assembled in the house of a third brother, Robert. In addition to gathering his neighbours at Robert's house, Roger had also brought a deathly-ill Simon. After the charter was read, Simon was asked if it expressed his wishes for the property. He answered that it did, although he went on to say, somewhat ambiguously, that he would willingly agree to anything they wanted. The charter was thus of uncertain validity because of questions about Simon's competency. In the end, however, Simon's status at the time the charter was made proved not to be the decisive issue; the jury decided to reject Roger's claim because he had not followed up on the charter by actually working the land.

Roger son of Jordan's behaviour is entirely understandable in light of the great emphasis that medieval people placed upon public notification as part of the charter-making process. Local courts were clearly preferred venues, but the value of having public notification and witnessing was so great that even a small gathering in a house was worth having if access to a local court was problematical. Daniel Smail reached a similar conclusion in his study of the legal culture of fourteenth-century Marseille: in spite of the great emphasis placed on notaries and written evidence, the city's judges routinely privileged public knowledge and public reputation over written records when deciding cases.[47] The drawing up of charters is thus best understood as part of a process that typically began with private negotiations and conversations but ultimately ended up as public acts with public consequences. Writing and speaking were both central to a successful conveyance. In spite of the precautions people took to make charters and to publicise them to contemporaries, however, disputes about the terms of conveyance still frequently broke out. Both litigants and courts thus found it necessary to find ways to handle cases in which the charters themselves were the primary bone of contention. One of the primary means by which they did so was to involve the charter witnesses in the adjudication process.

---

[46]   *CRR* xv, 192–3, no. 906.
[47]   Daniel Lord Smail, *The Consumption of Justice: Emotions, Publicity and Legal Culture in Marseille, 1264–1423* (Ithaca and London, 2003), 209–13.

Charter Witnesses and the Jury System

Witnesses were central to the chartering process. They were the first and foremost public audience for the notification of grants and sales, and they also served as the principal repository of public memory about conveyances. Both of these roles implicated them in the resolution of disputes associated with the use of charters. They were well situated to pronounce on the personal circumstances of a seller or a donor at the moment a charter was made, as well as to verify the terms and authenticity of the document produced as the formal record — or alleged record — of the transaction. With such a wide range of possibilities for contesting charters, it was almost inevitable that the witnesses would be called on to play a role in the adjudication of disputes.

Witnesses were involved in the making of charters long before the twelfth century, but their involvement in dispute resolution is difficult to trace in earlier periods. What is clear is that the nature of witness participation in resolving disputes underwent substantial transformation in the later twelfth century, as the procedures of the common law began to crystallise. The role of witnesses was influenced particularly heavily by the advent and subsequent popularity of the possessory assizes.[48] One of the key features of the possessory assizes was the use of juries charged with making substantive and determinative verdicts to resolve disputes about property rights.[49] Juries acting under the terms of one of the possessory assizes dealt with a relatively wide range of disputes, many of which did not involve the use of charters. On the other hand, many of the situations involving claims about the authenticity or legitimacy of a charter were amenable to process under the terms of one of the assizes. The king's courts found themselves with an interesting problem to resolve. The success of the possessory assizes was intimately bound up with the use of local people as jurors, people who could be called upon to serve in a particular case because they knew at first hand the circumstances underlying the dispute. The knowledge brought by jurors to a case was elemental in generating a fair and successful resolution. In disputes involving charters, however, there was a ready-made group of local people who had direct, even intimate, knowledge of how charters were drawn up, namely the witnesses. But though it was self-evident that the witnesses could be called upon to participate in the decision-making process, it was less clear how they might interact with the jury system prescribed by the possessory assizes. Could the witnesses serve as a surrogate form of jury when cases revolved around a charter? Or were the methods of juror selection that operated in cases when charters were marginal to the dispute or even non-existent — methods that were highly suc-

---

[48] D. W. Sutherland, *The Assize of Novel Disseisin* (Oxford, 1973); J. Biancalana, 'For Want of Justice: Legal Reforms of Henry II', *Columbia Law Review* 88 (1988), 433–536.

[49] J. Masschaele, *Jury, State, and Society in Medieval England* (New York, 2008).

cessful in other cases — worth maintaining even when witnesses were available? How exactly should witnesses and jurors be related to each other?

One option was to constitute witnesses as the jury and to charge them with finding a verdict under the terms of the assize relevant to the dispute. When Robert of Walton claimed that he had been disseised of land in Walton, Essex, by Richard Whitlether, for example, the court ordered that a jury made up of charter witnesses, who are specifically named in the record of the case, be constituted to deliver the verdict.[50] The same procedure was adopted to resolve the dispute described above between Margery Cumin and her brother Ralph. But on the whole this straightforward option of forming juries out of the charter witnesses failed to find much favour. The main problem it presented was the high potential for partiality. Charter-makers typically asked friends and relatives to serve as witnesses to their transactions, people who were sympathetic to their aims and who could be expected to uphold those aims when they were challenged. The common-law courts were deeply committed to the principle of juror impartiality, and while it was often possible for charter witnesses to meet the impartiality standard, the courts had good reason to be concerned about fairness when juries were made up of witnesses.

A second option was to treat witnesses as sources of evidence but not as bodies of judgment. When William de Scalebroc sued William de Mandeville for payment of arrears for the manor of Skelbrooke, Yorkshire, in 1221, for example, Mandeville stated that the manor had been conveyed to his father by a certain Olive, who had made a charter to document the transaction.[51] Mandeville showed the charter in court. The scribe recording the case summarised its essential details, listing the names of four witnesses and adding that other named witnesses were no longer alive. Scalebroc, who had married Olive in her widowhood, challenged the validity of Mandeville's charter. Recognising that the issue of validity hinged on the duration and circumstances of Olive's widowhood, the justices decided that the best way to establish the facts was to summon the four surviving witnesses to 'certify' (*ad certificandum*) how the charter had come to be made. Similarly, the record of a case in 1200 states that charter witnesses were summoned 'to testify' (*ad testificandum*) about the charter's validity.[52] In other cases from the early thirteenth century, the language describing the use made of witnesses who were summoned to court is more ambiguous, but appears to indicate a similar emphasis on the presentation of evidence about a charter rather than the delivery of a verdict.[53]

The summoning of witnesses to testify before royal justices had obvious

---

[50] *CRR* XII, 260–1, no. 1279.
[51] *CRR* X, 139.
[52] *CRR* I, 151–2.
[53] *CRR* I, 407–8; II, 26.

attractions as a mechanism for sorting out conflicting claims about the status of a charter, but it was not easily reconciled with the common law's deep commitment to using juries to establish facts and render verdicts. Roman law made the examination of witnesses by legal experts a central part of the judicial process, but the shapers of the common law had deliberately chosen to build their system on a different foundation, giving much of the responsibility for finding truth to juries rather than to judges. The common-law principle of using juries found especially fertile ground in the area of property law; and since clashes over charters usually involved land, the courts were reluctant to create an alternative procedure that departed so radically from existing practices. Instead, they found a compromise solution that continued to privilege jury verdicts while also making use of the extensive contextual knowledge available through witnesses. Essentially what the courts did was to create a modified form of jury to determine disputes involving charters. These modified juries were made up partly of jurors drawn from the local area in which a dispute arose and partly of charter witnesses. In effect, charter witnesses were drafted to serve as jurors, but they were required to serve in conjunction with other local people who were not as closely associated with the contending parties. The resulting hybrid juries allowed the courts to use the direct personal knowledge of the witnesses without sacrificing the legitimacy and impartiality associated with traditional jury forms. The merger worked well and became the standard method of handling disputes involving charters through to the end of the medieval period.

Collaboration between witnesses and other jurors took several forms. One arrangement was to constitute a group of charter witnesses as a separate jury that operated independently of the regular jury. A particularly clear example is provided by a case involving two alternative and conflicting charters concerning the same property, the manor of Rushock in Worcestershire.[54] Osbert D'Abbetot claimed possession of the manor by right of descent from his brother, Alexander, whose right had been conveyed in a charter of Reginald de Braose. Reginald, however, claimed that the manor had been conditionally conveyed to Alexander and any heirs that might result from Alexander's marriage, presumably to Reginald's sister or daughter. Since the marriage had not produced any offspring, Reginald claimed that the condition had not been met and that therefore the manor should revert to him. Reginald presented a second charter substantiating his version of the conveyance. The court appointed the charter witnesses named in one of the charters — it is not clear which one — to deliver a verdict about which charter was legitimate. They stated in their verdict that they knew of only one charter related to the manor and that they were certain that Reginald's version of the story was accurate. The justices also constituted a separate jury to render a verdict about which version of the conveyance was accurate. The jurors stated that they knew

54   CRR xiii, 25–6, no. 115.

nothing of either charter — they had 'neither seen nor heard any charter' — but they had seen Reginald take Alexander's homage and convey seisin to him. This left the justices in a bit of a quandary and they decided to set aside both charters and to seek a resolution on other grounds.

The practice of having two sworn groups weigh in on the same case had parallels in other legal settings. Some manor courts used juries of freeholders to confirm the presentments of villein juries in an arrangement known as double presentment.[55] From the end of the thirteenth century, county-wide juries of 'triers' were also often empanelled to confirm the presentments of hundred-based juries in peace sessions and other tribunals.[56] The most direct and influential parallel was no doubt the use of a trial jury to determine the innocence or guilt of someone who had been accused of a felony by a presentment jury. In spite of these parallels, however, the courts used the practice of constituting separate juries of witnesses only sparingly. They showed a much greater inclination towards forming truly hybrid juries, with some of the jurors appointed because they were witnesses and some of the jurors appointed as knowledgeable locals without any ties to the litigating parties.

In most cases in which witnesses and jurors were summoned to serve as a single panel, there is little or no evidence to indicate how the two types of juror interacted. In such cases, juries were typically summoned after initial pleading, during which charters were presented and examined by the justices. Knowledge that the witnesses might be summoned to serve on the jury must have been widespread, because many of the litigants offered to prove their case by placing themselves on the charter witnesses: litigants came to court knowing that witnesses could be drafted as jurors. If the parties and the justices were in accord that charter witnesses were suitable as jurors, the justices frequently instructed sheriffs to summon certain named witnesses along with a number of other people who could be placed on the jury in the usual way. The witnesses probably had a great deal of influence over the eventual verdict because they had more direct and extensive knowledge of the matter. But there is some evidence to suggest that the courts viewed the other jurors as more reliable and trustworthy because they were not personally invested in the case. This view is articulated with particular clarity in a Year Book discussion of a case heard in the Northamptonshire eyre of 1334.[57] The author of the account stated that the oath administered to the witnesses differed from that administered to the other jurors in that the phrase 'to the best of their knowledge' was not included, emphasising the fact that they were on the

---

[55] Masschaele, *Jury, State, and Society*, chap. 2.

[56] D. Crook, 'Triers and the Origin of the Grand Jury', *The Journal of Legal History* 12 (1991), 103–16.

[57] *The Eyre of Northamptonshire, 3–4 Edward III, A.D. 1329–1330*, ed. D. W. Sutherland (2 vols., Selden Society 97–8, 1983), II, 592.

panel because of their precise knowledge of the charter rather than their ability to evaluate all of the evidence related to a case. The Year Book entry goes on to state that one of the justices hearing the case instructed the regular jurors to take the charter witnesses aside one at a time to interrogate them about the charter. When they felt that they had a solid basis for a verdict, they were supposed to join together with the witnesses to render it. It is far from clear that this procedure was normative in other cases, but the fact that many combined juries included only a few witnesses alongside a larger number of regular jurors suggests that the dynamic may have been common.

An unusual case heard in the king's court in 1236–7 provides an exceptional account both of the relationship between witnesses and jurors and the circumstances in which charters were made and disputed.[58] The initial stages of the case were fairly run-of-the-mill, including the summoning of a jury made up of charter witnesses combined with other jurors. The jury was instructed to render a verdict on a claim by the monks of Osney abbey that Geoffrey Gibwin had conveyed land to them by charter a few years earlier. The two plaintiffs, Robert Brian and Robert de Insula, had questioned the charter's validity, asserting that Gibwin was not of sound mind when it was made. They contended furthermore that the abbot of Osney had been in possession of Gibwin's seal for some time before his death and had used it illicitly to seal the charter. Initially, at any rate, the case shared many features with other disputes involving the mental competency of a grantor, including the uncertainty inherent in charters drawn up during a period of retirement in a local monastery.

The court's first attempt to conclude the case failed when the charter witnesses missed their appointed court date. Significantly, the justices chose to postpone the case, even though the regular jurors had shown up; the record of the case states that the jury could not give its verdict without the witnesses. The witnesses' failure to appear was almost certainly related to the strange circumstances behind their being named as witnesses in the first place, as the justices ultimately learned when the witnesses and jurors finally convened in a subsequent court session. At that session both the jurors and the witnesses said that they could not evaluate the charter at the heart of the case because they had not been involved in its drafting or conveying. All they knew was that a few months before Gibwin had died, several representatives of Osney abbey had gone to the county court to read out a charter ostensibly conveying land from Gibwin to the abbey. When the charter was read out, Robert de Insula objected to it on the grounds that Gibwin was not mentally competent. The opportunity to mount this kind of direct public challenge without immediate resort to a formal lawsuit probably accounts for much of the emphasis placed on public readings of charters in the period.

De Insula's grievances ultimately led to a lawsuit. As part of the process in the

---

[58]   *Bracton's Note-Book*, III, 203–6, no. 1189.

king's court, the witnesses were called upon to explain how the charter came to be made. All but three of them said they knew nothing about the charter until it was read in the county court. One of the three who claimed to know something about it told the justices that he had visited Gibwin in the abbey about three years before he died. When he arrived at the abbey, the abbot showed him a copy of the charter and led him to see Gibwin, who was then of sound mind. Gibwin told this witness several important things: that the charter was of his making; that he wanted news of it to be spread as far as possible; and that he wanted the witness, who was presumably also his friend, to contact other friends who could attest that he wanted to convey his property to the abbey. The two other witnesses had a different but equally interesting story to tell. They claimed that they had been present when the charter was made and sealed. In fact, they gave a full description of when and where the charter was made, including the detail that Gibwin affixed his seal on top of a trunk that he had been using as a seat, which trunk was located near the side door of a hall in the abbey.

Both the jurors and witnesses then provided information about a number of other features related to the case, including how the property had been used in the final period of Gibwin's life and how the representatives that Osney sent to read the charter at the county court were related to the principals in the case. Ultimately, however, the court came back to the issue of the witnesses when rendering judgment in favour of the plaintiffs. The justices found it particularly significant that only three of the named witnesses knew anything about the charter when it was read in the county court, and furthermore that the three did not tell the same story about how the charter had been made. In light of these facts, the court not only awarded the land to the two plaintiffs but also nullified the charter and fined the abbot for having falsified it.

Conclusion

The dramatic expansion in charter use that characterised the twelfth and thirteenth centuries made a major contribution to expanding the role of writing in many facets of social and economic life. The emphasis on writing and record keeping that characterises the period was clearly associated with rising levels of literacy and increasing opportunities for education. But it is important to note that the cultural reorientation associated with the growing use of writing was a complex process that involved much more than the ability to write and read. Written records flourished in the period because medieval people proved to be adept at developing institutions and practices that enhanced trust in the integrity and reliability of writing. This trust was grounded in the recognition that private charters were part of public life, amenable to public scrutiny and evaluation, and ultimately without meaning if they failed to establish public confidence.

Charters were popular because they were adaptable and could be effectively integrated with other social and legal practices. But their popularity was also due to their ability to foster freedom and individual choice in the treatment and disposition of property. In this regard, their expanding use formed part of the broad process of commercialisation. Over the course of the high and later Middle Ages, land came to be treated more and more as a vehicle for investment, worth having because it generated income. People began to see it as a resource that could generate commodities and profits. Older conceptions of the value of possessing land did not disappear, but from the twelfth century these older notions had to compete with the commercial mind-set, which steadily gained ground throughout the period. From this perspective, it is clear that rising entrepreneurialism and the increasing use of charters went hand in hand. But it is also worth remembering that the entrepreneurial spirit at work in the conveying of land was not restricted to the realm of economics. Very often what people wanted to do with their increased freedom to traffic in land was not to generate profits or maximise income, but rather to provide for a non-inheriting child or to express their faith through gifts to churches and monasteries. The popularity of charters was, in short, driven by concepts of social value as much as by calculations of financial advantage. All societies make difficult choices when weighing the pursuit of wealth against the demands of social and familial obligation. Careful study of medieval charters allow us to see how people dealt with this challenge many centuries ago and can perhaps shed some light on how we might think about it today.

12

Luxury Goods in Medieval England

....

Christopher Dyer

WHAT WAS THE IMPORTANCE OF LUXURY GOODS in the medieval economy? It has often been assumed or implied that trade in high-value commodities and the manufacture of luxuries lay at the heart of medieval towns and their commercial life. Richard Britnell has done more than anyone to advance an alternative view, but no one has faced the subject head on, as this essay attempts to do.

Luxury is one of those difficult terms which cannot be strictly and easily defined. The word is constantly used by historians, who refer to 'luxury goods' and people involved in the 'luxury trades'. We think that we know a luxury when we see one, or read about it in a document: a piece of jewellery skilfully made from precious metals, like the fifteenth-century swan livery badge of enamelled gold found at Dunstable, or the 'silver pitcher for wine' weighing more than three pounds listed in the wardrobe inventory of Walter de Merton (along with many other items of silver plate) in 1277.[1] Dishes for a meal prepared elaborately by professional cooks and incorporating expensive ingredients such as spices would be easily categorised as luxurious, as would clothing tailored from imported textiles such as silks or fine woollens, and lined with furs from the Baltic. Leisure activities or pastimes which involved a lavish use of resources, such as court entertainments or hunting, could be included among luxuries. There are often difficulties in distinguishing between luxury and the everyday. As Braudel commented, luxury is 'an elusive, complex and contradictory entity'.[2] The concept depends on comparisons, so that luxury will vary from one rank of society to another, and over space and time.

Precious stones, silver plate, wine, spices and silks occupied a high and

---

[1] J. Cherry, 'The Dunstable Swan Jewel', *Journal of the British Archaeological Association* 32 (1969), 38–53; *The Early Rolls of Merton College Oxford*, ed. J. R. L. Highfield (Oxford Historical Society, new ser. 18, 1964), 91.

[2] F. Braudel, *Capitalism and Material Life 1400–1800* (London, 1973), 121–4; definitions are usefully discussed, but not resolved, in M. Berg and H. Clifford, 'Introduction', in *Consumers and Luxury: Consumer Culture in Europe 1650–1850*, ed. M. Berg and H. Clifford (Manchester, 1999), 1–16.

exclusive position within an English aristocratic household, as they were available mainly to the inner circle around the lord, and tended to be displayed or served on special occasions.[3] Many of those in daily attendance on the lord ate plain food and drank ale from wooden cups, wearing linen and woollen clothes, decorated with nothing more precious than a brass belt buckle. But for lesser peasants and artisans, and the general run of wage earners, the household servants' regular access to plenty of meat and ale and the routine renewal of their clothes would be rated as luxuries.

The cost of goods and services often depended on the labour devoted to them, which is especially evident in the building trades: constructing a manor house or castle with stone walls, glazed windows and lead roofing took months or even years for a numerous and skilled work force. By contrast, in a week or two a handful of workers with modest levels of skill could build a peasant's timber-framed house. In considering the social significance of luxury, price and scarcity were not the only basis for comparison. Some goods conveyed messages about social status, by demonstrating their owners' style of life. Falcons or hunting dogs did not always cost a great deal, but everyone knew what they meant.

The most striking geographical variation in luxury separated northern and southern Europe: wine was scarce north of the Rhine. In England dried fruits and almonds from the Mediterranean were expensive enough to be classified among the spices. In parts of northern England and Scotland where oats were the main cereal crop, wheat bread was a rarity.[4] As time passed, some luxuries died out of use and others developed in significance. Before about 1100 mead was drunk in quantity in wealthy households, but it disappears from view by the thirteenth century.[5] The meat of wild birds such as swans and herons was not always reckoned a high-status food, but around the eleventh century it became more strongly associated with the rich.[6] Squirrel fur from the Baltic, which had been highly regarded by the elite as a lining for clothes, fell out of favour after 1400 because it had become cheap enough for the newly affluent artisans.[7]

Luxury has complicated cultural and psychological dimensions. We debate why spices were valued and craved. It was not just a matter of a preference for their flavour, but also because they were thought to have medicinal properties and were associated with the magic and mystery of the earthly paradise.[8] Groups

---

[3] C. M. Woolgar, *The Great Household in Late Medieval England* (New Haven and London, 1999), 149–51, 154–9.

[4] C. Dyer, 'English Diet in the Late Middle Ages', in *Social Relations and Ideas: Essays in Honour of R. H. Hilton*, ed. T. H. Aston, P. R. Coss, C. Dyer and J. Thirsk (Cambridge, 1983), 205.

[5] *AHEW* I, pt. 2, 403, 438, 512, 514, refer to honey and mead.

[6] N. Sykes, 'The Dynamics of Status Symbols: Wildfowl Exploitation in England AD 410–1550', *Archaeological Journal* 161 (2004), 82–105.

[7] E. Veale, *The English Fur Trade in the Later Middle Ages* (Oxford, 1966), 138–9.

[8] P. Freedman, *Out of the East: Spices and the Medieval Imagination* (New Haven and London, 2008).

of people were bound together by the consumption of luxury goods, such as the monks in a wealthy monastery who enjoyed pittances — desirable food and drink — on special occasions, or the guildsmen who were served dishes at their annual feast to which they could not aspire in their own homes for the rest of the year.[9]

Morality entered into the definition of luxury. Preachers and churchmen in general regarded the consumption of costly goods as sinful. They linked expensive food and drink with gluttons; they pointed out that avaricious people maximised their wealth in order to afford high quality clothing and food; those afflicted by pride were driven to display their wealth.[10] For religious commentators the acquisition of luxuries was trivial, frivolous, corrupting and wasteful. These moral attitudes spilled over into public policy when the state condemned through sumptuary laws in 1363 and 1463 the 'excessive apparel' which distorted the social hierarchy (when the lower orders flaunted luxuries previously confined to their superiors), pushed up the price of fine cloth, and posed a potential threat to the economy by encouraging imports.[11] The selective disapproval of fine clothes for the lower orders was easily compatible with the idea that rulers should put on a show of 'magnificence' to demonstrate their superiority.[12]

To sum up a complex subject, luxury goods and services can be defined as not being merely utilitarian. They were scarce and expensive, they conferred status on those who used them, brought people of similar standing together, and excluded those who did not belong. Luxury status had economic significance, but cultural factors defined which goods were regarded as desirable. This brought into the picture pleasure, taste and fashion. Luxuries changed over space and time, and they were perceived differently at different social levels.

Historians writing about medieval European trade have given luxury goods a prominent place. Pirenne argued that the Arab invasions around 700 brought to an end the Mediterranean commerce in papyrus, spices, 'costly textiles', wine and oil. For a time Western Europe was thrown on to its own agricultural resources, and trade almost ceased. The cities of northern Europe that developed in the tenth and eleventh centuries were trading in such high-valued commodities as Flemish

[9] B. Harvey, 'Monastic Pittances in the Middle Ages', in *Food in Medieval England: Diet and Nutrition*, ed. C. M. Woolgar, D. Serjeantson and T. Waldron (Oxford, 2006), 215–27; G. Rosser, 'Going to the Fraternity Feast: Commensality and Social Relations in Late Medieval England', *Journal of British Studies* 33 (1994), 430–46.

[10] *The Riverside Chaucer*, ed. L. D. Benson (3rd edn, Oxford, 1987), 300–1, 313–16, 316–17, 321. All of these refer to The Parson's Tale, a prose sermon. The last reference is to a passage which criticises wives who wear expensive clothes in a discussion of the sin of lechery.

[11] N. B. Harte, 'State Control of Dress and Social Change in Pre-Industrial England', in *Trade, Government and Economy in Pre-Industrial England: Essays Presented to F. J. Fisher*, ed. D. C. Coleman and A. H. John (London, 1976), 132–65.

[12] S. Rigby, 'Ideology and Utopia: Prudence and Magnificence, Kingship and Tyranny in Chaucer's Knight's Tale', in *London and the Kingdom: Essays in Honour of Caroline M. Barron*, ed. M. Davies and A. Prescott (Donington, 2008), 316–34, esp. 327–32.

cloth and metal goods like the brass wares of Dinant.[13] The many critics of this thesis have demonstrated the continuities in commerce in the Carolingian period (730–900), when supplies of silk and spices were still available, and recent work on the ninth century has singled out the trade in spices, incense and silk from the east, while slaves, furs and Frankish swords were carried in the other direction.[14] A commonplace criticism of Pirenne's approach has been to emphasise regional trade throughout the early Middle Ages in commodities of modest value.

Duby set the revival of trade and towns in the eleventh and twelfth centuries in a wider social context. The new forms of lordly exploitation, called by later authors the 'feudal mutation', concentrated a growing quantity of wealth in the hands of the aristocracy, both secular and religious. This new money was spent on 'unfamiliar and exquisite commodities' imported from the Orient, together with fine cloth and wines.[15] Peasants had to sell produce to satisfy the lords' demands for rent, but they did not have much cash left for their own purchases.

A survey of late medieval commerce has highlighted the concentration of trade in the great European cities which were supplied by the mercantile business houses. The term 'court cities' is used to describe centres like Paris where magnates such as the dukes of Burgundy or the counts of Artois built grand houses, furnished them with precious textiles, and enjoyed the best food and wines. While they acquired expensive clothes, plate and armour, the peasants whose rents kept their lords in such style bought iron implements, horse harness and functional kitchen utensils, but soon after the harvest their purses were depleted.[16] None of these writers denies that trade existed partly to satisfy the needs of people below the aristocracy, but they all see demand for luxuries as a driving force behind the development and continued prosperity of towns.

Historical writing about Britain puts more emphasis on the everyday trade rather than luxury goods. How could it be otherwise when the staple commodity for international trade from the twelfth century, and probably earlier, wool, was bulky and not very precious? Of course, on the looms of Flanders and Tuscany around 1300, wool bought for 4*d.* per pound was transformed into valuable cloth worth 6*s.* per yard. An influential book on English towns refers to the 'cake of overseas commerce' which mattered less than the 'bread and butter' of regional trade.[17]

While this last view now has won widespread acceptance, the writings on the subject tend to show a distinct bias in favour of the more glamorous traffic at the

---

[13] H. Pirenne, *Medieval Cities: Their Origins and the Revival of Trade* (New York, 1956), II, 70–1, 110–11.

[14] M. McCormick, *The Origins of the European Economy* (Cambridge, 2001), 708–33.

[15] G. Duby, *The Early Growth of the European Economy: Warriors and Peasants from the Seventh to the Twelfth Century* (London, 1974), 234–40.

[16] P. Spufford, *Power and Profit: The Merchant in Medieval Europe* (London, 2002), 60–139.

[17] S. Reynolds, *An Introduction to the History of English Medieval Towns* (Oxford, 1977), 59.

higher end of the market. In recent decades monographs have featured the trade in wine, fur, spices, imported cloth and pewter, together with studies of wealthy merchants.[18] A book has been written about masons, but not carpenters, and there are studies of coal, ale and beer, but we badly need more work on bread, the fish trade, butchery and iron making. A single study has surveyed the urban artisans, and they deserve more attention.[19] The evidence exists in plenty, both written and material. Archaeologists have a more balanced record, with their research on timber buildings, pottery and animal bones, but they tend to become excited by high-quality metal work and pretentious architecture.[20]

Behind the focus on luxury trade lies the theory that wealth was concentrated in the hands of a small elite to an extreme degree. Estimates for *c.*1300, however, show that about fourteen or sixteen per cent of the English national income was received by the landed aristocracy, both lay and clerical. This was not very different from figures calculated from more reliable statistics in 1688, 1759 and 1801–3.[21]

We tend to think that the landed estates were enjoying a high point of power and wealth in *c.*1300, but their relatively thin slice of the national cake reflects the limited size of their demesnes (in some regions a fifth of the productive land), and their inability to squeeze the maximum from their own demesnes or from the peasantry. Although the thirteenth century, with its expanding markets, rising prices for agricultural produce and relatively low wages, offered the great landowners an opportunity to make profits, their incomes matched inflation but did not grow much beyond that figure.

The aristocratic consumers' share of spending money was not quite as modest as the income figures suggest, because rich people could devote a substantial proportion of their wealth to non-necessities. In many elite households food accounted for about a half of their annual expenditure, which included the cost of

[18] M. K. James, *Studies in the Medieval Wine Trade* (Oxford, 1971); Veale, *Fur Trade*; P. Nightingale, *A Medieval Mercantile Community: The Grocers' Company and the Politics and Trade of London, 1000–1485* (New Haven and London, 1995); A. Sutton, *The Mercery of London: Trade, Goods and People, 1130–1578* (Aldershot, 2005); J. Hatcher and T. C. Barker, *A History of British Pewter* (London, 1974). On the merchants, see T. H. Lloyd, *Alien Merchants in England in the High Middle Ages* (Brighton, 1982); A. Hanham, *The Celys and their World: An English Merchant Family of the Fifteenth Century* (Cambridge, 1985); J. Kermode, *Medieval Merchants: York, Beverley and Hull in the Later Middle Ages* (Cambridge, 1998); W. R Childs, *Anglo-Castilian Trade in the Later Middle Ages* (Manchester, 1978).

[19] D. Knoop and G. P. Jones, *The Medieval Mason* (3rd edn, Manchester, 1967); J. Hatcher, *History of the British Coal Industry*, 1: *Before 1700* (Oxford, 1993); J. Bennett, *Ale, Beer and Brewsters in England: Women's Work in a Changing World* (New York and Oxford, 1996); H. Swanson, *Medieval Artisans: An Urban Class in Late Medieval England* (Oxford, 1989).

[20] E.g. D. Hinton, *Gold and Gilt, Pots and Pins* (Oxford, 2005).

[21] B. M. S. Campbell, 'The Agrarian Problem in the Early Fourteenth Century', *P&P* 188 (2005), 10–18.

luxuries, notably wine and spices. They could have spent the other half on non-food items, and part of these purchases (on clothes and buildings in particular) can be regarded as luxuries.[22]

The lavishness of their spending should not be exaggerated. The fortunate survival of an account throws light on the purchases of an upper gentry family, the Catesbys of Northamptonshire and Warwickshire, whose landed income must have exceeded £150 per annum.[23] Emma Catesby's household based at Ashby St Ledgers in the year 1392/3 spent £18 on clothing, shoes and textiles. One is not immediately impressed by the family's conspicuous consumption, as much of the woollen cloth cost 11*d.* to 1*s.* 5*d.* per yard, with linen at 6*d.* to 9½*d.* per ell. Peasants could afford to buy cloth at 1*s.* per yard and linen at 4*d.* to 6*d.* per ell. The 'luxury' element in the expenditure of the Catesby family lay in its ample provision for many garments and pairs of shoes, and the superior quality of some of the woollens, with white, blue and black cloth at 2*s.* 9*d.* to 3*s.* 8*d.* per yard. One is constantly aware of careful economies: silk was bought, but only a half ounce, and clothes were lined with rabbit fur from the estate's own warren. Spices are mentioned, but venison came as a gift. Hiring a minstrel at Christmas for 3*s.* 4*d.* shows a tendency toward extravagance, and expenditure of more than £5 on building work on the parlour, including 21*s.* 4*d.* for a glazier, must be regarded as the biggest luxury of the year.

A somewhat higher level of expenditure by a family of similar standing is revealed by the wardrobe expenses of Sir John Mauduit of Oxfordshire and Wiltshire. He accounted for about £100 in twenty months in 1312–14, without reference to food, which would have appeared in another (lost) document. Minstrels cost him 6*s.* 8*d.*, and he bought imported furs for more than 20*s.*, but the main charge came from woollen cloth for liveries at 2*s.* to 3*s.* per yard, though the lowest grade of servants, the grooms, were dressed in cloth worth about 1*s.* 6*d.*[24] A similarly controlled extravagance is apparent from a 1358 account from the middling rank monastery of Southwick (Hampshire). The house enjoyed an income in the region of £250, but spent just under £20 at St Giles Fair in Winchester, on cloth for servants' liveries at 1*s.* 4*d.* per yard for the lowest grade to 2*s.* 7*d.* per yard for the highest. Fur cost 28*s.*, thirty-eight pewter vessels 16*s.*, and the rest went on spices, including 150 lb. of almonds and 7 lb. of ginger.[25]

For really major spending on the most expensive items we have to turn to the wardrobe accounts of a great magnate like the duke of Clarence in 1418–21, who, amidst expenditure of hundreds of pounds, bought a sword for 6*s.* 8*d.* and scarlet

[22] C. Dyer, *Standards of Living in the Later Middle Ages: Social Change in England, c.1200–1520* (rev. edn, Cambridge, 1998), 70–85.
[23] TNA, E101/511/15.
[24] *Household Accounts from Medieval England, Part 2*, ed. C. M. Woolgar (Oxford, 1992), 585–8.
[25] Hampshire Record Office, 5 M50/47.

cloth for 12s. per yard, and spent £12 13s. 4d. on a cloth of blue damask 'for a dress for the lady', which was then lined with marten skins for another £10 13s. 4d.[26] The existence of such accounts shows that even high-living lords were conscious of costs, and had an ambition to keep them under control.

Finds from archaeological work on aristocratic residences do not include large quantities of precious objects. We might hope that purchases from the 'privy purse', that is outside the formal accounting records, would find their way into deposits around castles, manor houses or palaces. Excavations at Barnard Castle (Co. Durham), which belonged in the later Middle Ages to the wealthy Balliol and Beauchamp families, produced some military iron work in the form of a crossbow bolt, thirteen arrowheads and four spearheads, with some fragments of scarce glass goblets of the fourteenth century, and gold thread from a top-quality silk garment. The bulk of the finds — thousands of pottery fragments, commonplace metalwork and objects of stone and bone — did not speak of great opulence. The excavator commented that 'what always surprises is the lack of high quality . . . artefacts given the long period of continuous use of the space by nobles and their retinues'. He reminds us that households were always on the move, and their possessions were packed and taken away.[27] One should not forget that the whole site, an elaborate masonry castle, itself must count as a luxury. Nonetheless, the lack of many high-value finds from the more cheaply-built manor houses of knights and gentry, who were often in continuous occupation, is partly explained by the scarcity of luxuries in such households and by the fact that any jewels or plate that they owned were kept with great care, and sold or recycled at the end of their period of use.

For the lower orders of society, food bulked large in their household budgets, and left them with much less to spend on other items. Much of the income of wage earners around 1300, varying from sixty per cent to ninety per cent, was spent on food. Many peasants obtained at least part of their grain, cheese, bacon and other needs from their own holding, which limited the proportion of their produce which they could sell. Although peasants and wage earners alike had modest sums available for non-food items, their cumulative spending power reflected their large numbers, as the combined surplus of a million households would have exceeded the expenditure of the approximately 30,000 wealthy lay and clerical households.[28]

---

[26] *Household Accounts, Part 2*, 631–82.

[27] D. Austin, *Acts of Perception: A Study of Barnard Castle in Teesdale* (2 vols., Durham, 2007), II, 511, 519–20, 534–7, 555. For similar comments on an even higher status continental site, see H. De Witte, 'Lifestyle! Luxury in Medieval Bruges', in *Lübecker Kolloquium zur Stadtar-chäologie im Hanseraum*, VI: *Luxus und Lifestyle*, ed. M. Gläser (Lübeck, 2008), 117–18. I am grateful to Brian Ayers for this last reference.

[28] N. Mayhew, 'Modelling Medieval Monetarisation', in *A Commercialising Economy: England 1086–c.1300*, ed. R. H. Britnell and B. M. S. Campbell (Manchester, 1995), 58.

Luxuries, 650–1100

To embark on an overview of the trade in luxuries, we can begin with the early history of the post-Roman exchange economy in the seventh to ninth centuries. Much is made of the barbaric splendours of early medieval kings, with their exotic and opulent possessions. The mainly seventh-century grave deposits found at Sutton Hoo, Prittlewell and Taplow, and the Staffordshire treasure of similar date, include jewellery made in England using imported materials, notably garnets from the Far East, and the silver dish from Sutton Hoo came from Byzantium. These objects belong to a world in which prestigious objects were made by craftsmen attached to a great household and were passed from hand to hand as gifts, or as tribute, or as plunder.

Trade should be well represented by excavations of the ports of the period c.650–850, such as Southampton (Hamwic) and London (Lundenwic).[29] They have produced a mass of material culture: remains of houses, streets, boundary fences, pits for various purposes, hearths and middens. The wealth of finds — potsherds, metal work, coins, industrial debris, bones, botanical material — does not contain much that was obviously precious or luxurious. This is not surprising, as valuable objects were not discarded along with household rubbish but kept carefully and, if lost, recovered by intensive searches. Even where there is evidence for silver or gold working, no scrap metal is found. Every fragment, together with old or broken objects, would have been recycled. In any case, many of the luxuries that may have been carried through these ports consisted of organic materials (textiles, spices, wine) which would leave no trace. In spite of this bias against recovering evidence for the import and distribution of luxuries, a few clues can be identified: broken glass vessels, made in the Rhineland, are found presumably because they broke in transit; and fragments have been recovered of Tating ware, a high-quality imported pottery distinctive because of its showy tin-foil decoration. Wine has been drunk and leaves no trace, but barrels in which it could have been transported have been found at Hamwic. From the same place comes equipment for trade: pans from small scales for weighing coins or precious metals. In the 'wic' settlements much debris is found from industrial processes, and Ipswich

[29] P. Holdsworth, *Excavations at Melbourne Street, Southampton, 1971–76* (Southampton Archaeological Research Committee Report 1, Council for British Archaeology Research Report 33, 1980); *Excavations at Hamwic*, 1: *Excavations 1946–83, excluding Six Dials and Melbourne Street*, ed. A. D. Morton (Council for British Archaeology Research Report 84, 1992); D. Hinton, *The Gold, Silver and Non-Ferrous Alloy Objects from Hamwic* (Southampton Archaeology Monograph 6, 1996); *Excavations at Hamwic*, II: *Excavations at Six Dials*, ed. P. Andrews (Council for British Archaeology Research Report 109, 1997); J. Hunter and M. P. Heyworth, *The Hamwic Glass* (Council for British Archaeology Research Report 116, 1998); G. Malcolm and D. Bowsher with R. Cowie, *Middle Saxon London: Excavations at the Royal Opera House 1989–99* (Museum of London Archaeology Service Monograph 15, 2003).

specialised in pottery making. Droitwich, a rare inland wic, produced salt for everyday use.[30] The other settlements were involved in bone working (particularly to make elaborate combs), metal working, textile manufacture, and food preparation. Many of these goods seem to be mundane and aimed at a general market, and the animal bones show local exchange with the surrounding countryside for wool, meat and hides.

High-status sites have yielded evidence for consumers' use of scarce and specialised objects. Flixborough (Lincolnshire) includes among its finds window glass and glass drinking cups, and styli (writing implements), some of which were made of copper alloy with rich decoration, silver trimming and occasional gilding. A gold book mount and silver-gilt pin have been found at an apparent minster site at Brandon in Suffolk.[31]

In the later pre-Conquest phase of urban and commercial growth after 850 literary texts tell us more about merchants and trade. In Ælfric's *Colloquy* of the early eleventh century, a merchant boasts that he is useful to the king, ealdorman and to the wealthy, but also 'to all people', but when he lists the goods that he buys and sells, they seem to be aimed at elite consumers: 'purple cloth and silk, gems and gold, ... cloth and dyes, and wine and oil,' and also brass, tin and glass.[32] A document giving details of tolls from the same period refers to overseas merchants visiting London to sell bulkier and less precious items: fish, whale meat, vinegar, 'melted fat', timber and cloth. Wine is the only commodity mentioned in both documents, though pepper is also mentioned in the toll list.[33]

An import trade in high-value goods is known from references to Anglo-Saxon merchants travelling to Italy, and from records of northern furs and walrus tusks. In Winchester, a centre of royal, noble and clerical residences, and also one of the most important English cities, finds include gold thread from sumptuous textiles buried in elite graves at the Old Minster, a tenth-century brooch made of gilded silver coins, and an alabaster jar from Egypt which may have belonged to the cathedral treasury.[34] Hoards of the late ninth and tenth centuries found throughout the country contain jewellery and household objects

---

[30] J. R. Maddicott, 'London and Droitwich, c. 650–750: Trade, Industry and the Rise of Mercia', *Anglo-Saxon England* 34 (2005), 24–58.

[31] C. Loveluck and D. Atkins, *The Early Medieval Settlement Remains from Flixborough, Lincolnshire: The Occupation Sequence, c. AD 600–1000* (Oxford, 2007); idem, *Rural Settlement, Lifestyle and Social Change in the Late First Millennium AD: Anglo-Saxon Flixborough in its Wider Context* (Oxford, 2007); *Life and Economy at Early Medieval Flixborough, c. AD 600–1000*, ed. D. Evans and C. Loveluck (Oxford, 2009), 103–15, 123–36, 159–64; J. Blair, *The Church in Anglo-Saxon Society* (Oxford, 2005), 206.

[32] *Ælfric's Colloquy*, ed. G. N. Garmonsway (2nd edn, London, 1947), 33–4.

[33] *The Laws of the Kings of England from Edmund to Henry I*, ed. A. J. Robertson (Cambridge, 1925), 70–3.

[34] M. Biddle, *Object and Economy in Medieval Winchester* (2 vols., Oxford, 1990), II, 480–1, 633, 928–33.

such as silver cups as well as coins, silver ingots and 'hacksilver'. These suggest the stock of precious possessions which were either at hand to be buried by their wealthy owner, or which could be acquired by fair means or foul from rich people by the person who buried his haul.[35] Wills (from the top rank of society, mainly of the tenth and eleventh centuries) refer to swords, rings, jewellery, drinking horns and cups made or adorned with precious metals, as well as high-quality clothing.[36] An important late-tenth-century churchman such as Oswald, bishop of Worcester, provided two of his goldsmiths with land, and they may have settled in the city of Worcester rather than travelling around with their patron.[37] The excavation of an artisan quarter in tenth- and eleventh-century York, the Coppergate site, yielded evidence of goods being made for the luxury end of the market, as well as the usual bone carving, leather working and mundane trades. Of the 867 crucibles found, seventeen had been used to melt gold and 294 for silver. The copper-alloy objects made in this area may also have included elaborately decorated types which would have been worn by the better off. Fragments of glass had probably been brought in as raw material by the metal workers to make enamel. In the damp conditions of Coppergate organic materials were preserved, including textiles. A high proportion of the pieces of cloth — twenty-three out of 106 — were of silk, and silk caps found in Dublin and Lincoln may have been made in York.[38]

To put these finds in a wider perspective, from the many tons of earth excavated from town sites of the period 850 to 1100, and the acres of urban space stripped and investigated, the great bulk of finds consists of everyday objects such as pottery and animal bones, and the typical urban activities were food processing (especially butchery), wood working, bone carving, leather working, textile manufacture, iron working and potting. Pottery has survived in abundance and provides evidence for the distribution of goods. The distinctive wares made in Thetford can be found scattered over many villages in Norfolk, as if the pots had been bought in the town by ordinary villagers, to be carried back to their homes, or brought by an itinerant trader into the countryside.[39] A similar picture is emerging from the small decorated metal belt fittings, designed in an Anglo-Scandinavian style and probably made in urban workshops, which are found

[35]   Hinton, Gold and Gilt, 108–16, 119.

[36]   Anglo-Saxon Wills, ed. D. Whitelock (Cambridge, 1930), e.g. 10–15, 20–5, 30–1.

[37]   N. Baker and R. Holt, 'The City of Worcester in the Tenth Century', in St Oswald of Worcester: Life and Influence, ed. N. Brooks and C. Cubitt (London, 1996), 137–8.

[38]   J. Bayley, Anglo-Scandinavian Non-Ferrous Metalworking from 16–22 Coppergate (London, 1992), 746–817; P. Walton, Textiles, Cordage and Raw Fibre from 16–22 Coppergate (London, 1989), 360–77, 419–20.

[39]   A distribution map of Late Saxon pottery (of which Thetford ware was the most plentiful) shows more than a thousand find spots in the county: Norfolk Historic Environment Record, provided by Alice Cattermole, to whom I am very grateful.

scattered over the fields of Lincolnshire, Norfolk and Suffolk, suggesting that the peasants of the region were in contact with towns.[40] The list of London tolls mentioned above also refers to the sale of poultry, eggs and dairy produce, by women presumably from the nearby countryside. The Graveney boat, which came to grief off the north coast of Kent in the tenth century, was apparently carrying a cargo of nothing more precious than hops and a few imported mill stones.[41]

How can we generalise about luxury goods in the period before 1100? A now well-rehearsed interpretation of the period 650 to 850 sees the 'wic' settlements as the creation of kings, who brought imported luxury goods such as wine into the country, for distribution to followers in a system of non-market exchange.[42] This view is not universally accepted, but it is widely agreed that the 'wic' settlements developed a relationship with their rural surroundings which involved much non-luxury trade in raw materials and foodstuffs.

In the next phase after 850, a new generation of towns grew until, by 1086, more than a hundred are recorded. The tenfold increase in the number of towns, and the fivefold multiplication of town dwellers from 20,000 to 100,000, suggests the rise of a widespread market for inexpensive goods. Not all of these people could have been employed entirely in providing kings, earls, thegns, bishops and abbots with luxuries. Industries making basic goods, such as cloth and pottery, were relocating from country to town, country people were being drawn into a cash economy to pay rents, church dues and taxes, and the peasants sold and bought in towns.[43]

Aristocrats were becoming more numerous and wealthy. An upheaval was created by the acquisition of rural land by thousands of thegns, who asserted themselves and expressed their identity by adopting new styles of life. They acquired impressive residences in the country, built stone churches and expanded their consumption of luxuries, which put pressure on the towns to cater for their needs. The thegns had close connections with the towns: they owned urban property, formed guilds and were generally attuned to urban life. The higher clergy also were heavily involved in towns and spent some of their wealth on merchandise.[44]

[40]   G. Thomas, 'Anglo-Scandinavian Metalwork from the Danelaw: Experiencing Social and Cultural Interaction', in *Cultures in Contact: Scandinavian Settlement in England in the Ninth and Tenth Centuries*, ed. D. M. Hadley and J. D. Richards (Turnhout, 2000), 237–55.

[41]   *Laws of Kings*, 72–3; *The Graveney Boat*, ed. V. Fenwick (British Archaeological Reports 53, 1978), 147.

[42]   D. Hill and R. Cowie, *Wics: The Early Mediaeval Trading Centres of Northern Europe* (Sheffield Archaeological Monograph 14, 2001).

[43]   R. H Britnell, *The Commercialisation of English Society, 1000–1500* (Cambridge, 1993), 47–52, discusses the flow of cash cautiously.

[44]   R. Fleming, 'The New Wealth, the New Rich and the New Political Style in Late Anglo-Saxon England', *Anglo-Norman Studies* 23 (2000), 1–23; idem, 'Rural Elites and Urban Communities in Late Saxon England', *P&P* 14 (1993), 3–37.

In the period between c.850 and 1100 not enough emphasis has been placed on the development of town economies in two tiers, with a stratum of traders and craftsmen catering for the luxury trades, and a large number profiting from the market which had grown further down the social scale.

Luxuries, 1100–1540

What part did the demand for luxuries play in the sizeable urban and commercial sector which developed in the later Middle Ages? Much of the evidence relates to the fourteenth and fifteenth centuries, and in analysing those records one cannot easily separate the contribution made by the phase of expansion up to c.1300 from any later retrenchment. Here the contribution of the luxury trades in small towns and local trade will be assessed, and then we will turn to their role in larger towns, international trade and London.

Small towns and local trade

The most revolutionary consequence of urbanisation between 1100 and 1300 was surely the proliferation of 500 small towns. In the midlands and the north in 1086 a rather thin scatter of shire towns is recorded, but by 1300 these were surrounded by smaller market towns which were so widely scattered as to serve the whole rural population. Derby was the only borough in its shire in 1086, but by 1300 ten Derbyshire towns had been established. The consequences of this change are too well known to rehearse in detail: everyone in the countryside had easy access to at least one market town; the availability of the market stimulated rural producers to sell produce and make purchases; lords collected rents in cash, and much of the labour for lords and other producers was obtained by paying wages; the towns, inhabited by people with varied non-agricultural occupations, functioned as administrative, social, religious and cultural centres as well as markets.

Within the hinterland of each market town lay manor houses and rectories which contained relatively wealthy consumers who expected to buy better quality clothes, shoes and household textiles. The secular lords were mainly gentry, who had acquired a taste for wine and spices, but with limited resources would consume them only occasionally. Every few years such households spent more heavily, on building schemes or on armour or on finery for a wedding. When they acquired property, or married, or after a death, they expected to consult lawyers.[45]

The luxury spending of the Catesbys and Mauduits has already been glimpsed. They were relatively wealthy, but the majority of gentry had modest incomes of £10 to £20 per annum. Even these lesser gentry households were limited in

---

[45] A small town hinterland has been anatomised in C. M. Newman, *Late Medieval Northaller-ton* (Stamford, 1999), 1–16, 41–5.

Table 12.1: Individuals pursuing luxury and non-luxury occupations in small towns

Town	Date	Luxury trades	Non-luxury trades	Total no. with known occupations
Birmingham	1296	7 (19%)	30 (81%)	37
Howden	1379	10 (12%)	71 (88%)	81
Melton Mowbray	1381	8 (14%)	50 (86%)	58
Thaxted	1381	9 (6%)	142 (94%)	151
Basingstoke	1464	12 (14%)	71 (86%)	83
Bishop's Waltham	1464	3 (6%)	49 (94%)	52
Oakham	1522	7 (24%)	22 (76%)	29
Sudbury	1522	30 (21%)	116 (79%)	146
Long Melford	1522	1 (2%)	63 (98%)	64

Note: The Birmingham occupations derive from surnames, the others from decisions by tax assessors; only specific non-agricultural occupations have been counted, so servants, yeomen, clergy, etc. have been excluded.

Sources: G. Demidowicz, *Medieval Birmingham: The Borough Rentals of 1296 and 1344–5* (Dugdale Society Occasional Papers 48, 2008), 35–49; *The Poll Taxes of 1377, 1379 and 1381*, ed. C. Fenwick (3 vols., Oxford, 1997–2005), III, 194–6; ibid., I, 588–90, 237–8; F. J. Baigent and J. E. Millard, *A History of the Ancient Town and Manor of Basingstoke* (Basingstoke, 1889), 289–90; H. G. Barstow, *1332 and 1464 Rentals of Bishop's Waltham Manor* (Chandlersford, 1992), 87–115; *The County Community under Henry VIII*, ed. J. Cornwall (Rutland Record Society 1, 1980), 76–9; *The Military Survey of 1522 for Babergh Hundred*, ed. J. F. Pound (Suffolk Records Society 28, 1986), 19–29, 83–7.

number: the hinterlands of many towns contained only a dozen resident gentry and not many more parish clergy of comparable wealth. Within these hinterlands there would often be at least one small monastery or collegiate church, and forty or so parish churches managed by churchwardens, and together they demanded a quantity of wax, incense, and materials to make or mend vestments, and like the gentry they needed the services of masons, plumbers and glaziers. Unlike the secular households they maintained organs and clocks.

Each hinterland would also contain about 2,000 households which were socially inferior to those of the gentry and beneficed clergy, and our problem is to decide the relative importance of the cumulative demand of these peasants, artisans and labourers. One route towards measuring the size of the luxury sector in small towns is to examine the occupational structure, and to identify those trades and crafts which were mainly concerned to satisfy the upper end of consumer spending.

This is a clumsy way of approaching the problem, because traders and artisans were too unspecialised to be easily pigeon-holed, and many pursued two or three occupations. Cornmongers, for example, do not appear in lists of trades, but many townspeople dealt in grain as a profitable sideline.[46] Here we can only concentrate on the primary activity which was regarded as an identifying characteristic by neighbours and officials. Only a very small number of occupations can be regarded as unequivocally committed to luxuries. Small towns often contained a single goldsmith, who typically made silver spoons, silver belt fittings and rings, and in addition engraved seals, and can be placed firmly among those providing luxury goods and services.[47] A spicer, if he derived a substantial part of his living from the sale of pepper and other imported spices, was likewise dealing in luxuries. Spicers and goldsmiths, with rarely more than one per town, can be found scattered over the country: a goldsmith appears in the Melton Mowbray list analysed above, and another was included in the Sudbury list. Two paid the poll tax at Thaxted. There were no spicers in the nine towns included in Table 12.1, but it was not uncommon for a small town to contain one. Richard Faytebrigge from Grantham bought spices worth 10s. at St Ives Fair in Huntingdonshire in 1275.[48] Spicers are even found in rather low-key towns, such as Bromsgrove in Worcestershire and Mansfield in Nottinghamshire.[49] Sudbury, the largest of the nine towns in the sample, included in its 1522 list four grocers, and there was one at Oakham: they dealt in spices among other commodities. Vintners are rarely mentioned in small towns, but wine was acquired from importers, and then sold locally, at such places as Evesham (Worcestershire) and Leominster (Herefordshire) in the late fifteenth century.[50] Perhaps the branch of the building trade most clearly defined as luxurious was that of the glazier, a number of whom worked at Thame in Oxfordshire in the early fourteenth century, but they were usually quite scarce in small towns.[51]

Among those with identified occupations in the sample of nine towns was an armourer at Birmingham and another at Sudbury, and a furbisher is found at

---

[46] A small town's involvement in the grain trade is indicated in R. H. Hilton, 'Low-Level Urbanization: The Seigneurial Borough of Thornbury in the Middle Ages', in *Medieval Society and the Manor Court*, ed. Z. Razi and R. Smith (Oxford, 1996), 498–500, 507–8. On the general issue of non-specialisation, see R. H. Britnell, 'Specialization of Work in England, 1100–1300', *EcHR* 54 (2001), 1–16.

[47] Goldsmiths' activities are revealed in J. Laughton, *Life in a Late Medieval City: Chester 1275–1520* (Oxford, 2008), 155–6.

[48] E. W. Moore, *The Fairs of Medieval England* (Toronto, 1985), 86.

[49] C. Dyer, *Bromsgrove: A Small Town in Worcestershire in the Middle Ages* (Worcestershire Historical Society Occasional Publications 9, 2000), 33; D. Crook, 'The Community of Mansfield from Domesday Book to the Reign of Edward III : pt 2', *Transactions of the Thoroton Society* 89 (1985), 16–29, esp. 25.

[50] J. Freeman, 'Simon Seman, Citizen and Vintner of London', in *London and the Kingdom*, ed. Davies and Prescott, 264; F. B. Andrews, 'The Compotus Rolls of the Monastery of Pershore', *Transactions of the Birmingham Archaeological Society* 57 (1933), 86; James, *Wine Trade*, 187.

[51] M. D. Lobel, 'Thame: Trade, Industry and Agriculture', in *Victoria County History of Oxfordshire*, VII, ed. M. D. Lobel (London, 1962), 180.

Oakham. These tradesmen, scarce in market towns, made and maintained plate armour or chain mail, which were definitely luxuries. The bulk of the 'luxury' trades which make up the numbers included in Table 12.1 were mercers, who are conventionally associated with the sale of linen, silks and other non-woollen cloth, but they were probably less specialised, and supplied dried fruits, for example. They probably dealt in cheap, locally made linens as well as those from the Low Countries and western Germany. They could prosper, judging from William le Mercer of Birmingham, who had accumulated nine burgages by 1296. Similarly the grocer in 1522 at Oakham was assessed at £50, a high figure, and the draper, who again could have dealt in cloth at both ends of the market, had goods worth an above-average £25. Large profits would be most easily earned from dealing in high-priced commodities. Masons have been counted in Table 12.1 because they built churches and superior houses, though a mason sometimes turned his hand to the foundations of a peasant's house. Skinners have been included as they sold expensive furs such as squirrel and marten, though one suspects that a small-town skinner would have handled lamb and rabbit skins. The minstrel at Oakham would have been employed by gentry or clerical households, though he may also have performed at fraternity feasts.

The occupations that have been regarded as lying outside the 'luxury' category consist mainly of those involved in providing food and drink, making cloth and leather goods, or building or working in wood and metal. Those providing every-day services, such as innkeepers, carters and barbers, may have been able to satisfy both wealthy and less affluent customers. Sir Edmund Don regularly visited a barber from the Buckinghamshire town of Wendover in 1518 and in subsequent years.[52] The barber, called John Wyer, must have been especially skilled, as he charged his knightly client 4*d*. If he had asked such a high price (a day's wages for a labourer) from the townsmen or peasants who were his regular customers, he would quickly have gone out of business. In the same way, the food traders would have raised their game when a magnate household moved into a castle or manor house nearby, and one imagines the ale-wives improving on their normal brew and the butchers buying in better-quality animals. Some tailors and glovers could similarly operate at different levels depending on whose clothes or gloves they were making.

In addition to seizing opportunities, small-town traders could do well out of luxury products if they could sell them far beyond their normal range of marketing. A goldsmith does not figure in the 1296 rental for Birmingham analysed in Table 12.1, but around that time a craftsman was evidently producing 'Birmingham pieces', twenty-two of which were listed among the possessions of the Master of the Templar Order in London in 1308. They were valued at between 2*s*. and

---

[52] *The Household Book (1510–1551) of Sir Edward Don: An Anglo-Welsh Knight and his Circle*, ed. R. A. Griffiths (Buckinghamshire Record Society 33, 2004), 2–27.

8s. each, and were probably small items of silver plate which were sufficiently distinctive to acquire a reputation in the capital. Another specialised luxury product which was sold far outside the normal hinterland of a market town was saffron (the most costly of all spices), grown and processed in the fifteenth century in and around Chipping Walden in Essex.[53] We can conclude from Table 12.1 that in most small towns between twelve and twenty-four per cent of traders are likely to have handled luxury goods, but in the towns with a specialised manufacturing base, such as the knife-making town of Thaxted and the clothing centre of Long Melford, the percentage fell to a lower level. Bishop's Waltham, probably the smallest of the towns in the sample, also receives a low score of six per cent.

Larger Towns

Involvement in the luxury trades should rise higher up the urban hierarchy, in the larger towns, those with populations between 2,000 and 10,000. The expectation would be that the gentry and higher aristocracy could make their purchases from more specialised merchants who would offer a better choice and more certain supply than the traders in the market towns. The Catesbys bought goods in Coventry, where they owned a house and other property, rather than market towns.

The occupations in Table 12.2 included in the 'luxury trade' category, as in the smaller towns, were armourers, furbishers, glaziers, goldsmiths, grocers, masons and spicers. The most numerous were drapers, mercers, saddlers and skinners. Trades which do not usually appear in the small towns are found in ones and twos in the larger towns (apothecaries, physicians, pewterers, organ makers), though the vintners were especially plentiful in Winchester and Coventry. Above all, the word 'merchant' is only occasionally used to describe the occupation of a small-town resident, yet it is found quite often in large towns. As with the small-town occupations, we doubt whether the description in the documents accurately describes the individual's range of activities.

The proportion of those identified as pursuing the luxury trades varies with the source of information. If the sample is based on deeds, in other words, if it includes only property holders, the proportion can rise to a third, as in the first two Coventry samples. However, if tax records are used, especially the poll taxes and the 1522 military survey, which included poorer artisans, then the proportion lies around sixteen to seventeen per cent. The Exeter calculation is a composite from a murage tax and other documents.

There can be no doubt that the larger towns played an important part in supplying luxury goods. They contained a wealthy elite which itself consumed luxuries: not just the merchants, but also lawyers, gentry and the higher clergy. This

---

[53]   E. A. Gooder, 'Birmingham Pieces', *Transactions of the Birmingham and Warwickshire Archaeological Society* 88 (1976–7), 135; J. S. Lee, *Cambridge and its Economic Region, 1450–1560* (Hatfield, 2005), 210–11.

Table 12.2: Individuals pursuing luxury and non-luxury occupations in large towns

Town	Date	Luxury trades	Non-luxury trades	Total no. with known occupations
Coventry	c.1180–1299	104 (34%)	200 (66%)	304
Coventry	1299–c.1450	277 (36%)	485 (64%)	762
Coventry	1522	93 (17%)	446 (83%)	539
Winchester	1200–1500	364 (20%)	1464 (80%)	1828
Exeter	1377	97 (23%)	316 (77%)	413
Worcester	1381	23 (16%)	122 (84%)	145
Northampton	1524	61 (16%)	312 (84%)	373

Note: The first two Coventry samples are based on deeds; Winchester and Exeter lists use a combination of sources, including deeds, and the others are based on fiscal assessments. As in Table 12.1, the sample is confined to urban occupations, and status descriptions, agricultural occupations and clergy are omitted.

Sources: 'The City of Coventry: Crafts and Industries: Medieval Industry and Trade', in *Victoria County History of Warwickshire*, VIII, ed. W. B. Stephens (London, 1969), 153–4; *Coventry and its People in the 1520s*, ed. M. H. M. Hulton (Dugdale Society 38, 1999), 57–127; D. Keene, *Survey of Medieval Winchester* (2 vols., Oxford, 1985), I, 352–65; M. Kowaleski, *Local Markets and Regional Trade in Medieval Exeter* (Cambridge, 1995), 375–95; C. M. Barron, 'The Fourteenth Century Poll Tax Returns for Worcester', *Midland History* 14 (1989), 1–29; A. Dyer, 'Northampton in 1524', *Northamptonshire Past and Present* 6 (1979), 73–80.

elite was frequently visited by members of the gentry, who were attending court sessions, fraternity feasts and other events. The provincial towns and regional capitals stretched out their hinterlands for more specialised goods and services beyond the usual seven miles. It was to them that churchwardens went to have their organ mended, or to find a craftsman who could maintain a clock. Potters, bellyeters or founders, all of whom cast bells, were only to be found in large urban centres. The merchants in large towns were connected to networks of supply by which they obtained the wine, spices, fine cloth and other goods at the higher end of the market. Mercers or drapers in large towns kept a sufficient stock of high quality goods to attract the more discerning and affluent customers. On the other hand, small towns and large towns might share activities, of which the carving of alabaster is a good example. The material was quarried in north Staffordshire, and craftsmen carved and painted devotional images for wealthy individuals and churches in Britain and on the Continent, and they produced effigies for the tombs of the aristocracy. The industry was practised in both Burton-on-Trent and the large urban centre of Nottingham.[54]

For all of the advantages that the large towns enjoyed in catering for the

[54] N. Ramsay, 'Alabaster', in *English Medieval Industries*, ed. J. Blair and N. Ramsay (London,

luxury trade, as Table 12.2 shows, four-fifths of their inhabitants were primarily involved in making and dealing in goods for a wide market. The rising and falling fortunes of a large town such as Colchester can be traced in trends in basic and mundane commodities: the grain trade, the number of corn mills, the numbers of brewers and bakers, the debts each of a few shillings which were sued through the borough court. The town's main product in the later Middle Ages — russet cloth at 1s. to 2s. per yard — was aimed at a wide market.[55] Merchants everywhere, whom we sometimes imagine trading in small quantities of valuable items over long distances, in most cases were buying and selling bulky cargoes of relatively cheap commodities: wool, grain, preserved fish, hides, salt, coal, tallow, lead and iron.[56]

Commercial economies worked in complex ways, and there is an element of artificiality in drawing a sharp distinction between luxury and non-luxury trades, not just because the same individual might supply a range of consumers, but because so many middlemen handled materials which cannot be classified. Dyestuffs, alum, oil, teasels, soap and goods such as iron wire (which was made into cards for wool processing) were constantly being moved about by traders, and all of them contributed to making cloth, both the cheap and the high-quality varieties.

Archaeological evidence cannot be expected to provide simple and direct material remains of the luxury trades. As we have seen, problems of non-survival of organic materials, selective disposal of rubbish and careful recycling, mean that scarlet cloth and silver plate are very unlikely to be found among the debris left on the site of an urban house. Many excavations have been carried out on late medieval deposits, and their results published, in a dozen larger towns. Anecdotal evidence can be cited of finds of rare and costly objects, such as the silk veil found in Lincoln, or a glass beaker recovered from the ashes of the Norwich fire of 1507, or a thirteenth-century gold ring set with a pearl and garnets among the finds at Coppergate in York.[57] The scarcity of such items serves to point up the rather dull general picture. Urban sites, even near the centre of large towns, produce much pottery, and many small finds of iron, copper alloy, bone and stone, and, in wet conditions in which organic materials are preserved, the mass of functional wood

1991), 29–40; N. Saul, *English Church Monuments in the Middle Ages: History and Representation* (Oxford, 2009), 70–1.

[55] R. H. Britnell, *Growth and Decline in Colchester, 1300–1520* (Cambridge, 1986).

[56] R. H. Britnell, *Britain and Ireland 1050–1530: Economy and Society* (Oxford, 2004), 331–8.

[57] M. Jones, D. Stocker and A. Vince, *The City by the Pool* (Oxford, 2005), 294; R. Tyson, *Medieval Glass Vessels Found in England, AD 1200–1500* (Council for British Archaeology Research Report 121, 2000), 82; P. Ottaway and N. Rogers, *Craft, Industry and Everyday Life: Finds from Medieval York* (London, 2002), 2923–5. For an overview see the essays on English and continental towns in *Lübecker Kolloquium*, ed. Gläser.

and leather objects which were once present on every site but were usually lost from decay.[58]

We should not arrive at the unexciting conclusion that medieval towns were full of not-very-wealthy people who had ordinary functional possessions, but instead note that the great variety and intensity of life in large towns was reflected in their rich material culture. Their houses differ a great deal: each town had its own architectural style; buildings varied with social rank; individual landlords and tenants had different needs and tastes. Luxury is apparent in the minority of houses built of stone, and in their fixtures and fittings. Pottery of many forms and fabrics were gathered into the town from widely scattered centres of manufacture, and households put them not just to practical uses in the kitchen, but also to decorate the table. For artisans of modest wealth, occupying unpretentious houses, serving ale on the table in a decorated jug, or towards the end of the period drinking from well-made glazed cups and tankards, brought a touch of colour and style to their daily lives. The botanical remains found in pits and ditches also reveal the town as a centre of consumption, attracting every variety of edible and useful plant from the surrounding countryside. Townspeople enjoyed a diet of fruits and berries, wild and cultivated, which may not have cost a great deal of money, but must have given them a sense of enjoying good things.[59]

Finally, in considering the economy of the larger towns, a head count of individual businesses, which has been one of the methods of analysis here, is an unsatisfactory way of judging the economic significance of different branches of trade. The list of occupations is sometimes combined with fiscal assessments, as in the military survey and lay subsidies of the 1520s. A large share of the town's wealth was evidently held by the drapers, mercers, grocers, vintners and similar occupations, which shows the benefit of the trade in luxuries. The great majority of those assessed at Coventry in 1522 (see Table 12.2 above) had their goods rated at £2 or less, but every draper and all but two of the mercers rose above £2. The majority of those pursuing the occupations of drapery and mercery were said to have goods worth more than £20, and the wealthiest, a mercer, was worth £1,333. Selling fine cloth (and other expensive goods) to the rich did not generate much employment, but it made large profits.

Large towns, a dozen of which were also ports, played an important part in importing and distributing luxury goods from overseas. Not all imports fall into the 'luxury' category, as many cargoes that entered Bristol and Chester from across the Irish Sea consisted of fish and hides, with the occasional goshawk and

---

[58]   H. Clarke and A. Carter, *Excavations in King's Lynn 1963–1970* (Society for Medieval Archaeology Monograph 7, 1977), 349–74.

[59]   L. Moffett, 'The Archaeology of Medieval Plant Foods', in *Food in Medieval England*, ed. Woolgar, Serjeantson and Waldron, 46.

some cloth and fur.[60] Likewise the large-scale traffic from Scandinavia and the Baltic depended on fish, timber, tar and salt, with furs as the main high-value item, together with wax. Ships from the Low Countries and northern France, which left England mainly with wool and cloth, came back sometimes with cabbages, garlic and onions. High-value goods, however, occupied much space in the holds of ships entering English ports from the Continent. Wine was especially prominent through the whole period, which, at prices in the range of 4d. to 8d. per gallon, was confined to the rich.

By the early years of the fourteenth century, before the surge in English cloth making, more than 10,000 cloths mainly from Flanders were imported each year, and from the late fourteenth century onwards we know of very large quantities of linen: 200,000 ells in 1384, 380,000 in 1390, 221,000 in 1450, and 420,000 in 1480–1.[61] Imported cloths, both woollen and linen, tended to be highly priced and were mostly purchased by the great households. Silks were being brought into the country in impressive quantities, reaching in 1390 a peak of 412 cloths of gold (silk with gold thread woven into the fabric), worth £5,483. Most of these must have been destined for the royal household and a few super-rich aristocrats. Small silk items, such as garters, which are known from their occasional survival in the damp soil of the London waterfront, were more affordable by the less well-off.[62] A wide range of consumers bought the brassware, above all pots and pans, which came across the Channel. In the late fifteenth century ships were filling up with miscellaneous continental manufactures after discharging their wool and cloth, and these included ribbons, hats, playing cards, mirrors, purses and spectacles. These are best described as petty luxuries, many of them inessential or even frivolous, but attractive to lower-class fair goers on pay day.[63]

A growing proportion of overseas trade throughout the fourteenth and fifteenth centuries was focused on London, at the expense of the provincial ports and the great fairs. London's role as the principal location of the luxury trades is the subject of this final section. In 1500 London received sixty-five per cent of the goods coming into England on which customs were paid (excluding wine).[64] London was the place to which cloths of gold and continental linen were brought.

[60]   Bristol's Trade with Ireland and the Continent, ed, S. Flavin and E. T. Jones (Bristol Record Society 61, 2009); Laughton, Late Medieval City, 173–9.

[61]   J. H. Munro, 'The "Industrial Crisis" of the English Textile Towns, c.1290–c.1330', Thirteenth Century England 7, ed. M. Prestwich, R. Britnell and R. Frame (Woodbridge, 1999), 103–42; Sutton, Mercery, 152–4, 295–7.

[62]   W. Childs, 'Cloth of Gold and Gold Thread: Luxury Imports to England in the Fourteenth Century', in War, Government and Aristocracy in the British Isles, c.1150–1500, ed. C. Given-Wilson, A. Kettle and L. Scales (Woodbridge, 2008), 267–85; E. Crowfoot, F. Pritchard and K. Staniland, Textiles and Clothing c. 1150–c.1450 (London, 1992), 82–149.

[63]   The Overseas Trade of London: Exchequer Customs Accounts 1480–1, ed. H. S. Cobb (London Record Society 27, 1990), pp. xxxvi–xxxviii.

[64]   C. M. Barron, London in the Later Middle Ages: Government and People (Oxford, 2004), 117.

London merchants were no more confined to one trade than their provincial counterparts, so we cannot be sure whose warehouses were crammed with luxury goods. It can be said, however, that many merchants pursued trades closely associated with luxuries, and they played key roles in the social and political life of the city. The pepperers, vintners, mercers, drapers, skinners, goldsmiths and saddlers paid a good share of the city's taxes in 1332, and most of these (the pepperers having become grocers) figured among the leading livery companies, who, according to Thrupp, accounted for 1,900 of the adult males active in trade in 1501–2. The majority of the city's mayors and sheriffs came from the first six of these occupations.[65] Merchants such as the mercers ran retail shops as well as acting as wholesalers who sold goods into the provinces. By the fifteenth century, many larger towns and other provincial outlets received supplies of imported linen from Londoners, and affluent customers, like Durham Priory, sometimes bought linen directly from London.[66]

The leading customers, the bishops, abbots and secular magnates, who needed to stay in the capital to attend to their official duties, or to consult their lawyers, acquired town houses on the edge of the city. These were not just residences but also bases from which negotiations could be conducted with merchants. The magnates also set up wardrobes in the city for assembling and storing their purchases.[67] London provided an opportunity for artisans such as tailors, whose skill and awareness of fashion ensured that they were sought out by the rich. John Bourwill made clothes regularly for the Dinham family from Devon in the years 1379 to 1394.[68] Some specialist crafts were confined to London, or at least the artisans of the city who made luxuries were numerous and produced a much superior product. The London silkwomen had no counterparts in other towns, nor could embroiderers be easily found elsewhere. The monumental brasses coming from the London marblers were recognised for their quality and were bought throughout the country.[69] The advantages of the city for the luxury trades lay not just in the proximity of the Continent, the busy port, the presence of the customers, and

---

[65] M. Curtis, 'The London Lay Subsidy of 1332', in *Finance and Trade under Edward III*, ed. G. Unwin (Manchester, 1918), 45–6; S. Thrupp, *The Merchant Class of Medieval London* (Ann Arbor, 1948), 42–5; Barron, *London*, 308–55.

[66] D. Keene, 'Changes in London's Economic Hinterland as Indicated by Debt Cases in the Court of Common Pleas', in *Trade, Urban Hinterlands and Market Integration c.1300–1600*, ed. J. Galloway (Centre for Metropolitan History Working Paper 3, 2000), 74–6; M. Threlfall-Holmes, *Monks and Markets: Durham Cathedral Priory 1460–1520* (Oxford, 2005), 174 (though the priory bought most of its luxuries from Newcastle).

[67] C. Barron, 'Centres of Conspicuous Consumption: The Aristocratic Town House in London, 1200–1500', *London Journal* 20 (1995), 1–16; D. Keene, 'Wardrobes in the City: Houses of Consumption, Finance and Power', *Thirteenth Century England*, ed. Prestwich, Britnell and Frame, 61–79.

[68] Barron, *London*, 69–70.

[69] M. Norris, *Monumental Brasses: The Memorials* (London, 1977), 23, 52–92, 132–53.

the easy communications with the regions, but also in the availability of credit for merchants needing to lay out large sums to acquire expensive merchandise.

Even in the case of London, the dominance of the luxury trades must be doubted, on the same grounds as have been argued for other towns. Most of the population gained their living by making and selling ordinary commodities, and providing mundane services. Not all of the eighty-five young men who were enrolled as apprentice tailors each year in the 1460s went on to work in the trade, but even if half of them did so, if they were to be fully employed, they would have had to spend time making relatively ordinary clothing.[70] The great majority of London's working population similarly supplied food, housing, footwear, fuel and the other needs of its fellow citizens and out-of-town customers in London's region. The occupations of the two largest suburbs, Southwark and Westminster, included a couple of goldsmiths in both cases, a scatter of vintners and skinners in Southwark, and specialists attracted by the presence of the abbey at Westminster, such as a glazier and a book binder, but otherwise the innkeepers, victuallers, retailers and providers of services predominated.[71]

Conclusion

As Richard Britnell has shown in his most important book to date, commercialisation permeated the whole of medieval society. The rich helped to keep trade flowing, by their own demand for luxuries, their demesne production and preference for cash rents, all of which stimulated the urban economy. Their contribution as consumers, however, should not be exaggerated, even in the early stages before 850, or in the case of late medieval London. The commercial life of the Middle Ages was based on the solid foundations of exchange of ordinary goods, which had a broad base throughout society.

[70] *The Merchant Taylors' Company of London: Court Minutes 1486–1493*, ed. M. Davies (Stamford, 2000), 31–2.

[71] M. Carlin, *Medieval Southwark* (London, 1996), 170–89, 259–69, 280–4; G. Rosser, *Medieval Westminster* (Oxford, 1989), 119–65.

Index of People and Places

....

Bibliography of the Writings of Richard Britnell

1964
'History of Cold Brayfield', *The Bucks Standard* (28 February – 27 March)
'History of Lavendon', *The Bucks Standard* (17 April – 29 May)

1966
'Production for the Market on a Small Fourteenth-Century Estate', *EcHR* 19, 380–7

1968
'The Making of Witham', *History Studies* 1, 13–21

1977
'Agricultural Technology and the Margin of Cultivation in the Fourteenth Century', *EcHR* 30, 53–66
'Finchingfield Park under the Plough, 1341–2', *Essex Archaeology and History* 9, 107–12
'The Origins of Stony Stratford', *Records of Buckinghamshire* 20, 451–3

1978
'English Markets and Royal Administration before 1200', *EcHR* 31, 183–96

1979
'King John's Early Grants of Markets and Fairs', *EHR* 94, 90–6

1980
'Avantagium Mercatoris: A Custom in Medieval Trade', *Nottingham Medieval Studies* 24, 37–50
'Minor Landlords in England and Medieval Agrarian Capitalism', *P&P* 89, 3–22
'Abingdon: A Lost Buckinghamshire Village', *Records of Buckinghamshire* 22, 48–52

1981
'The Proliferation of Markets in England, 1200–1349', *EcHR* 34, 209–21
'Burghal Characteristics of Market Towns in Medieval England', *Durham University Journal* 73, 147–51
'Essex Markets before 1350', *Essex Archaeology and History* 13, 15–21

1982

'The Oath Book of Colchester and the Borough Constitution, 1372–1404', *Essex Archaeology and History* 14, 94–101

1983

'Agriculture in a Region of Ancient Enclosure, 1185–1500', *Nottingham Medieval Studies* 27, 37–55

1986

Growth and Decline in Colchester, 1300–1525 (Cambridge)
'Colchester Courts and Court Records, 1310–1525', *Essex Archaeology and History* 17, 133–40

1987

'Forstall, Forestalling and the Statute of Forestallers', *EHR* 102, 89–102
'Minor Landlords in England and Medieval Agrarian Capitalism' [1980], repr. in *Landlords, Peasants and Politics in Medieval England*, ed. T. H. Aston (Cambridge), 227–46

1988

Colchester in the Early Fifteenth Century: A Portrait (Durham)
'The Fields and Pastures of Colchester, 1280–1350', *Essex Archaeology and History* 19, 159–65
'The Pastons and their Norfolk', *AgHR* 36, 32–44
'The Langley Survey of Durham Bishopric Estates, 1418–21', *Archaeologia Aeliana* 16, 213–21

1989

'England and Northern Italy in the Early Fourteenth Century: The Economic Contrasts', *TRHS* 39, 167–83

1990

'Feudal Reaction after the Black Death in the Palatinate of Durham', *P&P* 128, 28–47
'Bailiffs and Burgess of Colchester, 1400–1525', *Essex Archaeology and History* 45, 154–63
'Third Anglo-American Seminar on the Medieval Economy and Society, July 1989', *Journal of Historical Geography* 16, 153–4

1991

'The Towns of England and Northern Italy in the Early Fourteenth Century', *EcHR* 44, 21–35
'Occupation of the Land: Eastern England', in *AHEW* (Cambridge), III, 53–67
'Farming Practice and Technique: Eastern England', ibid., 194–210
'Tenant Farming and Tenant Farmers: Eastern England', ibid., 611–24

1992
Review: Review of Periodical Literature [for 1990]: 'Medieval', *EcHR* 45, 154–63

1993
The Commercialisation of English Society, 1000–1500 (Cambridge)
'Morals, Laws and Ale in Medieval England', in *Le Droit et sa perception dans la littérature et les mentalités médiévales*, ed. D. Buschinger (Göppingen), 21–9
'Commerce and Capitalism in Late Medieval England: Problems of Description and Theory', *Journal of Historical Sociology* 6, 359–76
Review: Review of Periodical Literature [for 1991]: 'Medieval', *EcHR* 46, 163–70

1994
'Rochester Bridge, 1382–1530', in *Traffic and Politics: The Construction and Management of Rochester Bridge, A.D. 43–1993*, ed. N. Yates and J. M. Gibson (Woodbridge), 41–106
'The Black Death in English Towns', *Urban History* 21, 195–210
'Price Setting and Rules against Monopoly in Medieval English Markets', in *Production Networks: Market Rules and Social Norms*, ed. C. Poni and R. Scazzieri (Bologna), 23–34
Review: Review of Periodical Literature [for 1992]: 'Medieval', *EcHR* 47, 165–73

1995
A Commercialising Economy: England 1086 to c.1300, ed. with B. M. S. Campbell (Manchester)
'Commercialisation and Economic Development in England, 1000–1300', ibid., 7–26
The McFarlane Legacy: Studies in Late Medieval Politics and Society, ed. with A. J. Pollard (Stroud)
'Cardinal Wolsey's Loan for the Northern Campaigns of 1523', *Durham County Local History Society Bulletin* 53, 3–8
'Richard, Duke of Gloucester, and the Death of Thomas Fauconberg', *The Ricardian* 10, 174–84
'The Economic Context', in *The Wars of the Roses*, ed. A. J. Pollard (London), 41–64
'Sedentary Long-Distance Trade and the English Merchant Class', in *Thirteenth Century England v*, ed. P. R. Coss and S. D. Lloyd (Woodbridge), 129–39
Review: Review of Periodical Literature [for 1993]: 'Medieval', *EcHR* 48, 151–9

1996
The Commercialisation of English Society, 1000–1500 (2nd edn, Manchester)
Progress and Problems in Medieval England: Essays in Honour of Edward Miller, ed. with J. Hatcher (Cambridge)
'Boroughs, Markets and Trade in Northern England, 1000–1216', ibid., 46–67
'Price-Setting in English Borough Markets, 1349–1500', *Canadian Journal of History* 31, 1–15
Review: Review of Periodical Literature [for 1994]: 'Medieval', *EcHR* 49, 154–62

1997

The Closing of the Middle Ages? England, 1471–1529 (Oxford)

Pragmatic Literacy, East and West, 1200–1330, ed. (Woodbridge)

'Pragmatic Literacy in Latin Christendom', ibid., 3–24

'Pragmatic Literacy beyond Latin Christendom', ibid., 167–88

'Records and Record-Keeping in Yuan China', ibid., 217–34

Thirteenth Century England VI, ed. with M. Prestwich and R. Frame (Woodbridge)

'Les Marchés hebdomadaires dans les îles Britanniques avant 1200', in *Foires et marchés dans les campagnes de l'Europe médiévale et moderne*, ed. C. Desplat (Toulouse), 27–46

'Penitence and Prophecy: George Cavendish on the Last State of Cardinal Wolsey', *Journal of Ecclesiastical History* 48, 263–81

'La commercializzazione dei ceriali in Inghilterra (1250–1350)', *Quaderni storici* 96, 631–61

Review: Review of Periodical Literature [for 1995]: 'Medieval', *EcHR* 50, 133–42

1998

Daily Life in the Late Middle Ages, ed. (Stroud)

'York under the Yorkists', ibid., 175–94, 220–3

'The English Economy and the Government, 1450–1550', in *The End of the Middle Ages*, ed. J. Watts (Stroud), 89–116

'Food and the Food Trades', in *Medieval England: An Encyclopedia*, ed. P. E. Szarmach with M. T. Tavormina and J. T. Rosenthal (New York and London), 299–301

Review: Review of Periodical Literature [for 1996]: 'Medieval', *EcHR* 51, 155–65

1999

Thirteenth Century England VII, ed. with M. Prestwich and R. Frame (Woodbridge)

'The Exercise of Power in English Towns, 1200–1550', in *Poteri economici e poteri politici: Secc. XIII–XVIII*, ed. S. Cavaciocchi (Florence), 161–84

'The Black Death in Durham', *Cleveland History* 76, 42–51

Review: Review of Periodical Literature [for 1997]: 'Medieval', *EcHR* 52, 103–13

2000

Vernacular Literature and Current Affairs in the Early Sixteenth Century: France, England and Scotland, ed. with J. Britnell (Aldershot)

'Introduction', ibid., pp. xiv–xxv

'Urban Demand in the English Economy, 1300–1600', in *Trade, Urban Hinterlands and Market Integration c.1300–1600*, ed. J. A. Galloway (London), 1–21

'The Economy of British Towns, 600–1300', in *The Cambridge Urban History of Britain*, I: *600–1540*, ed. D. M. Palliser (Cambridge), 105–26

'The Economy of British Towns, 1300–1540', ibid., 313–33

Review: Review of Periodical Literature [for 1998]: 'Medieval', *EcHR* 53, 127–36

2001

Thirteenth Century England VIII, ed. with M. Prestwich and R. Frame (Woodbridge)

'Social Bonds and Economic Change', in *The Twelfth and Thirteenth Centuries*, ed. B. Harvey (Oxford), 101–33

'Specialisation of Work in England, 1100–1300', *EcHR* 54, 1–16

'Local Trade, Remote Trade: Institutions, Information and Market Integration, 1050–1330', in *Fiere e mercati nella integrazione delle economie europee: Secc. XIII–XVIII*, ed. S. Cavaciocchi (Florence), 185–203

Review: Review of Periodical Literature [for 1999]: 'Medieval', *EcHR* 54, 115–27

2002

Review: Review of Periodical Literature [for 2000]: 'Medieval', *EcHR* 55, 128–39

Obituary: 'Rodney Hilton', *The Times* (21 June)

2003

The Winchester Pipe Rolls: Studies in Medieval English Economy and Society, ed. (Woodbridge)

'The Winchester Pipe Rolls and their Historians', ibid., 1–19

Thirteenth Century England IX, ed. with M. Prestwich and R. Frame (Woodbridge)

'England: Towns, Trade and Industry', in *A Companion to Britain in the Later Middle Ages*, ed. S. H. Rigby (Oxford), 47–64

'The Woollen Textile Industry of Suffolk in the Later Middle Ages', in *Tant d'Emprises — So Many Undertakings: Essays in Honour of Anne Sutton*, ed. L. Visser-Fuchs, *The Ricardian* 23, 86–99

'Medieval Boroughs, Markets and Fairs of North Yorkshire', in *Historical Atlas of North Yorkshire*, ed. R. A. Butlin (Otley), 103–5

'Agricultural Marketing and Regional Trade', in *The Oxford Encyclopedia of Economic History*, ed. J. Mokyr (5 vols., Oxford), I, 26–9

'Domesday Book', ibid., II, 97–8

'England: Early and Medieval Periods up to 1500', ibid., II, 200–5

Review: Review of Periodical Literature [for 2001]: 'Medieval', *EcHR* 56, 131–42

2004

Britain and Ireland 1050–1530: Economy and Society (Oxford)

'Fields, Farms and Sun-Division in a Moorland Region, 1100–1400', *AgHR* 52, 20–37

'Uses of Money in Medieval Britain', in *Medieval Money Matters*, ed. D. Wood (Oxford), 16–30

'John Goldbeter', in *Oxford Dictionary of National Biography*, ed. H. C. G. Matthew and B. Harrison (60 vols., Oxford), XXII, 646–7

'Thomas Paycocke', ibid., XLIII, 188

'Commercialization', in *Dictionary of the Middle Ages: Supplement 1*, ed. W. C. Jordan (New York and London), 129–32

2005

Thirteenth Century England x, ed. with M. Prestwich and R. Frame (Woodbridge)

North-East England in the Later Middle Ages, ed. with C. D. Liddy (Woodbridge)

'Service, Loyalty, and Betrayal in Cavendish's *The Life and Death of Cardinal Wolsey*', *Moreana* 42, 3–30

2006

'Town Life', in *A Social History of England, 1200–1500*, ed. R. Horrox and W. M. Ormrod (Cambridge), 134–78

'Markets, Shops, Inns, Taverns and Private Houses in Medieval English Trade', in *Buyers, Sellers: Retail Circuits and Practices in Medieval and Early Modern Europe*, ed. B. Blondé, P. Stabel, J. Stobart and I. Van Damme (Turnhout), 109–23

'Tax-collecting in Colchester, 1489–1502', *Historical Research* 79, 477–87

'Medieval English Wool and Woollen Textile Trade', *Microsoft® Encarta® Encyclopedia 2007* [DVD], Microsoft Corporation

2007

'Movable Goods before the Consumer Revolution: England *c.*1300', in *In but not of the Market: Movable Goods in the Late Medieval and Early Modern Economy*, ed. M. Boone and M. Howell (Brussels), 71–80

'La Communication écrite et son rôle dans la société médiévale de l'Europe du Nord', in *Rome et l'état moderne européen*, ed. J.-P. Genet (Rome), 251–63

2008

Rural Society and Agriculture after the Black Death: Common Themes and Regional Variations, ed. with B. Dodds (Hertford)

'Markets and Incentives: Common Themes and Regional Variations', ibid., 3–19

'English Agricultural Output, 1350–1450: National Trends and Regional Divergences', ibid., 20–39

'Land and Lordship: Common Themes and Regional Variations', ibid., 149–67

Records of the Borough of Crossgate, Durham, 1312–1531, ed. (Surtees Society 212)

2009

Markets, Trade and Economic Development in England and Europe, 1050–1550 (Variorum Collected Studies Series, Farnham)

'Bureaucracy and Literacy', in *A Companion to the Medieval World*, ed. C. Lansing and E. D. English (Chichester), 413–34

'Uses of French Language in Medieval English Towns', in *Language and Culture in Medieval Britain: The French of England c.1100–c.1500*, ed. J. Wogan-Brown, C. Collette, M. Kowaleski, L. Mooney, A. Putter and D. Trotter (Woodbridge), 81–9

'Agriculture, Marketing and Rural Change, 1100–1500', in *A Common Agricultural Heritage? Revising French and British Rural Divergence*, ed. J. Broad (Agricultural History Review Supplement Series, Exeter), 107–20

'Medieval Gateshead', in *A History of Newcastle Before 1700*, ed. D. Newton and A. J. Pollard (Chichester), 137–70

2010
Land and Family: Trends and Local Variations in the Peasant Land Market on the Winchester Bishopric Estates, 1263–1415, with J. Mullan (Hertford)

'Postan's Fifteenth Century', in *Survival and Discord in Medieval Society: Essays in Honour of Christopher Dyer*, ed. R. Goddard, J. Langdon and M. Müller (Turnhout), 49–67

Tabula Gratulatoria

Martin Allen
Andrew Ayton
Mark Bailey
Caroline Barron
G. W. S. Barrow
Adrian R. Bell
Judith M. Bennett
Paul Brand
Chris Briggs
Timothy Brook
Bruce M. S. Campbell
Martha Carlin
Christine Carpenter
Jeremy Catto
Peter Coss
Anne Curry
David D'Avray
James Davis
Barrie Dobson
Ben Dodds
Caroline Dunn and Paul Clark
Christopher Dyer
Ralph Evans
Robin Frame
Constance Fraser

Giles E. M. Gasper
Elizabeth Gemmill
John Gillingham
Richard Goddard
Jeremy Goldberg
Adrian Green
David Green
Ralph A. Griffiths
John Hare
Simon J. Harris
Barbara Harvey
Margaret Harvey
Yvonne and Paul Harvey
John Hatcher
Alan Heesom
Hipólito Rafael Oliva Herrer
Emilia Jamroziak
Derek Keene
Ann Kettle
Edmund King
Maryanne Kowaleski
Craig Lambert
John Langdon
Peter L. Larson
John S. Lee
Christian D. Liddy

John and Judy McKinnell
James A. McKinstry
John Maddicott
James Masschaele
Elizabeth Matthew
Ronald and Dinah Michie
Roger Middleton
John H. Munro
Christine M. Newman
Anne Orde
W. Mark Ormrod
Tony Pollard
Michael Prestwich
Stephen H. Rigby
Miri Rubin
Corinne Saunders
Len Scales
Phillipp R. Schofield
Philip Slavin
Brendan Smith
Richard Smith
Peter Stabel
Sheila Sweetinburgh
Miranda Threlfall-Holmes
Nicholas Vincent

COMMERCIAL ACTIVITY,
MARKETS AND ENTREPRENEURS
IN THE MIDDLE AGES

....

ESSAYS IN HONOUR OF RICHARD BRITNELL

The publishers gratefully acknowledge the generous
financial support of the Marc Fitch Fund in the
production
of this volume